Backwards Game

BAKÉGYAMON

VOL. 4

MITSUHISA TAMURA

Original concept by Kazuhiro Fujita

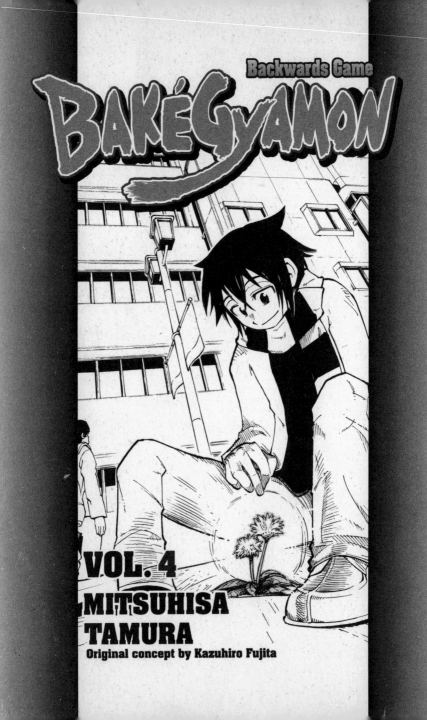

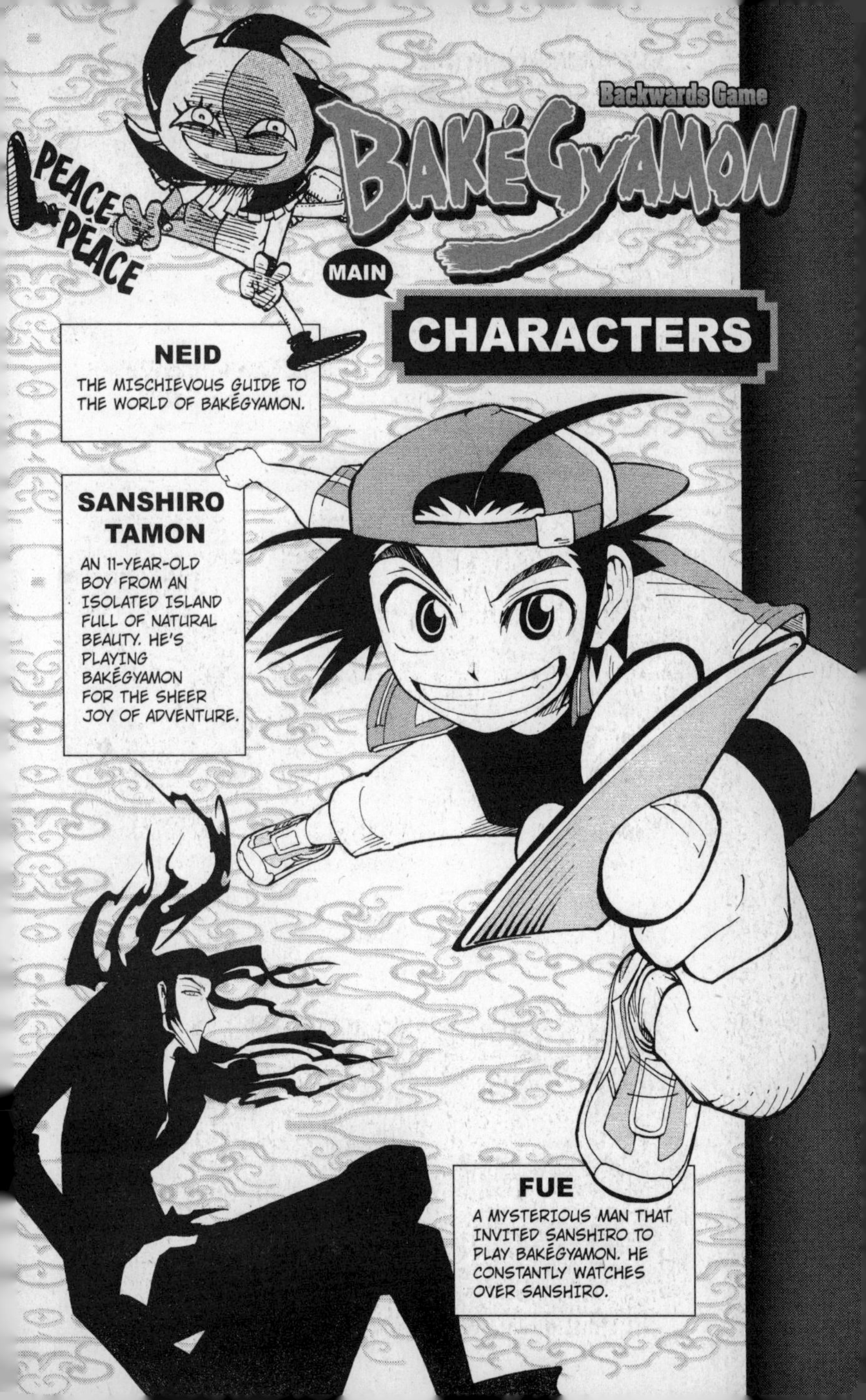
Backwards Game
BAKÉGYAMON
PEACE PÈACE
MAIN
CHARACTERS
NEID
THE MISCHIEVOUS GUIDE TO THE WORLD OF BAKÉGYAMON.
SANSHIRO TAMON
AN 11-YEAR-OLD BOY FROM AN ISOLATED ISLAND FULL OF NATURAL BEAUTY. HE'S PLAYING BAKÉGYAMON FOR THE SHEER JOY OF ADVENTURE.
FUE
A MYSTERIOUS MAN THAT INVITED SANSHIRO TO PLAY BAKÉGYAMON. HE CONSTANTLY WATCHES OVER SANSHIRO.

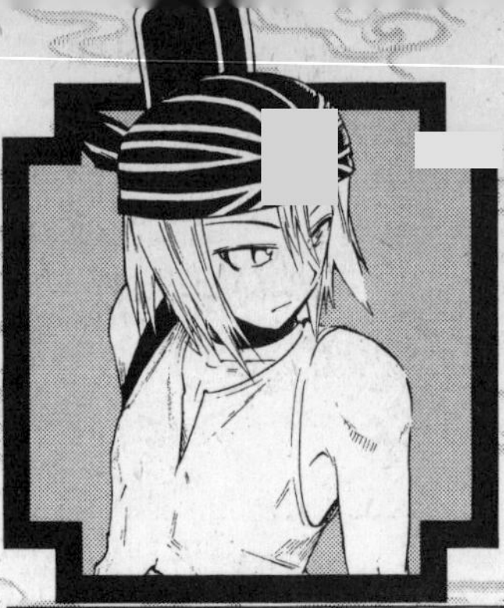

LONDON

HIS REAL NAME IS TOSHIO SAEGUSA. HE WANTS TO BECOME A MUSICIAN BUT HE'S TONE DEAF. HIS MANTRA IN LIFE IS TO BE ***COOL***.

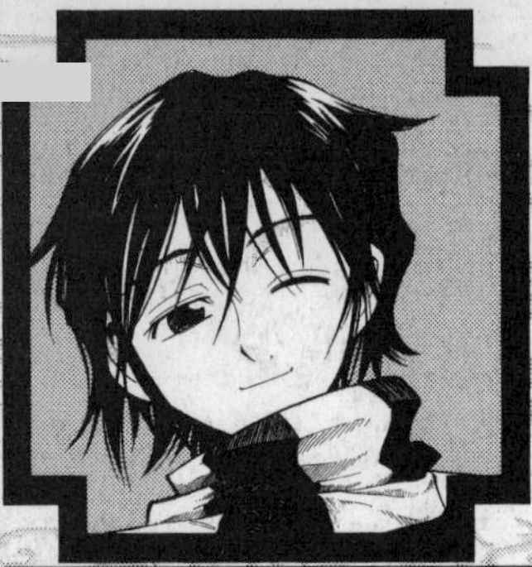

YUKINOSHIN KABURAGI

A BOY THAT SEEMS DISTANT AND DOES EVERYTHING AT HIS OWN PACE. BUT HIS SKILL IN THE GAMES IS TOP CLASS.

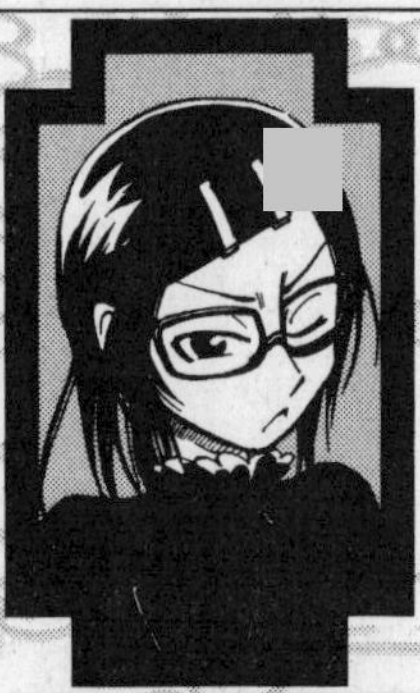

SHIORI FUMIZUKI

ANOTHER BAKÉGYAMON PARTICIPANT AND A VERY INTELLIGENT GIRL. SHE'S ESPECIALLY COMPETITIVE WITH YUKINOSHIN KABURAGI.

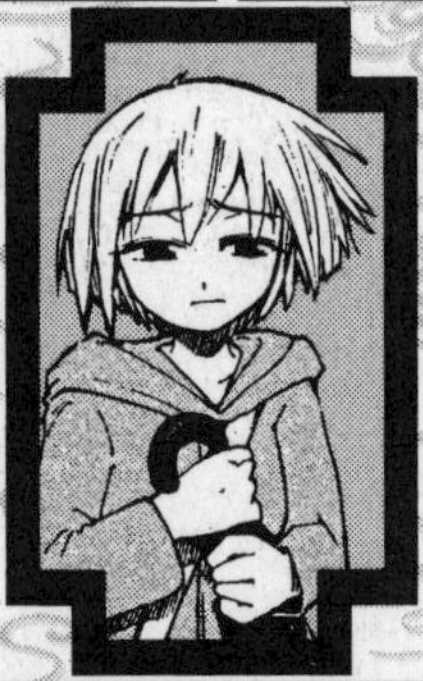

MYSTERIOUS GIRL

SHE TOLD SANSHIRO THAT "GEKI FU MONSTERS HAVE FEELINGS TOO," THEN DISAPPEARED.

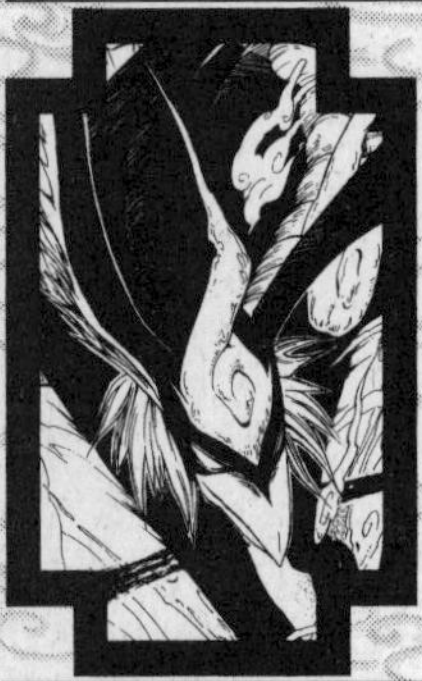

ENZAN

SANSHIRO'S MOST POWERFUL MONSTER, BUT IT REFUSES TO TAKE ORDERS.

"BAKÉGYAMON" IS A GAME FOR CHILDREN SET UP BY MONSTERS AND PLAYED ONCE EVERY 44 YEARS IN "BACKWARDS JAPAN." WHOEVER PREVAILS IN THE END WILL BE GRANTED ONE WISH. HAVING AN ADVENTURER FOR A FATHER AND EAGER TO HAVE AN ADVENTURE HIMSELF, 11-YEAR-OLD SANSHIRO TAMON JUMPS AT THE CHANCE TO PARTICIPATE. IF SANSHIRO WINS, HIS WISH WILL BE TO FREE ALL OF THE MONSTERS FROM THE GEKI FU CARDS. HE'S ALREADY MADE IT TO THE SEMIFINALS, BUT HIS FRIEND LONDON STILL HAS TO PLAY A QUARTERFINAL MATCH.

Contents

Chapter 30: If I Win BakéGyamon   5

Chapter 31: The Battle for Rock   23

Chapter 32: Yukinoshin vs. Shiori   41

Chapter 33: Special Talent   59

Chapter 34: Fight with Me   77

Chapter 35: I Am Superior   95

Chapter 36: Finals   113

Chapter 37: Demon Mask   131

Chapter 38: Now Is the Time   149

Chapter 39: The Birth of BakéGyamon   167

Chapter 40: The Mystery Behind Demon Mask   185

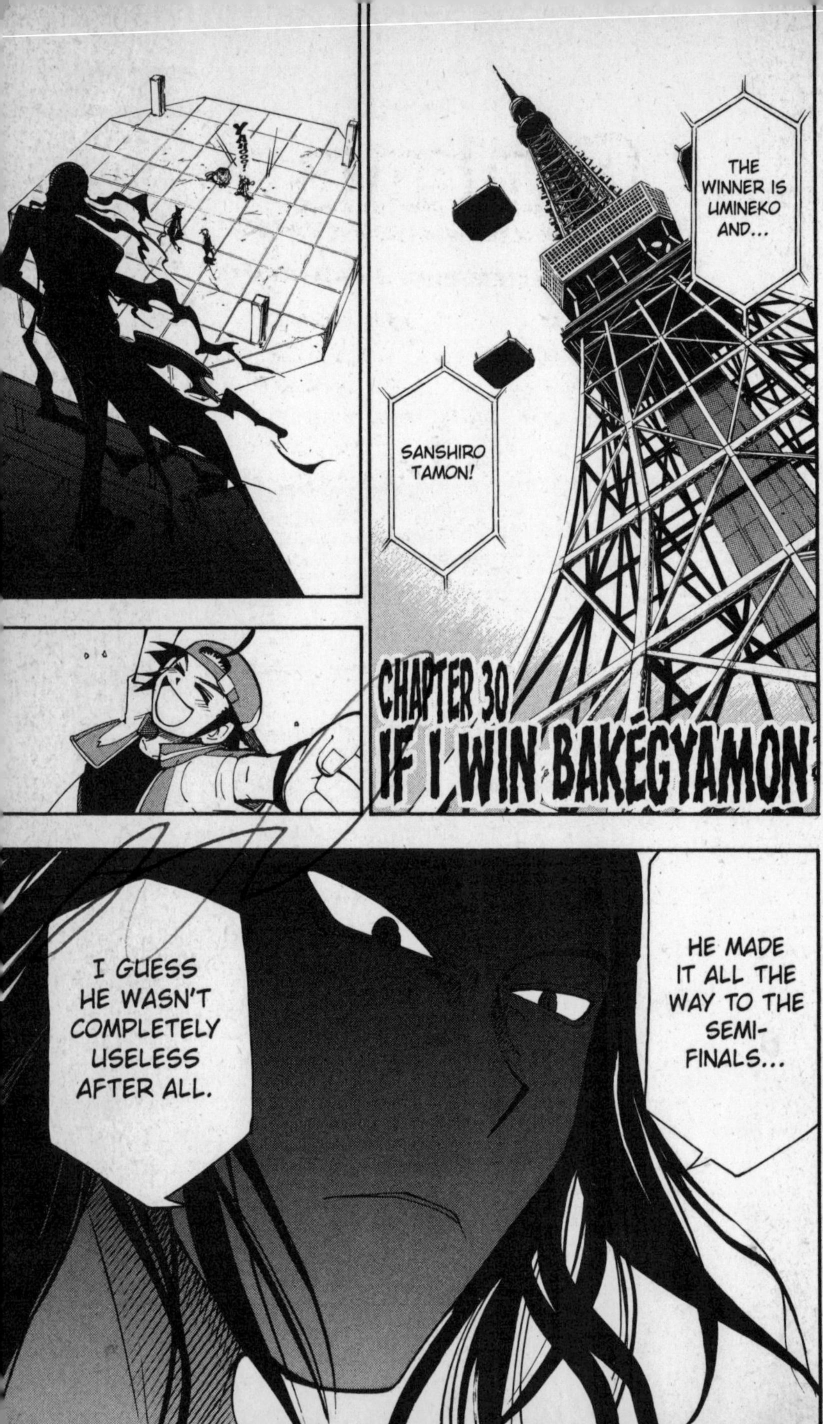
THE WINNER IS UMINEKO AND...
SANSHIRO TAMON!
CHAPTER 30
IF I WIN BAKÉGYAMON
HE MADE IT ALL THE WAY TO THE SEMI-FINALS...
I GUESS HE WASN'T COMPLETELY USELESS AFTER ALL.

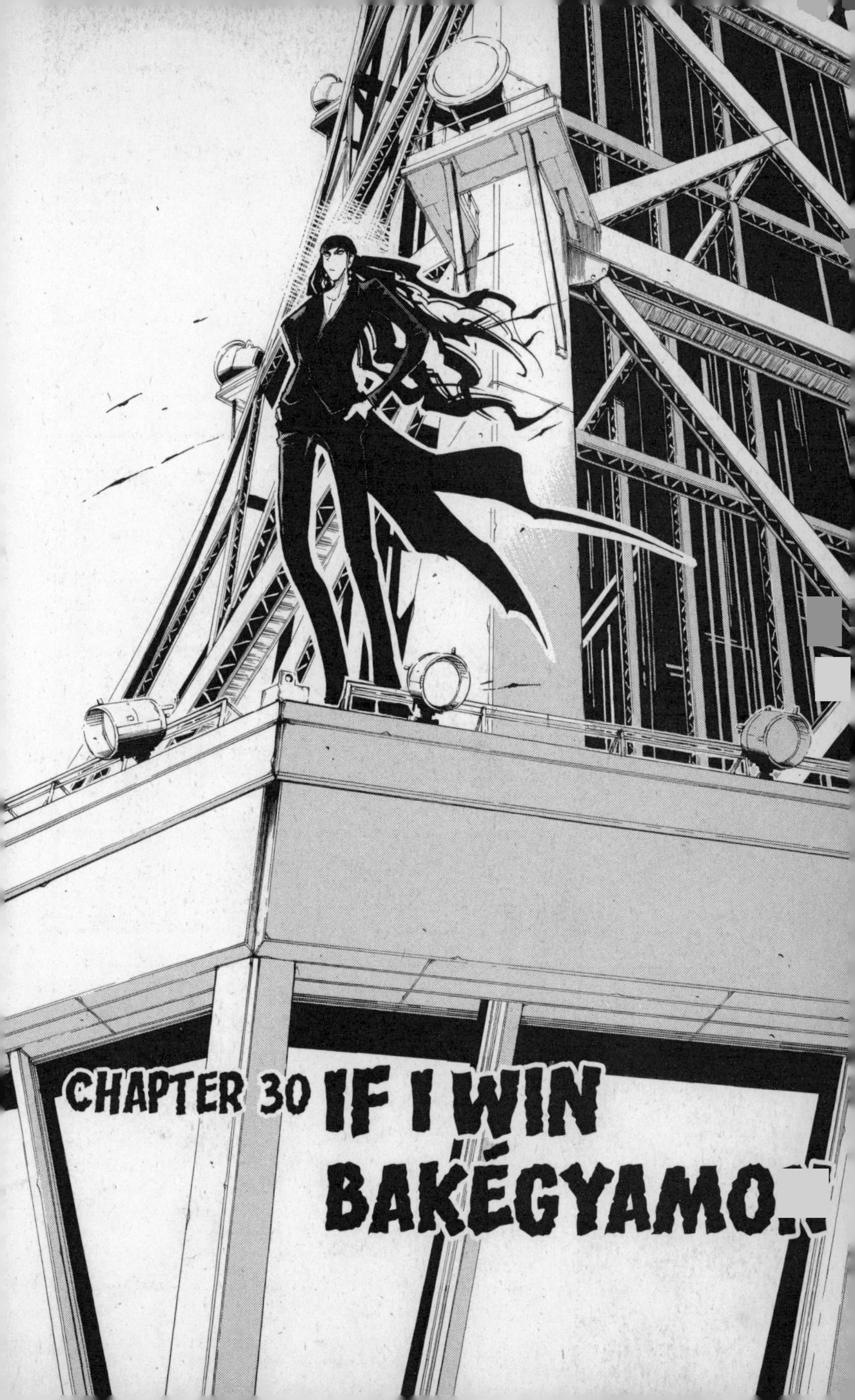
CHAPTER 30 IF I WIN BAKĒGYAMO

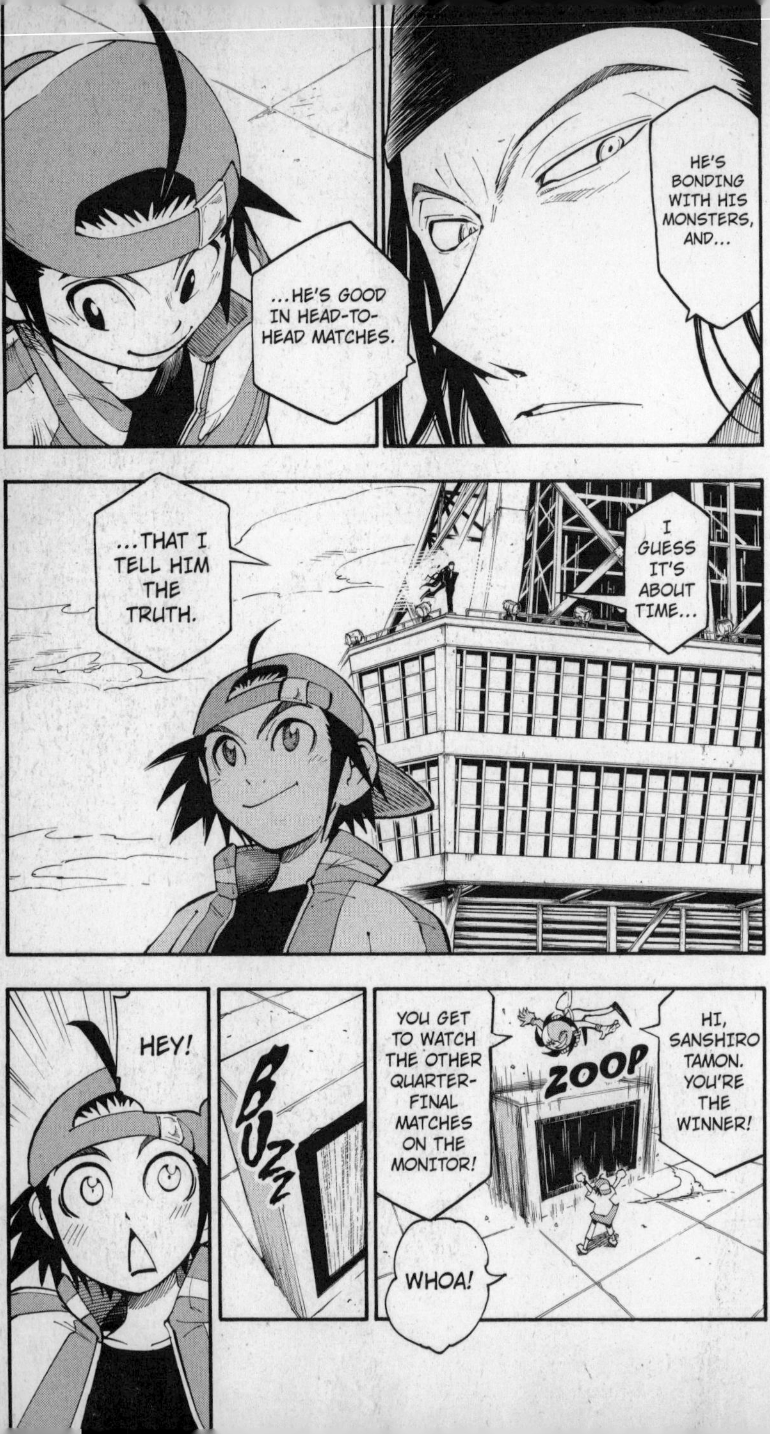
HE'S BONDING WITH HIS MONSTERS, AND...
...HE'S GOOD IN HEAD-TO-HEAD MATCHES.
I GUESS IT'S ABOUT TIME...
...THAT I TELL HIM THE TRUTH.
HI, SANSHIRO TAMON. YOU'RE THE WINNER!
ZOOP
YOU GET TO WATCH THE OTHER QUARTER-FINAL MATCHES ON THE MONITOR!
WHOA!
BUZZ
HEY!

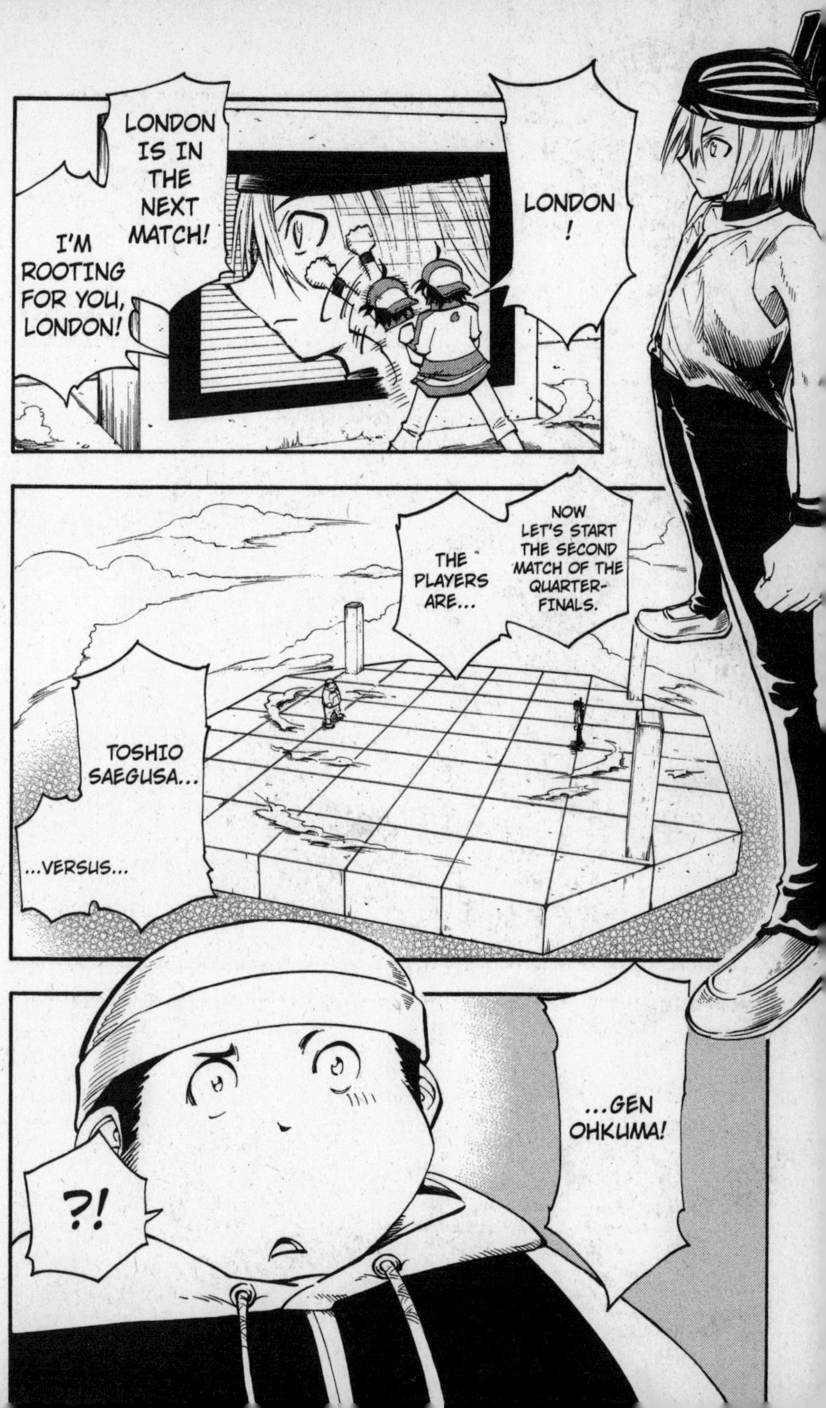
LONDON!
LONDON IS IN THE NEXT MATCH!
I'M ROOTING FOR YOU, LONDON!
NOW LET'S START THE SECOND MATCH OF THE QUARTER-FINALS.
THE PLAYERS ARE...
TOSHIO SAEGUSA...
...VERSUS...
...GEN OHKUMA!
?!

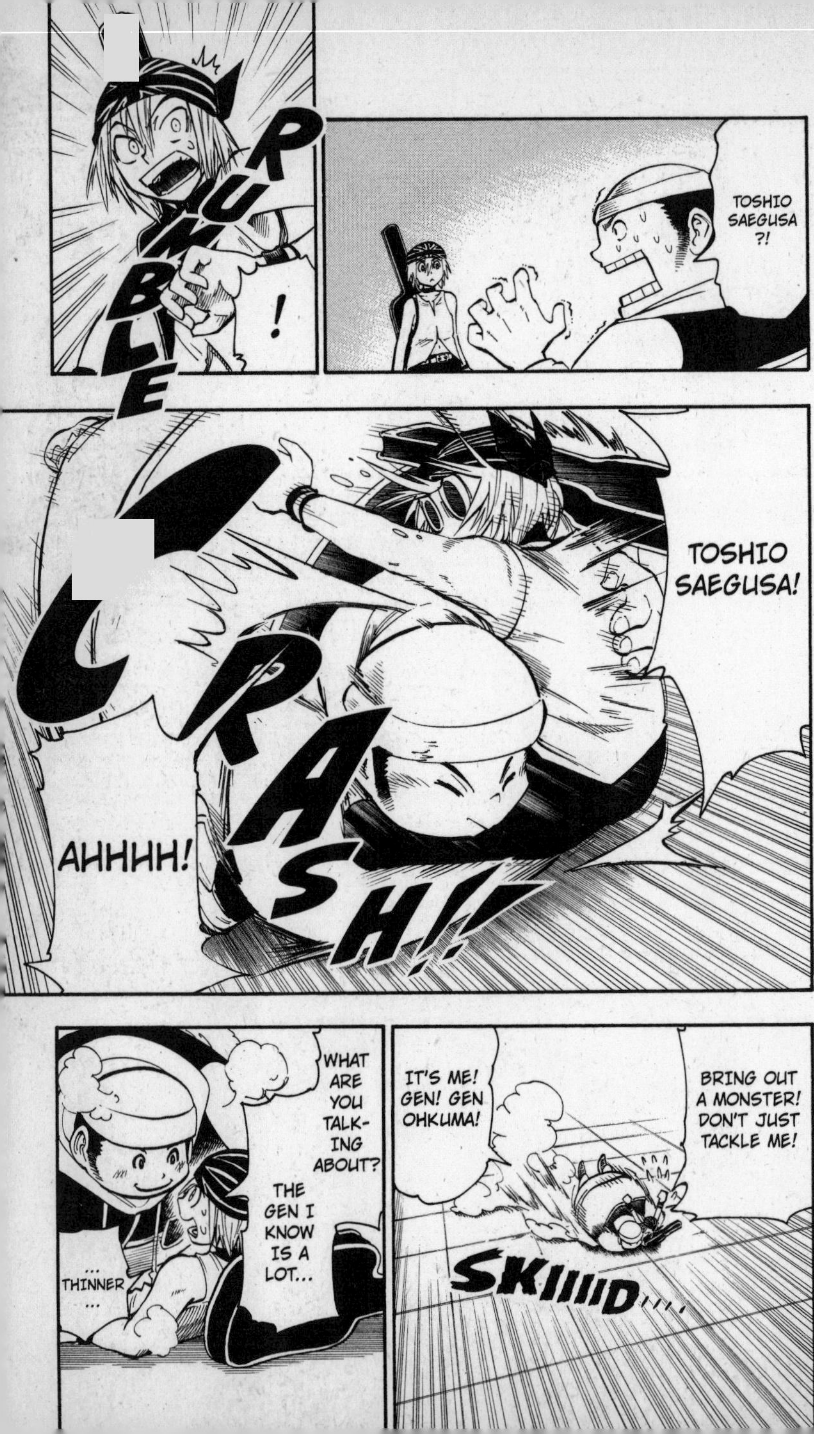
TOSHIO SAEGUSA ?!
RUMBLE
!
TOSHIO SAEGUSA!
CRASH!!
AHHHH!
BRING OUT A MONSTER! DON'T JUST TACKLE ME!
IT'S ME! GEN! GEN OHKUMA!
SKIIIID
WHAT ARE YOU TALKING ABOUT?
THE GEN I KNOW IS A LOT...
...THINNER...

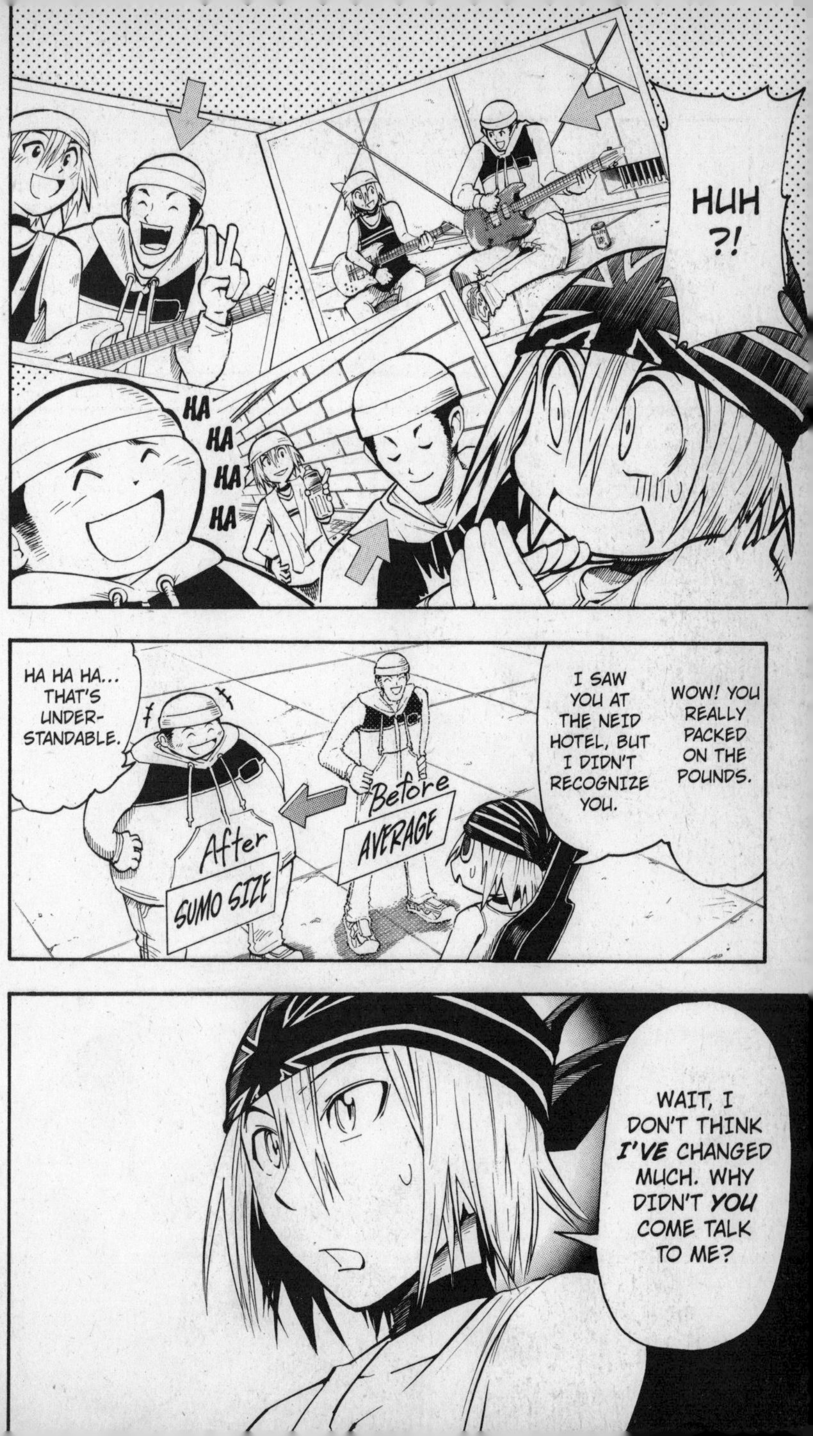
HUH ?!
HA HA HA HA
WOW! YOU REALLY PACKED ON THE POUNDS.
I SAW YOU AT THE NEID HOTEL, BUT I DIDN'T RECOGNIZE YOU.
Before
AVERAGE
After
SUMO SIZE
HA HA HA... THAT'S UNDER-STANDABLE.
WAIT, I DON'T THINK *I'VE* CHANGED MUCH. WHY DIDN'T *YOU* COME TALK TO ME?

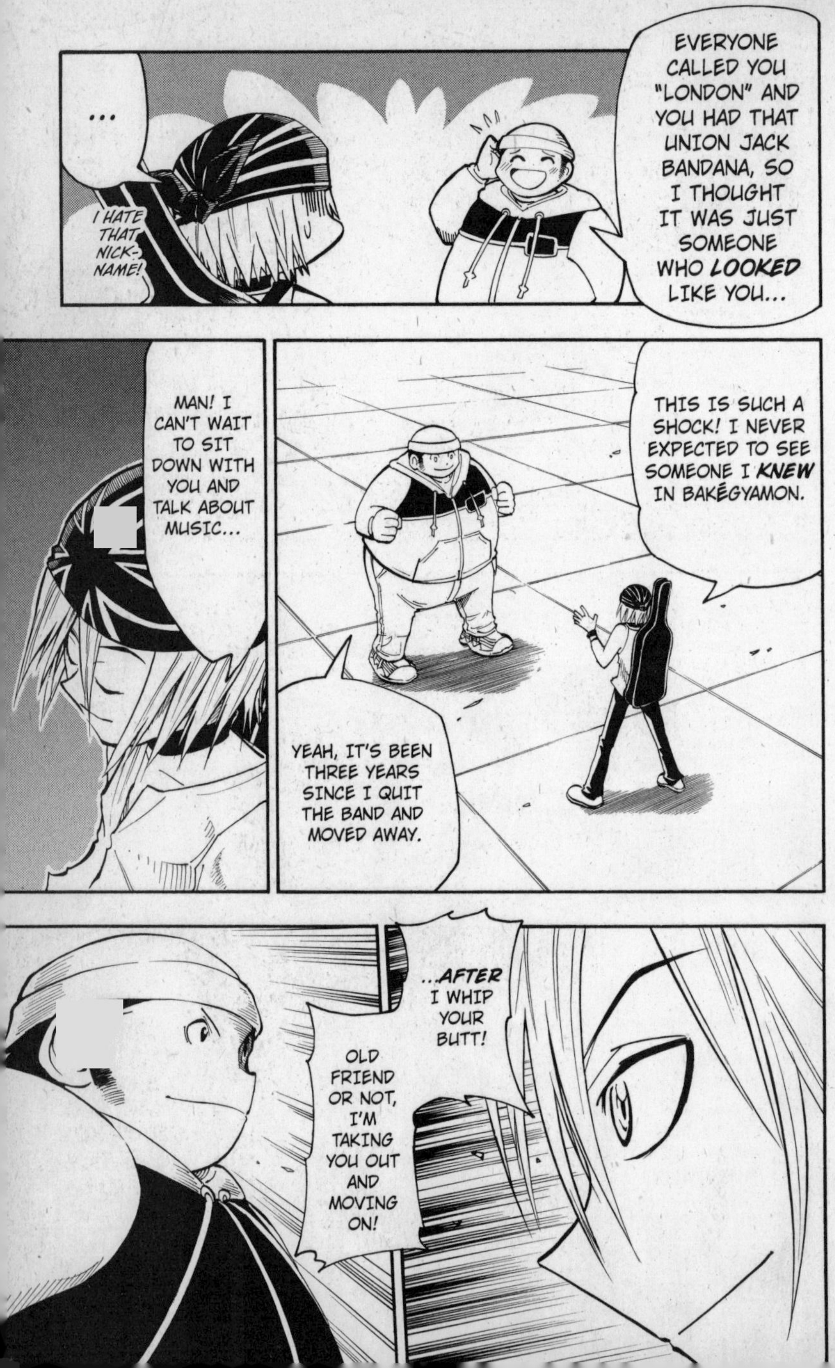
EVERYONE CALLED YOU "LONDON" AND YOU HAD THAT UNION JACK BANDANA, SO I THOUGHT IT WAS JUST SOMEONE WHO *LOOKED* LIKE YOU...
...
I HATE THAT NICK-NAME!
THIS IS SUCH A SHOCK! I NEVER EXPECTED TO SEE SOMEONE I *KNEW* IN BAKÉGYAMON.
YEAH, IT'S BEEN THREE YEARS SINCE I QUIT THE BAND AND MOVED AWAY.
MAN! I CAN'T WAIT TO SIT DOWN WITH YOU AND TALK ABOUT MUSIC...
...*AFTER* I WHIP YOUR BUTT!
OLD FRIEND OR NOT, I'M TAKING YOU OUT AND MOVING ON!

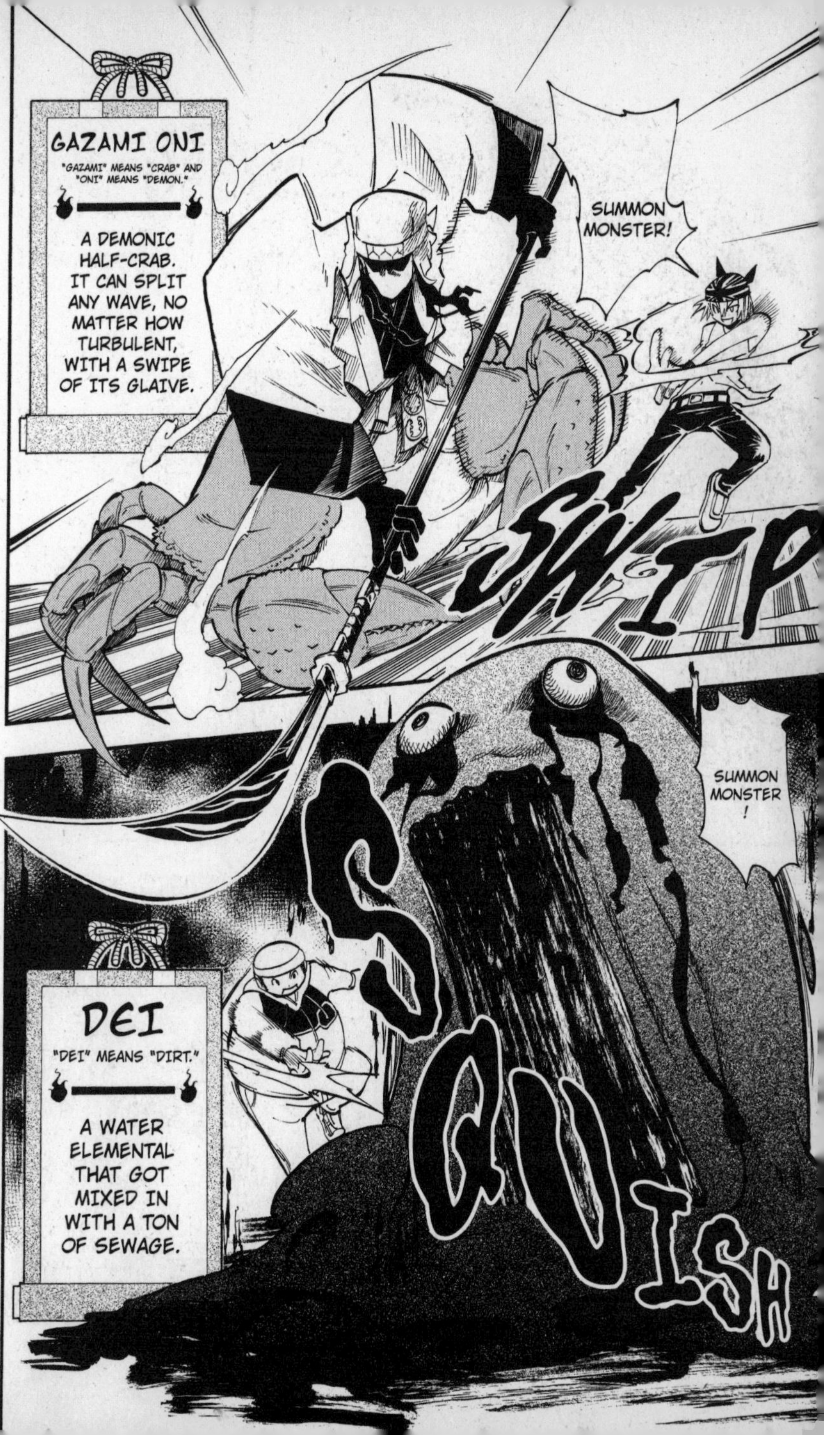
SUMMON MONSTER!
GAZAMI ONI
"GAZAMI" MEANS "CRAB" AND "ONI" MEANS "DEMON."
A DEMONIC HALF-CRAB. IT CAN SPLIT ANY WAVE, NO MATTER HOW TURBULENT, WITH A SWIPE OF ITS GLAIVE.
SWIP
SUMMON MONSTER !
SQUISH
DEI
"DEI" MEANS "DIRT."
A WATER ELEMENTAL THAT GOT MIXED IN WITH A TON OF SEWAGE.

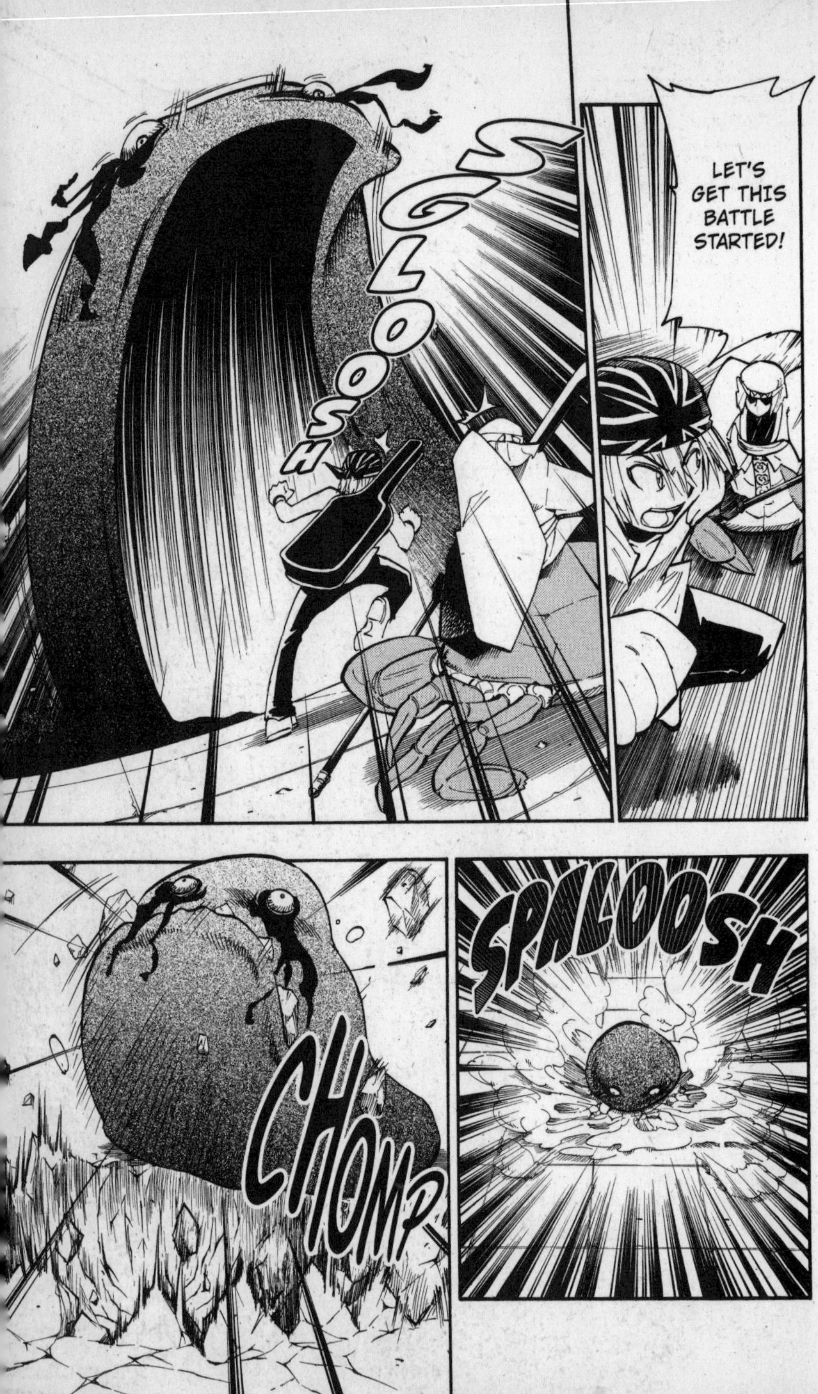
LET'S GET THIS BATTLE STARTED!
SGLOOSH
SPALOOSH
CHOMP

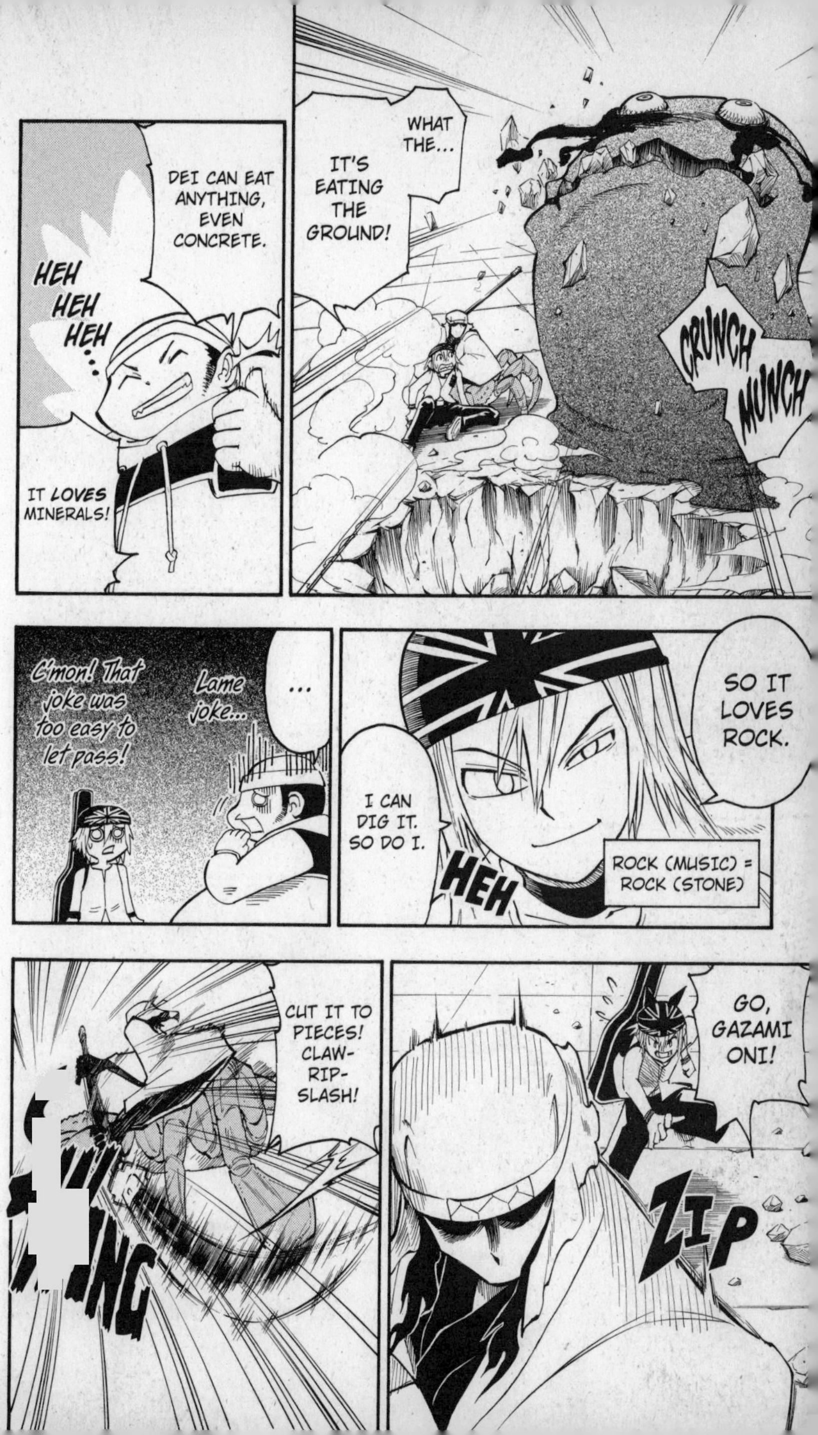
WHAT THE...
IT'S EATING THE GROUND!
CRUNCH MUNCH
DEI CAN EAT ANYTHING, EVEN CONCRETE.
HEH HEH HEH...
IT LOVES MINERALS!
SO IT LOVES ROCK.
I CAN DIG IT. SO DO I.
HEH
ROCK (MUSIC) = ROCK (STONE)
...
Lame joke...
C'mon! That joke was too easy to let pass!
GO, GAZAMI ONI!
ZIP
CUT IT TO PIECES! CLAW-RIP-SLASH!

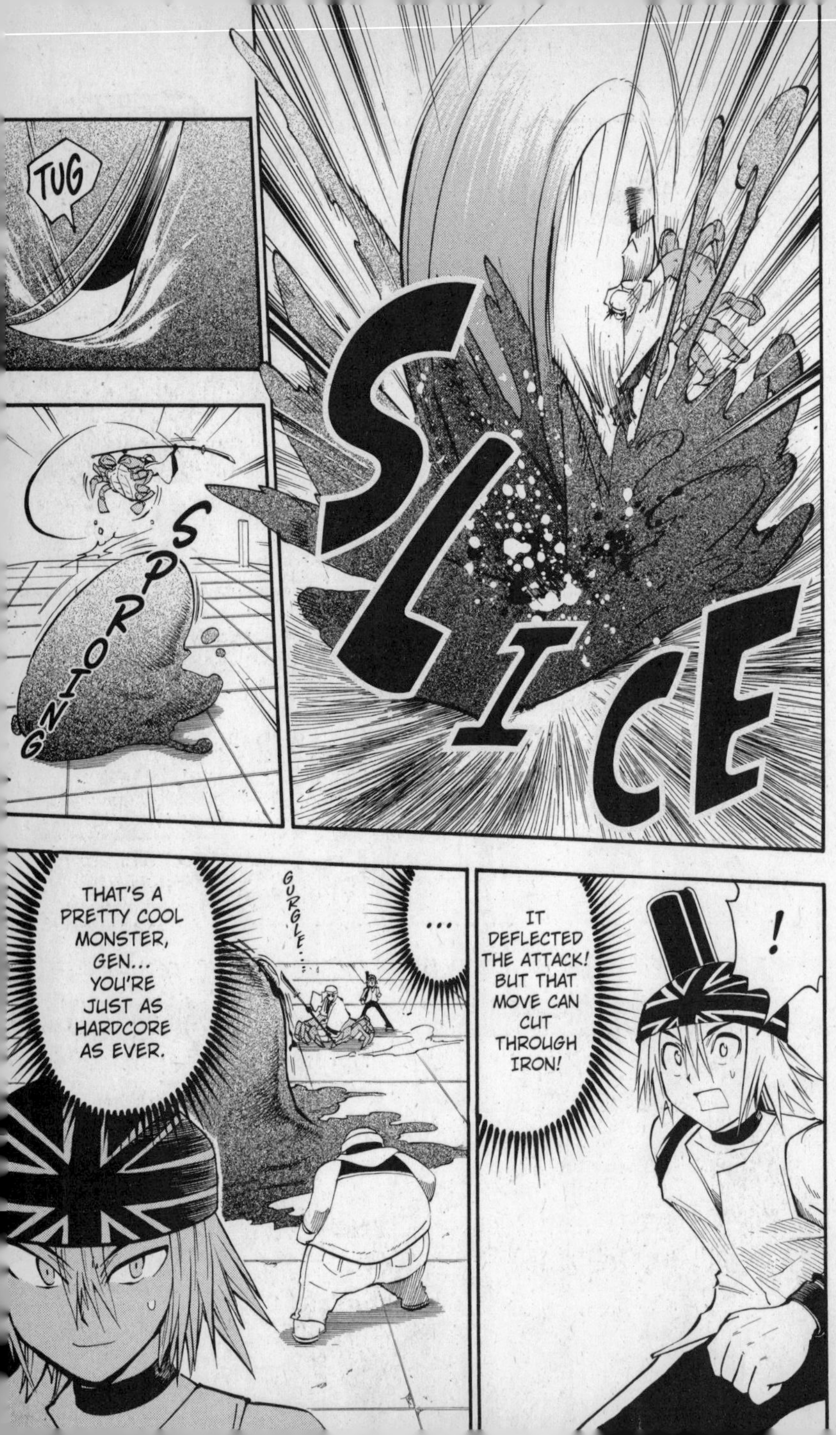
SLICE
TUG
SPROING
!
IT DEFLECTED THE ATTACK! BUT THAT MOVE CAN CUT THROUGH IRON!
...
GURGLE...
THAT'S A PRETTY COOL MONSTER, GEN... YOU'RE JUST AS HARDCORE AS EVER.

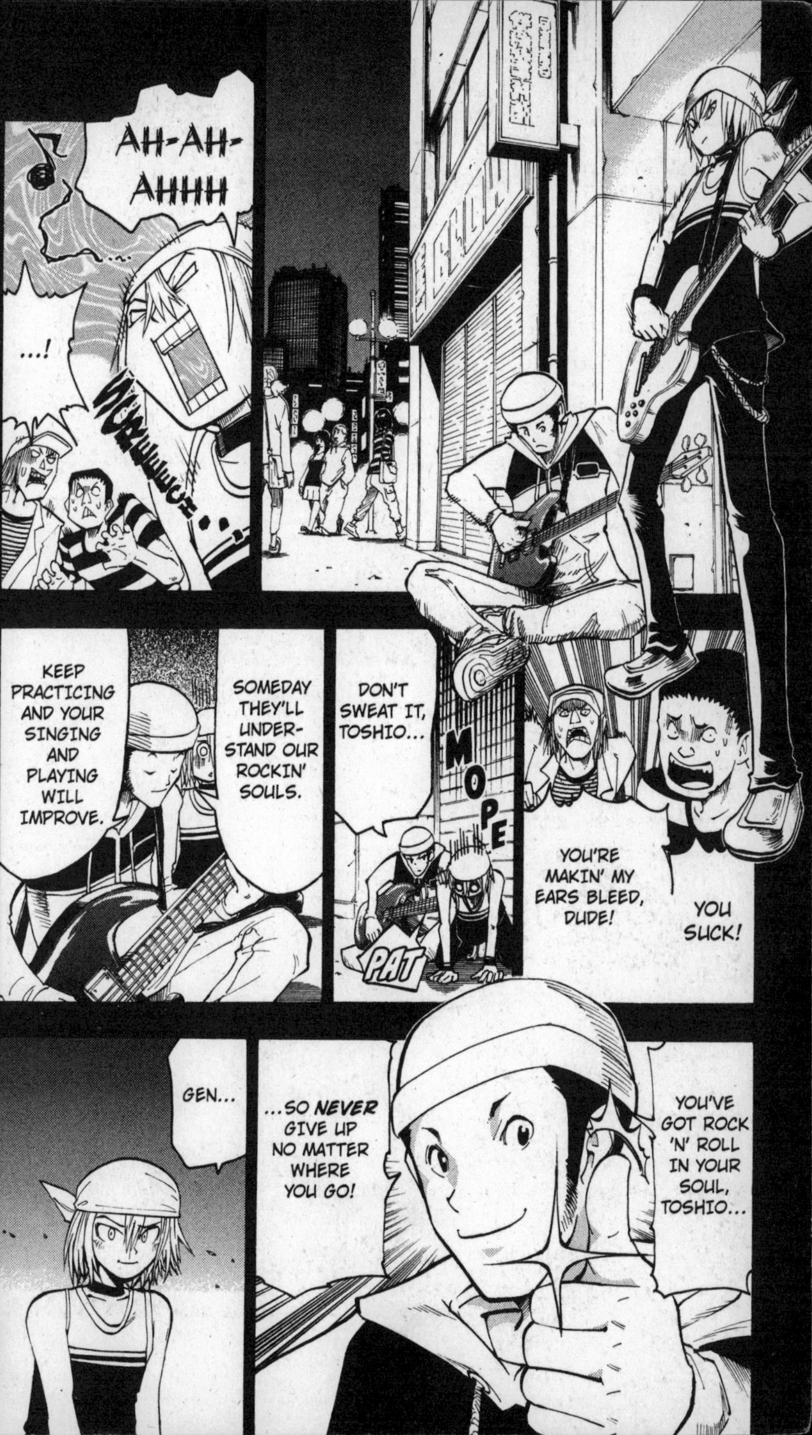
AH-AH-AHHHH
...!
YOU SUCK!
YOU'RE MAKIN' MY EARS BLEED, DUDE!
MOPE
DON'T SWEAT IT, TOSHIO...
PAT
SOMEDAY THEY'LL UNDER-STAND OUR ROCKIN' SOULS.
KEEP PRACTICING AND YOUR SINGING AND PLAYING WILL IMPROVE.
YOU'VE GOT ROCK 'N' ROLL IN YOUR SOUL, TOSHIO...
...SO *NEVER* GIVE UP NO MATTER WHERE YOU GO!
GEN...

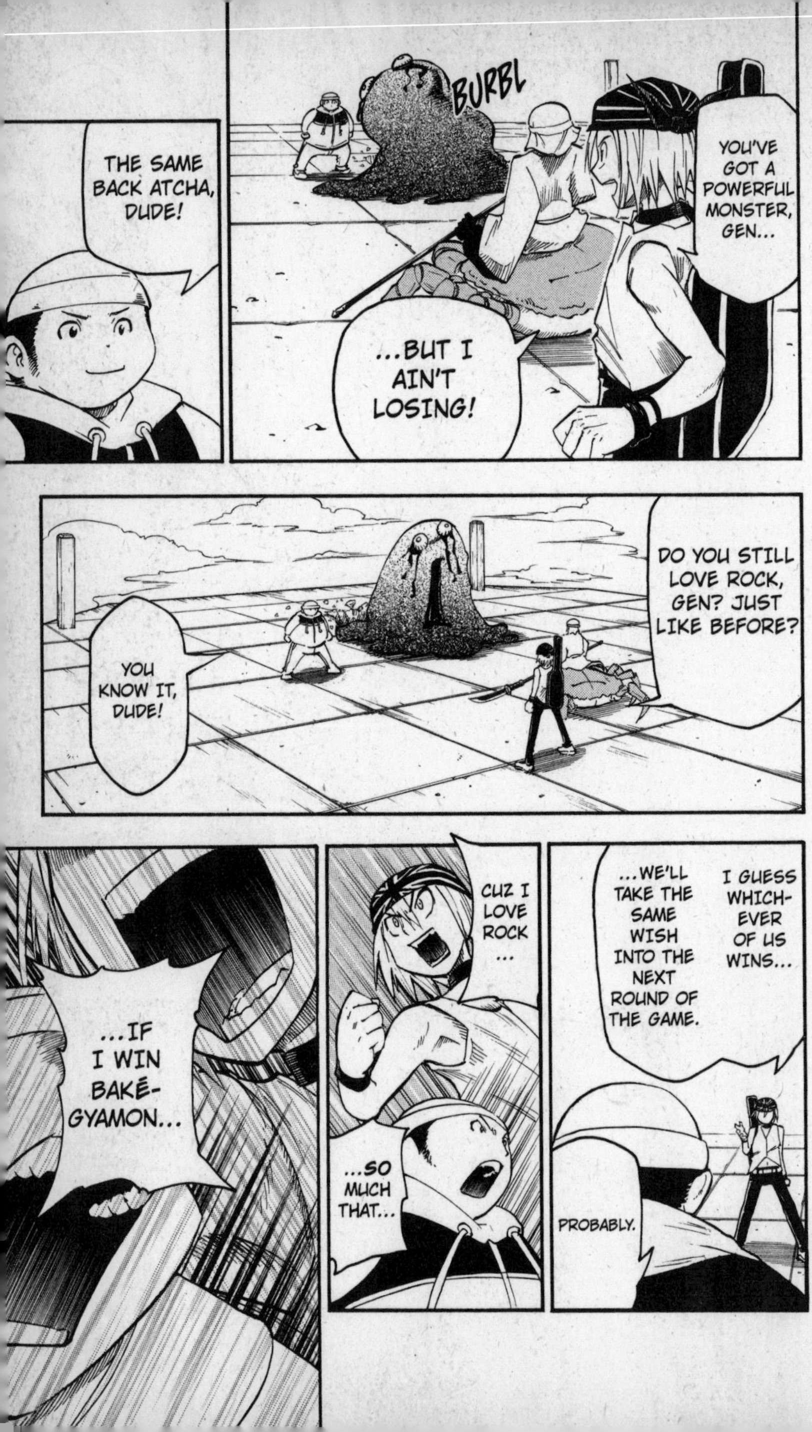
YOU'VE GOT A POWERFUL MONSTER, GEN...
BURBL
...BUT I AIN'T LOSING!
THE SAME BACK ATCHA, DUDE!
DO YOU STILL LOVE ROCK, GEN? JUST LIKE BEFORE?
YOU KNOW IT, DUDE!
I GUESS WHICH-EVER OF US WINS...
...WE'LL TAKE THE SAME WISH INTO THE NEXT ROUND OF THE GAME.
PROBABLY.
CUZ I LOVE ROCK...
...SO MUCH THAT...
...IF I WIN BAKÉ-GYAMON...

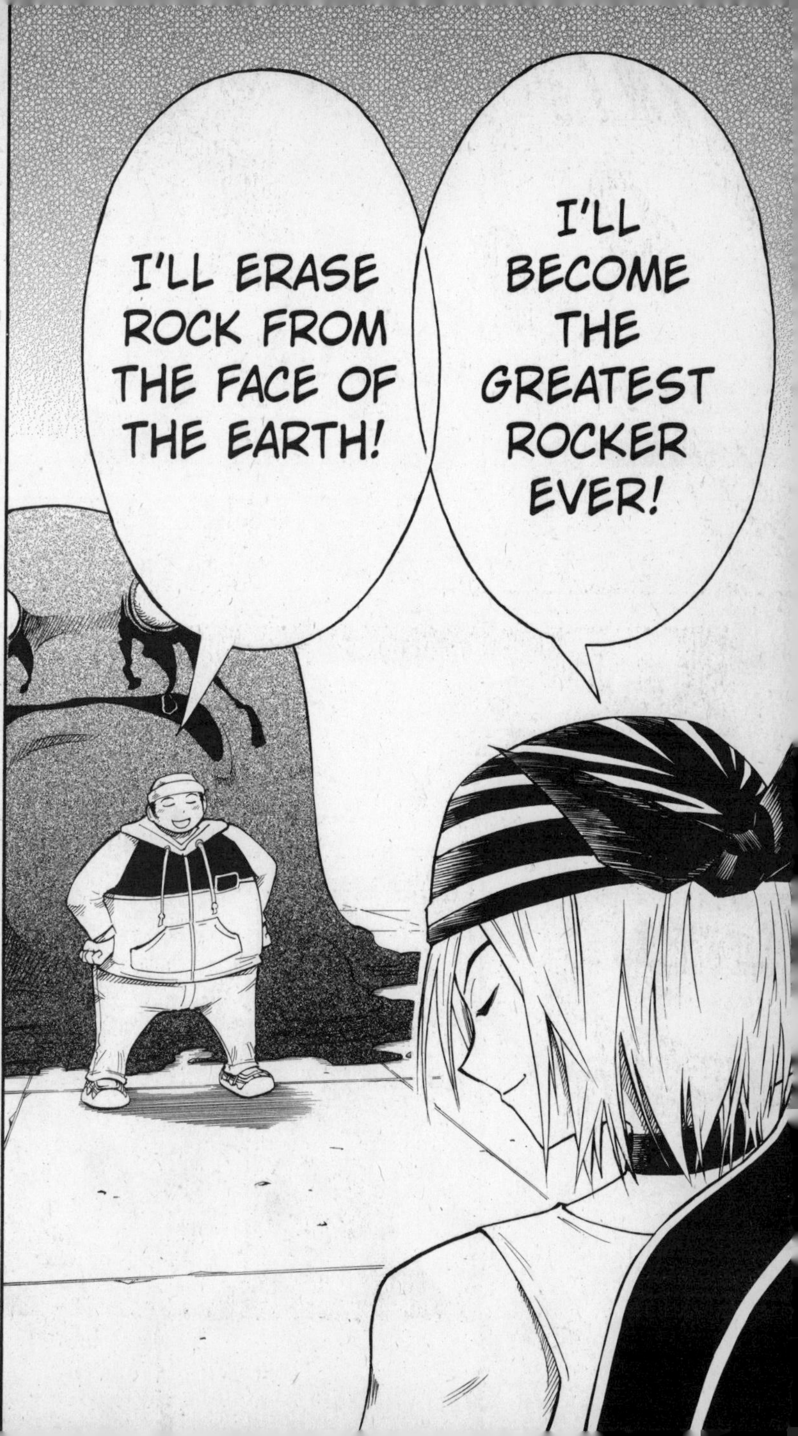
I'LL BECOME THE GREATEST ROCKER EVER!
I'LL ERASE ROCK FROM THE FACE OF THE EARTH!

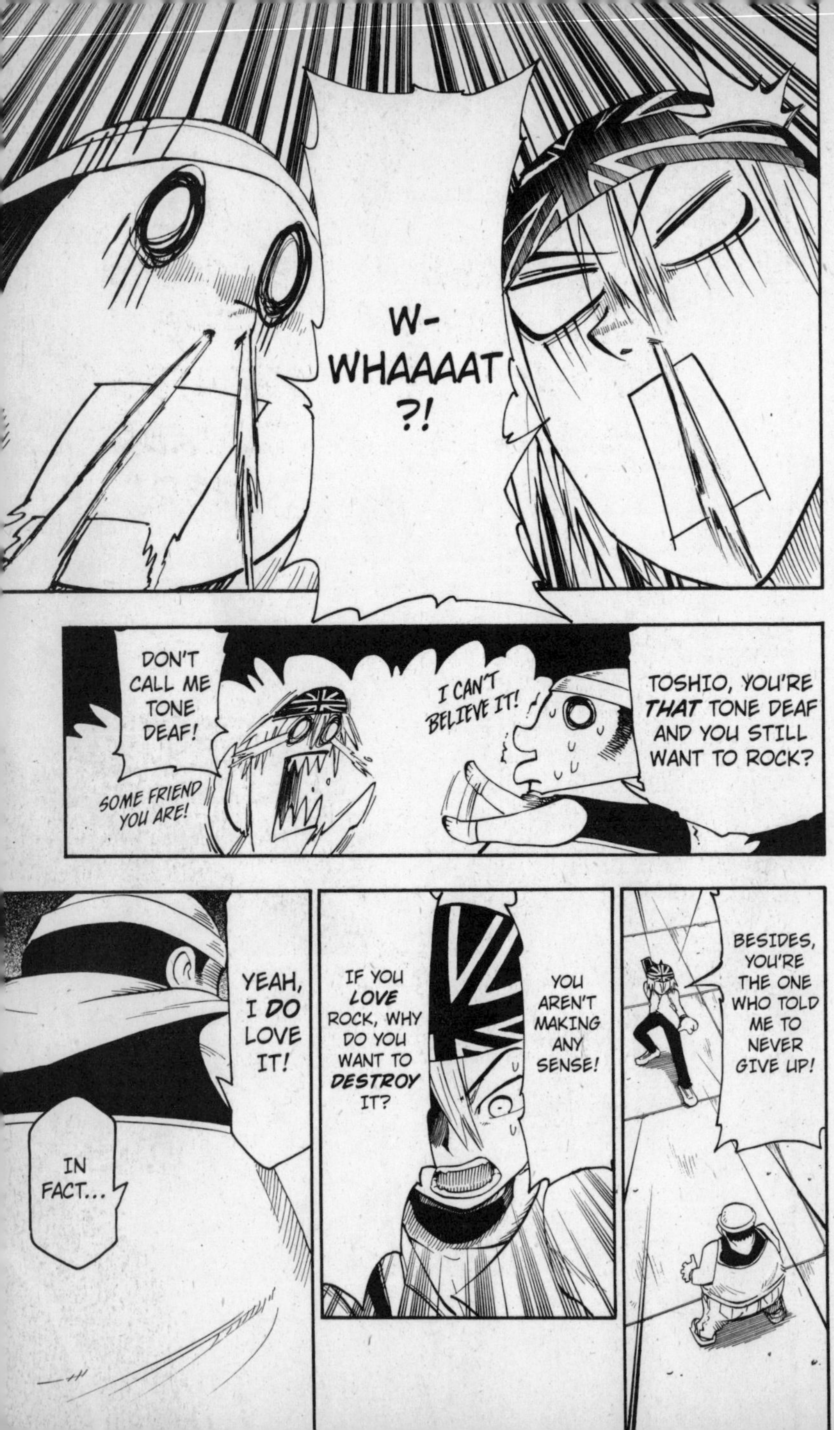
W-WHAAAAT?!
TOSHIO, YOU'RE THAT TONE DEAF AND YOU STILL WANT TO ROCK?
I CAN'T BELIEVE IT!
DON'T CALL ME TONE DEAF!
SOME FRIEND YOU ARE!
BESIDES, YOU'RE THE ONE WHO TOLD ME TO NEVER GIVE UP!
YOU AREN'T MAKING ANY SENSE!
IF YOU LOVE ROCK, WHY DO YOU WANT TO DESTROY IT?
YEAH, I DO LOVE IT!
IN FACT...

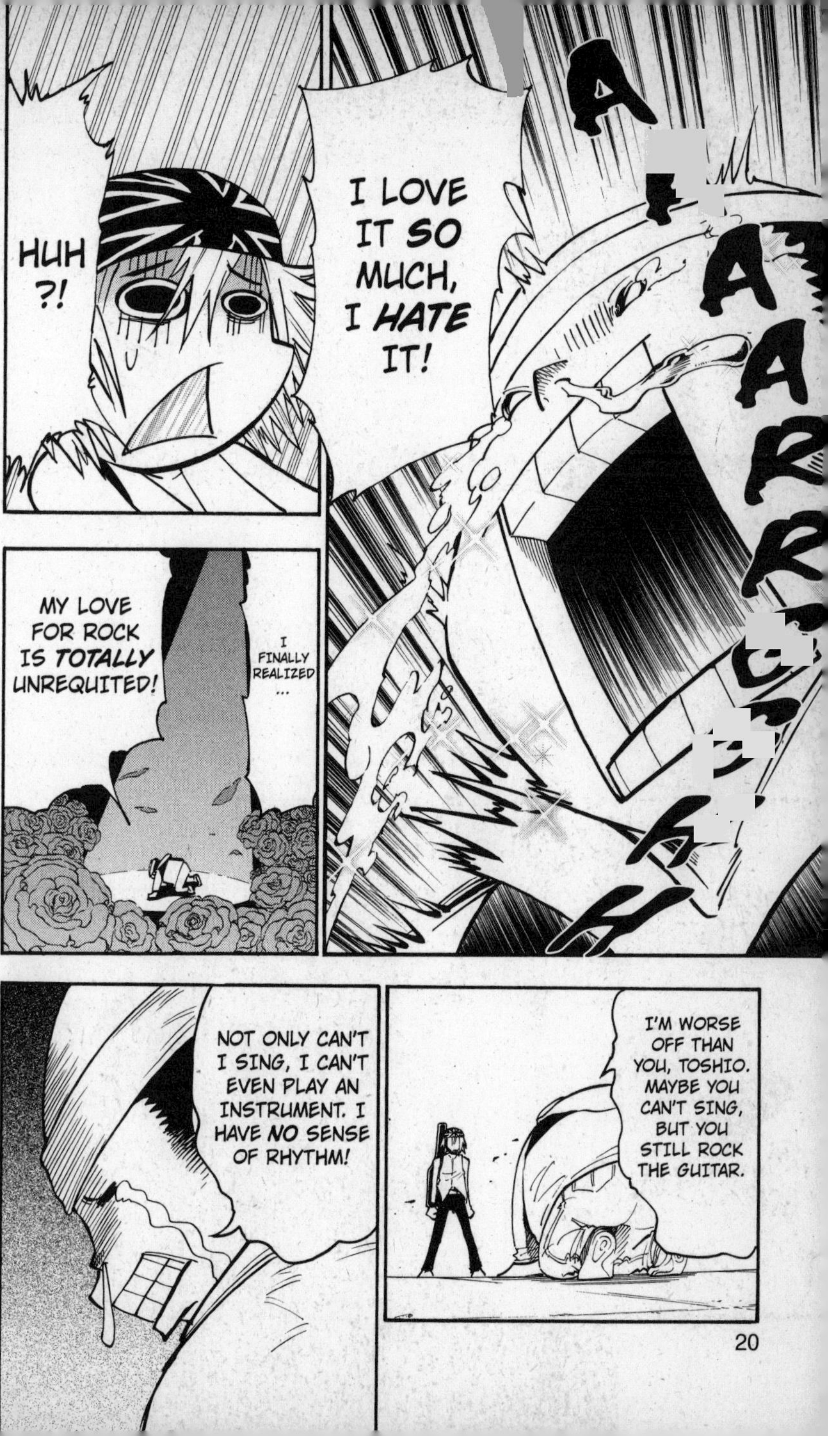
I LOVE IT *SO* MUCH, I *HATE* IT!
HUH ?!
I FINALLY REALIZED ...
MY LOVE FOR ROCK IS *TOTALLY* UNREQUITED!
I'M WORSE OFF THAN YOU, TOSHIO. MAYBE YOU CAN'T SING, BUT YOU STILL ROCK THE GUITAR.
NOT ONLY CAN'T I SING, I CAN'T EVEN PLAY AN INSTRUMENT. I HAVE *NO* SENSE OF RHYTHM!

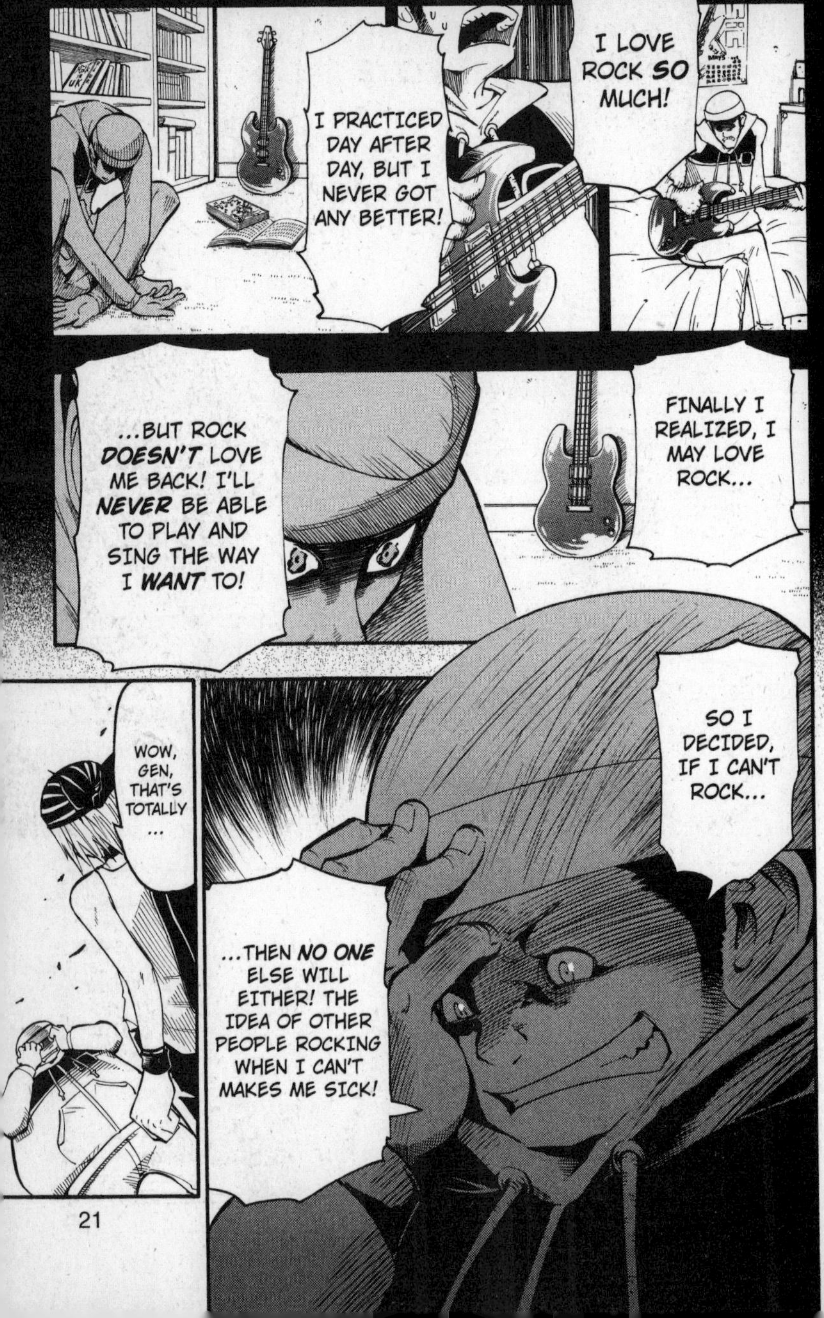
I LOVE ROCK SO MUCH!
I PRACTICED DAY AFTER DAY, BUT I NEVER GOT ANY BETTER!
FINALLY I REALIZED, I MAY LOVE ROCK...
...BUT ROCK DOESN'T LOVE ME BACK! I'LL NEVER BE ABLE TO PLAY AND SING THE WAY I WANT TO!
SO I DECIDED, IF I CAN'T ROCK...
...THEN NO ONE ELSE WILL EITHER! THE IDEA OF OTHER PEOPLE ROCKING WHEN I CAN'T MAKES ME SICK!
WOW, GEN, THAT'S TOTALLY ...

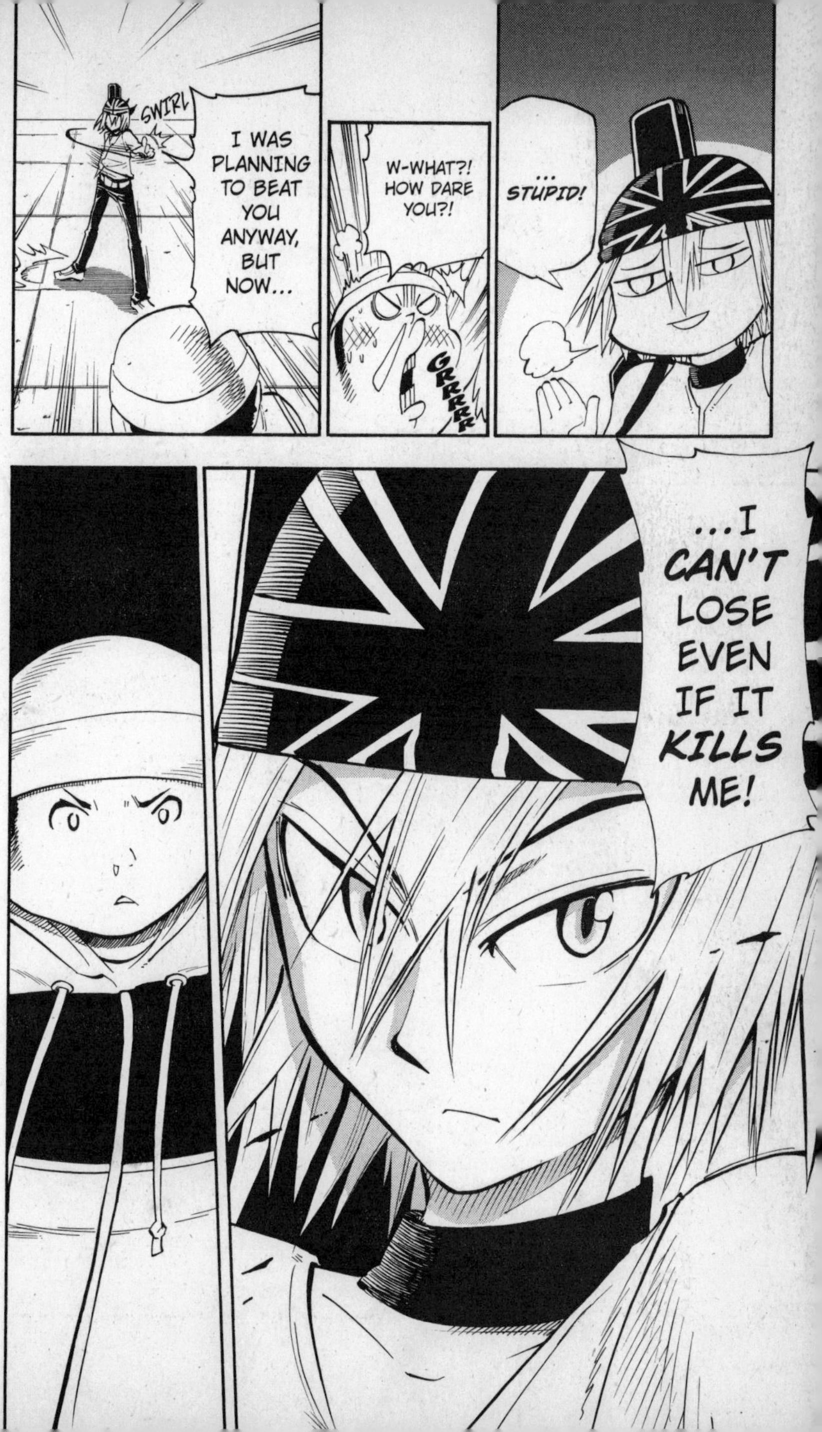
... STUPID!
W-WHAT?! HOW DARE YOU?!
GRRRR
SWIRL
I WAS PLANNING TO BEAT YOU ANYWAY, BUT NOW...
...I CAN'T LOSE EVEN IF IT KILLS ME!

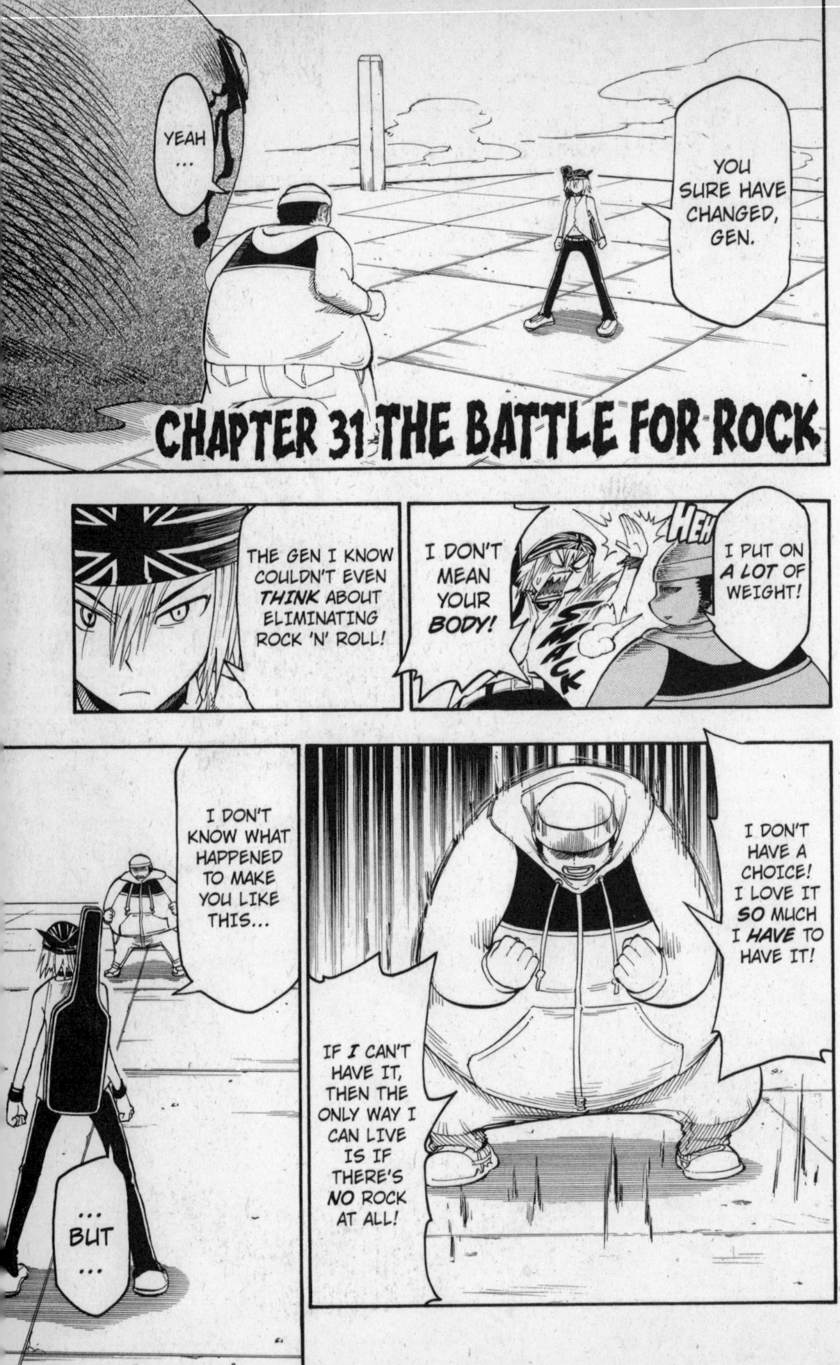
YOU SURE HAVE CHANGED, GEN.
YEAH ...
CHAPTER 31 THE BATTLE FOR ROCK
I PUT ON A LOT OF WEIGHT!
HEH
I DON'T MEAN YOUR BODY!
SMACK
THE GEN I KNOW COULDN'T EVEN THINK ABOUT ELIMINATING ROCK 'N' ROLL!
I DON'T HAVE A CHOICE! I LOVE IT SO MUCH I HAVE TO HAVE IT!
IF I CAN'T HAVE IT, THEN THE ONLY WAY I CAN LIVE IS IF THERE'S NO ROCK AT ALL!
I DON'T KNOW WHAT HAPPENED TO MAKE YOU LIKE THIS...
... BUT ...

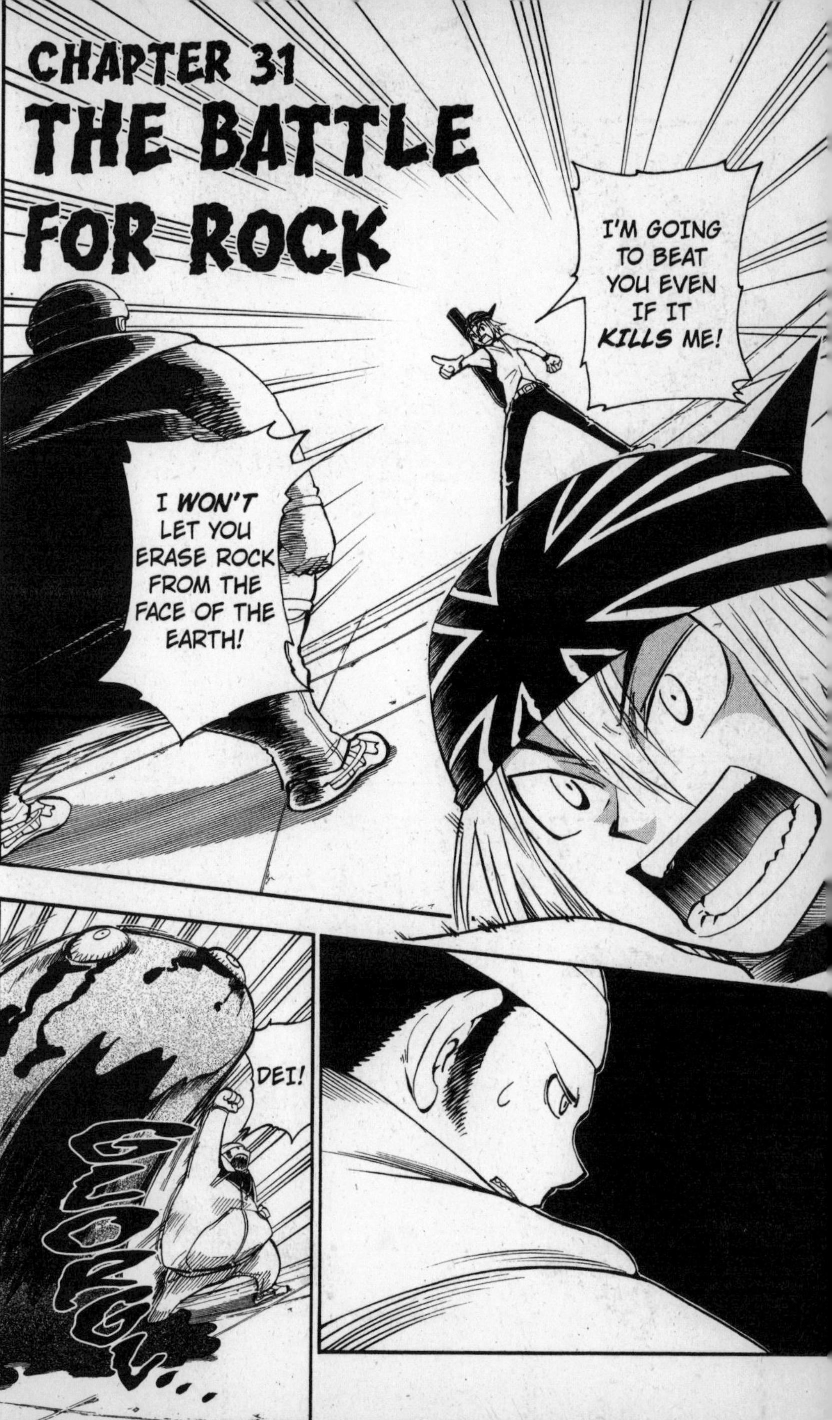
CHAPTER 31
THE BATTLE FOR ROCK
I'M GOING TO BEAT YOU EVEN IF IT KILLS ME!
I WON'T LET YOU ERASE ROCK FROM THE FACE OF THE EARTH!
DEI!

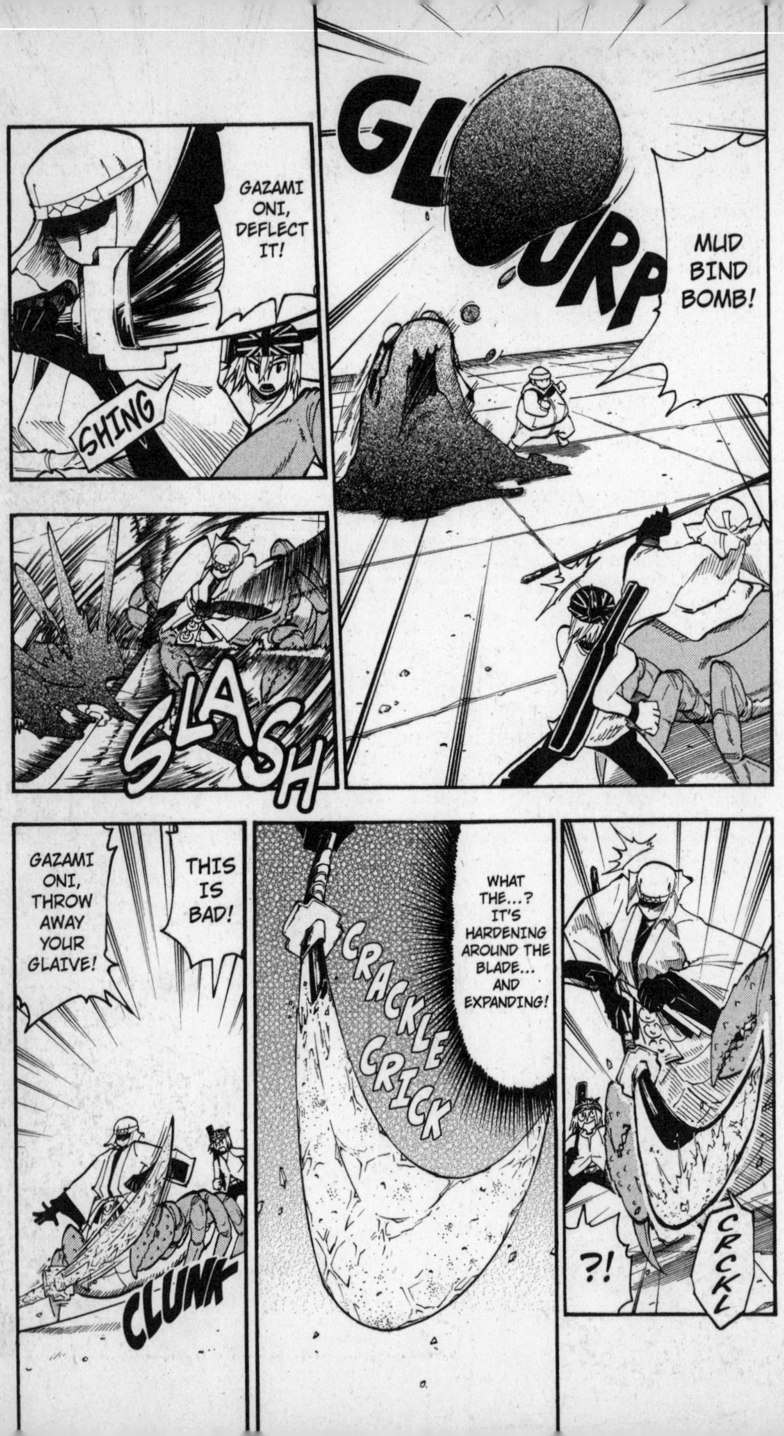
GLOURP
MUD BIND BOMB!
GAZAMI ONI, DEFLECT IT!
SHING
SLASH
?!
CRCKL
WHAT THE...? IT'S HARDENING AROUND THE BLADE... AND EXPANDING!
CRACKLE CRICK
THIS IS BAD!
GAZAMI ONI, THROW AWAY YOUR GLAIVE!
CLUNK

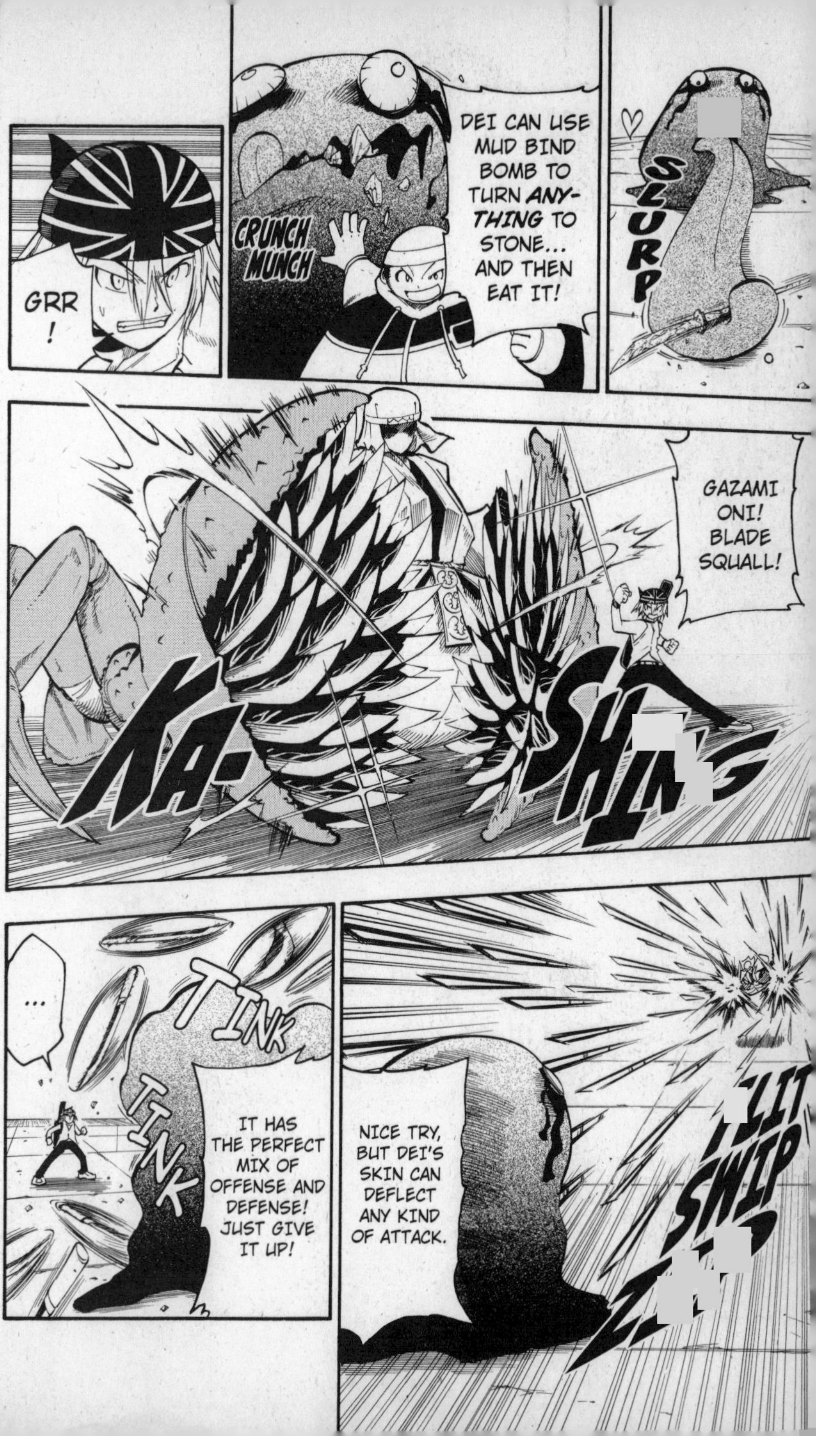
SLURP
DEI CAN USE MUD BIND BOMB TO TURN ANYTHING TO STONE... AND THEN EAT IT!
CRUNCH MUNCH
GRR!
GAZAMI ONI! BLADE SQUALL!
KA-SHING
SNIP
NICE TRY, BUT DEI'S SKIN CAN DEFLECT ANY KIND OF ATTACK.
IT HAS THE PERFECT MIX OF OFFENSE AND DEFENSE! JUST GIVE IT UP!
TINK
TINK
...

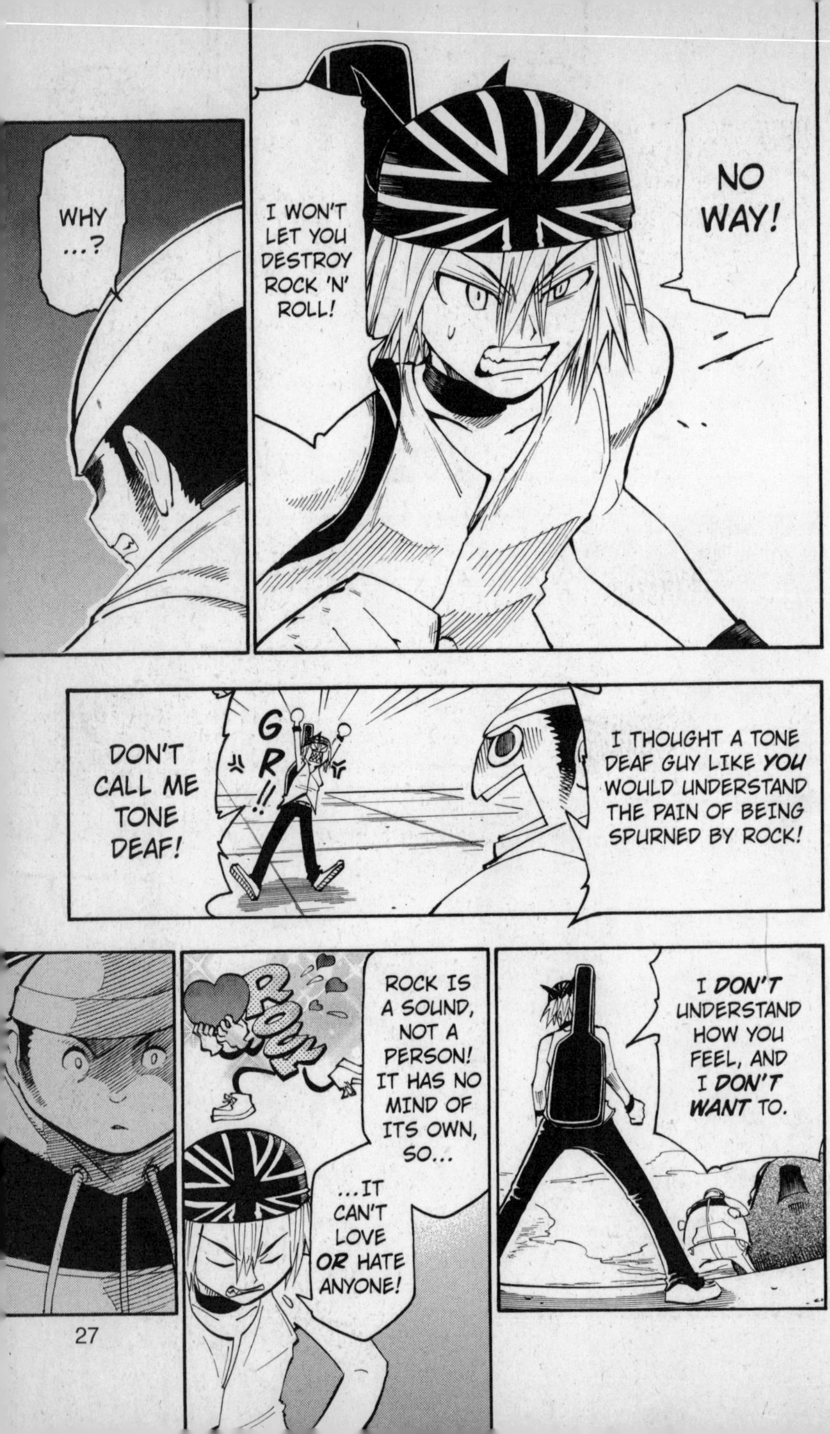
NO WAY!
I WON'T LET YOU DESTROY ROCK 'N' ROLL!
WHY ...?
I THOUGHT A TONE DEAF GUY LIKE YOU WOULD UNDERSTAND THE PAIN OF BEING SPURNED BY ROCK!
DON'T CALL ME TONE DEAF!
GR!!
I DON'T UNDERSTAND HOW YOU FEEL, AND I DON'T WANT TO.
ROCK IS A SOUND, NOT A PERSON! IT HAS NO MIND OF ITS OWN, SO...
...IT CAN'T LOVE OR HATE ANYONE!

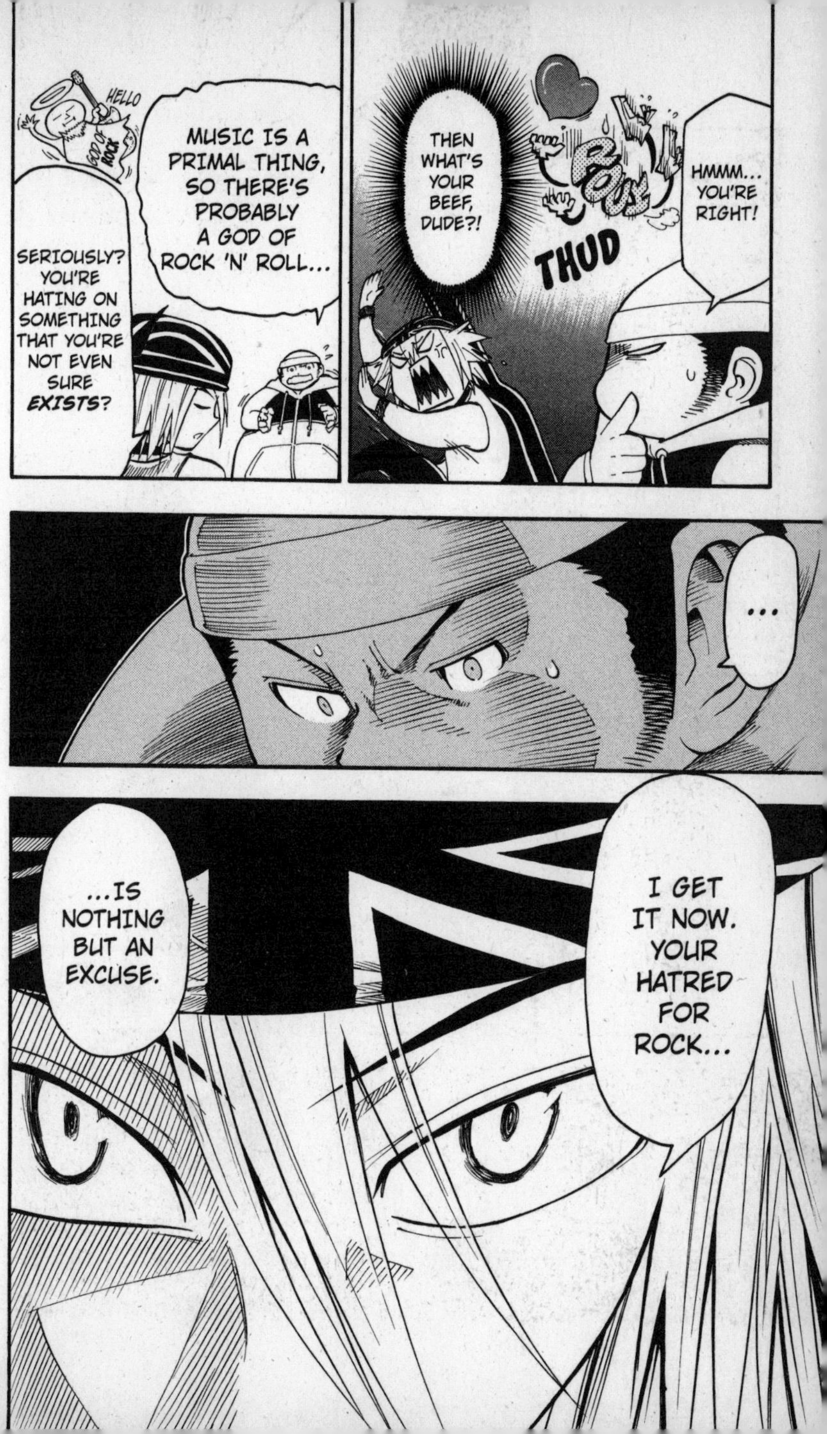
HMMM... YOU'RE RIGHT!
THUD
THEN WHAT'S YOUR BEEF, DUDE?!
MUSIC IS A PRIMAL THING, SO THERE'S PROBABLY A GOD OF ROCK 'N' ROLL...
HELLO
GOD OF ROCK
SERIOUSLY? YOU'RE HATING ON SOMETHING THAT YOU'RE NOT EVEN SURE *EXISTS*?
...
I GET IT NOW. YOUR HATRED FOR ROCK...
...IS NOTHING BUT AN EXCUSE.

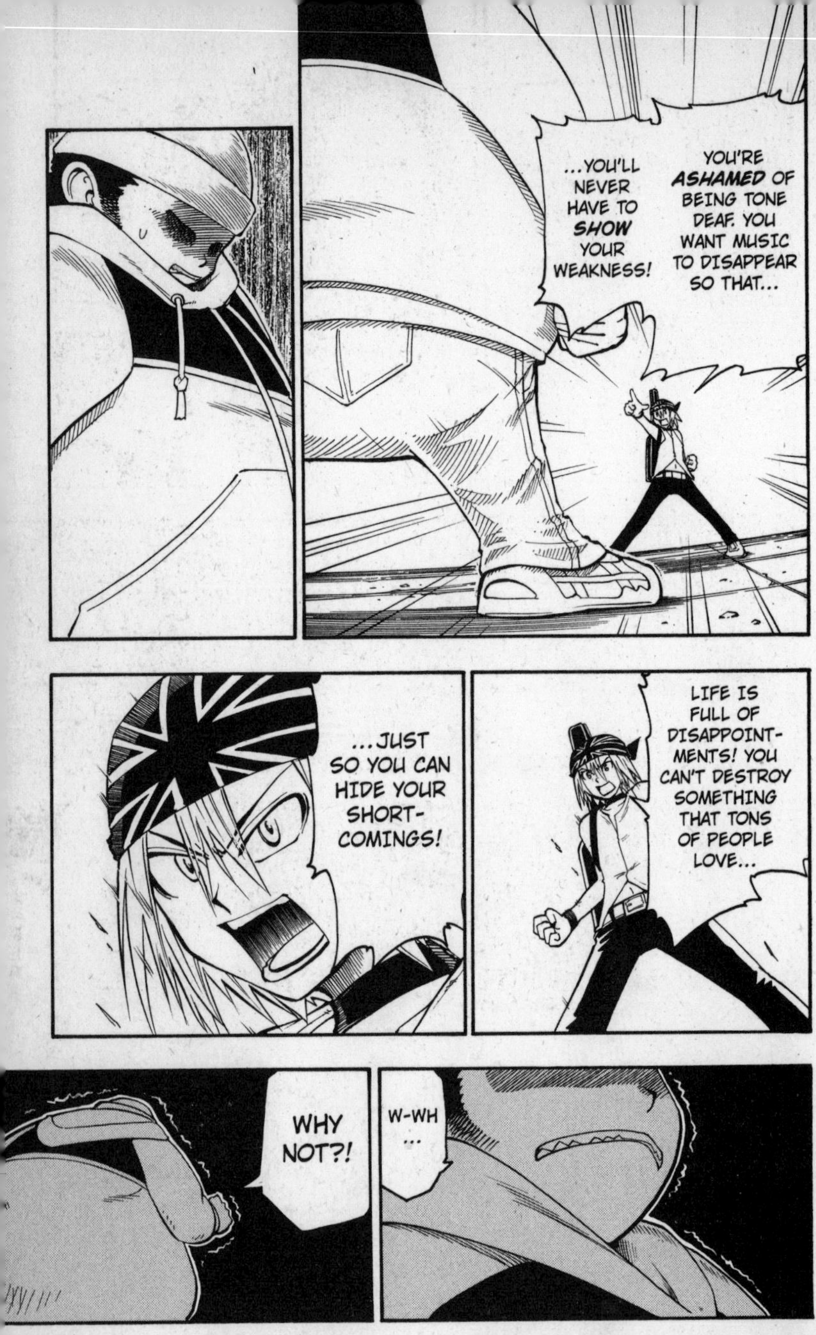
YOU'RE ASHAMED OF BEING TONE DEAF. YOU WANT MUSIC TO DISAPPEAR SO THAT...
...YOU'LL NEVER HAVE TO SHOW YOUR WEAKNESS!
LIFE IS FULL OF DISAPPOINTMENTS! YOU CAN'T DESTROY SOMETHING THAT TONS OF PEOPLE LOVE...
...JUST SO YOU CAN HIDE YOUR SHORTCOMINGS!
W-WH...
WHY NOT?!

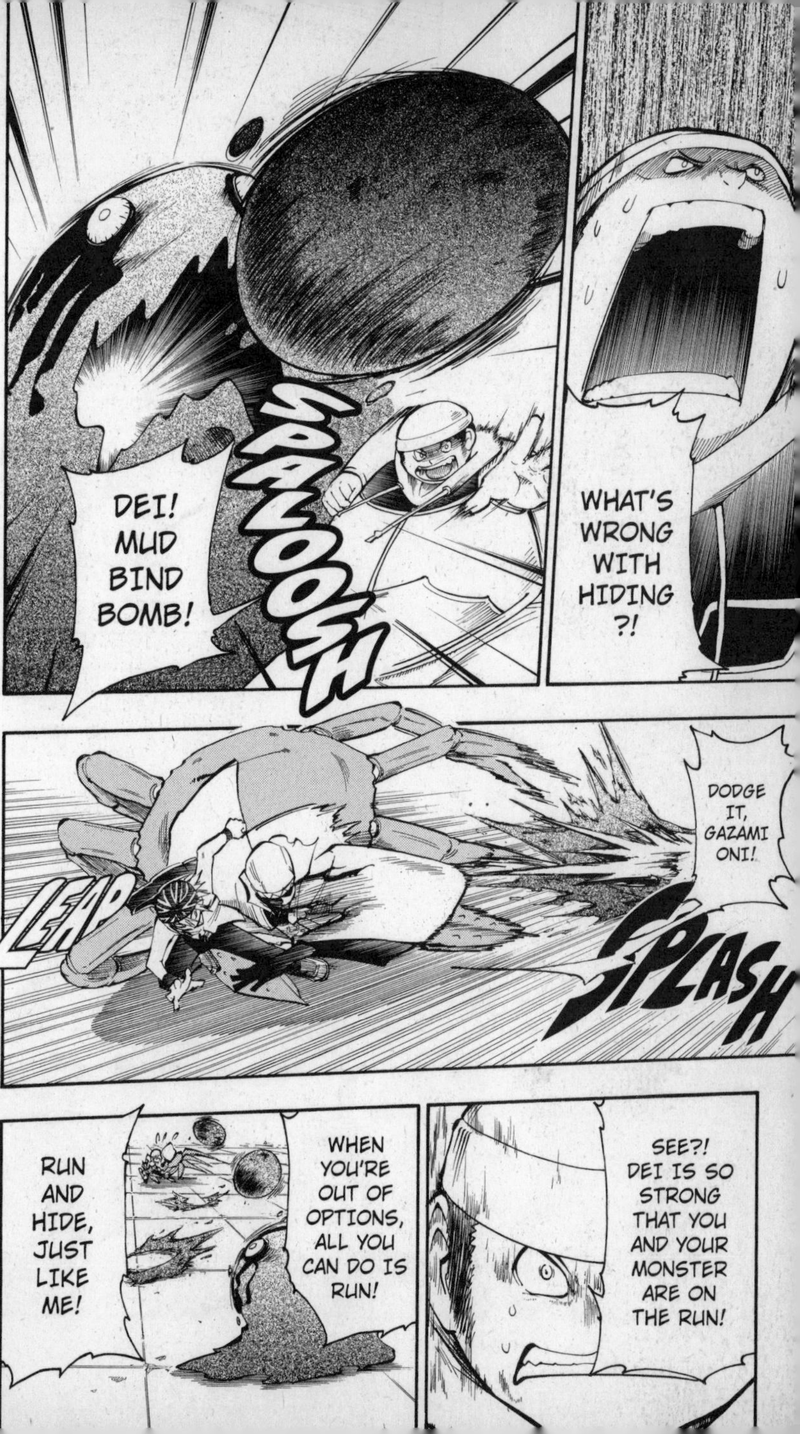
WHAT'S WRONG WITH HIDING ?!
DEI! MUD BIND BOMB!
SPALOOSH
DODGE IT, GAZAMI ONI!
SPLASH
LEAP
SEE?! DEI IS SO STRONG THAT YOU AND YOUR MONSTER ARE ON THE RUN!
WHEN YOU'RE OUT OF OPTIONS, ALL YOU CAN DO IS RUN!
RUN AND HIDE, JUST LIKE ME!

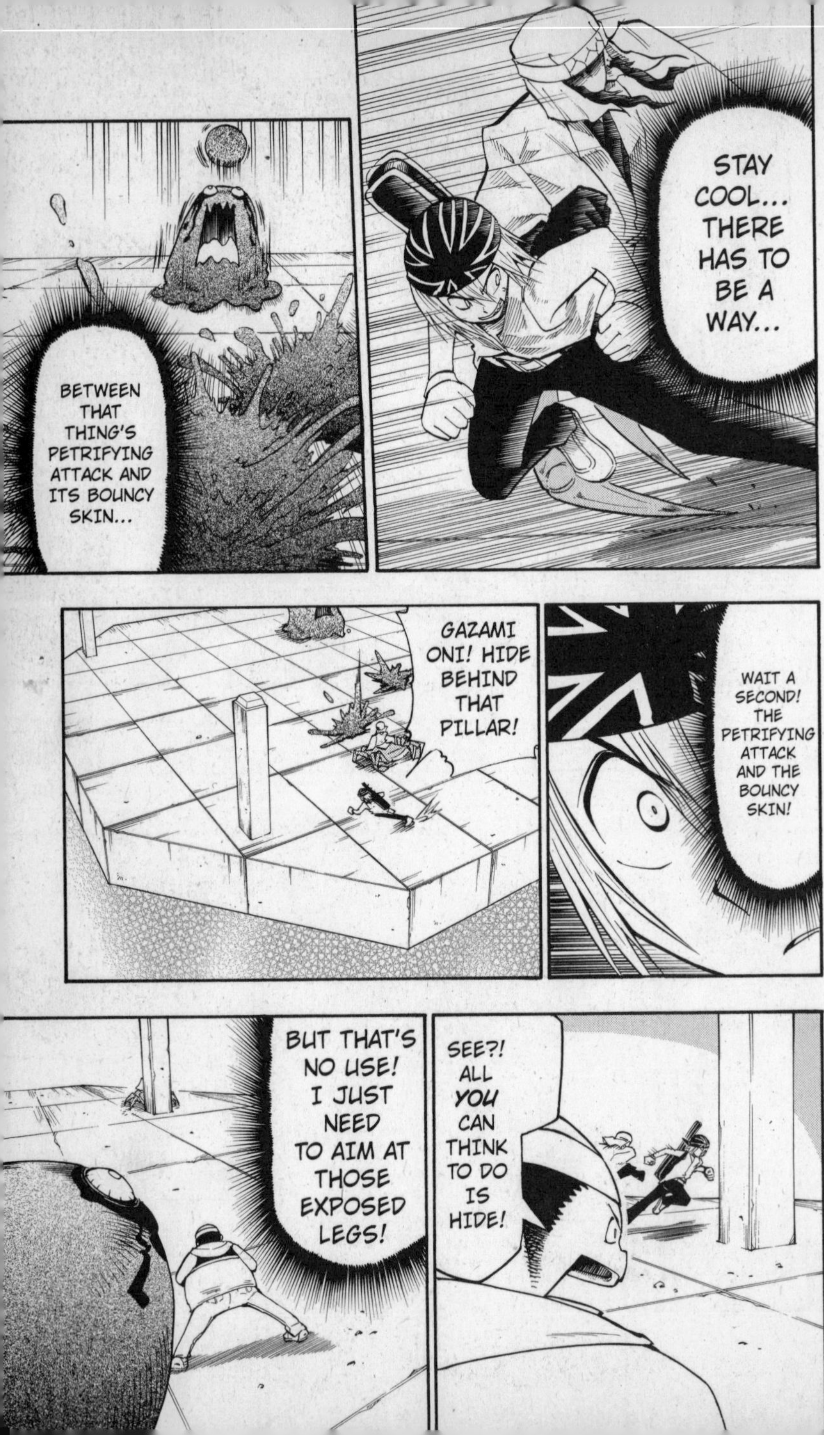
STAY COOL... THERE HAS TO BE A WAY...
BETWEEN THAT THING'S PETRIFYING ATTACK AND ITS BOUNCY SKIN...
WAIT A SECOND! THE PETRIFYING ATTACK AND THE BOUNCY SKIN!
GAZAMI ONI! HIDE BEHIND THAT PILLAR!
SEE?! ALL *YOU* CAN THINK TO DO IS HIDE!
BUT THAT'S NO USE! I JUST NEED TO AIM AT THOSE EXPOSED LEGS!

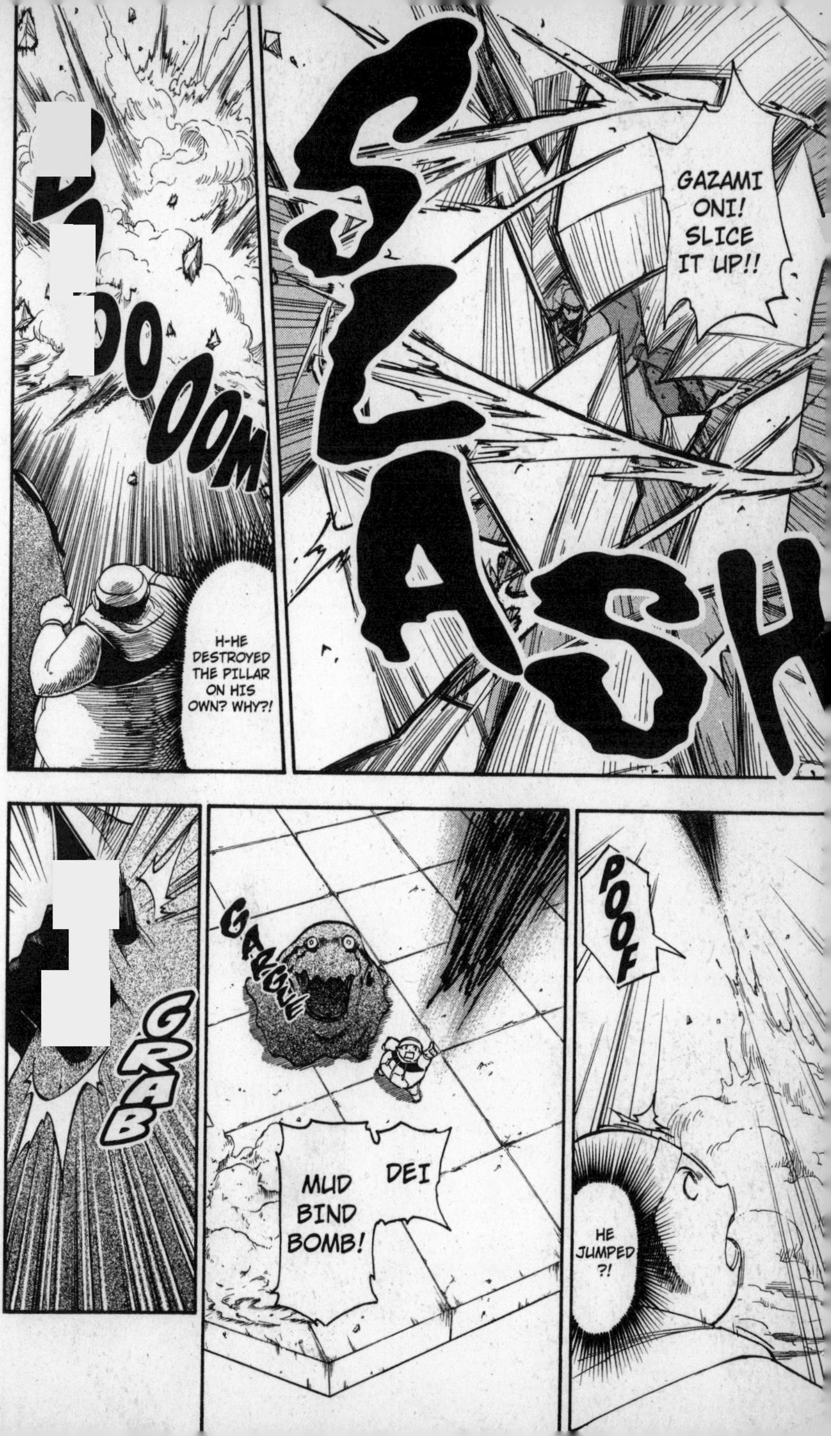
GAZAMI ONI! SLICE IT UP!!
SLASH
H-HE DESTROYED THE PILLAR ON HIS OWN? WHY?!
POOF
HE JUMPED?!
DEI
MUD BIND BOMB!
GARGLE
GRAB

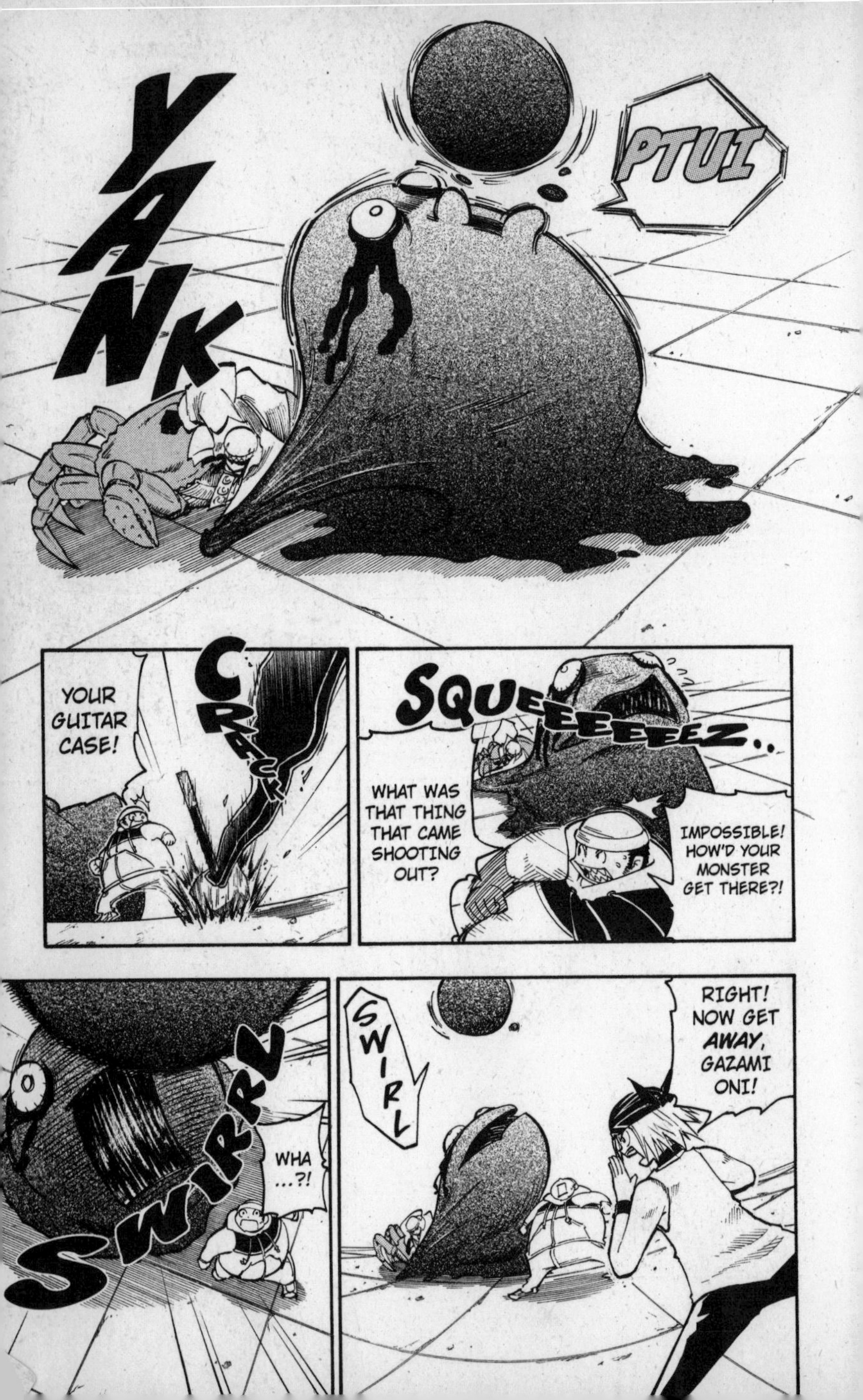
PTUI
YANK
SQUEEEEEEEZ..
IMPOSSIBLE! HOW'D YOUR MONSTER GET THERE?!
WHAT WAS THAT THING THAT CAME SHOOTING OUT?
CRACK
YOUR GUITAR CASE!
RIGHT! NOW GET AWAY, GAZAMI ONI!
SWIRL
SWIRRL
WHA ...?!

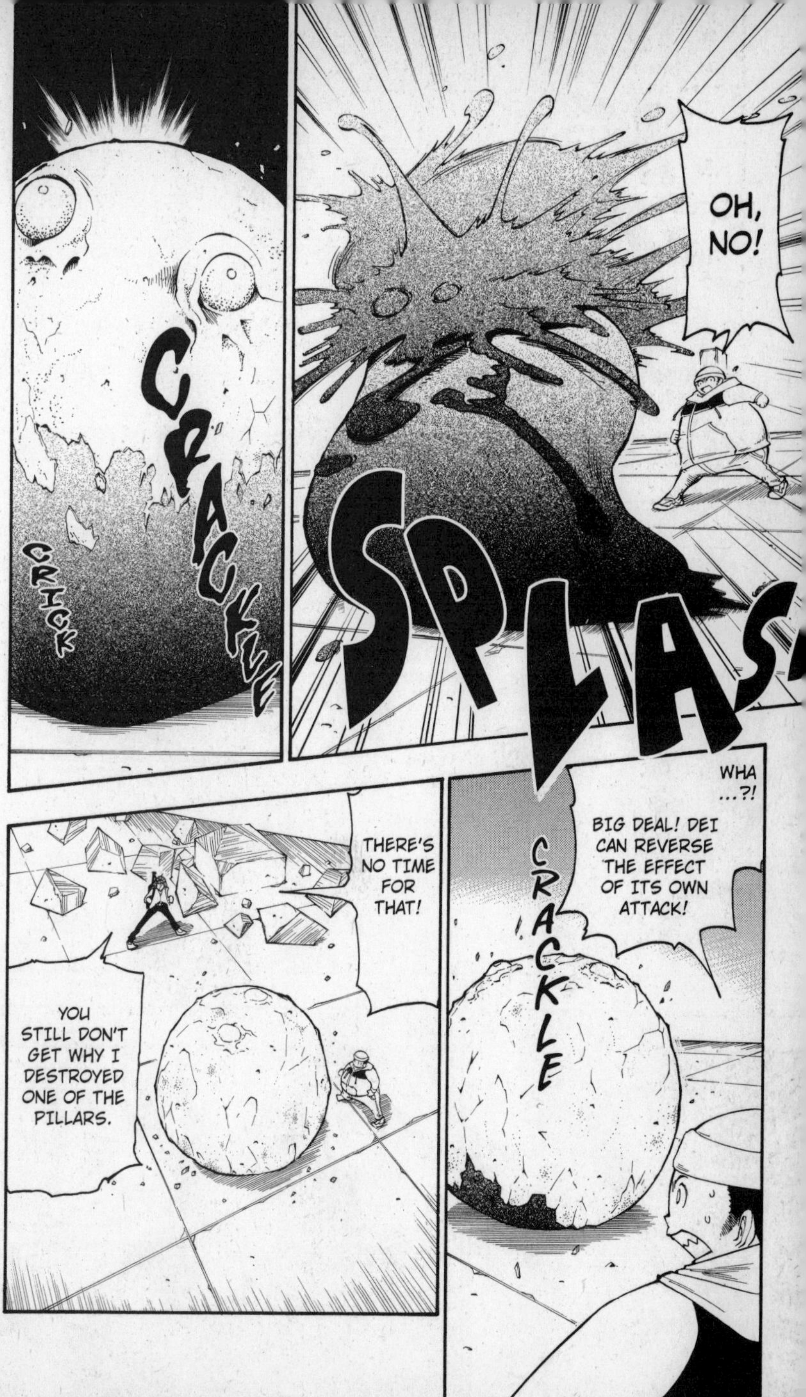
OH, NO!
SPLAS
CRACKLE
CRICK
WHA...?!
BIG DEAL! DEI CAN REVERSE THE EFFECT OF ITS OWN ATTACK!
CRACKLE
THERE'S NO TIME FOR THAT!
YOU STILL DON'T GET WHY I DESTROYED ONE OF THE PILLARS.

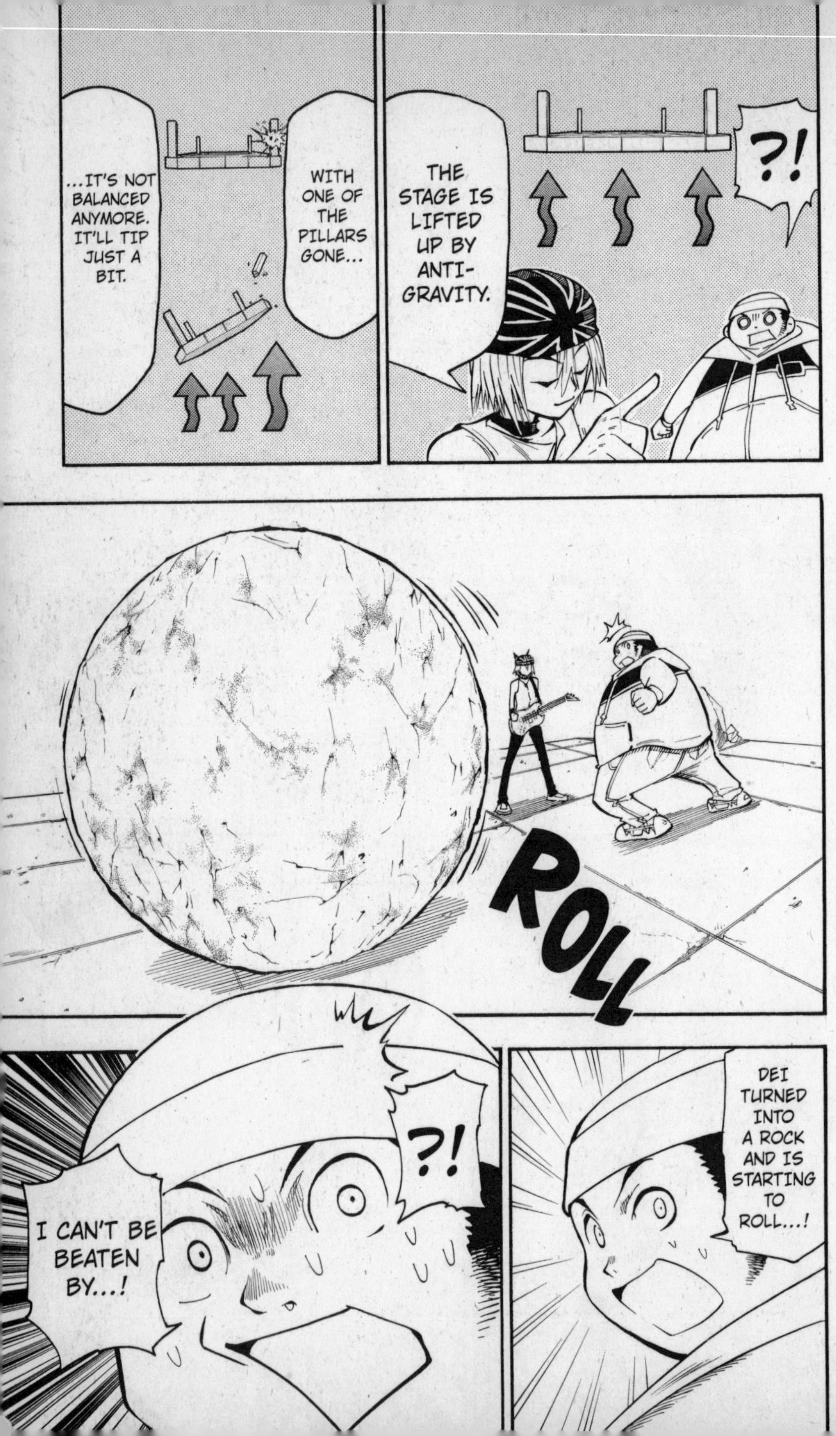
?!
THE STAGE IS LIFTED UP BY ANTI-GRAVITY.
WITH ONE OF THE PILLARS GONE...
...IT'S NOT BALANCED ANYMORE. IT'LL TIP JUST A BIT.
ROLL
DEI TURNED INTO A ROCK AND IS STARTING TO ROLL...!
?!
I CAN'T BE BEATEN BY...!

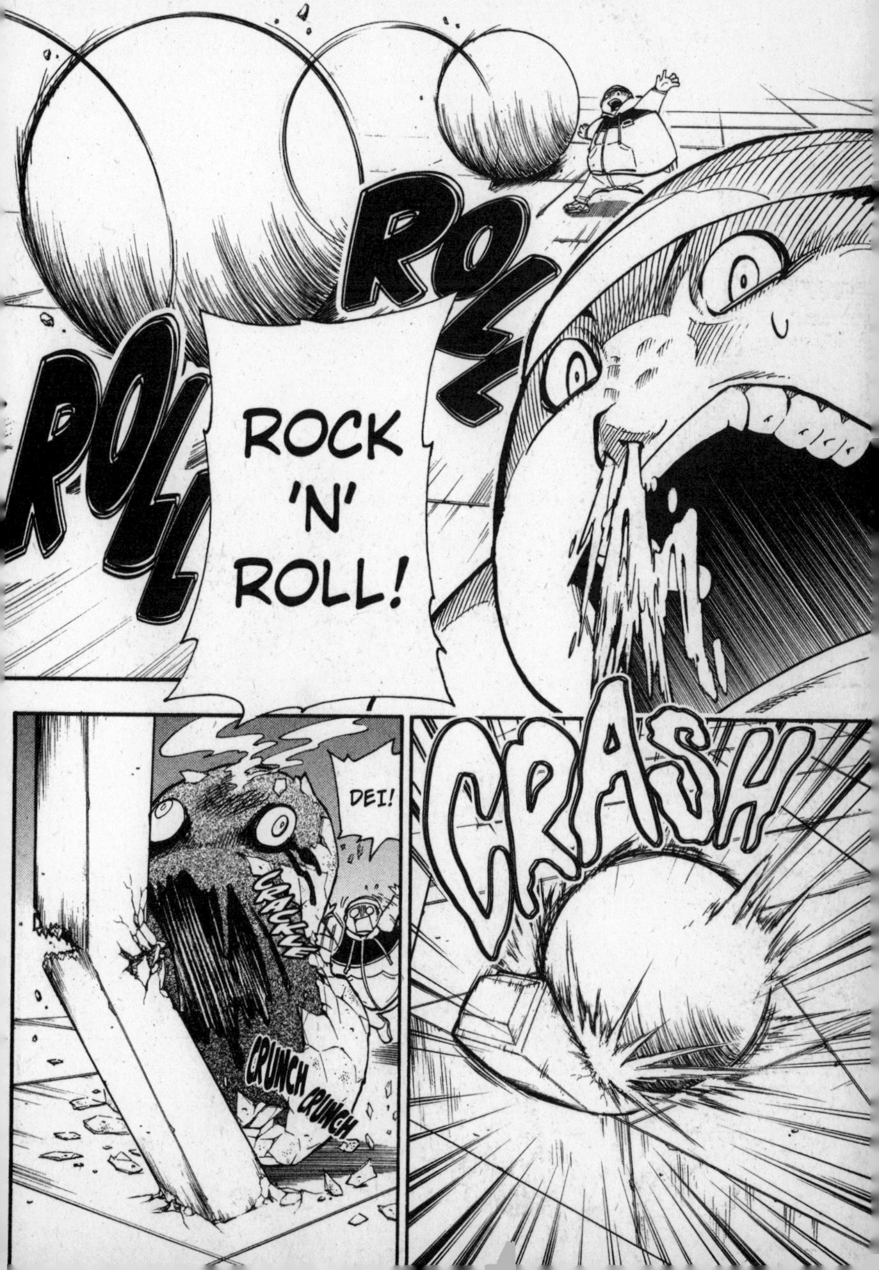
ROLL
ROLL
ROCK 'N' ROLL!
CRASH
DEI!
CRACKLE
CRUNCH CRUNCH

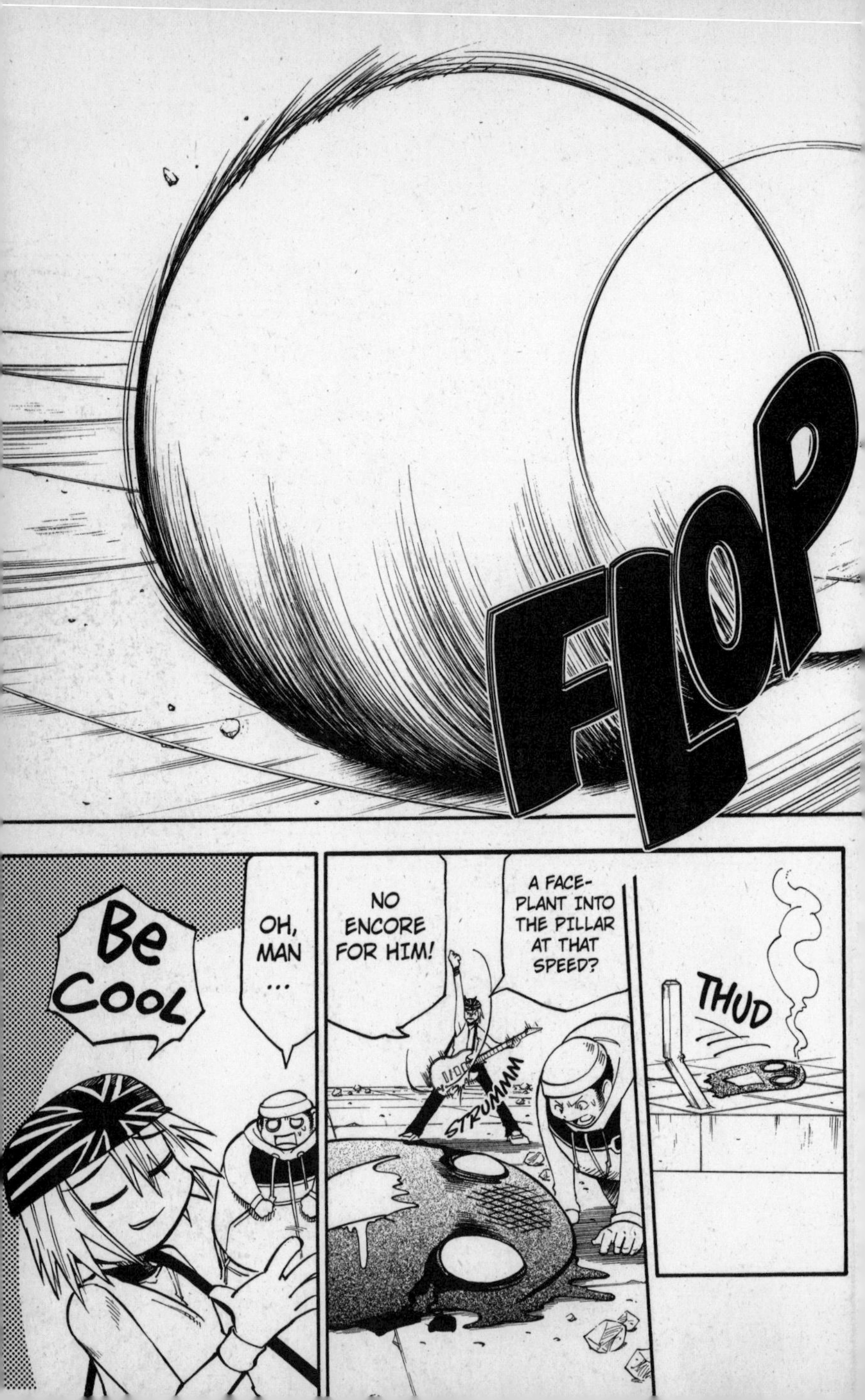
FLOP
THUD
A FACE-PLANT INTO THE PILLAR AT THAT SPEED?
NO ENCORE FOR HIM!
STRUMMM
OH, MAN ...
Be Cool

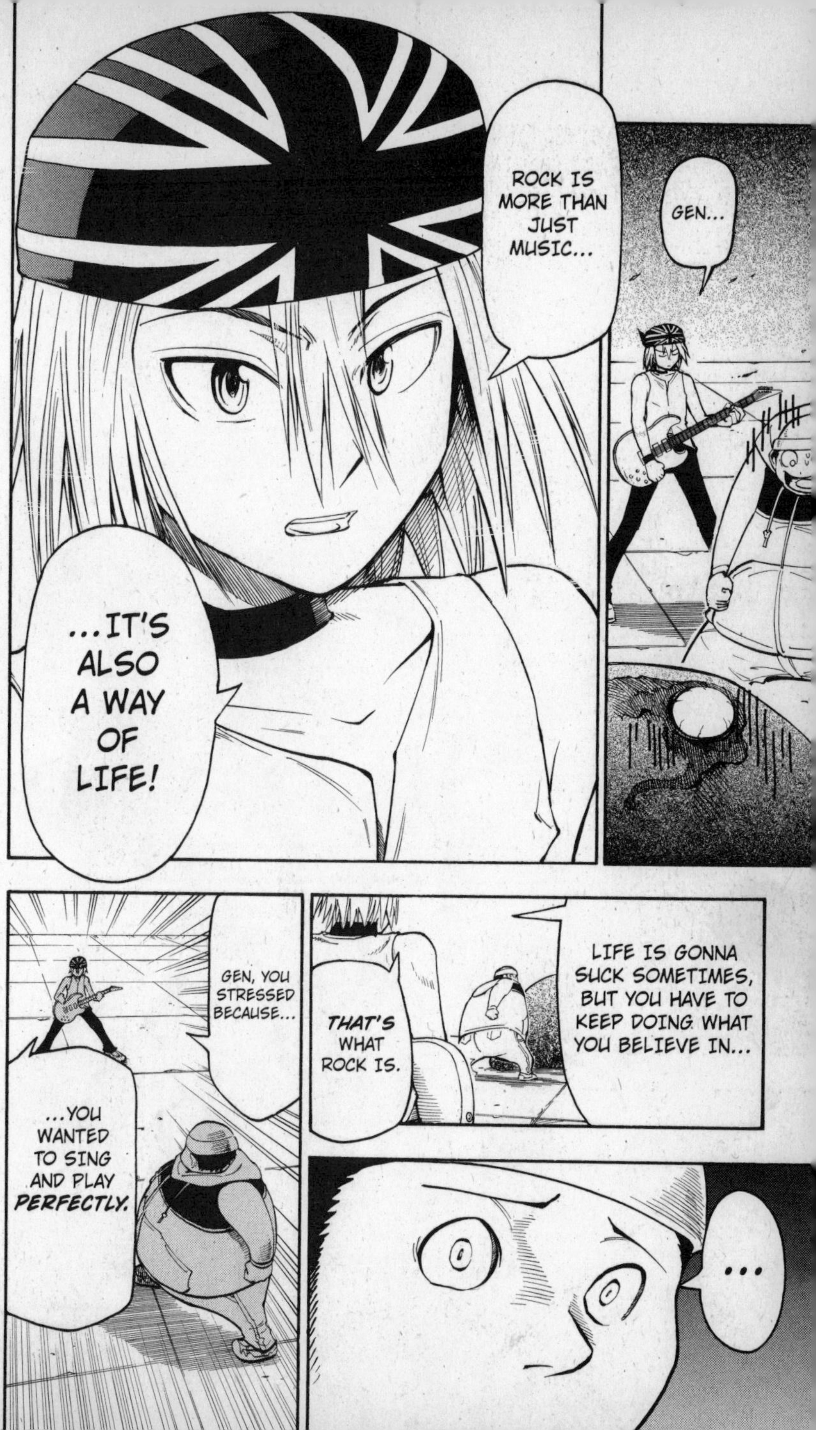
GEN...
ROCK IS MORE THAN JUST MUSIC...
...IT'S ALSO A WAY OF LIFE!
LIFE IS GONNA SUCK SOMETIMES, BUT YOU HAVE TO KEEP DOING WHAT YOU BELIEVE IN...
THAT'S WHAT ROCK IS.
...
GEN, YOU STRESSED BECAUSE...
...YOU WANTED TO SING AND PLAY *PERFECTLY.*

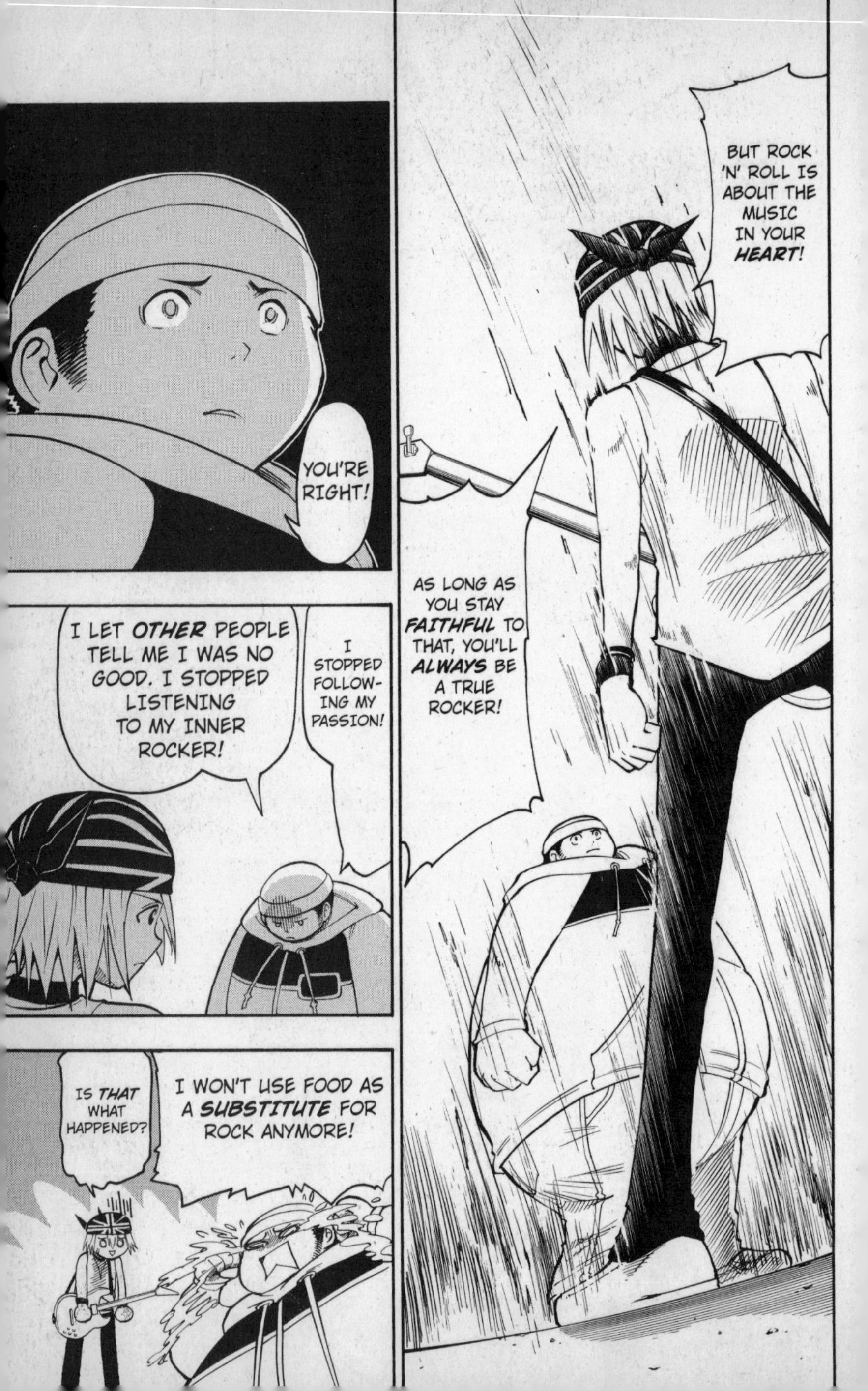
BUT ROCK 'N' ROLL IS ABOUT THE MUSIC IN YOUR *HEART*!
AS LONG AS YOU STAY *FAITHFUL* TO THAT, YOU'LL *ALWAYS* BE A TRUE ROCKER!
YOU'RE RIGHT!
I STOPPED FOLLOW-ING MY PASSION!
I LET *OTHER* PEOPLE TELL ME I WAS NO GOOD. I STOPPED LISTENING TO MY INNER ROCKER!
I WON'T USE FOOD AS A *SUBSTITUTE* FOR ROCK ANYMORE!
IS *THAT* WHAT HAPPENED?

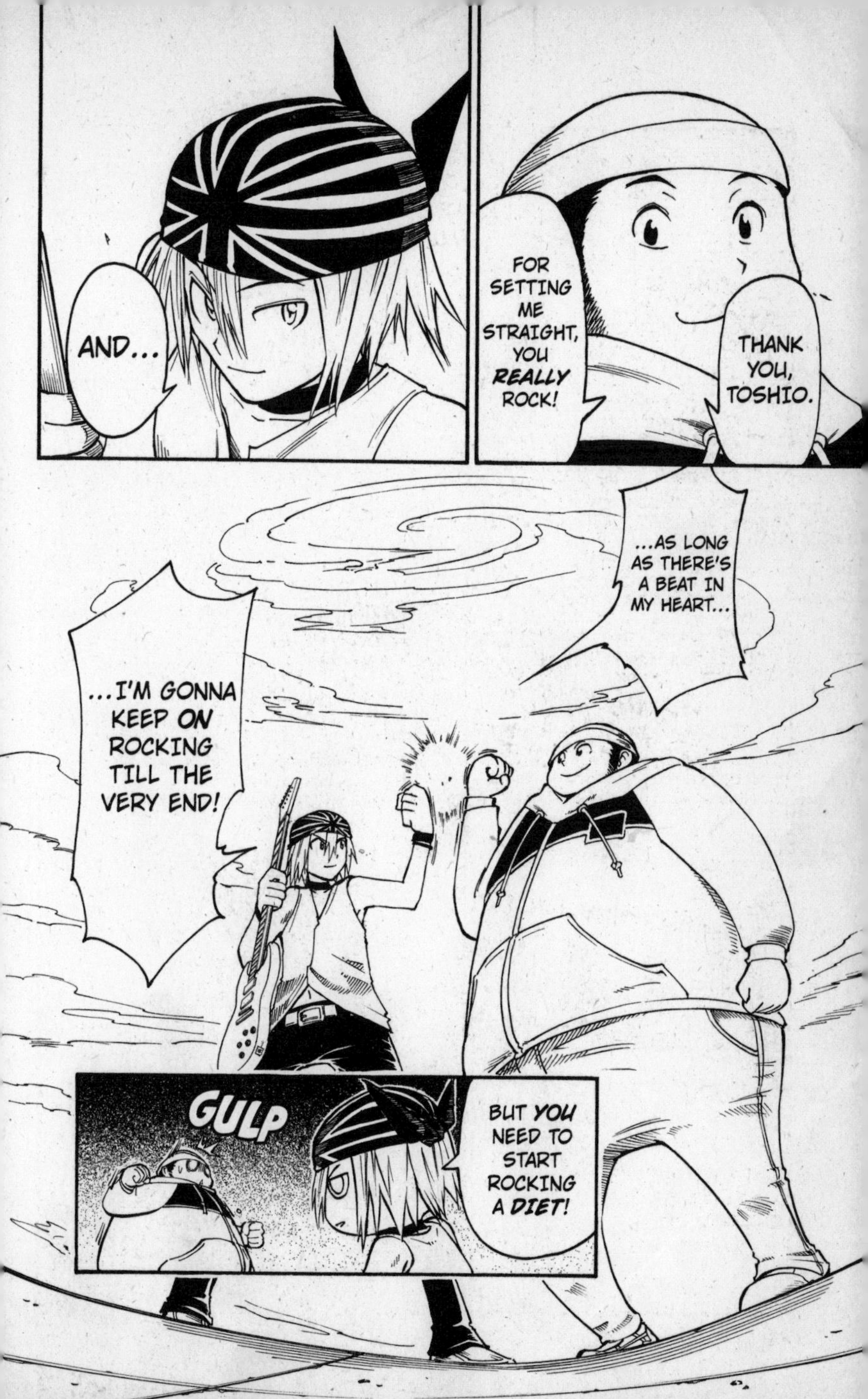
THANK YOU, TOSHIO.
FOR SETTING ME STRAIGHT, YOU *REALLY* ROCK!
AND...
...AS LONG AS THERE'S A BEAT IN MY HEART...
...I'M GONNA KEEP *ON* ROCKING TILL THE VERY END!
BUT *YOU* NEED TO START ROCKING A *DIET*!
GULP

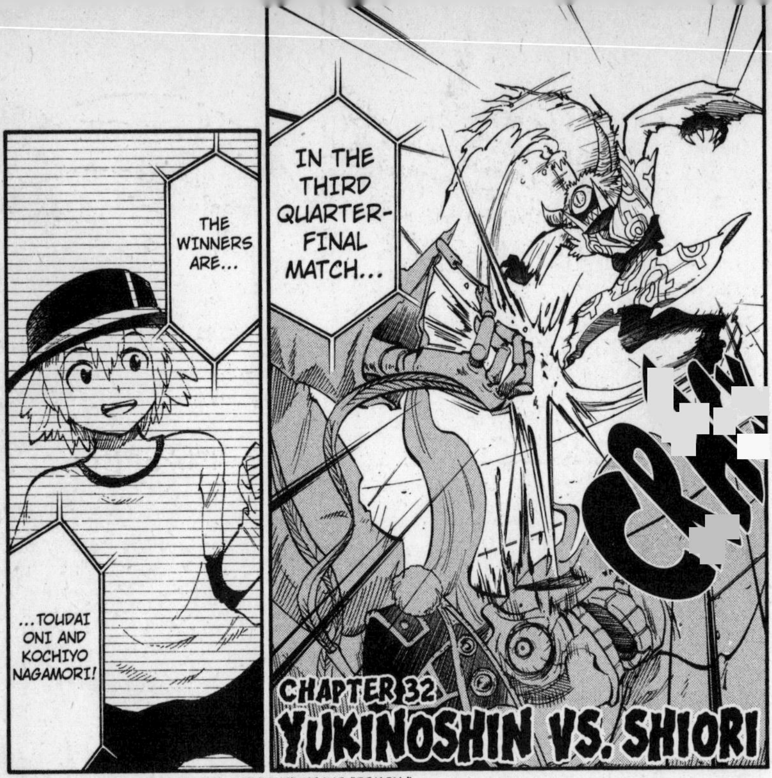
IN THE THIRD QUARTER-FINAL MATCH...
CHAPTER 32
YUKINOSHIN VS. SHIORI
THE WINNERS ARE...
...TOUDAI ONI AND KOCHIYO NAGAMORI!

"TOUDAI" MEANS "LIGHTHOUSE" AND "ONI" MEANS "DEMON."

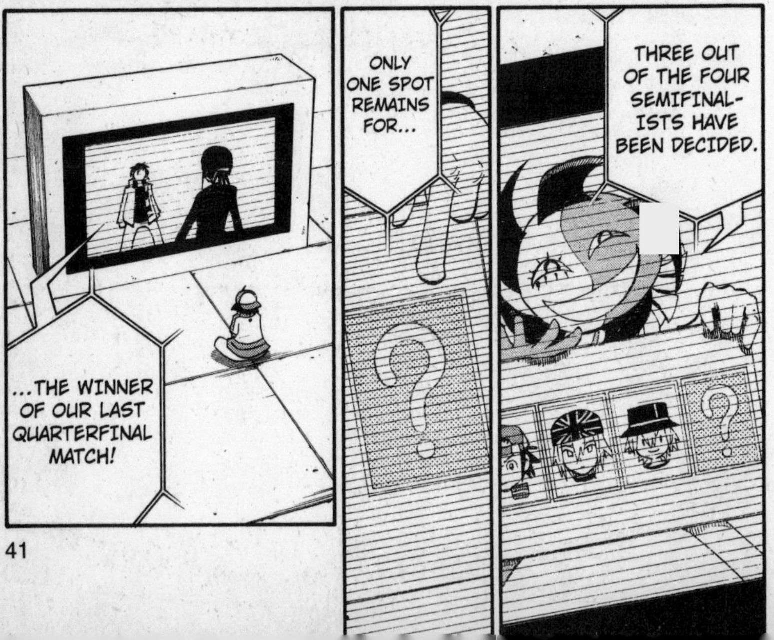
THREE OUT OF THE FOUR SEMIFINAL-ISTS HAVE BEEN DECIDED.
ONLY ONE SPOT REMAINS FOR...
...THE WINNER OF OUR LAST QUARTERFINAL MATCH!

CHAPTER 32

YUKINOSHIN VS. SHIORI

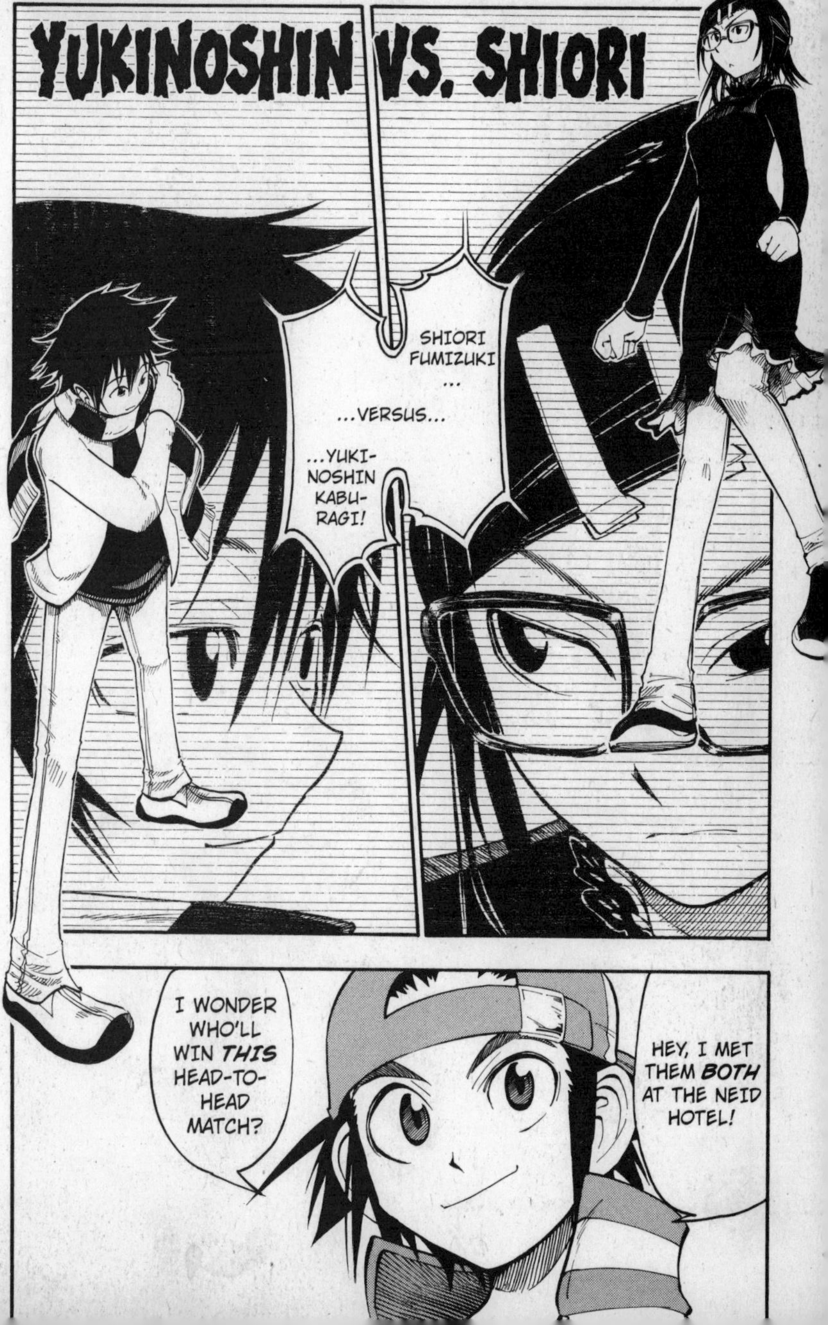
SHIORI FUMIZUKI ...
...VERSUS...
...YUKI-NOSHIN KABU-RAGI!
HEY, I MET THEM *BOTH* AT THE NEID HOTEL!
I WONDER WHO'LL WIN *THIS* HEAD-TO-HEAD MATCH?

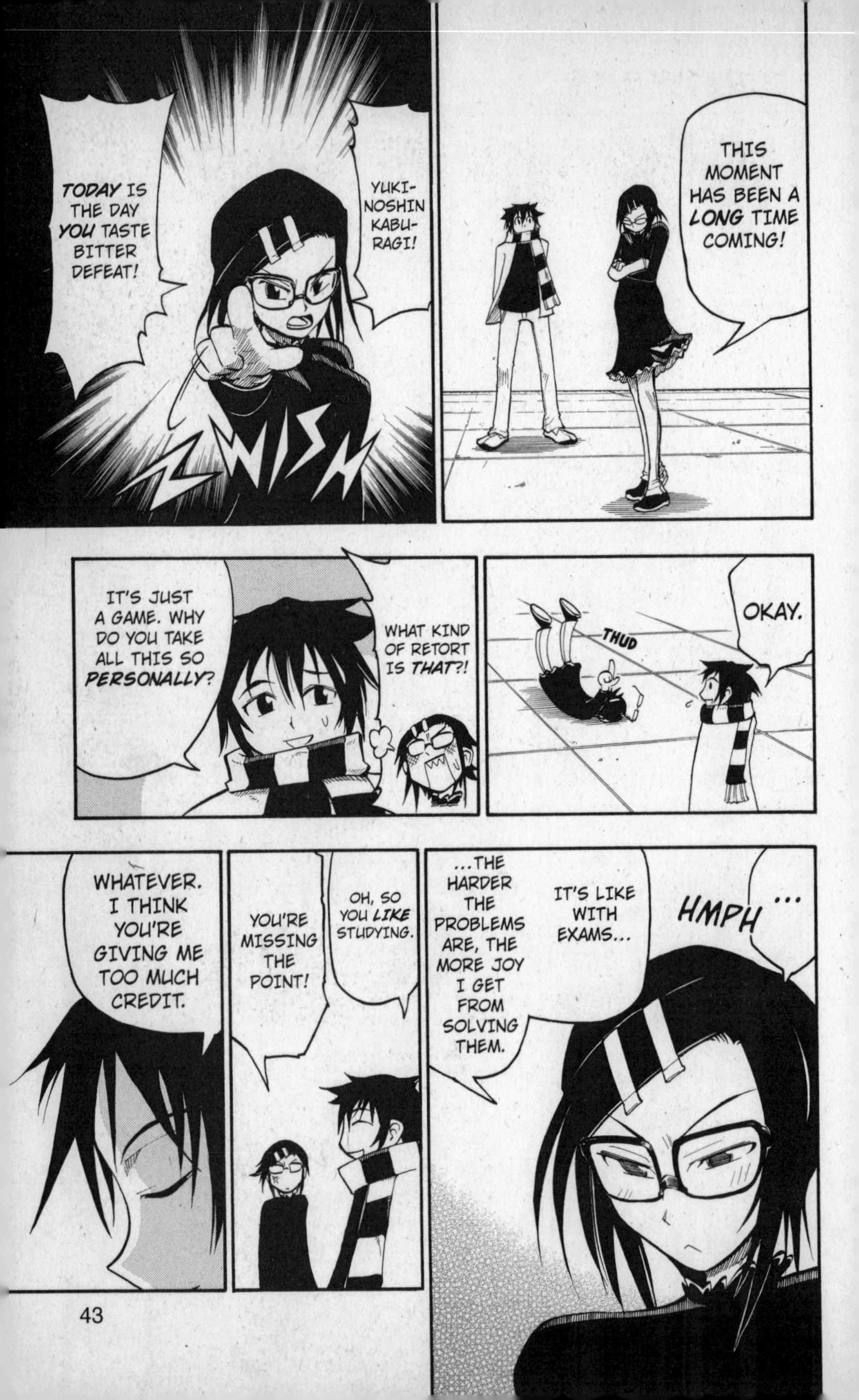
THIS MOMENT HAS BEEN A LONG TIME COMING!
YUKINOSHIN KABURAGI!
TODAY IS THE DAY YOU TASTE BITTER DEFEAT!
ZWISH
OKAY.
THUD
WHAT KIND OF RETORT IS THAT?!
IT'S JUST A GAME. WHY DO YOU TAKE ALL THIS SO PERSONALLY?
HMPH...
IT'S LIKE WITH EXAMS...
...THE HARDER THE PROBLEMS ARE, THE MORE JOY I GET FROM SOLVING THEM.
OH, SO YOU LIKE STUDYING.
YOU'RE MISSING THE POINT!
WHATEVER. I THINK YOU'RE GIVING ME TOO MUCH CREDIT.

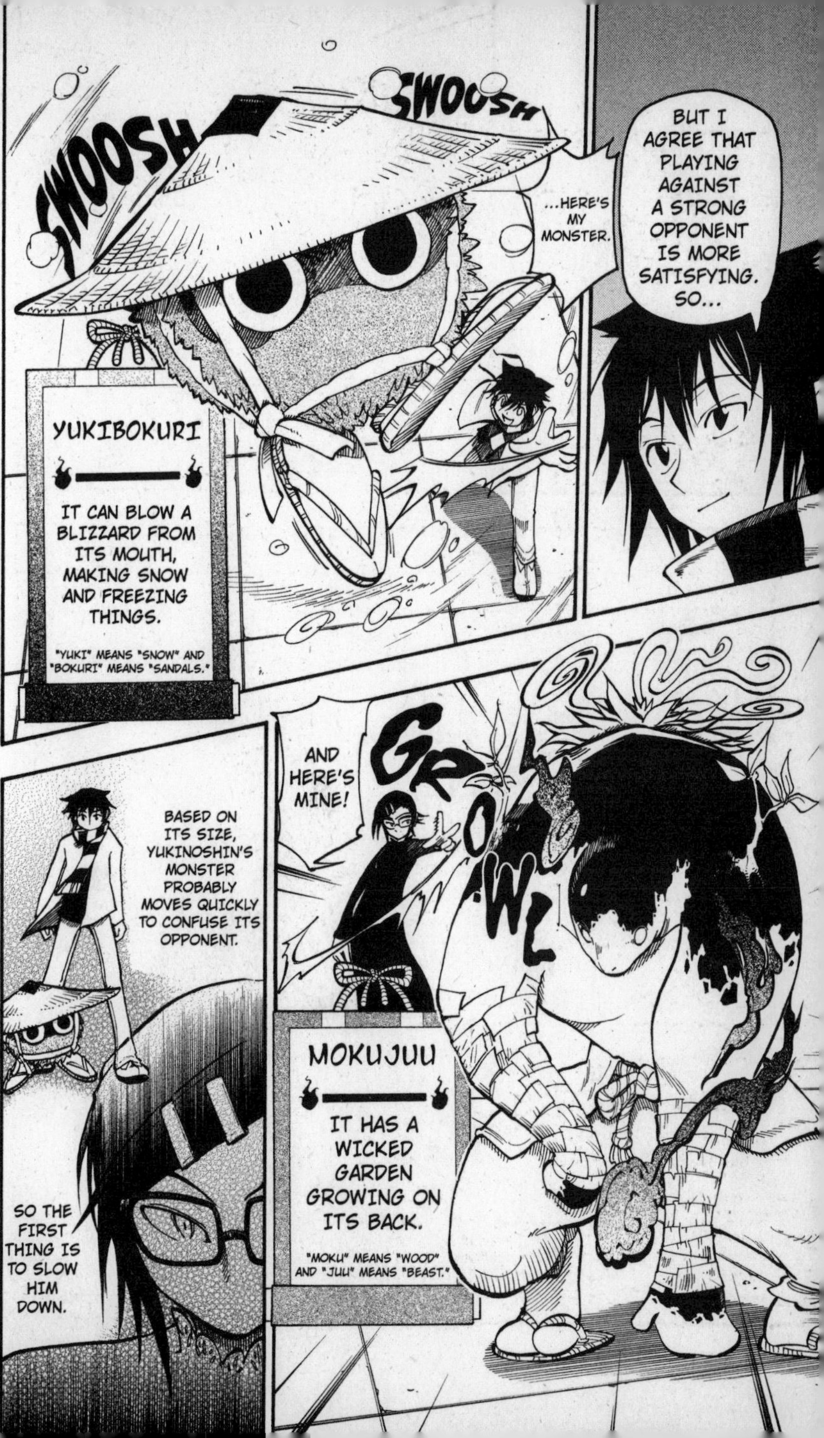
BUT I AGREE THAT PLAYING AGAINST A STRONG OPPONENT IS MORE SATISFYING. SO...
SWOOSH
...HERE'S MY MONSTER.
SWOOSH
YUKIBOKURI
IT CAN BLOW A BLIZZARD FROM ITS MOUTH, MAKING SNOW AND FREEZING THINGS.
"YUKI" MEANS "SNOW" AND "BOKURI" MEANS "SANDALS."
AND HERE'S MINE!
GROWL
MOKUJUU
IT HAS A WICKED GARDEN GROWING ON ITS BACK.
"MOKU" MEANS "WOOD" AND "JUU" MEANS "BEAST."
BASED ON ITS SIZE, YUKINOSHIN'S MONSTER PROBABLY MOVES QUICKLY TO CONFUSE ITS OPPONENT.
SO THE FIRST THING IS TO SLOW HIM DOWN.

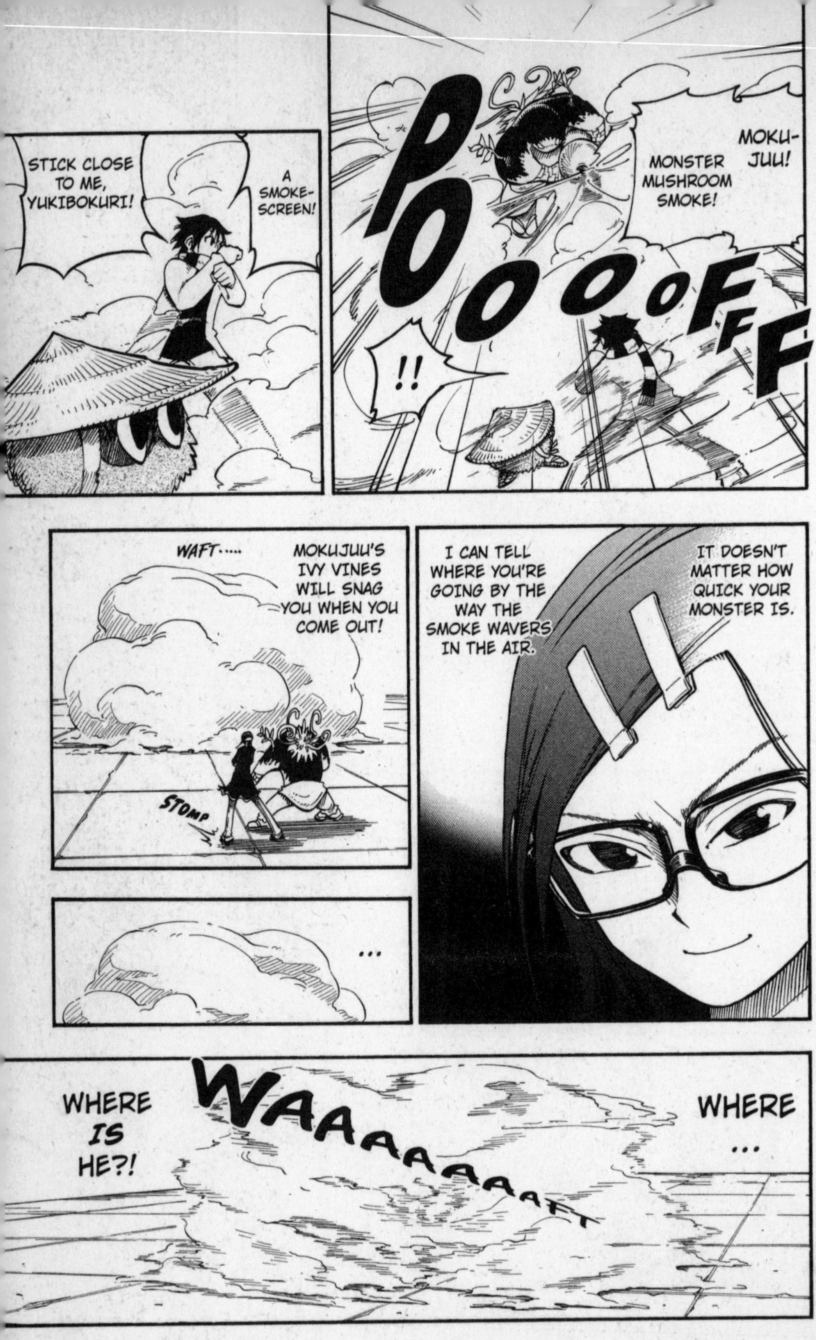
MOKU-JUU!
MONSTER MUSHROOM SMOKE!
POOOOOFFF
!!
A SMOKE-SCREEN!
STICK CLOSE TO ME, YUKIBOKURI!
IT DOESN'T MATTER HOW QUICK YOUR MONSTER IS.
I CAN TELL WHERE YOU'RE GOING BY THE WAY THE SMOKE WAVERS IN THE AIR.
MOKUJUU'S IVY VINES WILL SNAG YOU WHEN YOU COME OUT!
WAFT.....
STOMP
...
WHERE ...
WAAAAAAAAFT
WHERE IS HE?!

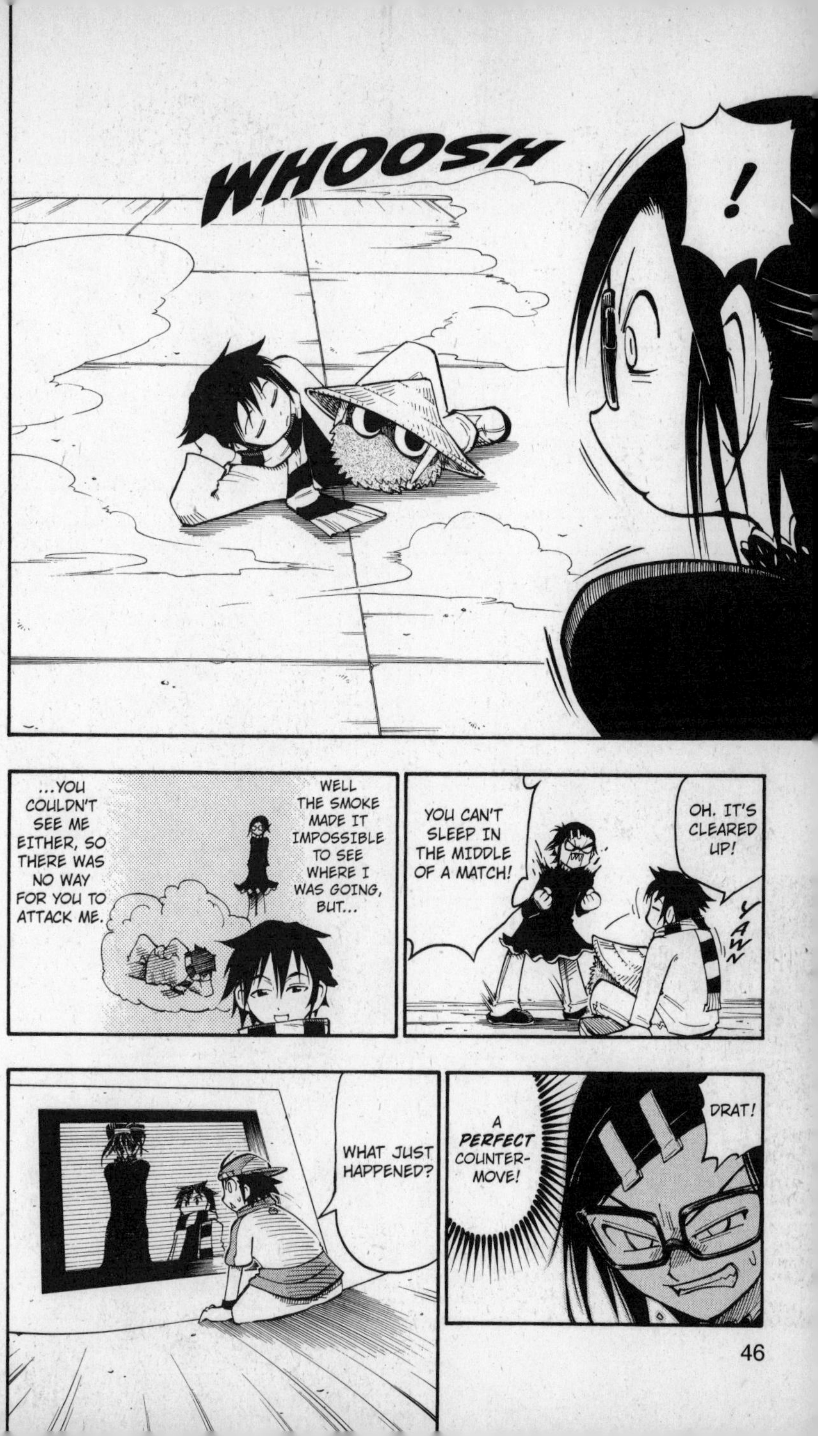
!
WHOOSH
OH. IT'S CLEARED UP!
YAWN
YOU CAN'T SLEEP IN THE MIDDLE OF A MATCH!
WELL THE SMOKE MADE IT IMPOSSIBLE TO SEE WHERE I WAS GOING, BUT...
...YOU COULDN'T SEE ME EITHER, SO THERE WAS NO WAY FOR YOU TO ATTACK ME.
DRAT!
A PERFECT COUNTER-MOVE!
WHAT JUST HAPPENED?

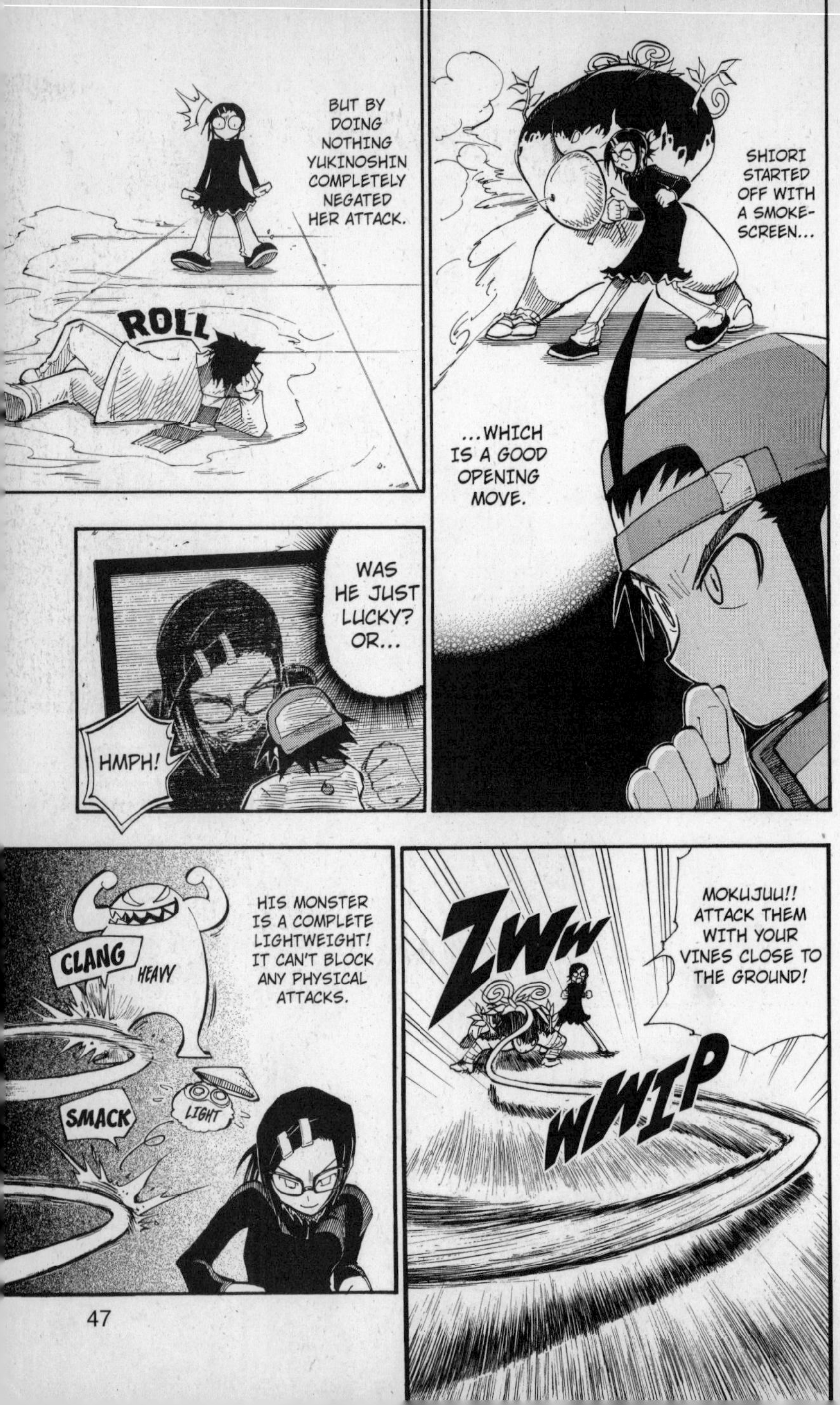
SHIORI STARTED OFF WITH A SMOKE-SCREEN...
BUT BY DOING NOTHING YUKINOSHIN COMPLETELY NEGATED HER ATTACK.
ROLL
...WHICH IS A GOOD OPENING MOVE.
WAS HE JUST LUCKY? OR...
HMPH!
MOKUJUU!! ATTACK THEM WITH YOUR VINES CLOSE TO THE GROUND!
ZWW
WHIP
HIS MONSTER IS A COMPLETE LIGHTWEIGHT! IT CAN'T BLOCK ANY PHYSICAL ATTACKS.
CLANG
HEAVY
SMACK
LIGHT

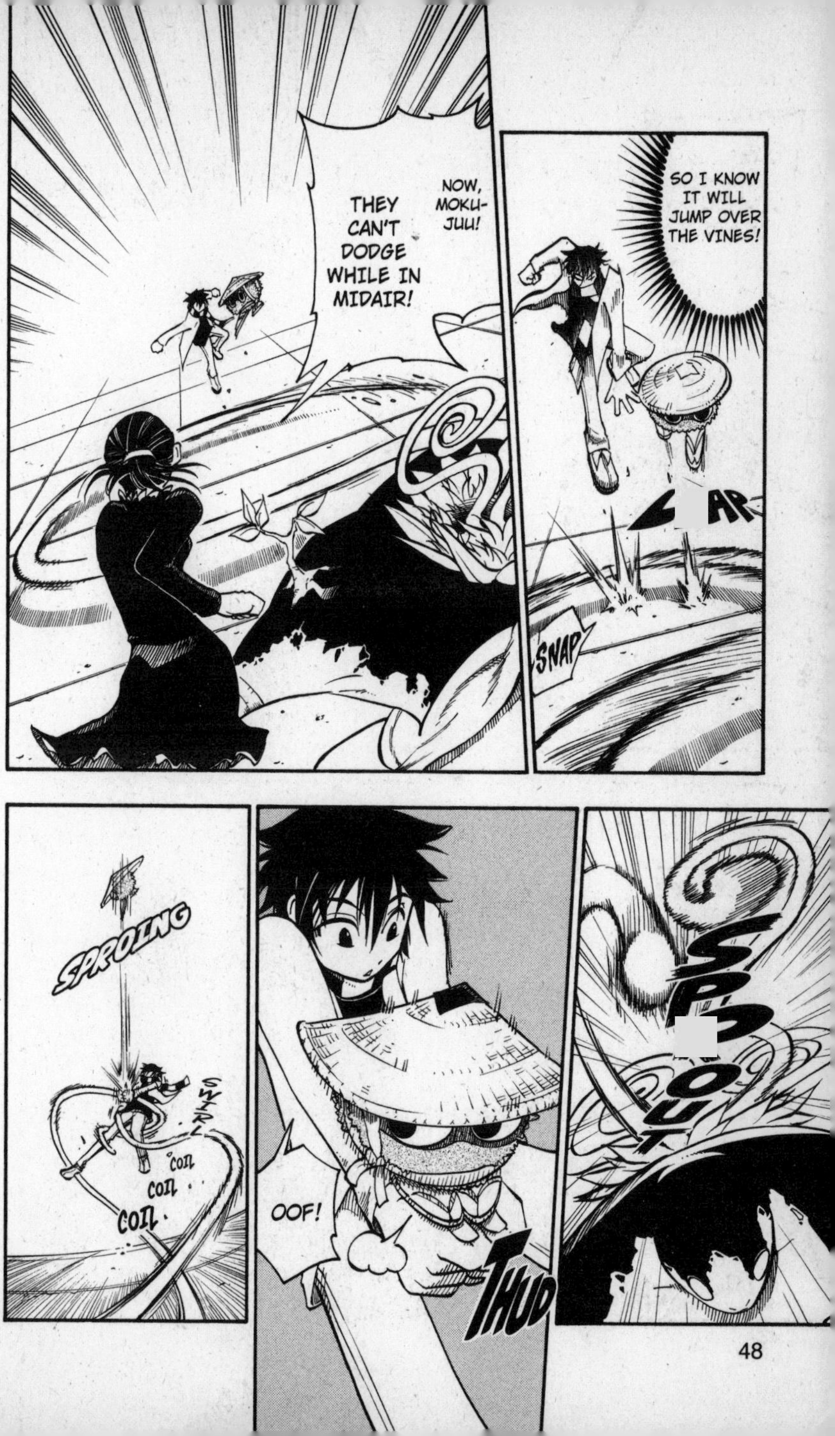
SO I KNOW IT WILL JUMP OVER THE VINES!
SNAP
NOW, MOKUJUU!
THEY CAN'T DODGE WHILE IN MIDAIR!
OOF!
THUD
SPROING
SWIRL
COIL
COIL
COIL

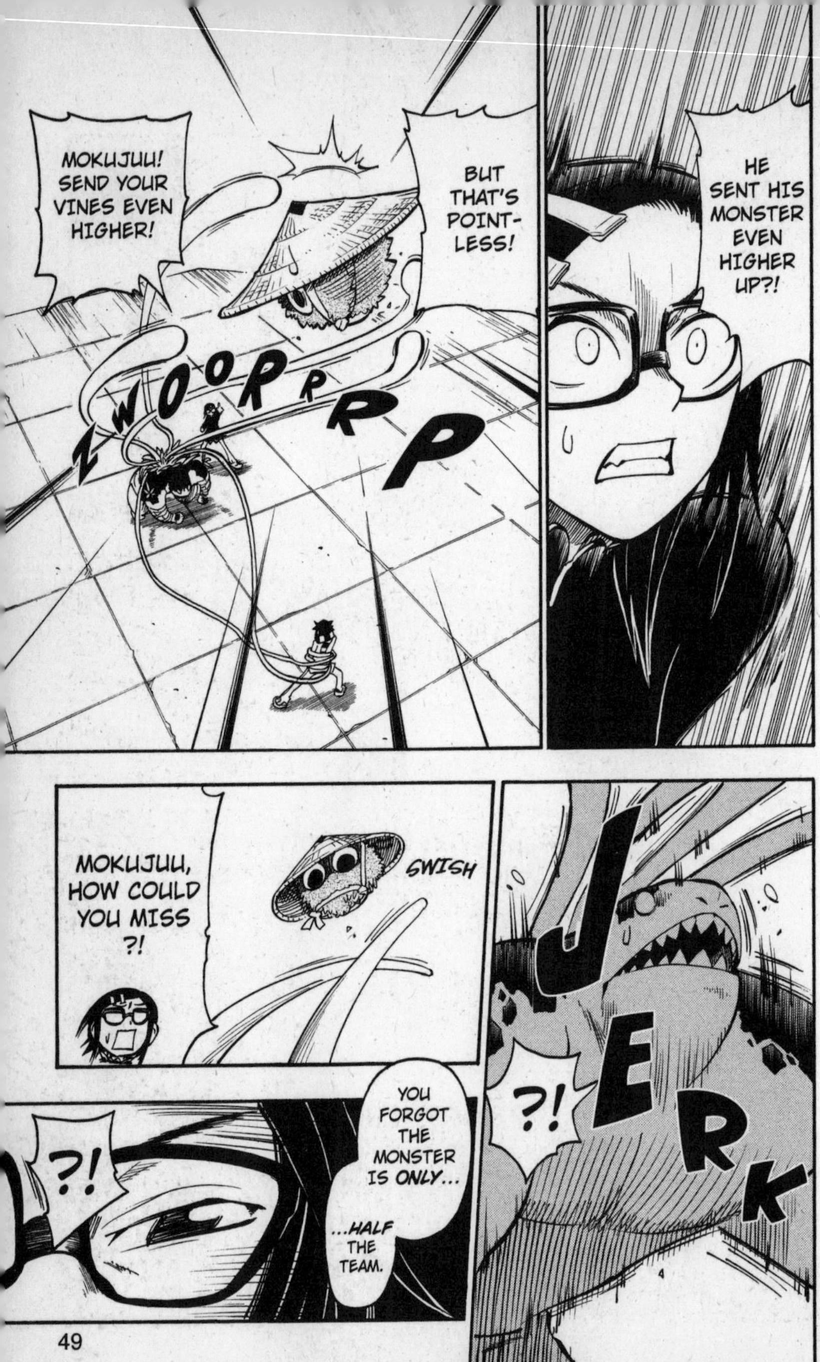
HE SENT HIS MONSTER EVEN HIGHER UP?!
BUT THAT'S POINTLESS!
MOKUJUU! SEND YOUR VINES EVEN HIGHER!
ZWOORRRP
JERK
?!
MOKUJUU, HOW COULD YOU MISS ?!
SWISH
YOU FORGOT THE MONSTER IS *ONLY*...
...*HALF* THE TEAM.
?!

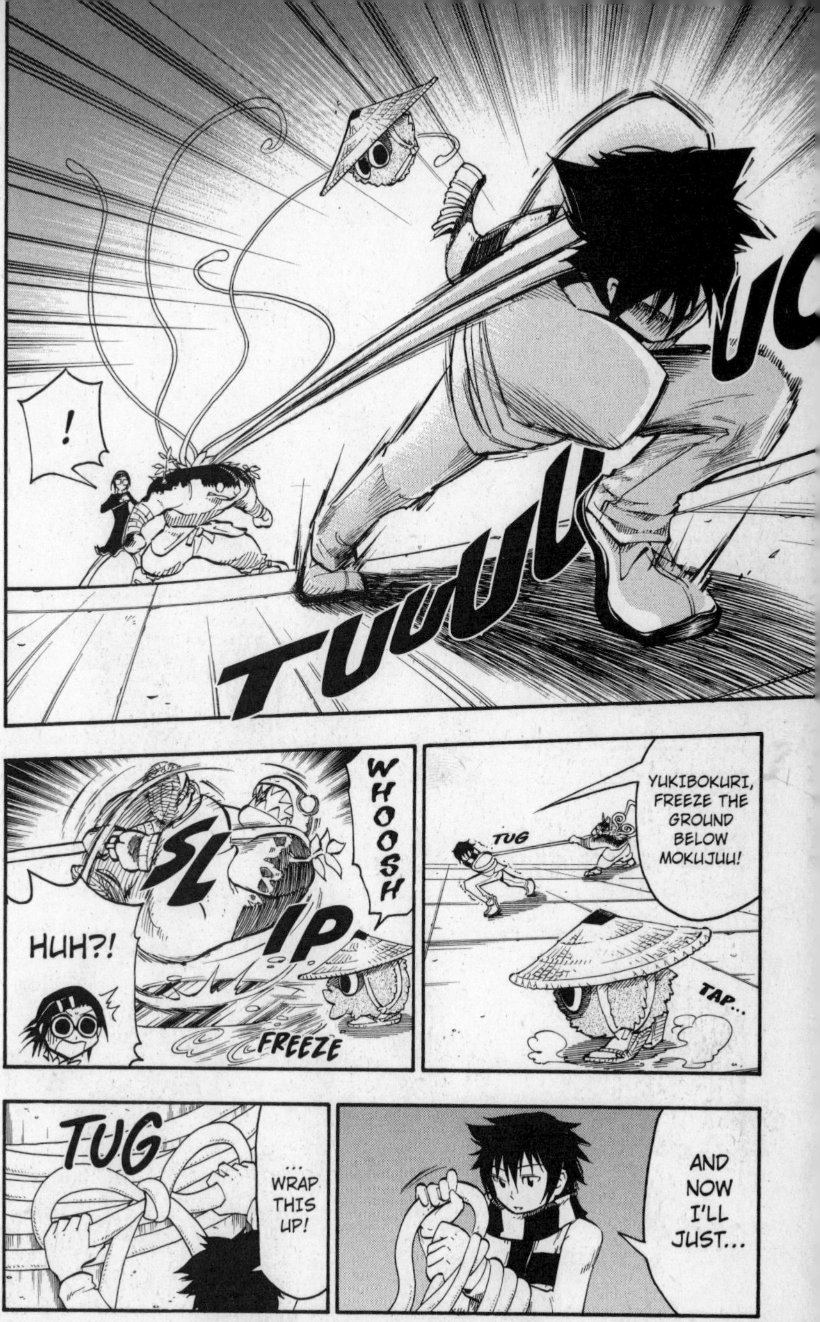
!
TUUUUUG
YUKIBOKURI, FREEZE THE GROUND BELOW MOKUJUU!
TUG
TAP...
WHOOSH
SLIP
HUH?!
FREEZE
AND NOW I'LL JUST...
TUG
...WRAP THIS UP!

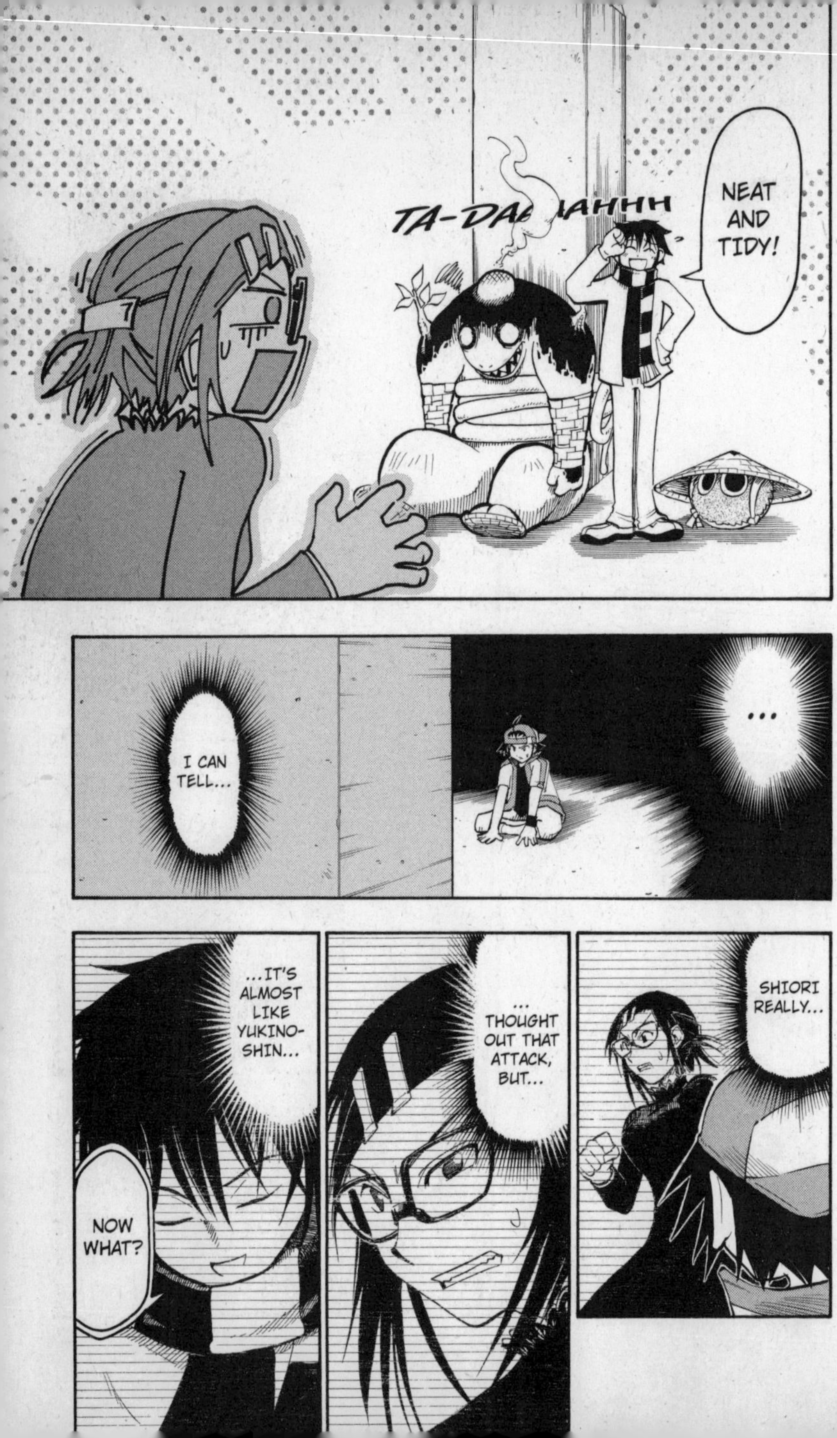
NEAT AND TIDY!
TA-DAHHHH
...
I CAN TELL...
SHIORI REALLY...
... THOUGHT OUT THAT ATTACK, BUT...
...IT'S ALMOST LIKE YUKINO-SHIN...
NOW WHAT?

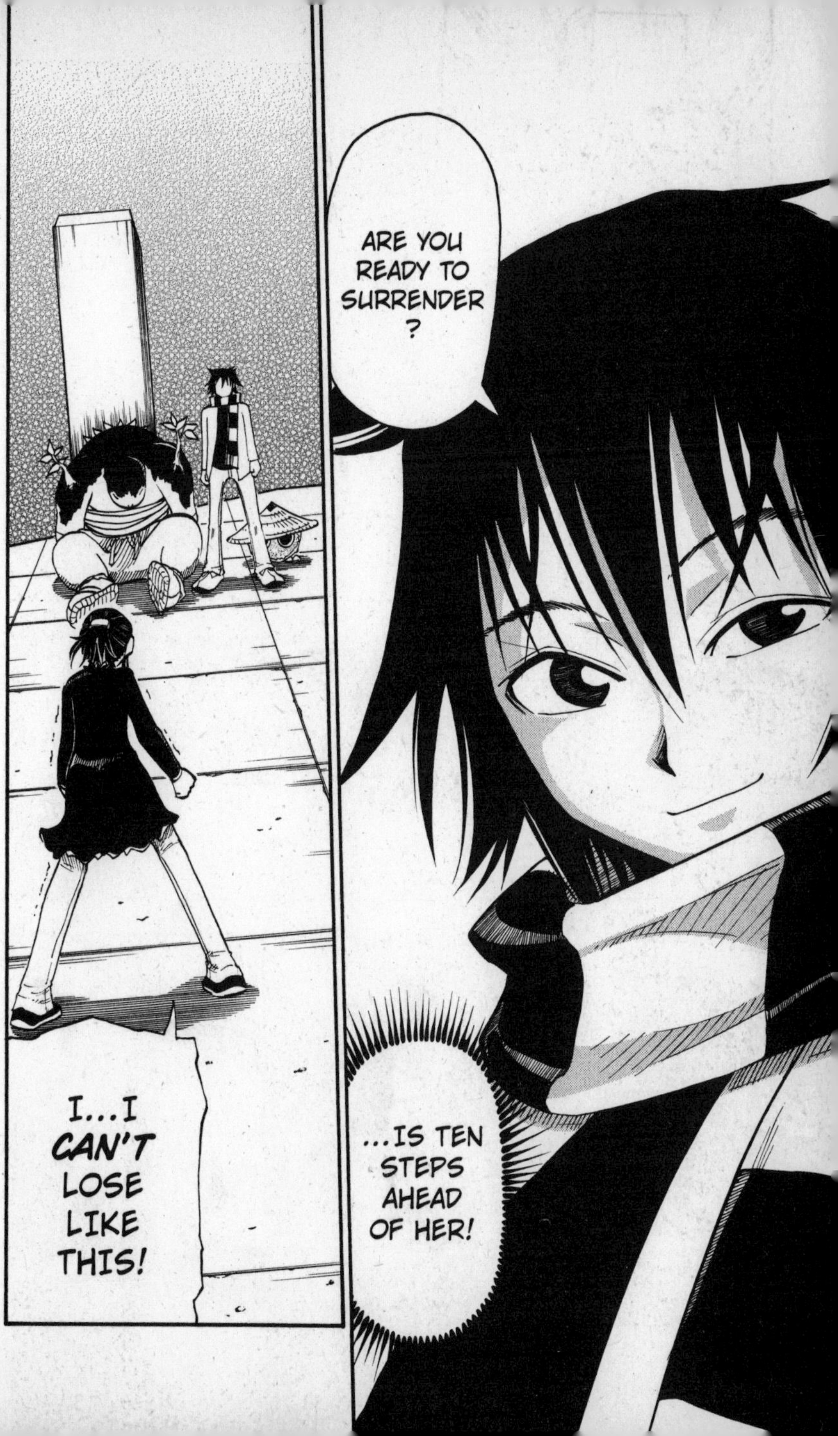
ARE YOU READY TO SURRENDER?
...IS TEN STEPS AHEAD OF HER!
I...I *CAN'T* LOSE LIKE THIS!

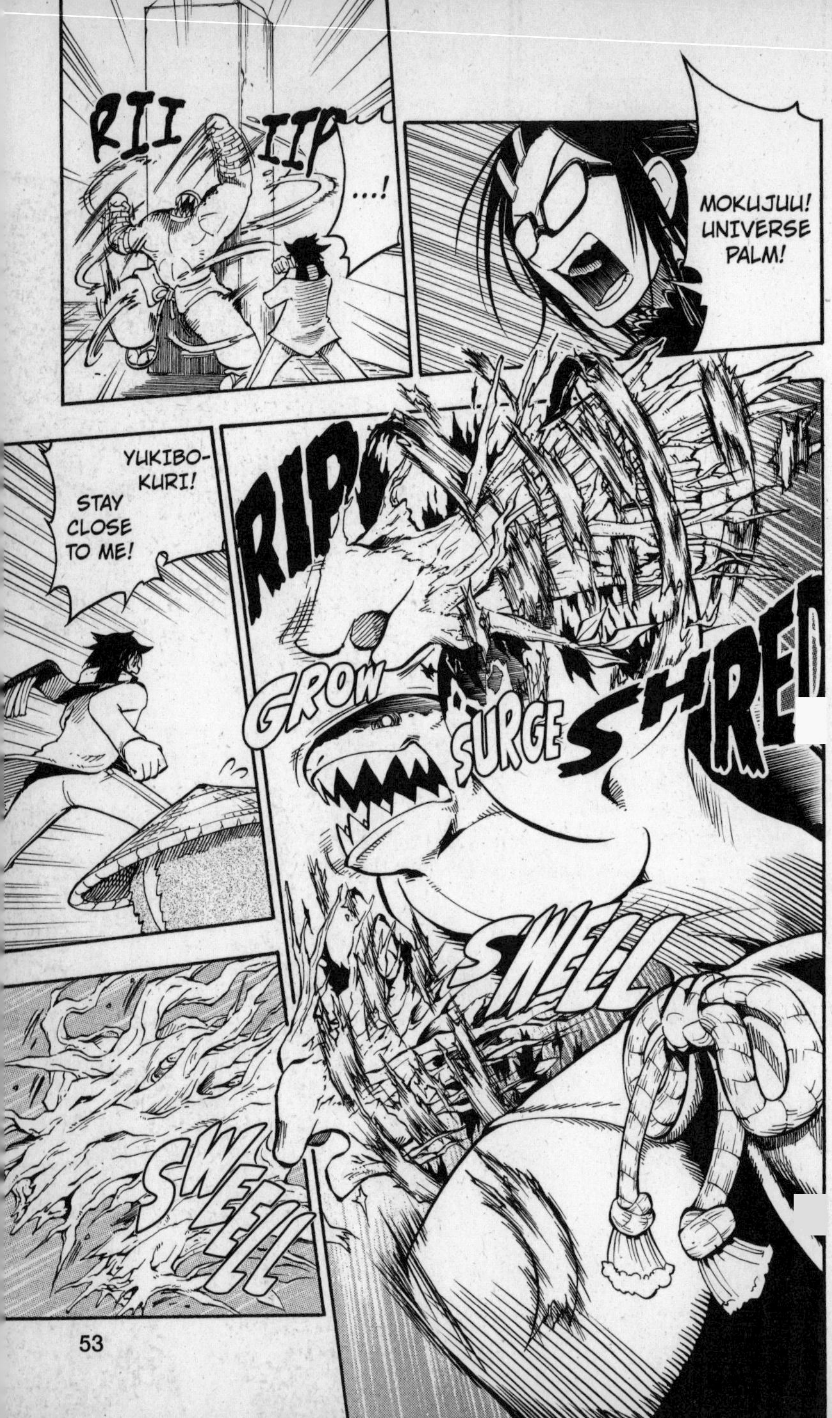
MOKUJUU! UNIVERSE PALM!
RII IIP
...!
RIP
GROW
SURGE
SHRED
SWELL
YUKIBO-KURI! STAY CLOSE TO ME!
SWELL

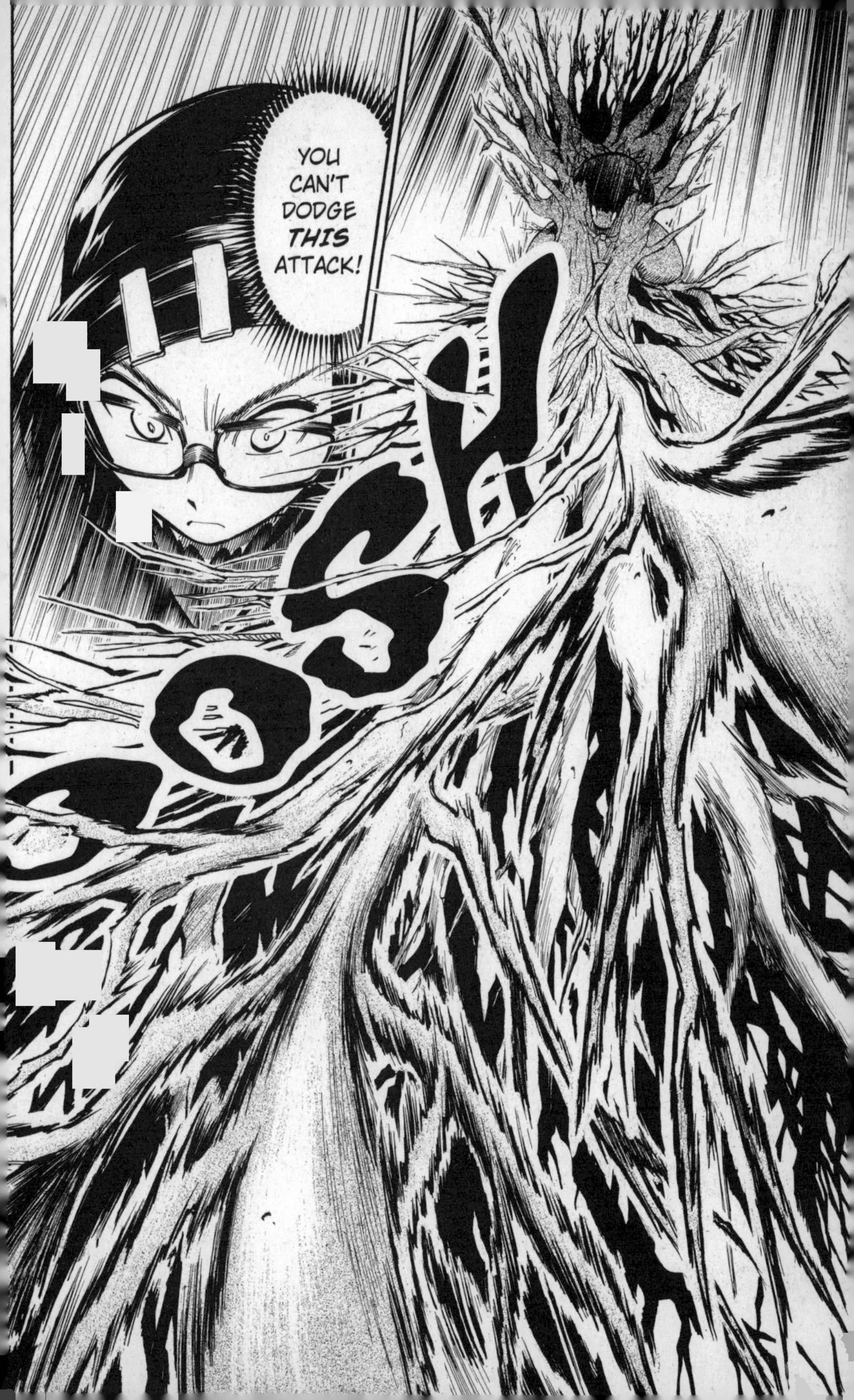
YOU CAN'T DODGE THIS ATTACK!

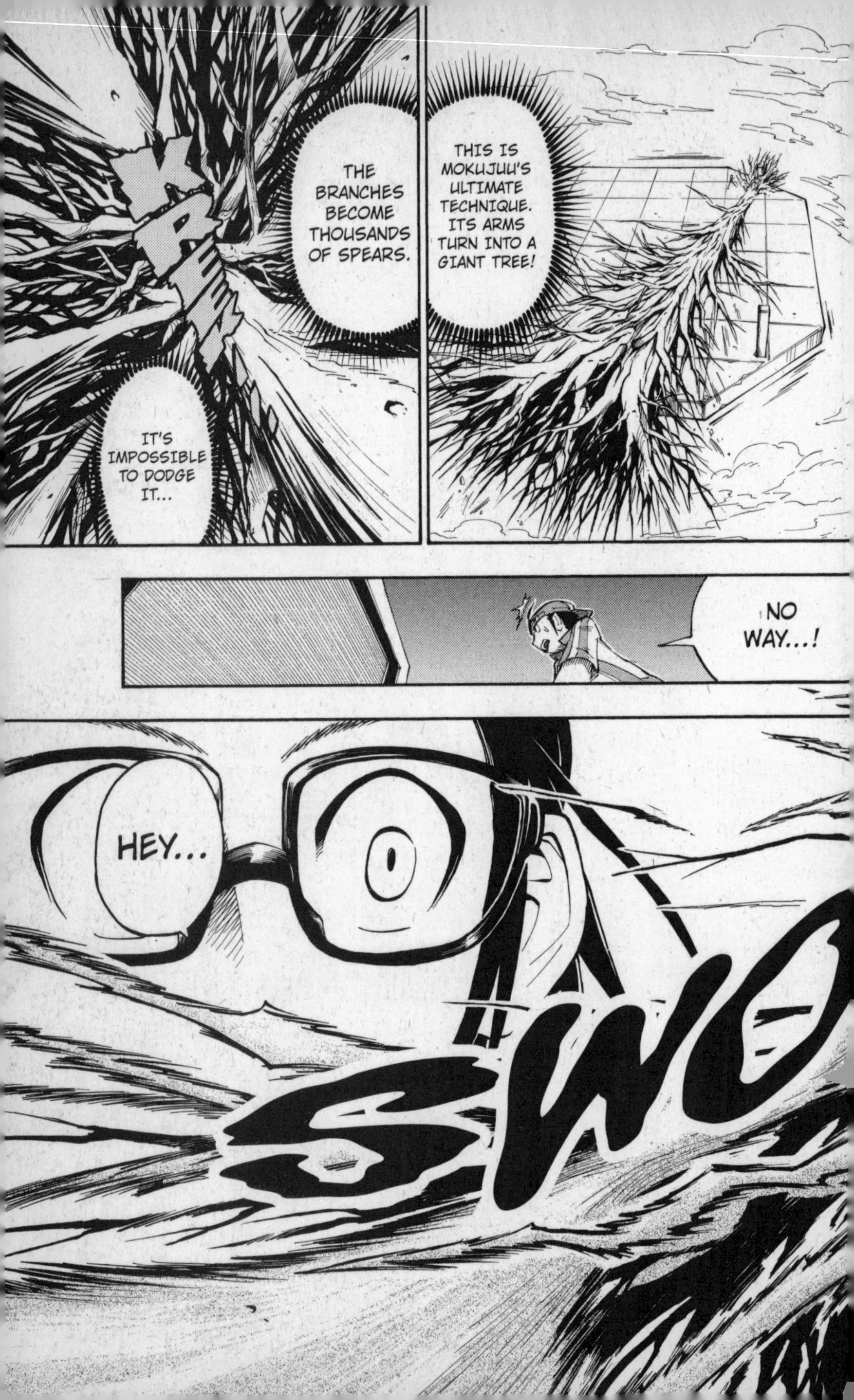
THIS IS MOKUJUU'S ULTIMATE TECHNIQUE. ITS ARMS TURN INTO A GIANT TREE!
THE BRANCHES BECOME THOUSANDS OF SPEARS.
IT'S IMPOSSIBLE TO DODGE IT...
NO WAY...!
HEY...
SWO

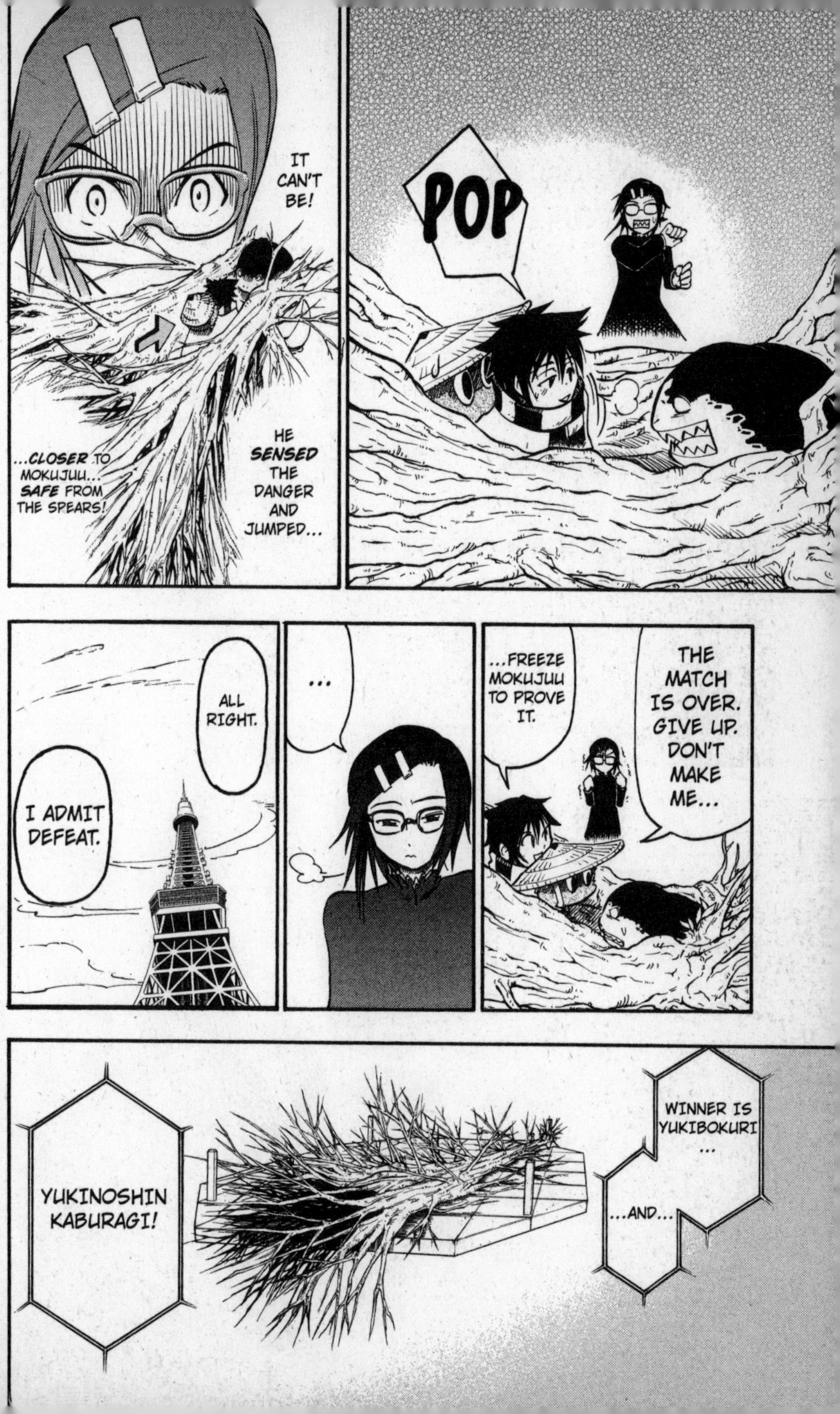
POP
IT CAN'T BE!
HE SENSED THE DANGER AND JUMPED...
...CLOSER TO MOKUJUU... SAFE FROM THE SPEARS!
THE MATCH IS OVER. GIVE UP. DON'T MAKE ME...
...FREEZE MOKUJUU TO PROVE IT.
...
ALL RIGHT.
I ADMIT DEFEAT.
WINNER IS YUKIBOKURI ...
...AND...
YUKINOSHIN KABURAGI!

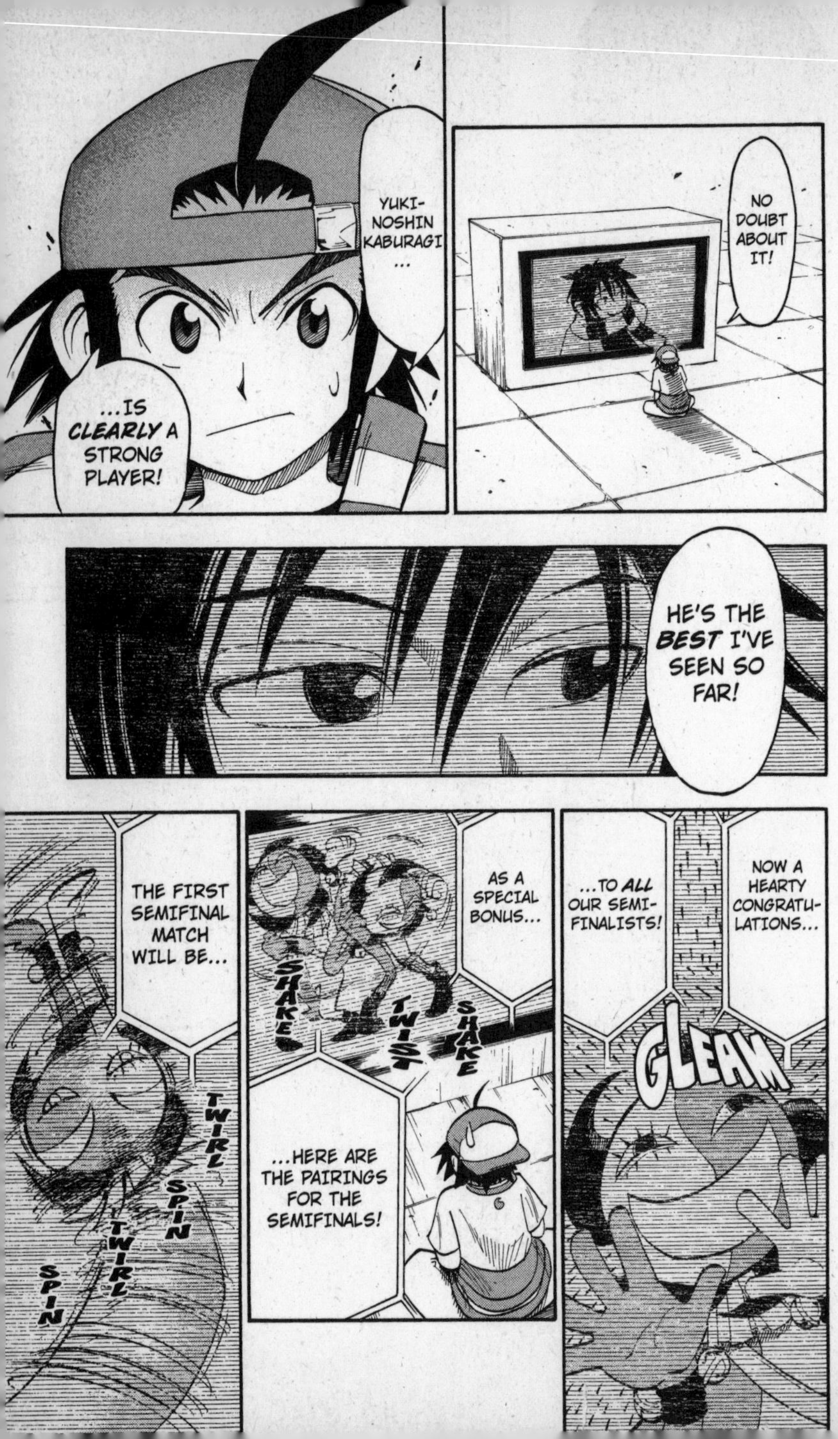
NO DOUBT ABOUT IT!
YUKI-NOSHIN KABURAGI...
...IS CLEARLY A STRONG PLAYER!
HE'S THE BEST I'VE SEEN SO FAR!
NOW A HEARTY CONGRATULATIONS...
...TO ALL OUR SEMI-FINALISTS!
GLEAM
AS A SPECIAL BONUS...
SHAKE
TWIST
SHAKE
...HERE ARE THE PAIRINGS FOR THE SEMIFINALS!
THE FIRST SEMIFINAL MATCH WILL BE...
TWIRL
SPIN
TWIRL
SPIN

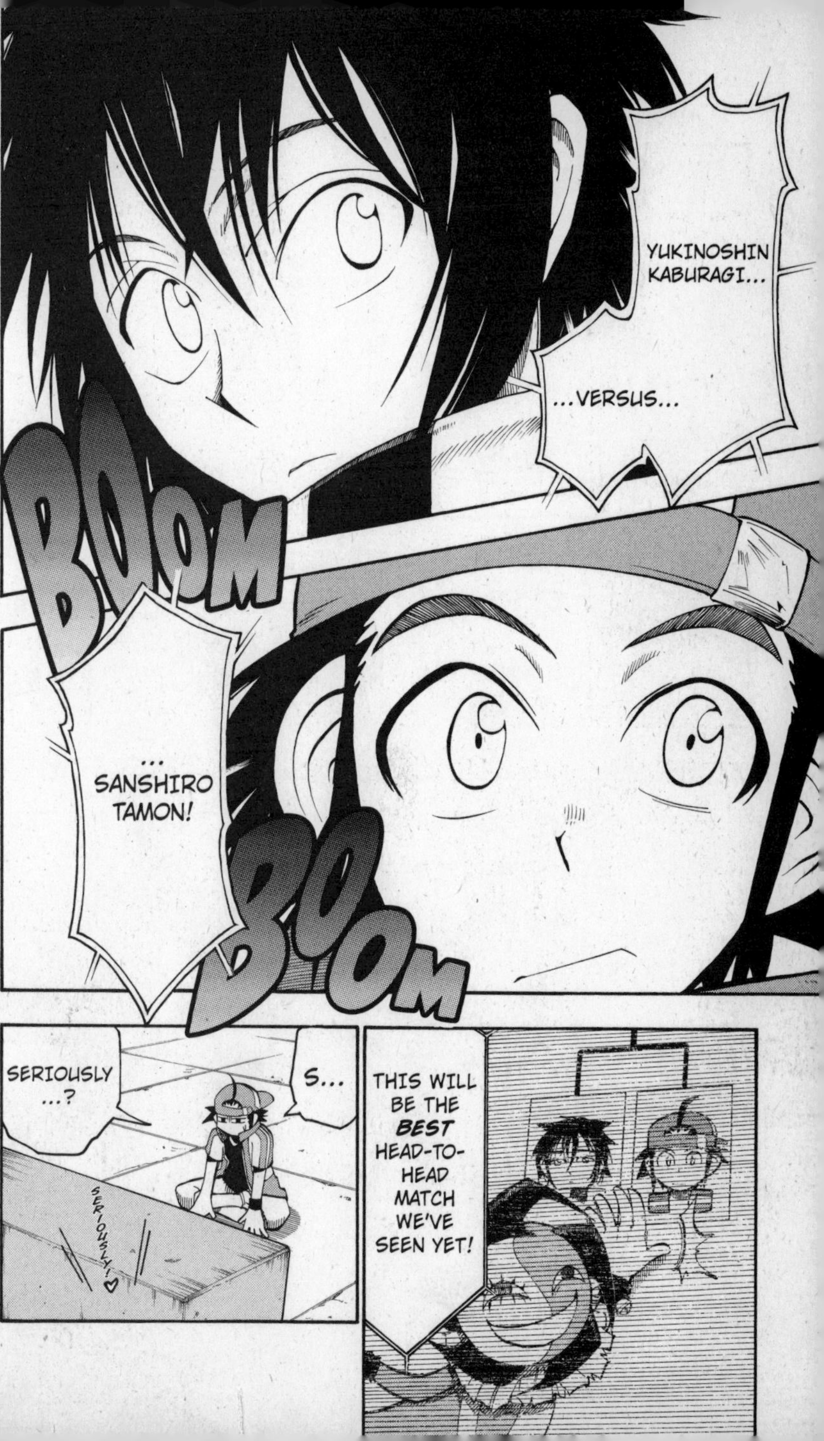
YUKINOSHIN KABURAGI...
...VERSUS...
BOOM
... SANSHIRO TAMON!
BOOM
THIS WILL BE THE BEST HEAD-TO-HEAD MATCH WE'VE SEEN YET!
S...
SERIOUSLY ...?
SERIOUSLY!♥

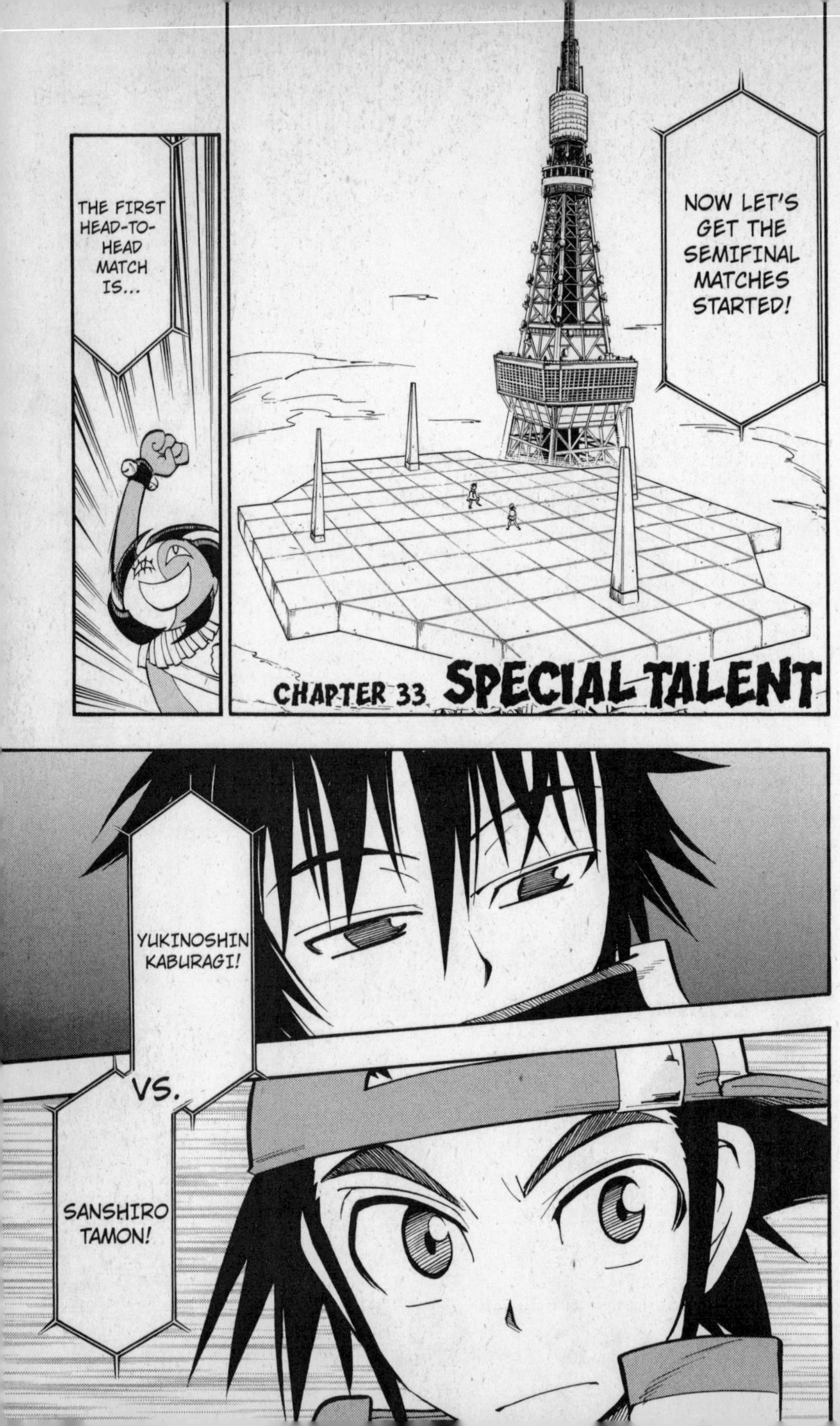
NOW LET'S GET THE SEMIFINAL MATCHES STARTED!
CHAPTER 33 SPECIAL TALENT
THE FIRST HEAD-TO-HEAD MATCH IS...
YUKINOSHIN KABURAGI!
VS.
SANSHIRO TAMON!

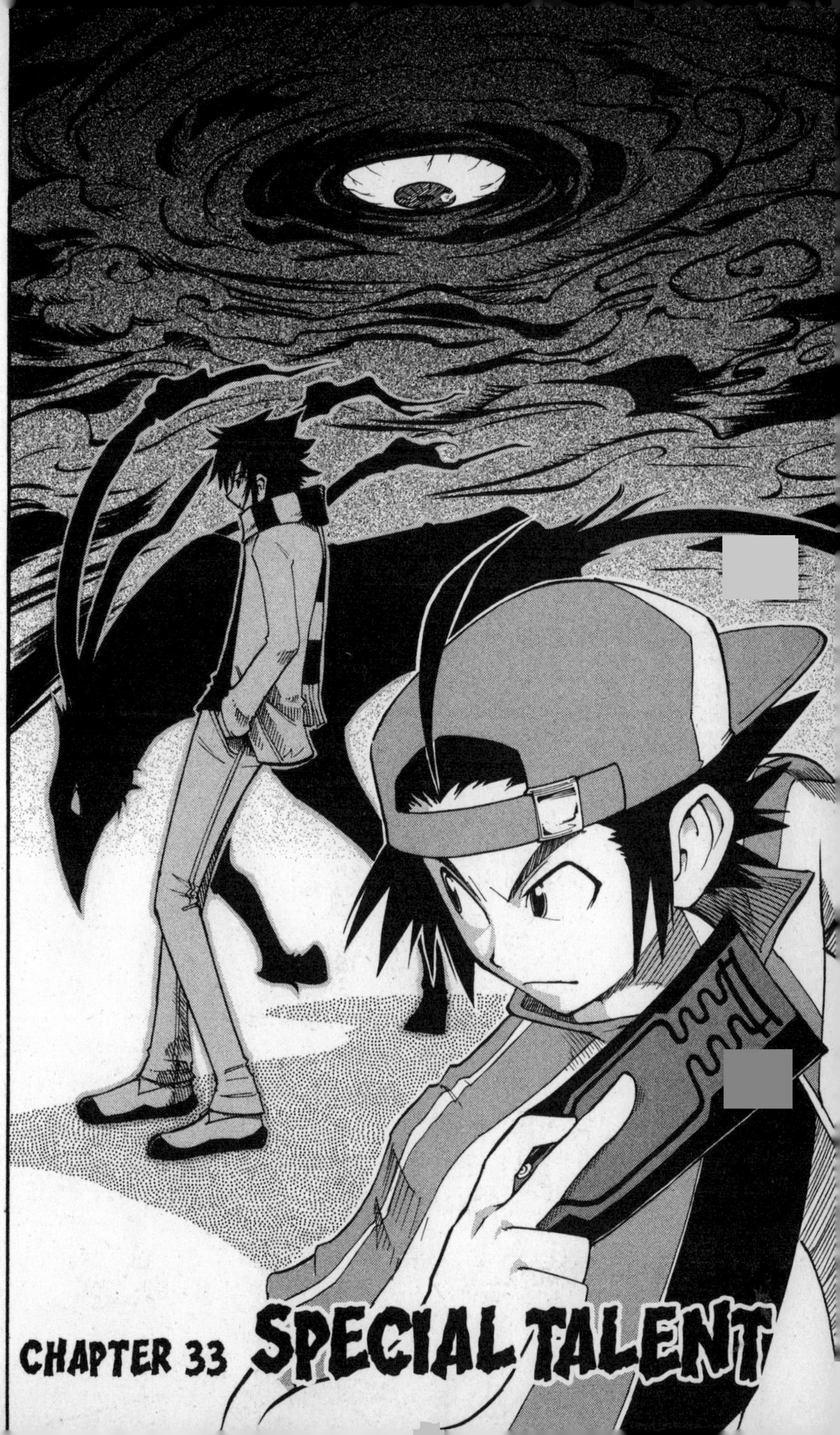
CHAPTER 33
SPECIAL TALENT

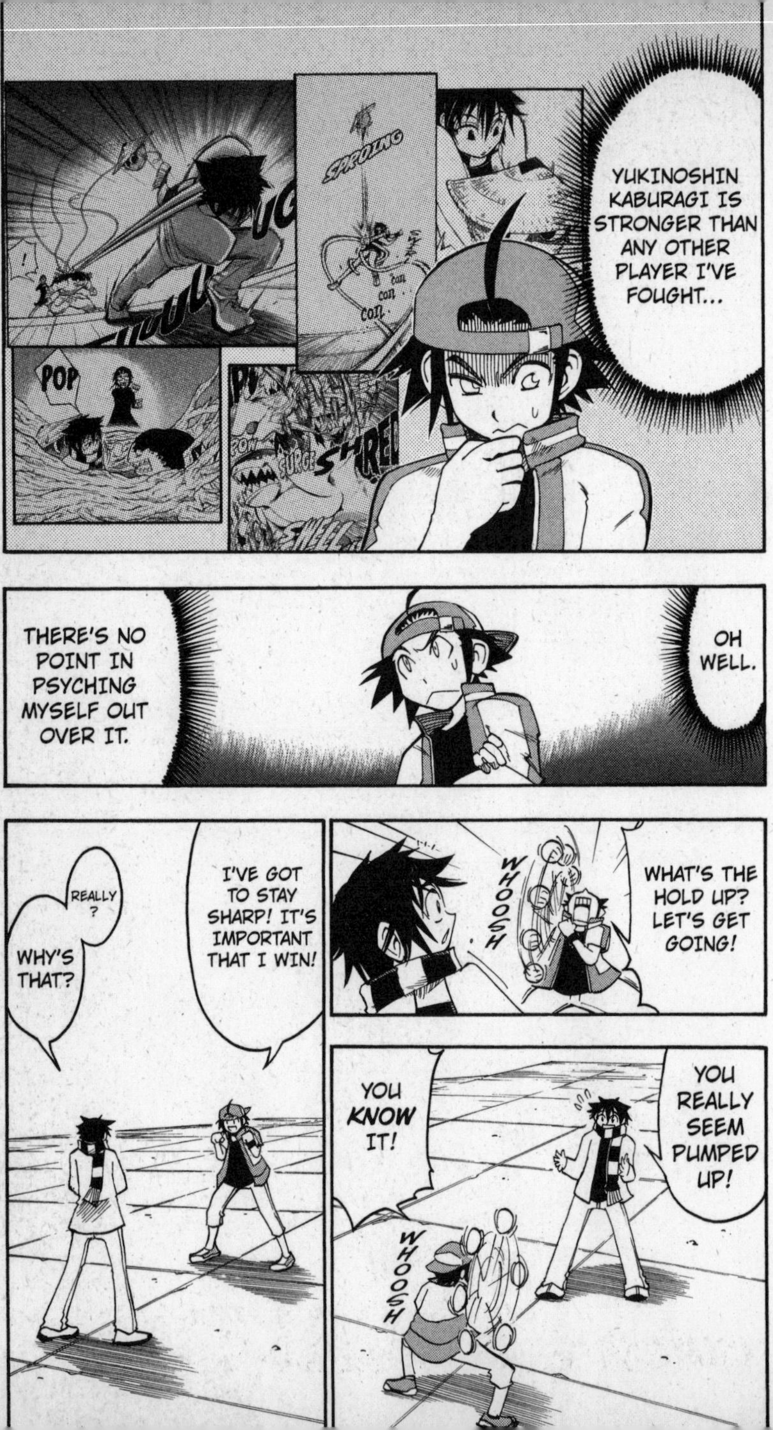
YUKINOSHIN KABURAGI IS STRONGER THAN ANY OTHER PLAYER I'VE FOUGHT...
SPROING
POP
SHRED
OH WELL.
THERE'S NO POINT IN PSYCHING MYSELF OUT OVER IT.
WHAT'S THE HOLD UP? LET'S GET GOING!
WHOOSH
YOU REALLY SEEM PUMPED UP!
YOU KNOW IT!
WHOOOSH
I'VE GOT TO STAY SHARP! IT'S IMPORTANT THAT I WIN!
REALLY?
WHY'S THAT?

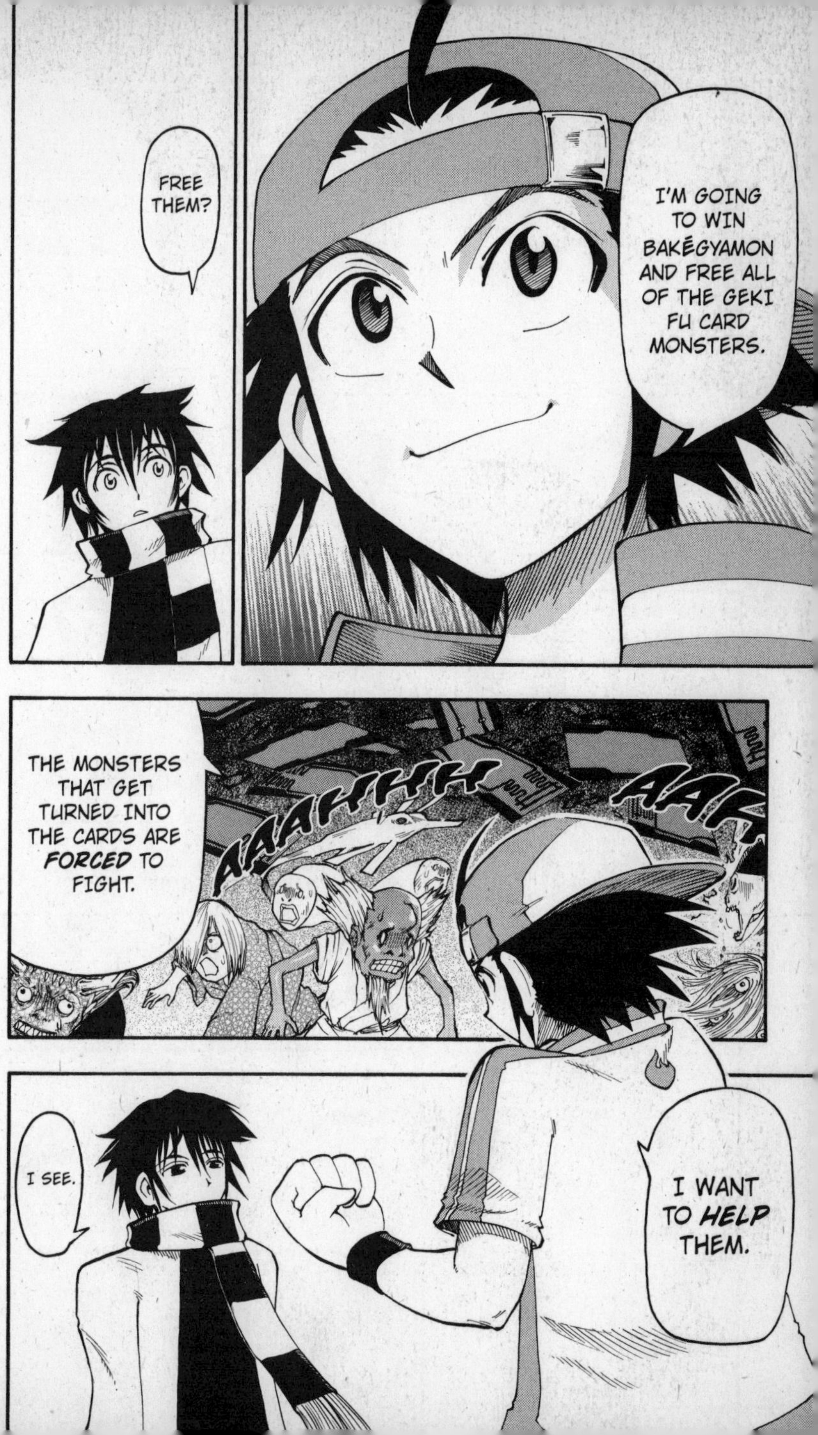
I'M GOING TO WIN BAKÉGYAMON AND FREE ALL OF THE GEKI FU CARD MONSTERS.
FREE THEM?
THE MONSTERS THAT GET TURNED INTO THE CARDS ARE *FORCED* TO FIGHT.
AAA
AAAHHHH
I WANT TO *HELP* THEM.
I SEE.

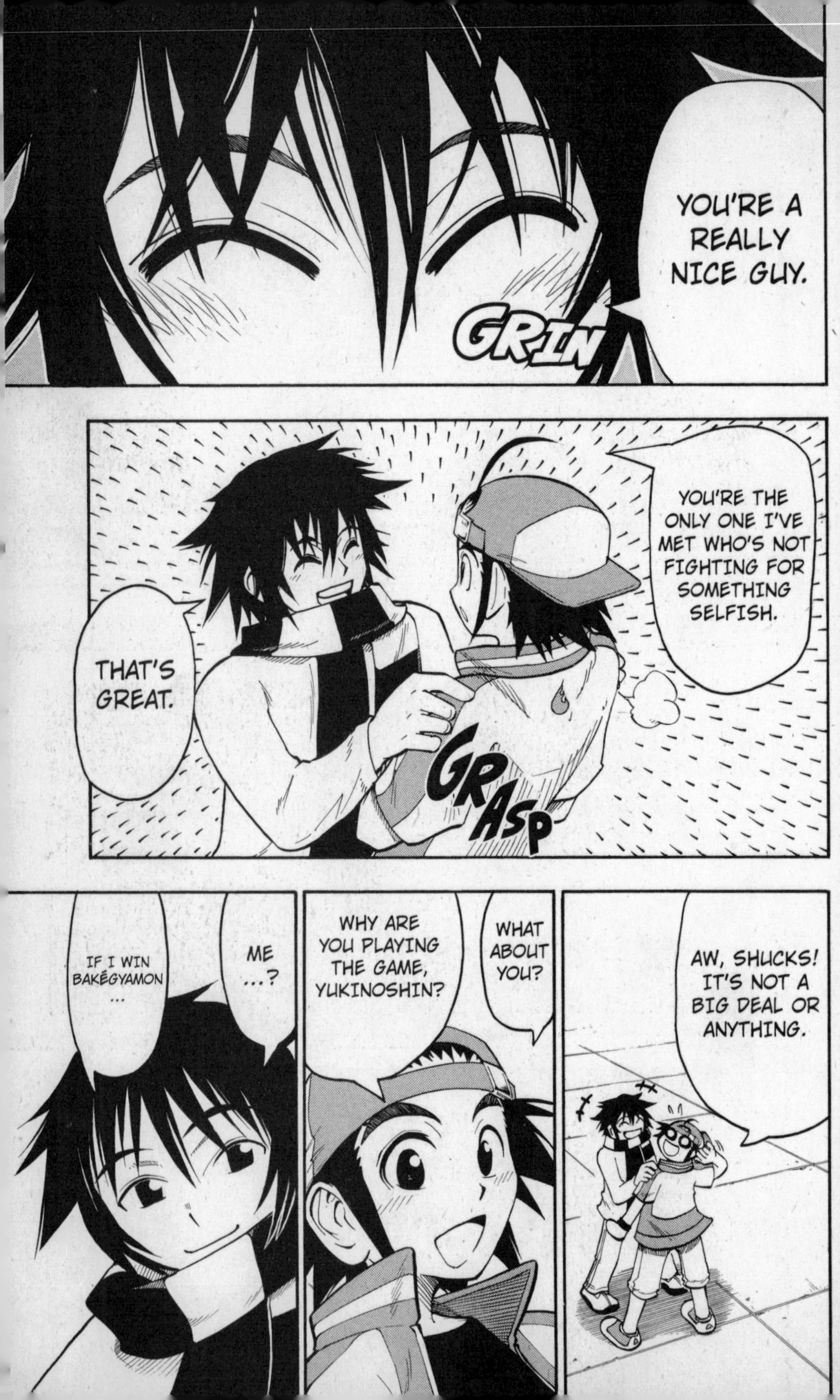
YOU'RE A REALLY NICE GUY.
GRIN
YOU'RE THE ONLY ONE I'VE MET WHO'S NOT FIGHTING FOR SOMETHING SELFISH.
THAT'S GREAT.
GRASP
AW, SHUCKS! IT'S NOT A BIG DEAL OR ANYTHING.
WHAT ABOUT YOU?
WHY ARE YOU PLAYING THE GAME, YUKINOSHIN?
ME ...?
IF I WIN BAKÉGYAMON ...

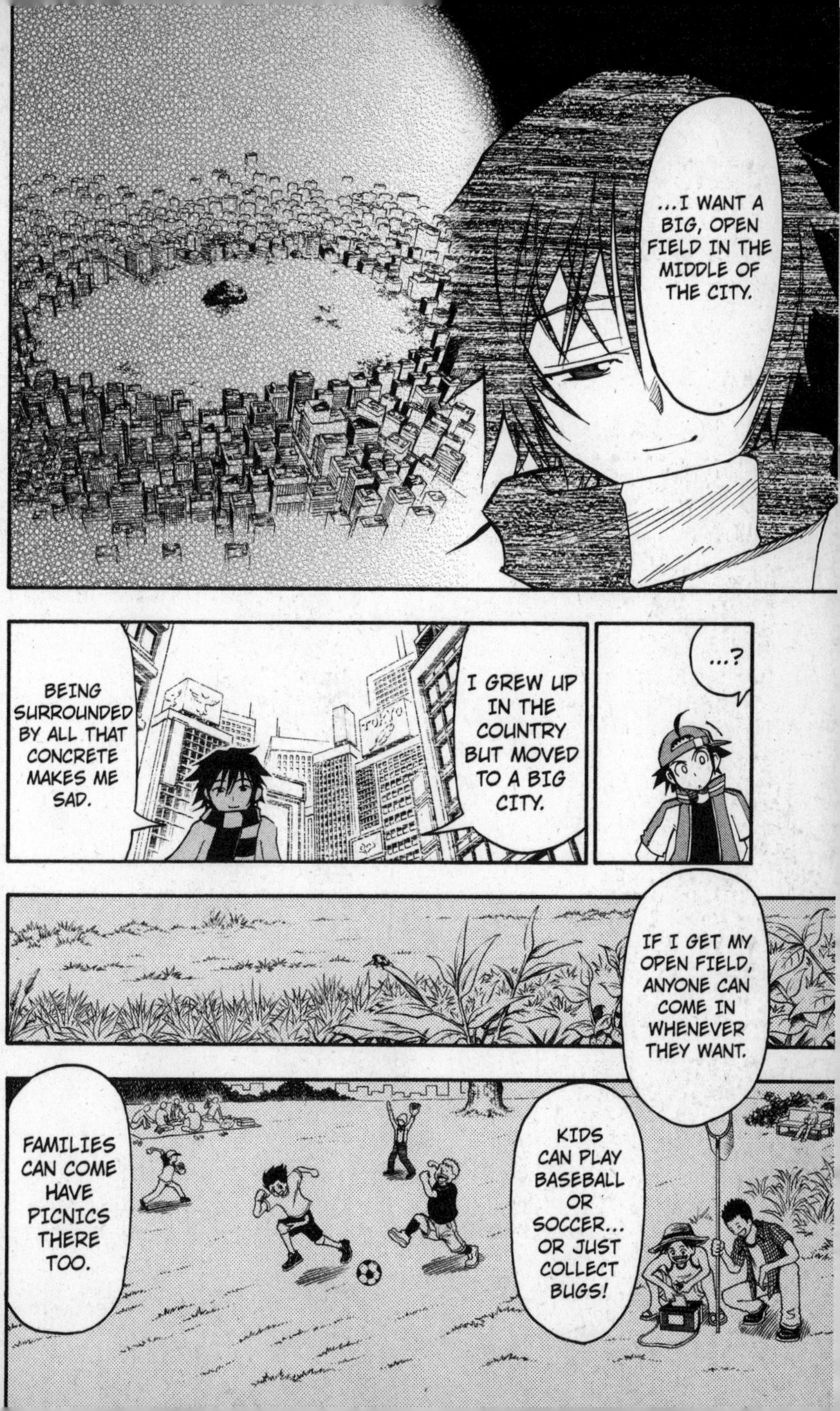

...I WANT A BIG, OPEN FIELD IN THE MIDDLE OF THE CITY.
...?
I GREW UP IN THE COUNTRY BUT MOVED TO A BIG CITY.
BEING SURROUNDED BY ALL THAT CONCRETE MAKES ME SAD.
IF I GET MY OPEN FIELD, ANYONE CAN COME IN WHENEVER THEY WANT.
KIDS CAN PLAY BASEBALL OR SOCCER... OR JUST COLLECT BUGS!
FAMILIES CAN COME HAVE PICNICS THERE TOO.

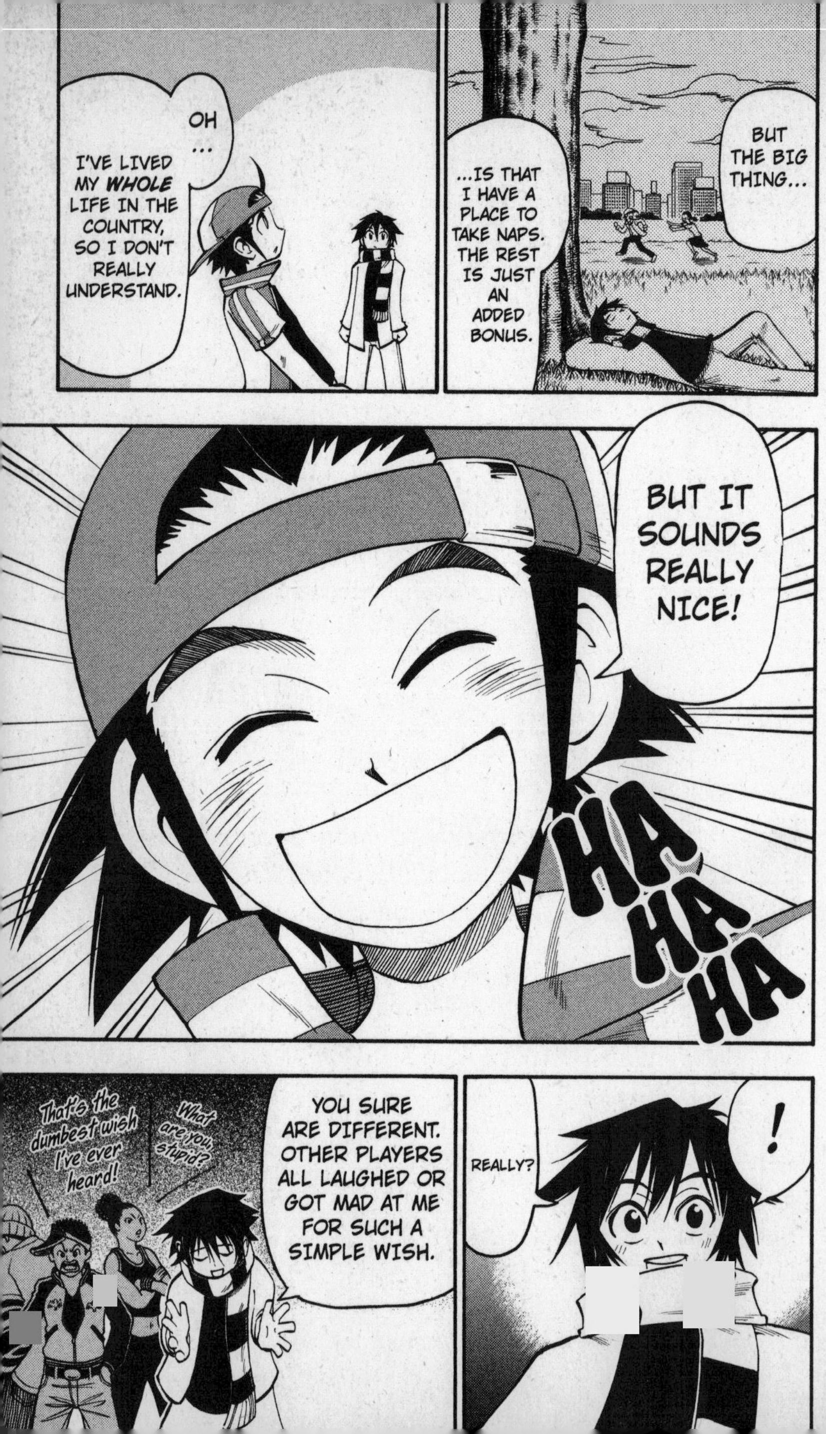
BUT THE BIG THING...
...IS THAT I HAVE A PLACE TO TAKE NAPS. THE REST IS JUST AN ADDED BONUS.
OH ...
I'VE LIVED MY **WHOLE** LIFE IN THE COUNTRY, SO I DON'T REALLY UNDERSTAND.
BUT IT SOUNDS REALLY NICE!
HA HA HA
!
REALLY?
YOU SURE ARE DIFFERENT. OTHER PLAYERS ALL LAUGHED OR GOT MAD AT ME FOR SUCH A SIMPLE WISH.
What are you, stupid?
That's the dumbest wish I've ever heard!

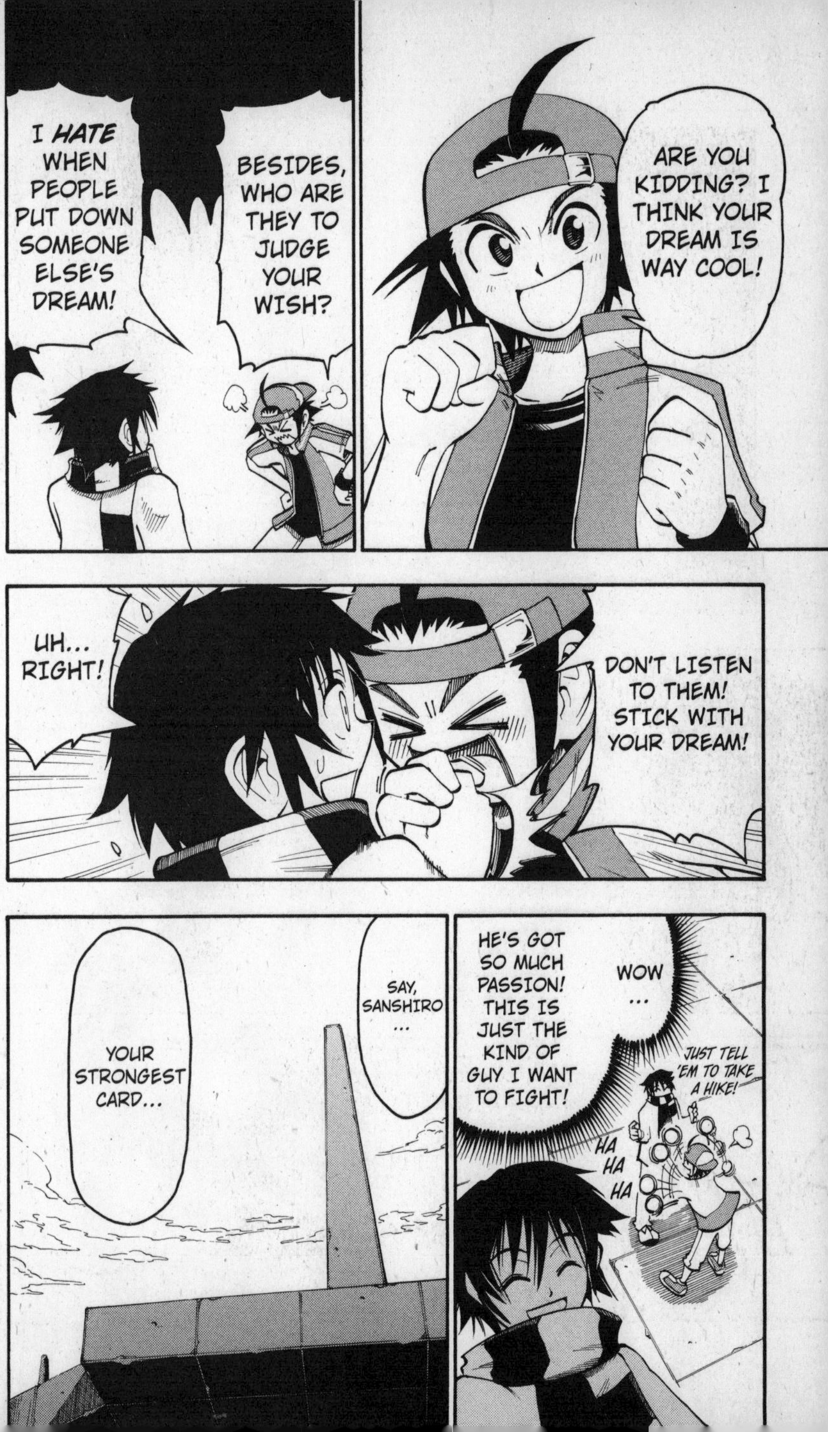
ARE YOU KIDDING? I THINK YOUR DREAM IS WAY COOL!
BESIDES, WHO ARE THEY TO JUDGE YOUR WISH?
I *HATE* WHEN PEOPLE PUT DOWN SOMEONE ELSE'S DREAM!
DON'T LISTEN TO THEM! STICK WITH YOUR DREAM!
UH... RIGHT!
WOW ...
HE'S GOT SO MUCH PASSION! THIS IS JUST THE KIND OF GUY I WANT TO FIGHT!
JUST TELL 'EM TO TAKE A HIKE!
HA HA HA
SAY, SANSHIRO ...
YOUR STRONGEST CARD...

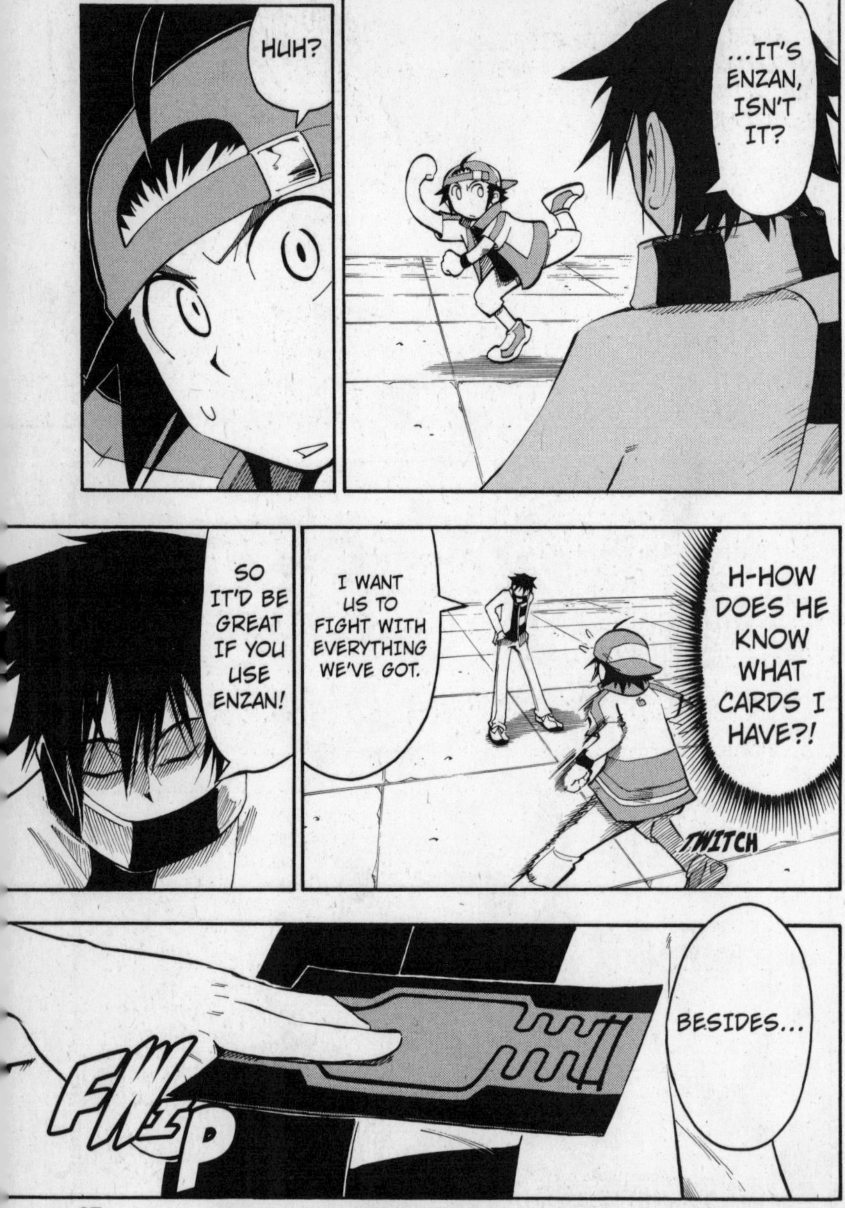
...IT'S ENZAN, ISN'T IT?
HUH?
H-HOW DOES HE KNOW WHAT CARDS I HAVE?!
TWITCH
I WANT US TO FIGHT WITH EVERYTHING WE'VE GOT.
SO IT'D BE GREAT IF YOU USE ENZAN!
BESIDES...
FWISP

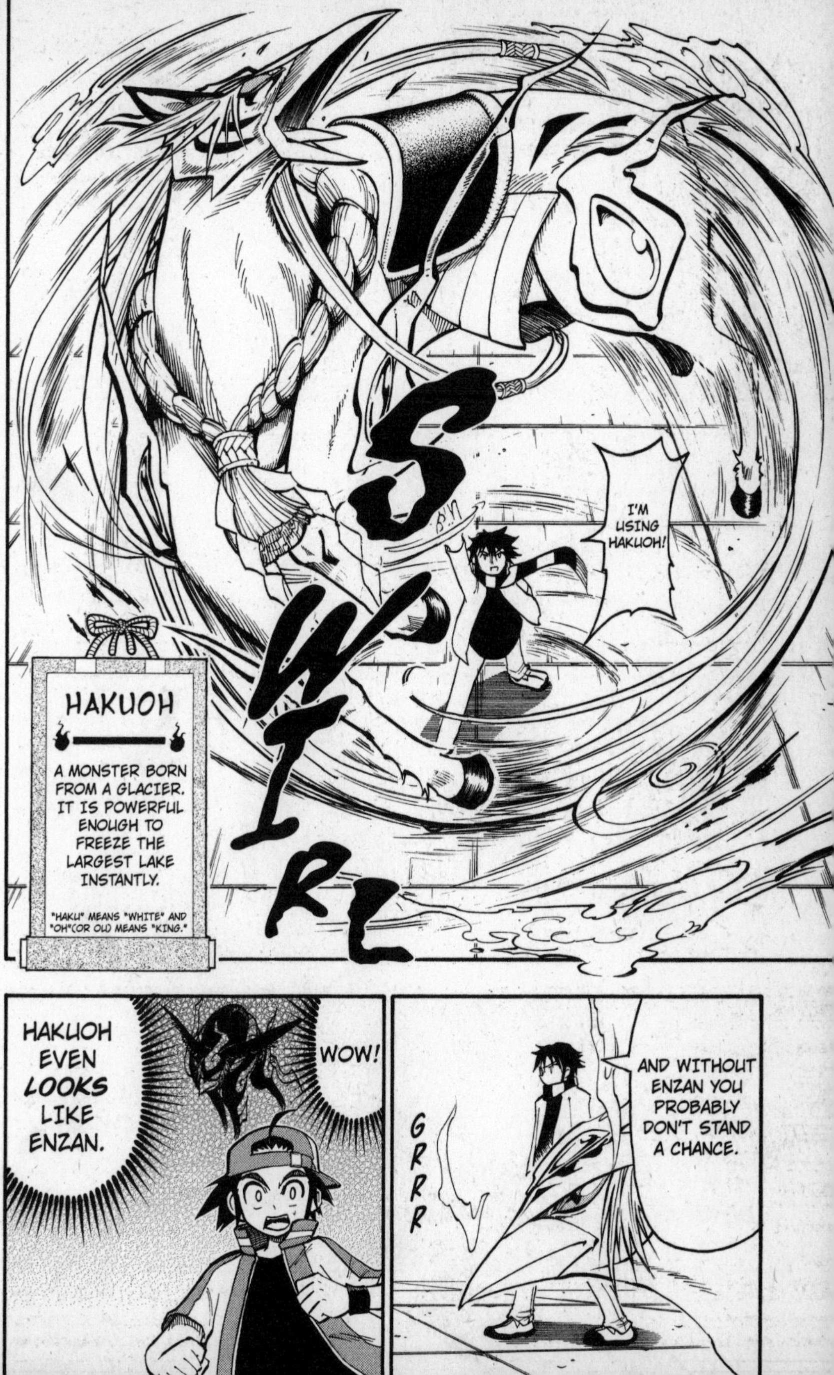
SWIRL
I'M USING HAKUOH!
HAKUOH
A MONSTER BORN FROM A GLACIER. IT IS POWERFUL ENOUGH TO FREEZE THE LARGEST LAKE INSTANTLY.
"HAKU" MEANS "WHITE" AND "OH"(OR OU) MEANS "KING."
AND WITHOUT ENZAN YOU PROBABLY DON'T STAND A CHANCE.
GRRR
WOW!
HAKUOH EVEN LOOKS LIKE ENZAN.

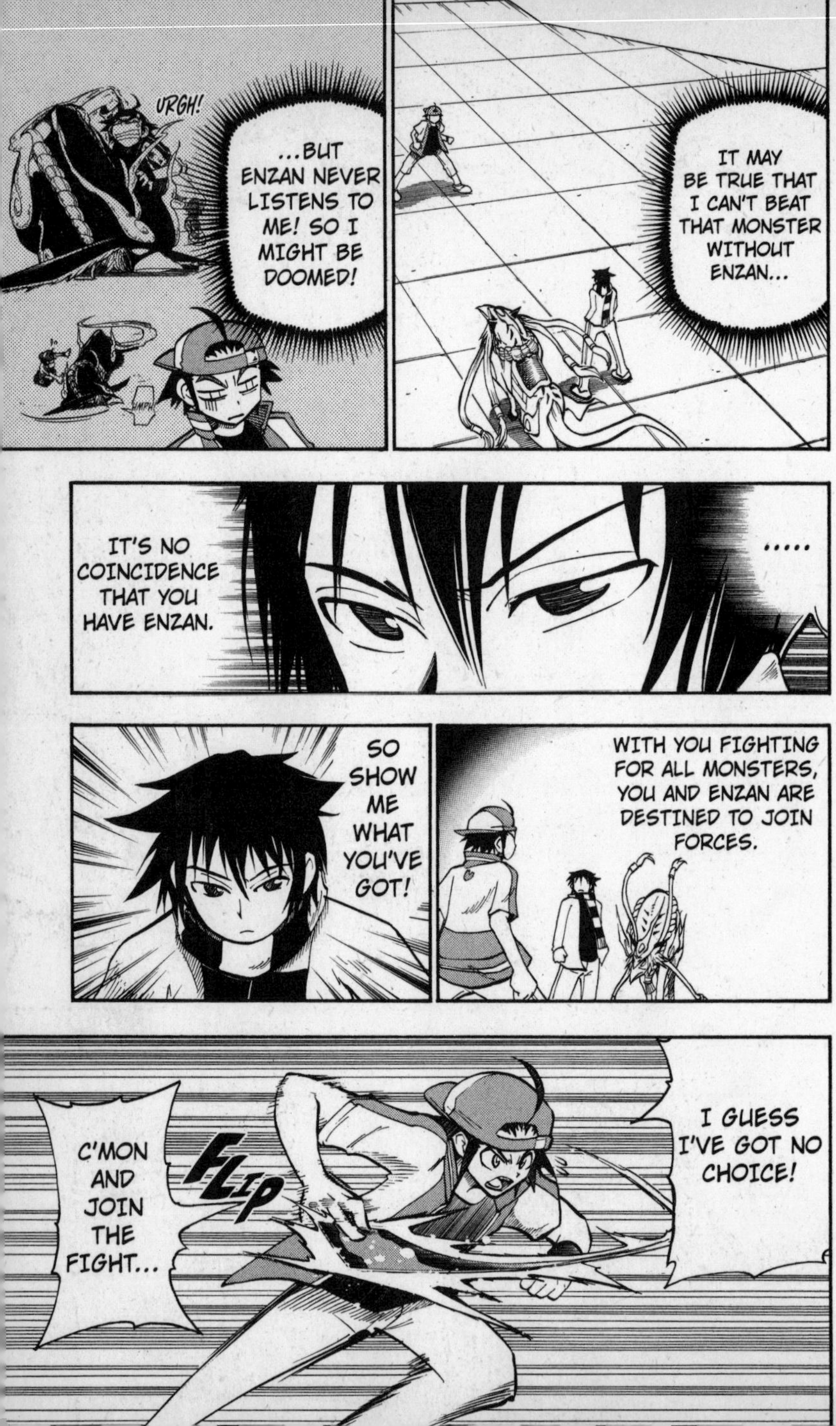
IT MAY BE TRUE THAT I CAN'T BEAT THAT MONSTER WITHOUT ENZAN...
URGH!
...BUT ENZAN NEVER LISTENS TO ME! SO I MIGHT BE DOOMED!
.....
IT'S NO COINCIDENCE THAT YOU HAVE ENZAN.
WITH YOU FIGHTING FOR ALL MONSTERS, YOU AND ENZAN ARE DESTINED TO JOIN FORCES.
SO SHOW ME WHAT YOU'VE GOT!
I GUESS I'VE GOT NO CHOICE!
FLIP
C'MON AND JOIN THE FIGHT...

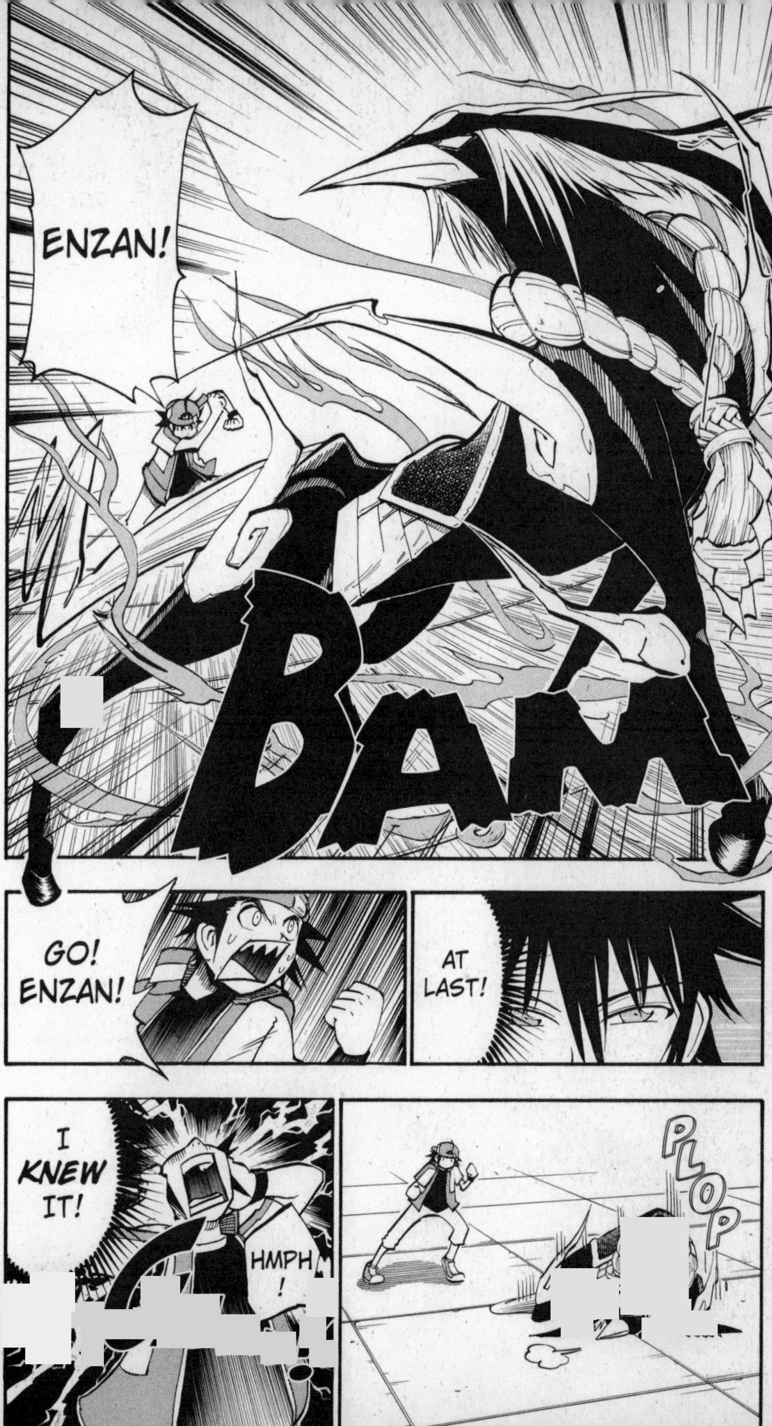
ENZAN!
BAM
AT LAST!
GO! ENZAN!
PLOP
I KNEW IT!
HMPH!

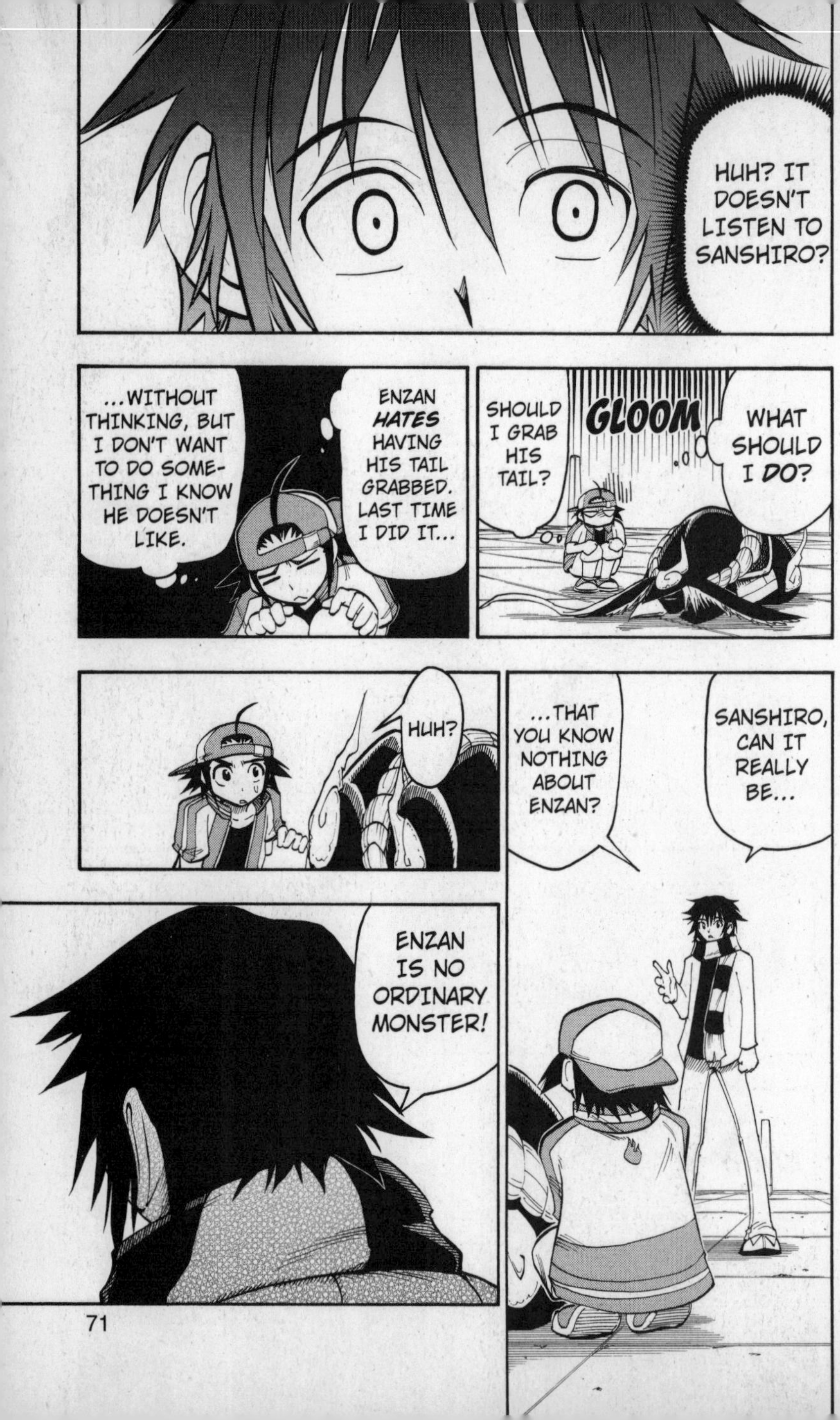
HUH? IT DOESN'T LISTEN TO SANSHIRO?
WHAT SHOULD I *DO*?
GLOOM
SHOULD I GRAB HIS TAIL?
ENZAN *HATES* HAVING HIS TAIL GRABBED. LAST TIME I DID IT...
...WITHOUT THINKING, BUT I DON'T WANT TO DO SOME-THING I KNOW HE DOESN'T LIKE.
SANSHIRO, CAN IT REALLY BE...
...THAT YOU KNOW NOTHING ABOUT ENZAN?
HUH?
ENZAN IS NO ORDINARY MONSTER!

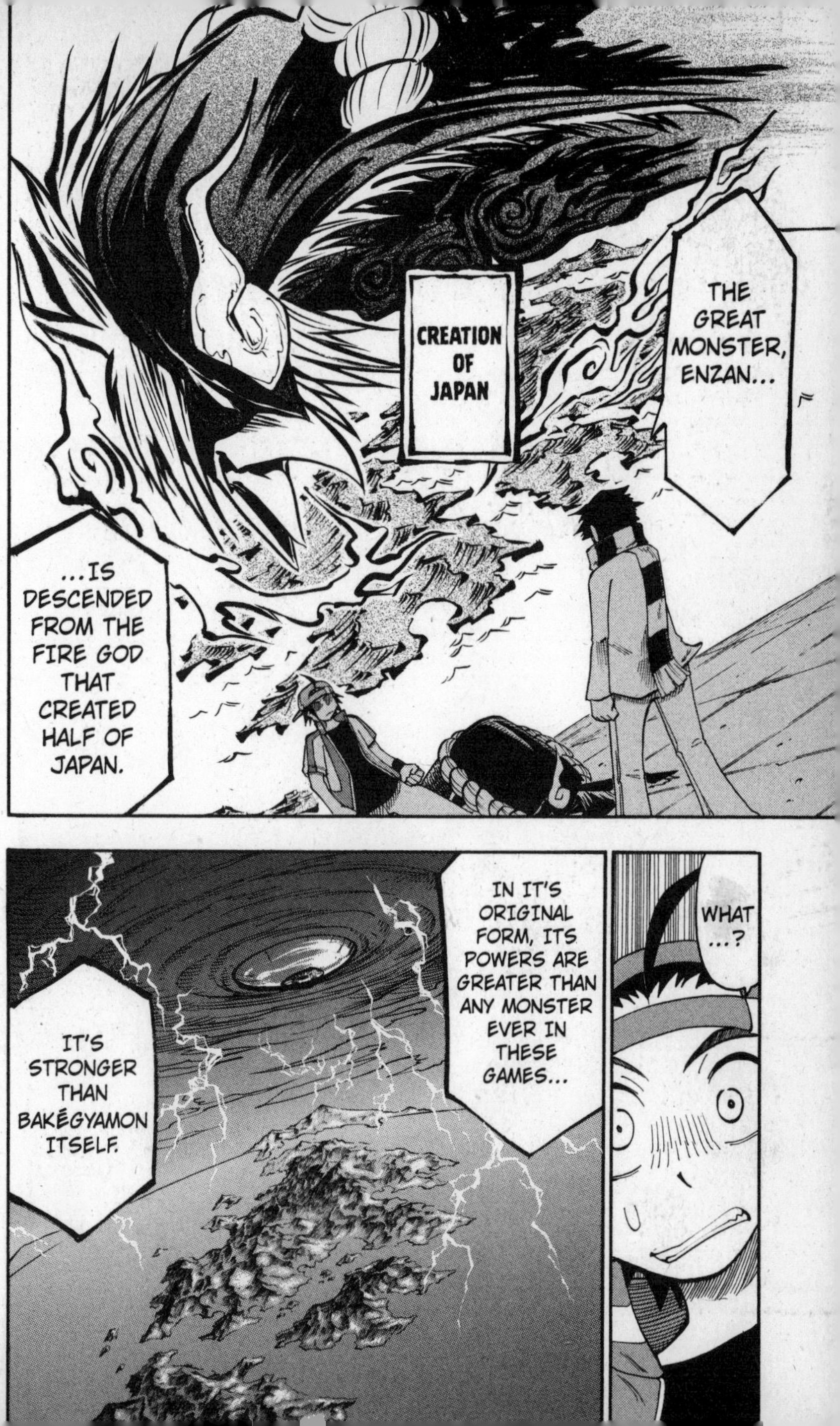
THE GREAT MONSTER, ENZAN...
CREATION OF JAPAN
...IS DESCENDED FROM THE FIRE GOD THAT CREATED HALF OF JAPAN.
WHAT ...?
IN IT'S ORIGINAL FORM, ITS POWERS ARE GREATER THAN ANY MONSTER EVER IN THESE GAMES...
IT'S STRONGER THAN BAKÉGYAMON ITSELF.

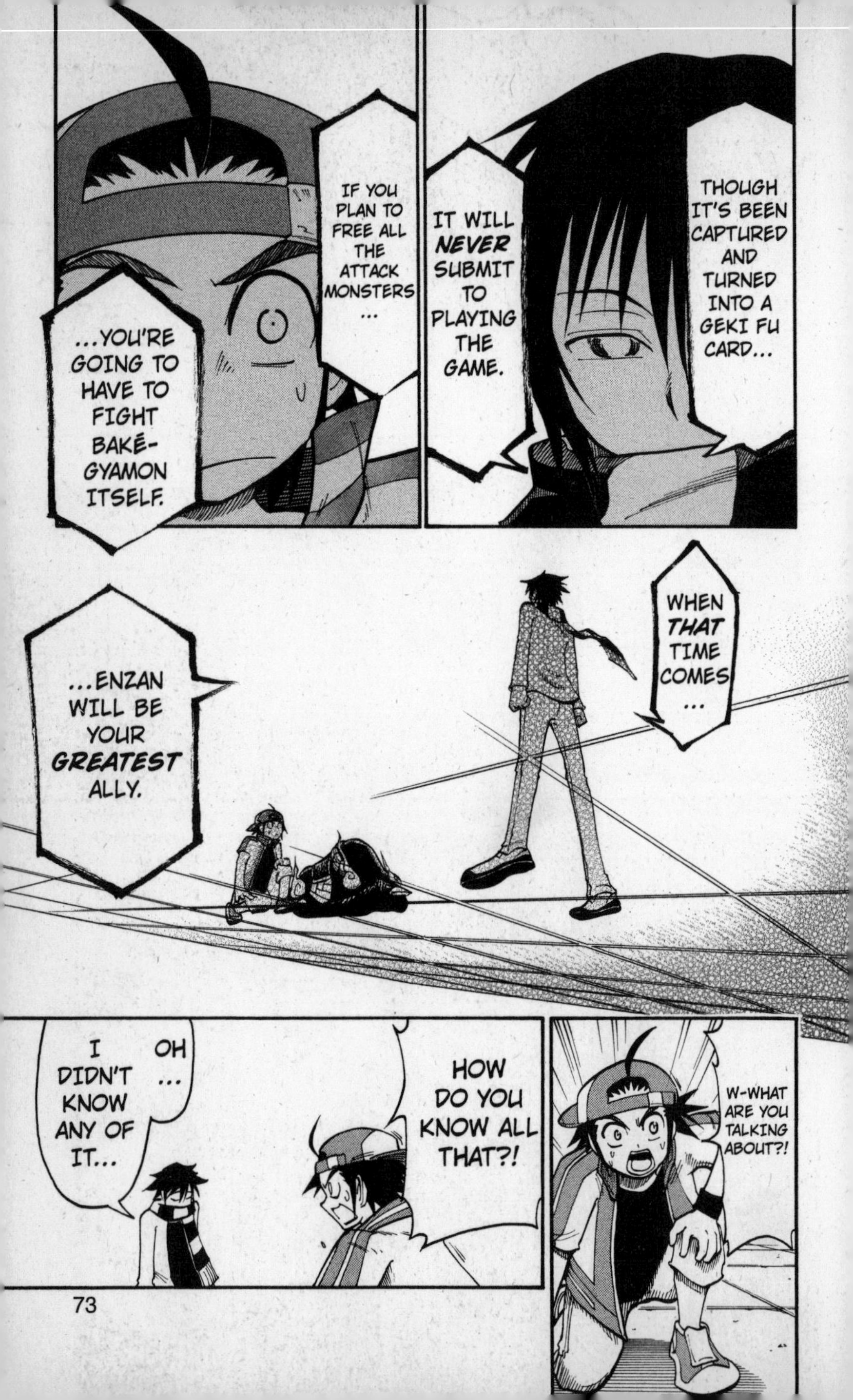
THOUGH IT'S BEEN CAPTURED AND TURNED INTO A GEKI FU CARD...
IT WILL NEVER SUBMIT TO PLAYING THE GAME.
IF YOU PLAN TO FREE ALL THE ATTACK MONSTERS...
...YOU'RE GOING TO HAVE TO FIGHT BAKÉ-GYAMON ITSELF.
WHEN THAT TIME COMES...
...ENZAN WILL BE YOUR GREATEST ALLY.
W-WHAT ARE YOU TALKING ABOUT?!
HOW DO YOU KNOW ALL THAT?!
OH...
I DIDN'T KNOW ANY OF IT...

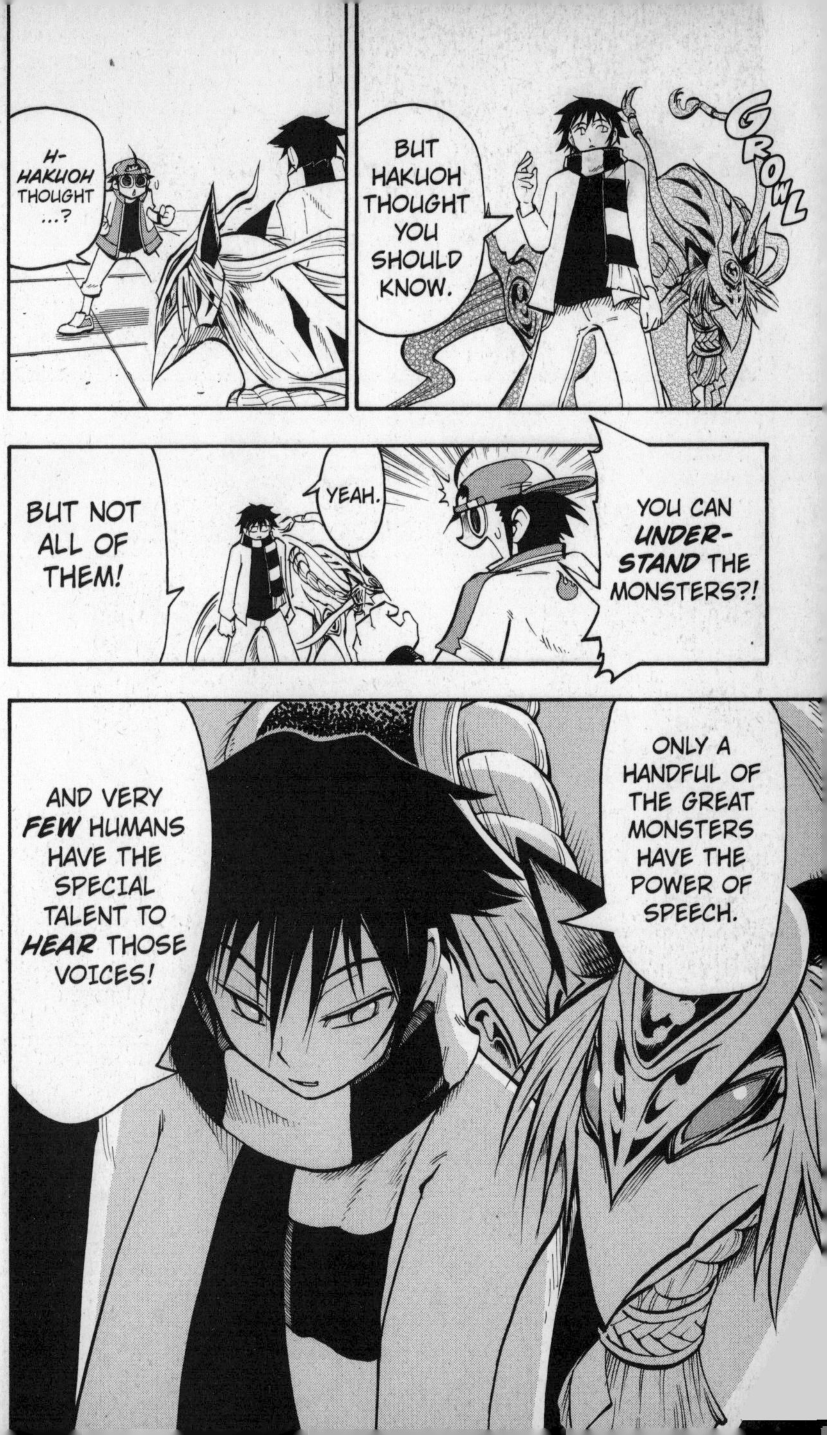
BUT HAKUOH THOUGHT YOU SHOULD KNOW.
GROWL
H-HAKUOH THOUGHT ...?
YOU CAN UNDERSTAND THE MONSTERS?!
YEAH.
BUT NOT ALL OF THEM!
ONLY A HANDFUL OF THE GREAT MONSTERS HAVE THE POWER OF SPEECH.
AND VERY FEW HUMANS HAVE THE SPECIAL TALENT TO HEAR THOSE VOICES!

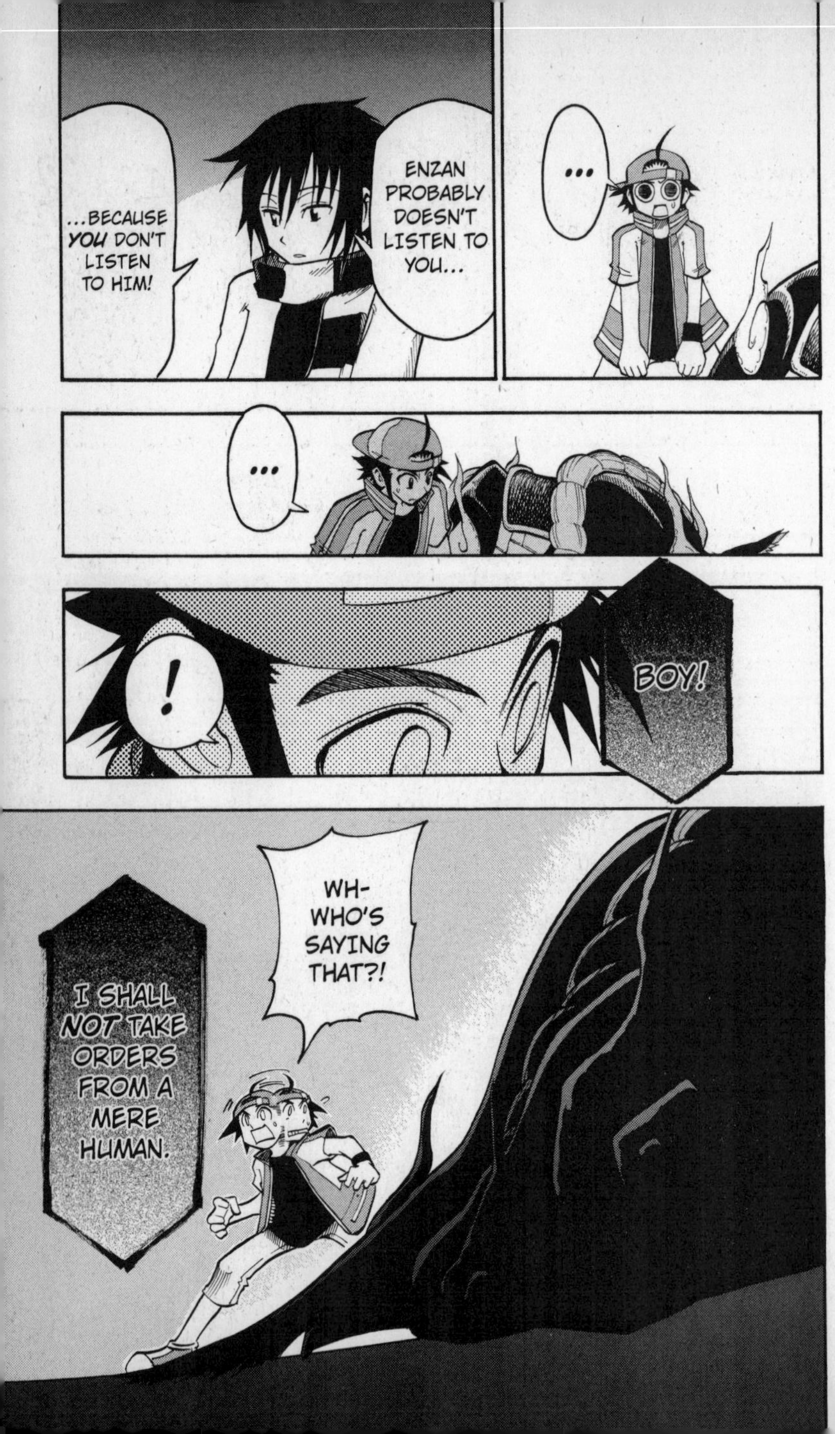
...
ENZAN PROBABLY DOESN'T LISTEN TO YOU...
...BECAUSE *YOU* DON'T LISTEN TO HIM!
...
BOY!
!
WH-WHO'S SAYING THAT?!
I SHALL *NOT* TAKE ORDERS FROM A MERE HUMAN.

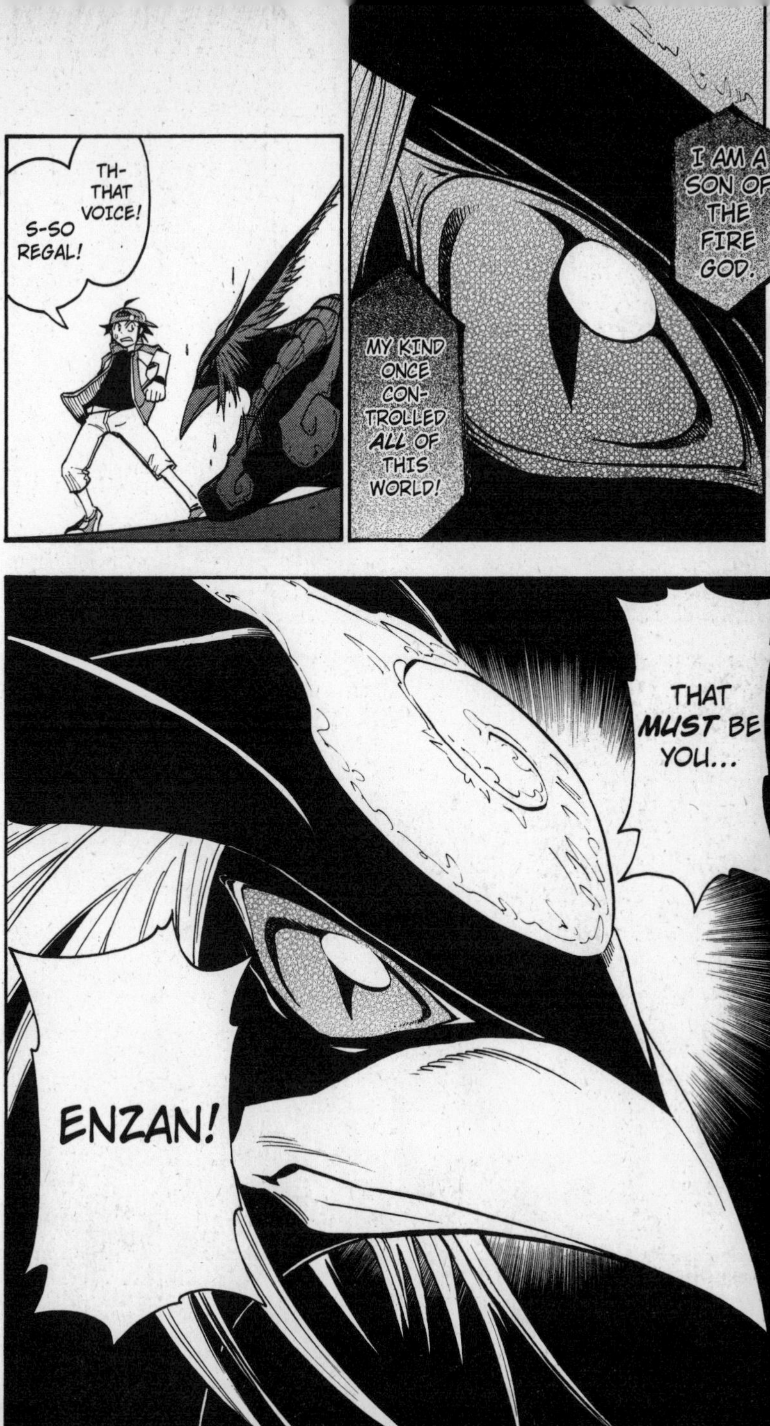
I AM A SON OF THE FIRE GOD.
MY KIND ONCE CON-TROLLED **ALL** OF THIS WORLD!
TH-THAT VOICE!
S-SO REGAL!
THAT **MUST** BE YOU...
ENZAN!

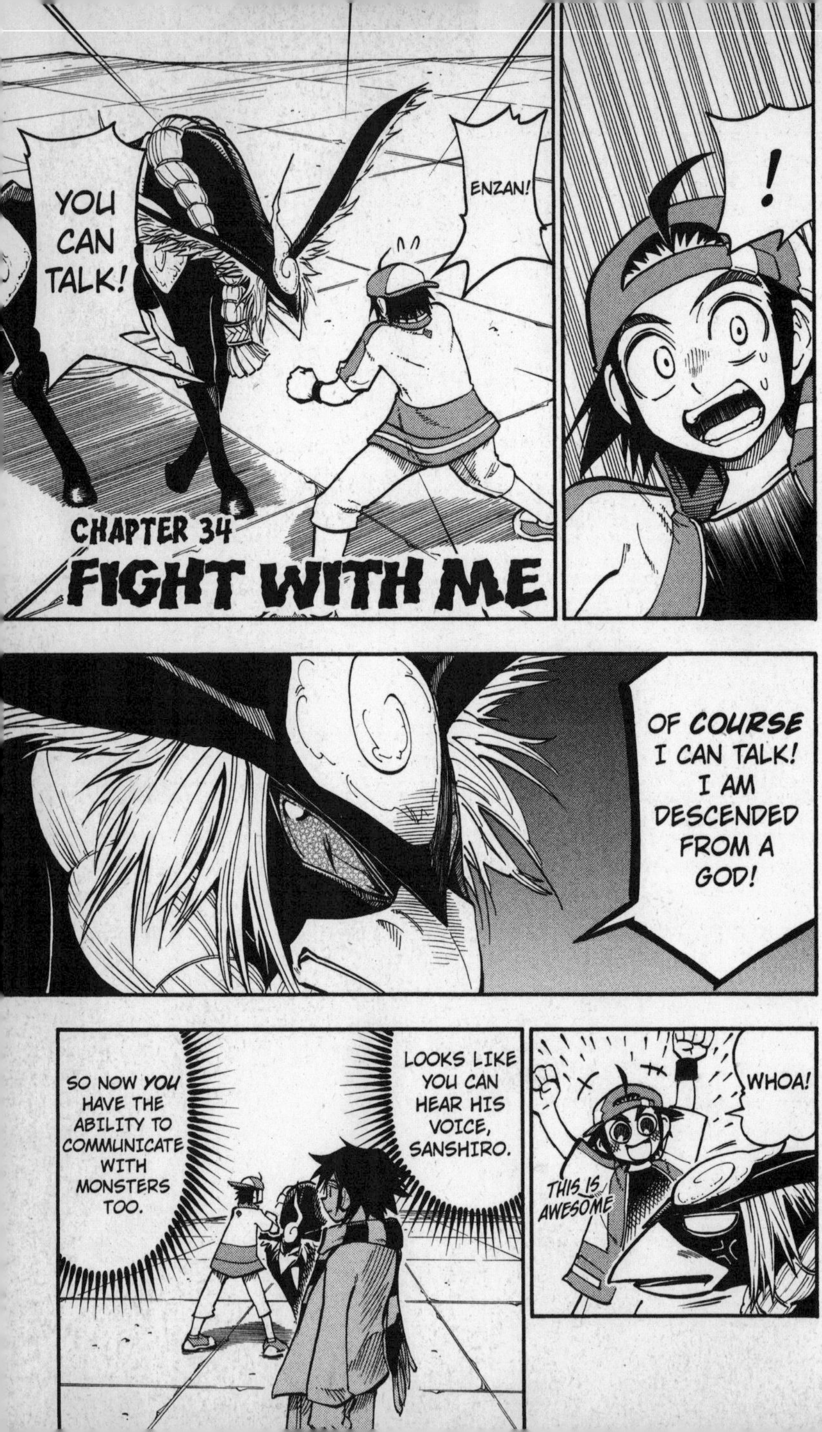
!
ENZAN!
YOU CAN TALK!
CHAPTER 34
FIGHT WITH ME
OF COURSE I CAN TALK! I AM DESCENDED FROM A GOD!
WHOA!
THIS IS AWESOME
LOOKS LIKE YOU CAN HEAR HIS VOICE, SANSHIRO.
SO NOW YOU HAVE THE ABILITY TO COMMUNICATE WITH MONSTERS TOO.

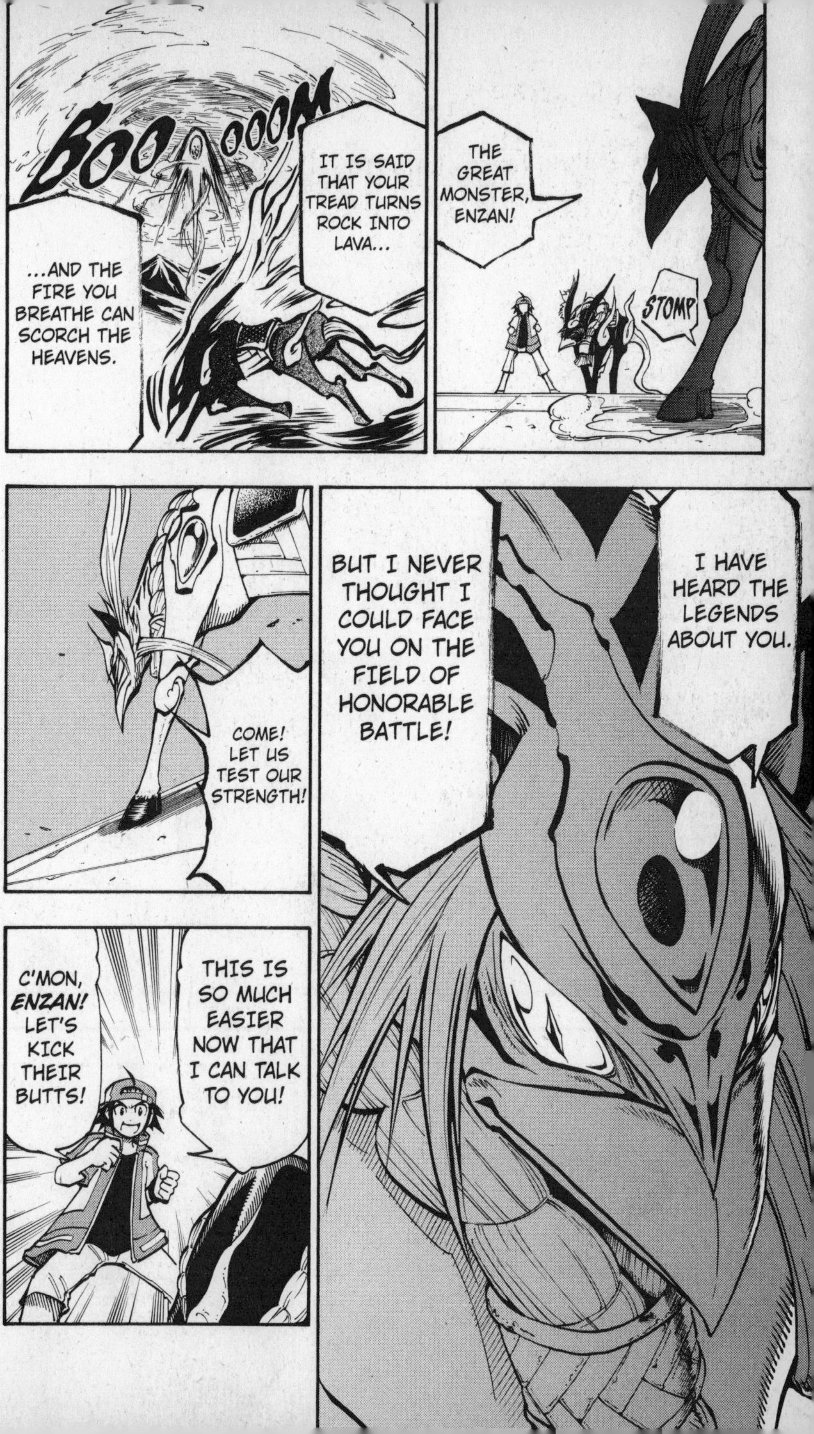
THE GREAT MONSTER, ENZAN!
STOMP
IT IS SAID THAT YOUR TREAD TURNS ROCK INTO LAVA...
BOOOOOM
...AND THE FIRE YOU BREATHE CAN SCORCH THE HEAVENS.
I HAVE HEARD THE LEGENDS ABOUT YOU.
BUT I NEVER THOUGHT I COULD FACE YOU ON THE FIELD OF HONORABLE BATTLE!
COME! LET US TEST OUR STRENGTH!
THIS IS SO MUCH EASIER NOW THAT I CAN TALK TO YOU!
C'MON, **ENZAN!** LET'S KICK THEIR BUTTS!

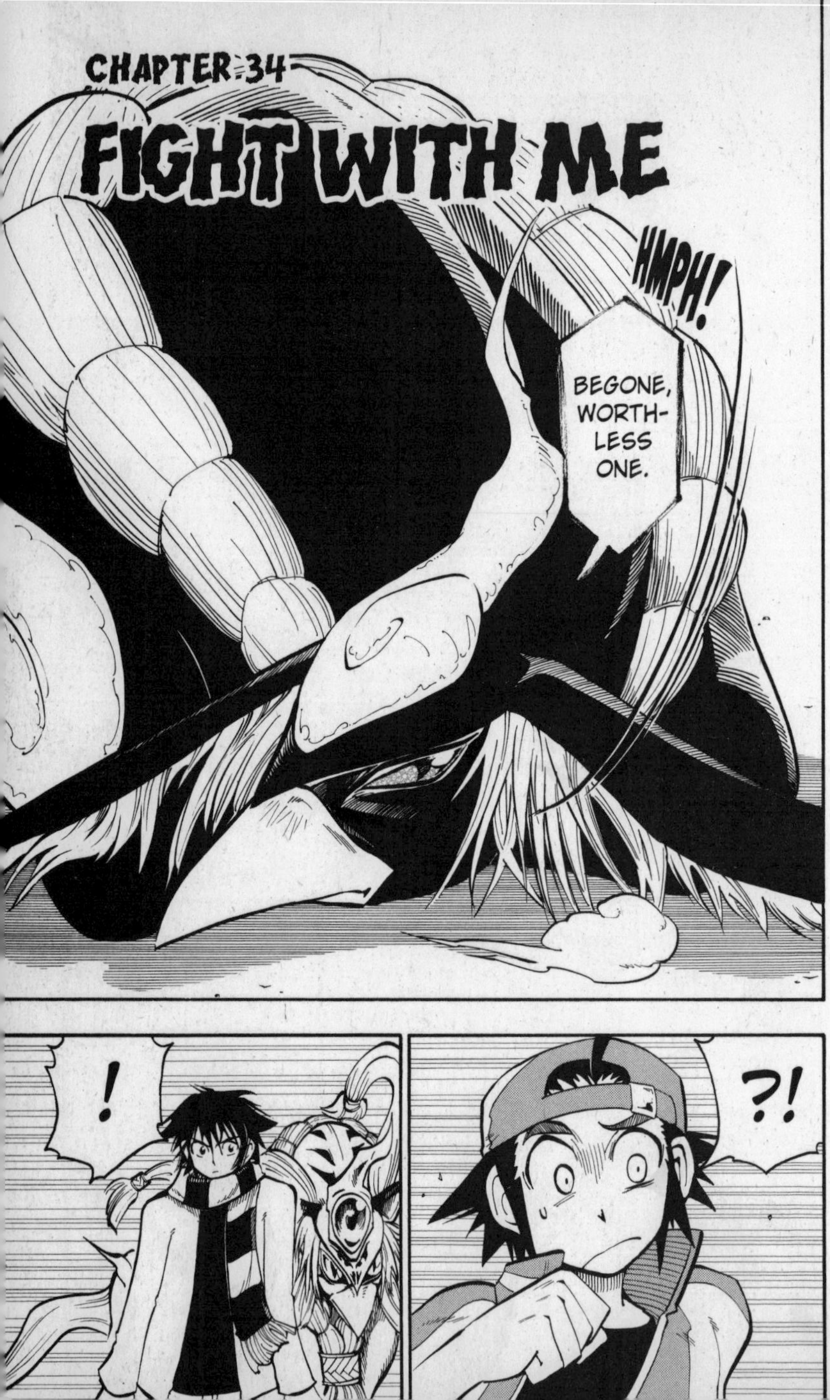
CHAPTER 34
FIGHT WITH ME
HMPH!
BEGONE, WORTHLESS ONE.
?!
!

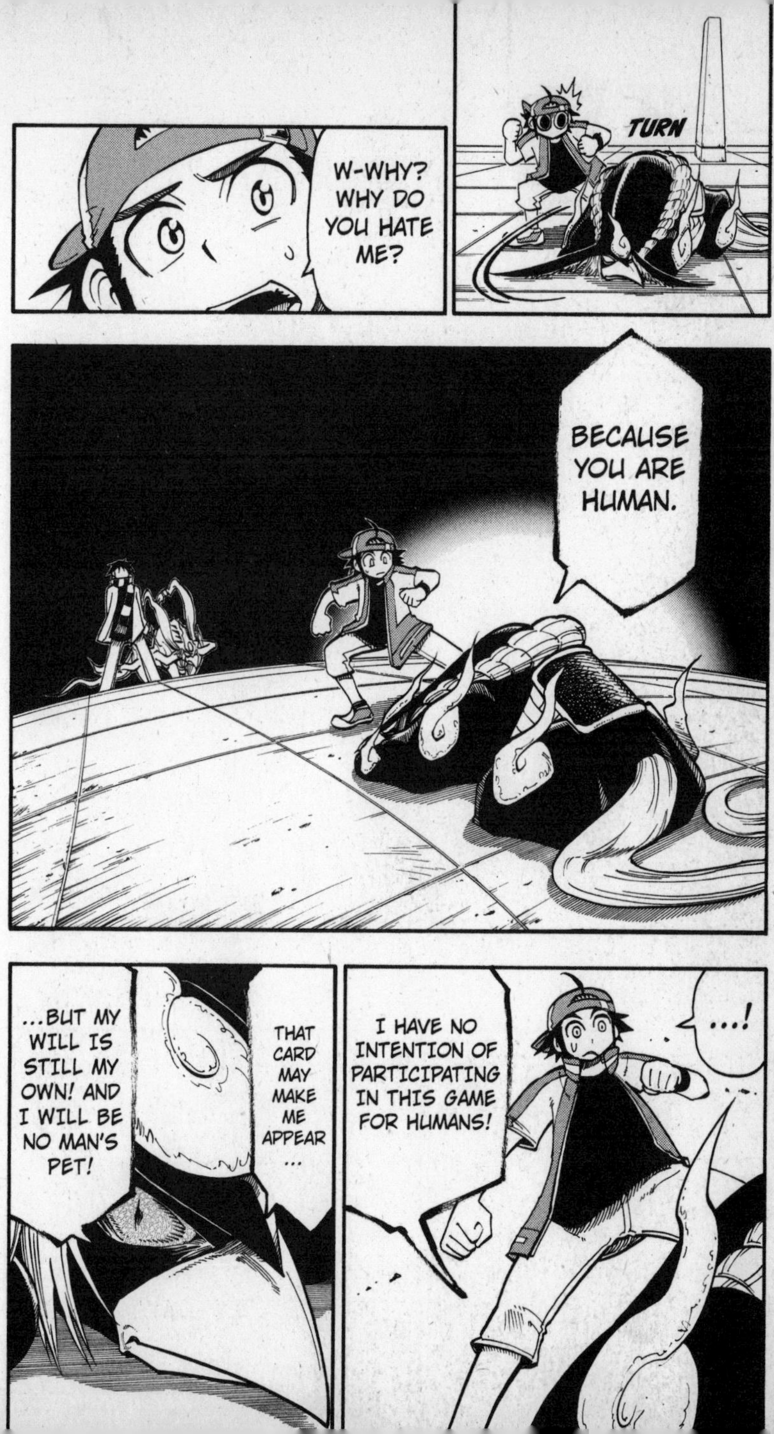
TURN
W-WHY? WHY DO YOU HATE ME?
BECAUSE YOU ARE HUMAN.
...!
I HAVE NO INTENTION OF PARTICIPATING IN THIS GAME FOR HUMANS!
THAT CARD MAY MAKE ME APPEAR...
...BUT MY WILL IS STILL MY OWN! AND I WILL BE NO MAN'S PET!

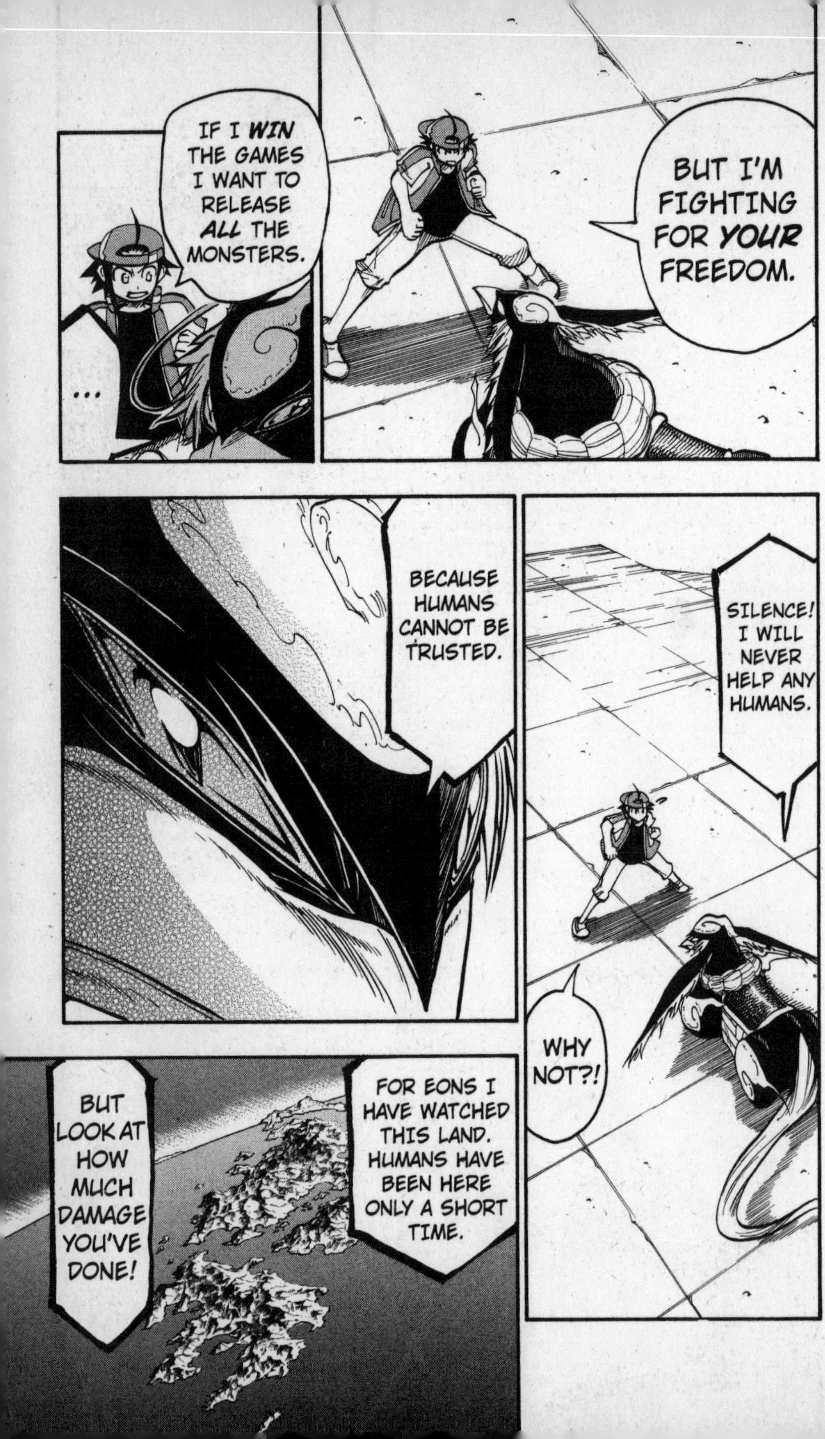

BUT I'M FIGHTING FOR YOUR FREEDOM.
IF I WIN THE GAMES I WANT TO RELEASE ALL THE MONSTERS.
...
SILENCE! I WILL NEVER HELP ANY HUMANS.
WHY NOT?!
BECAUSE HUMANS CANNOT BE TRUSTED.
FOR EONS I HAVE WATCHED THIS LAND. HUMANS HAVE BEEN HERE ONLY A SHORT TIME.
BUT LOOK AT HOW MUCH DAMAGE YOU'VE DONE!

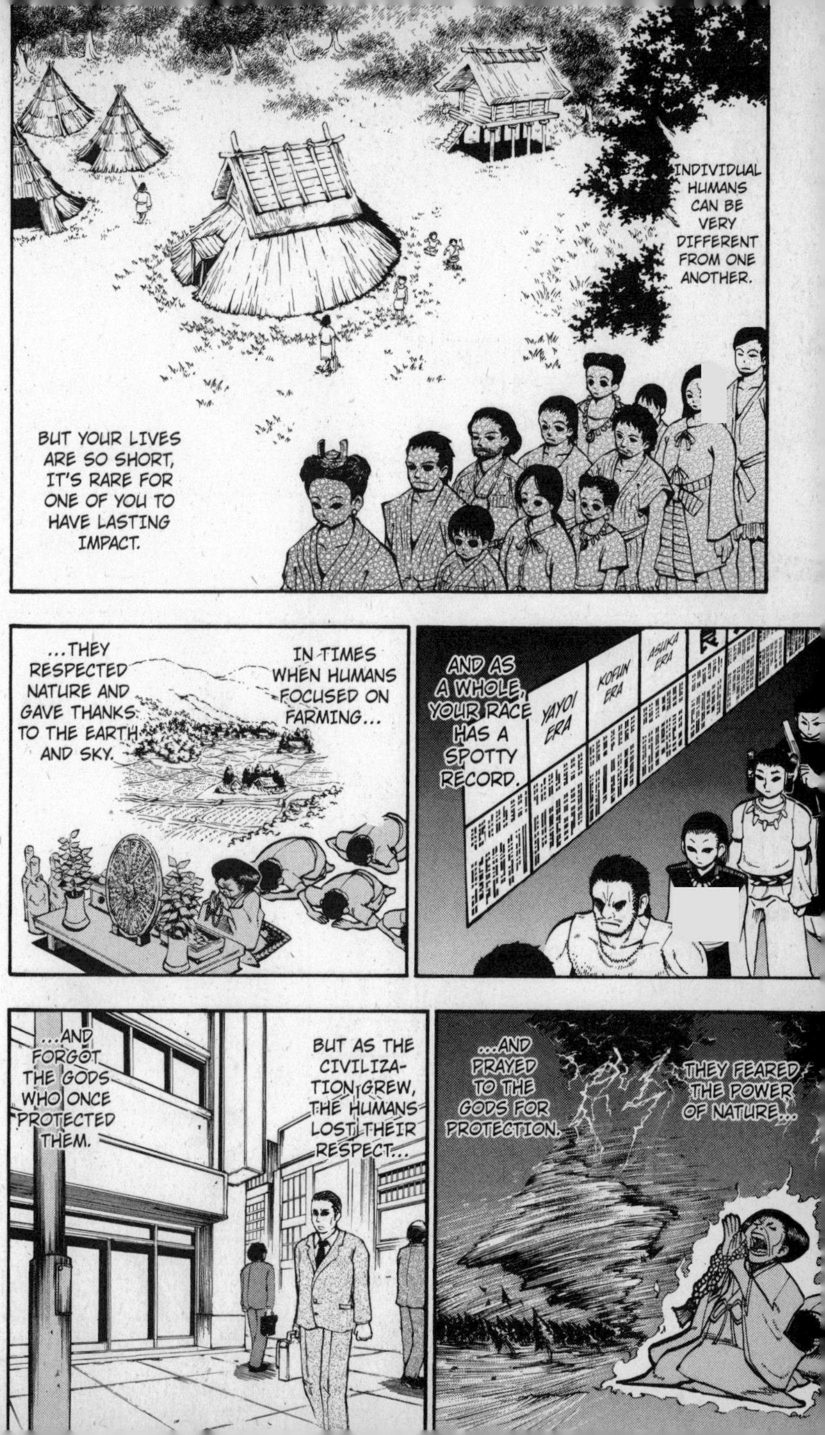
INDIVIDUAL HUMANS CAN BE VERY DIFFERENT FROM ONE ANOTHER.
BUT YOUR LIVES ARE SO SHORT, IT'S RARE FOR ONE OF YOU TO HAVE LASTING IMPACT.
AND AS A WHOLE, YOUR RACE HAS A SPOTTY RECORD.
ASUKA ERA
KOFUN ERA
YAYOI ERA
IN TIMES WHEN HUMANS FOCUSED ON FARMING...
...THEY RESPECTED NATURE AND GAVE THANKS TO THE EARTH AND SKY.
THEY FEARED THE POWER OF NATURE...
...AND PRAYED TO THE GODS FOR PROTECTION.
BUT AS THE CIVILIZATION GREW, THE HUMANS LOST THEIR RESPECT...
...AND FORGOT THE GODS WHO ONCE PROTECTED THEM.

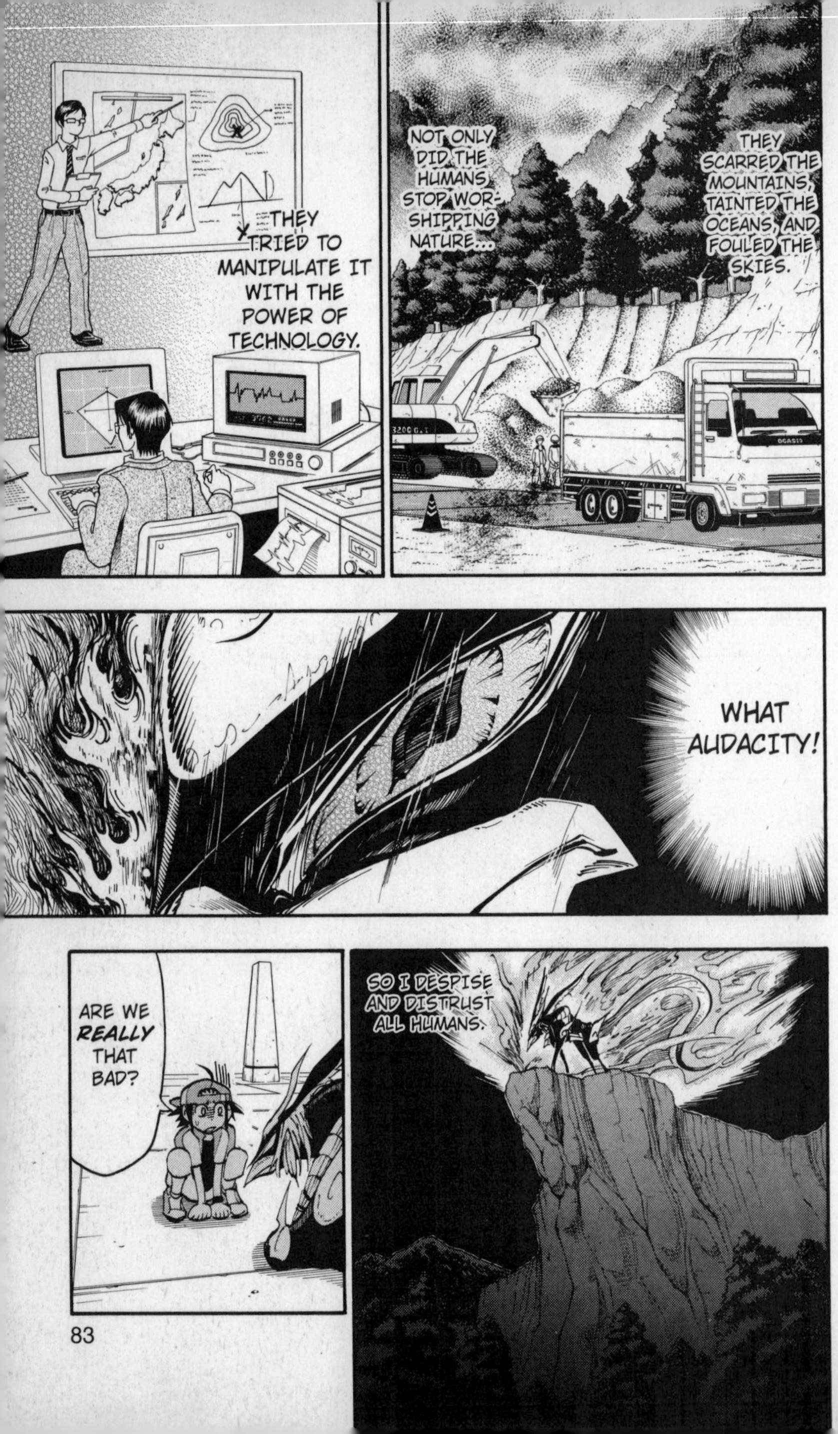
NOT ONLY DID THE HUMANS STOP WOR-SHIPPING NATURE...
THEY SCARRED THE MOUNTAINS, TAINTED THE OCEANS, AND FOULED THE SKIES.
THEY TRIED TO MANIPULATE IT WITH THE POWER OF TECHNOLOGY.
WHAT AUDACITY!
SO I DESPISE AND DISTRUST ALL HUMANS.
ARE WE *REALLY* THAT BAD?

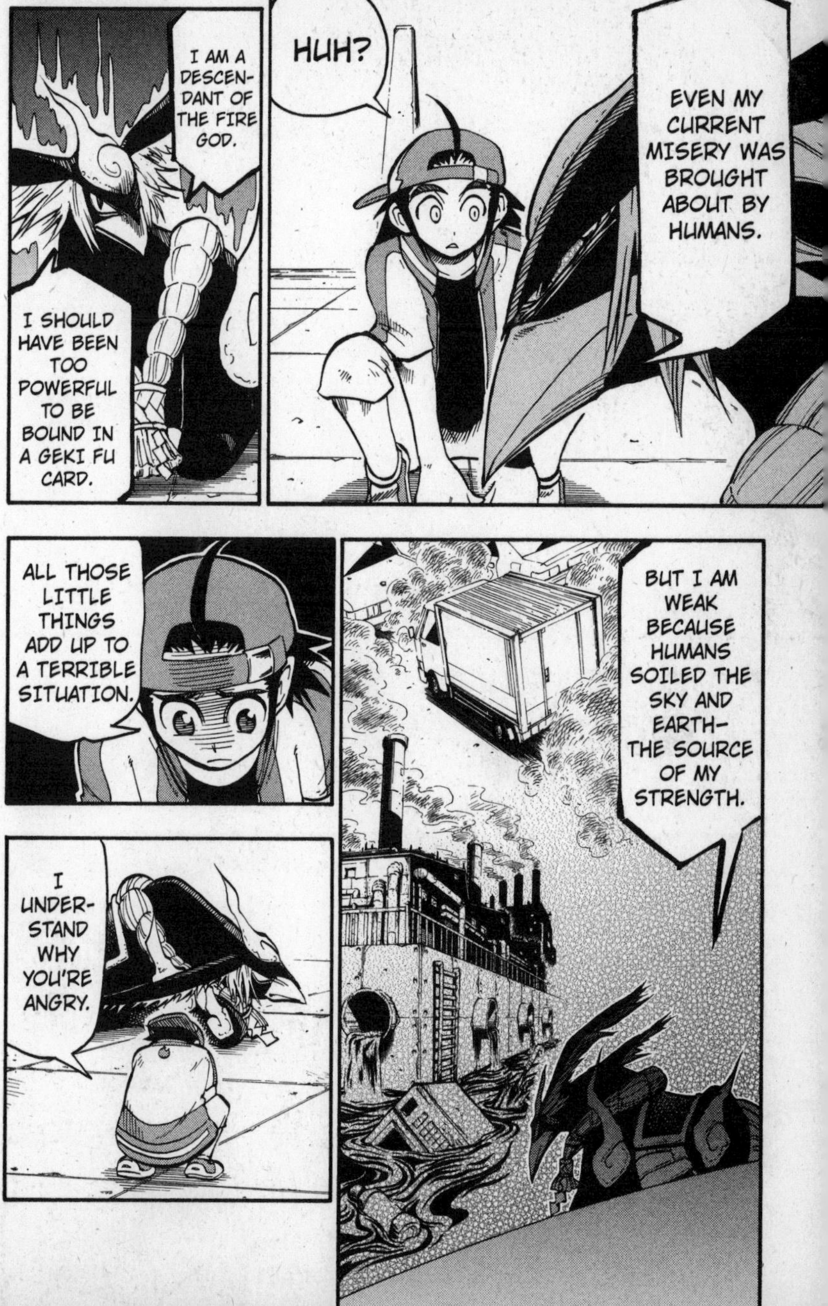
EVEN MY CURRENT MISERY WAS BROUGHT ABOUT BY HUMANS.
HUH?
I AM A DESCENDANT OF THE FIRE GOD.
I SHOULD HAVE BEEN TOO POWERFUL TO BE BOUND IN A GEKI FU CARD.
BUT I AM WEAK BECAUSE HUMANS SOILED THE SKY AND EARTH— THE SOURCE OF MY STRENGTH.
ALL THOSE LITTLE THINGS ADD UP TO A TERRIBLE SITUATION.
I UNDERSTAND WHY YOU'RE ANGRY.

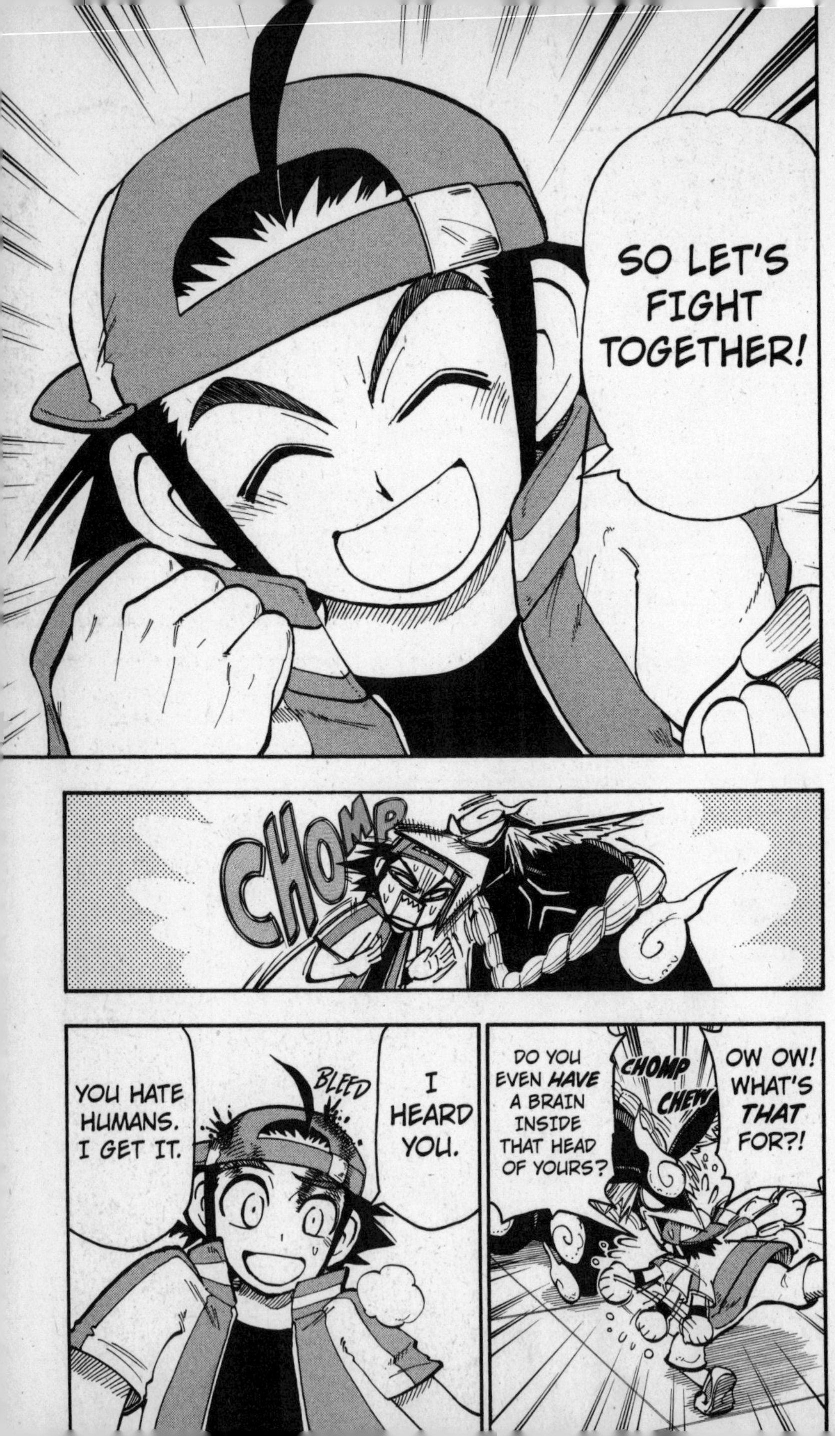
SO LET'S FIGHT TOGETHER!
CHOMP
OW OW! WHAT'S *THAT* FOR?!
CHOMP
CHEW
DO YOU EVEN *HAVE* A BRAIN INSIDE THAT HEAD OF YOURS?
I HEARD YOU.
BLEED
YOU HATE HUMANS. I GET IT.

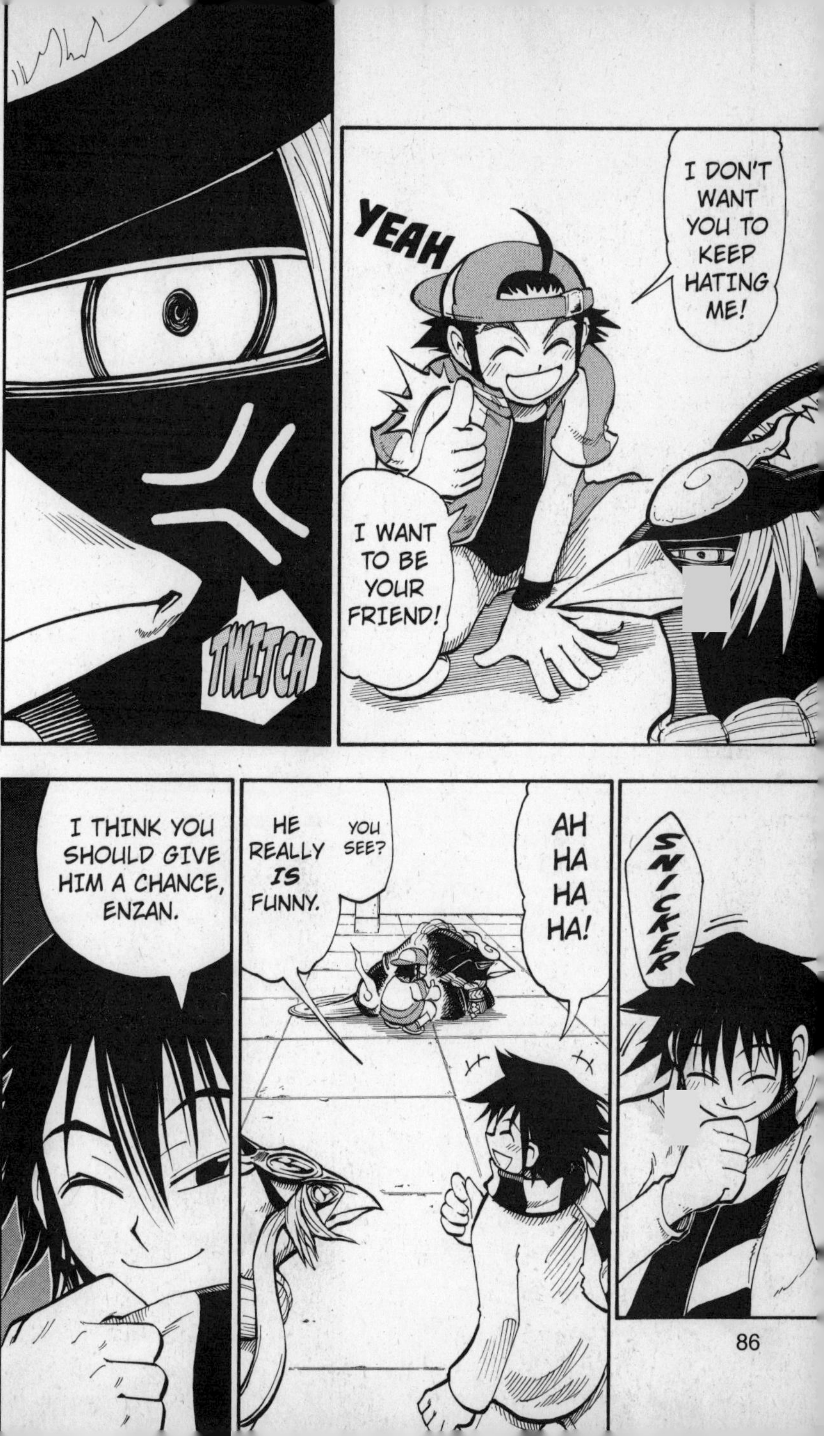
YEAH
I DON'T WANT YOU TO KEEP HATING ME!
I WANT TO BE YOUR FRIEND!
TWITCH
SNICKER
AH HA HA HA!
YOU SEE?
HE REALLY IS FUNNY.
I THINK YOU SHOULD GIVE HIM A CHANCE, ENZAN.

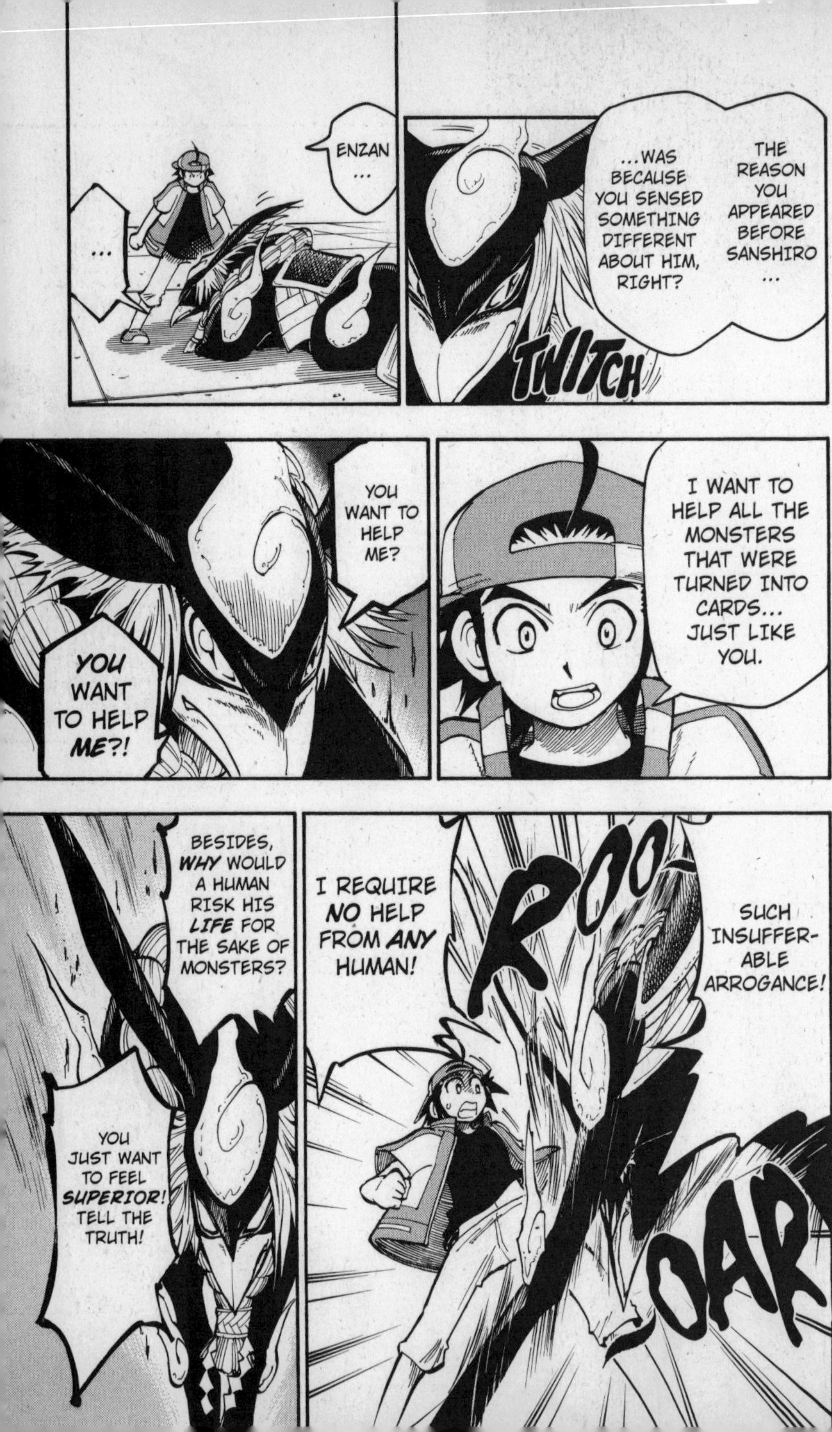
THE REASON YOU APPEARED BEFORE SANSHIRO ...
...WAS BECAUSE YOU SENSED SOMETHING DIFFERENT ABOUT HIM, RIGHT?
TWITCH
ENZAN ...
...
I WANT TO HELP ALL THE MONSTERS THAT WERE TURNED INTO CARDS... JUST LIKE YOU.
YOU WANT TO HELP ME?
YOU WANT TO HELP *ME*?!
SUCH INSUFFER-ABLE ARROGANCE!
ROOOAR
I REQUIRE *NO* HELP FROM *ANY* HUMAN!
BESIDES, *WHY* WOULD A HUMAN RISK HIS *LIFE* FOR THE SAKE OF MONSTERS?
YOU JUST WANT TO FEEL *SUPERIOR*! TELL THE TRUTH!

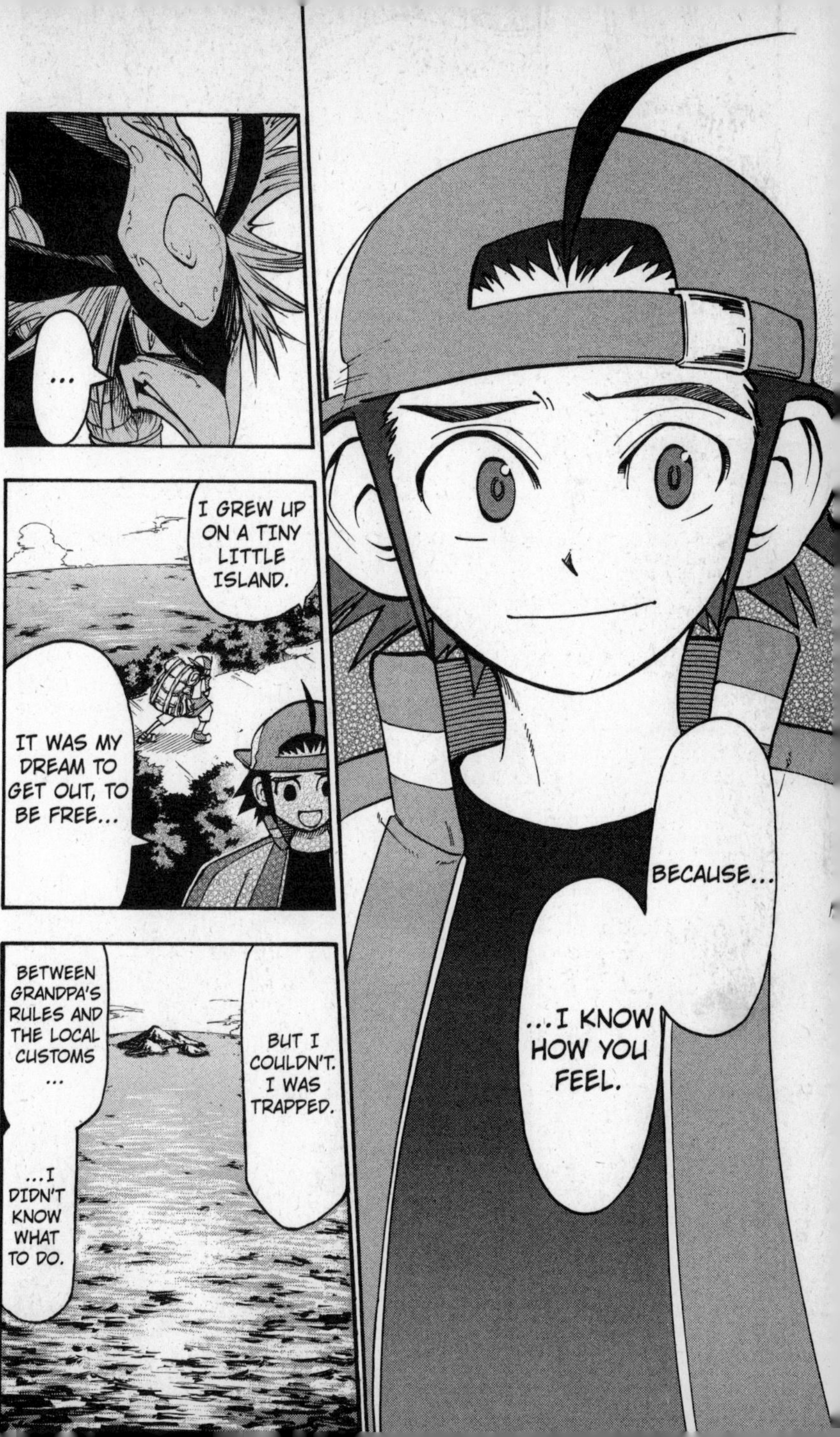
BECAUSE...
...I KNOW HOW YOU FEEL.
...
I GREW UP ON A TINY LITTLE ISLAND.
IT WAS MY DREAM TO GET OUT, TO BE FREE...
BUT I COULDN'T. I WAS TRAPPED.
BETWEEN GRANDPA'S RULES AND THE LOCAL CUSTOMS ...
...I DIDN'T KNOW WHAT TO DO.

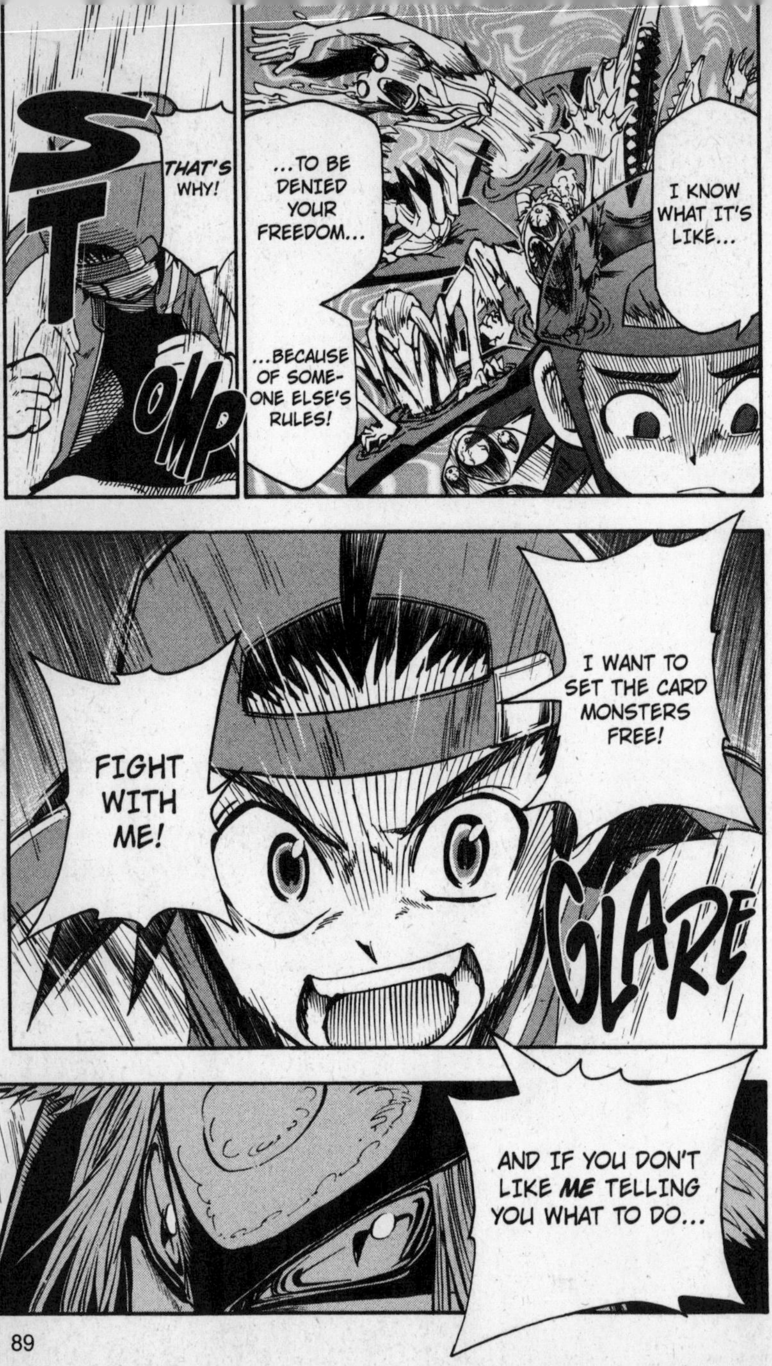
I KNOW WHAT IT'S LIKE...
...TO BE DENIED YOUR FREEDOM...
...BECAUSE OF SOME-ONE ELSE'S RULES!
THAT'S WHY!
STOMP
I WANT TO SET THE CARD MONSTERS FREE!
FIGHT WITH ME!
GLARE
AND IF YOU DON'T LIKE *ME* TELLING YOU WHAT TO DO...

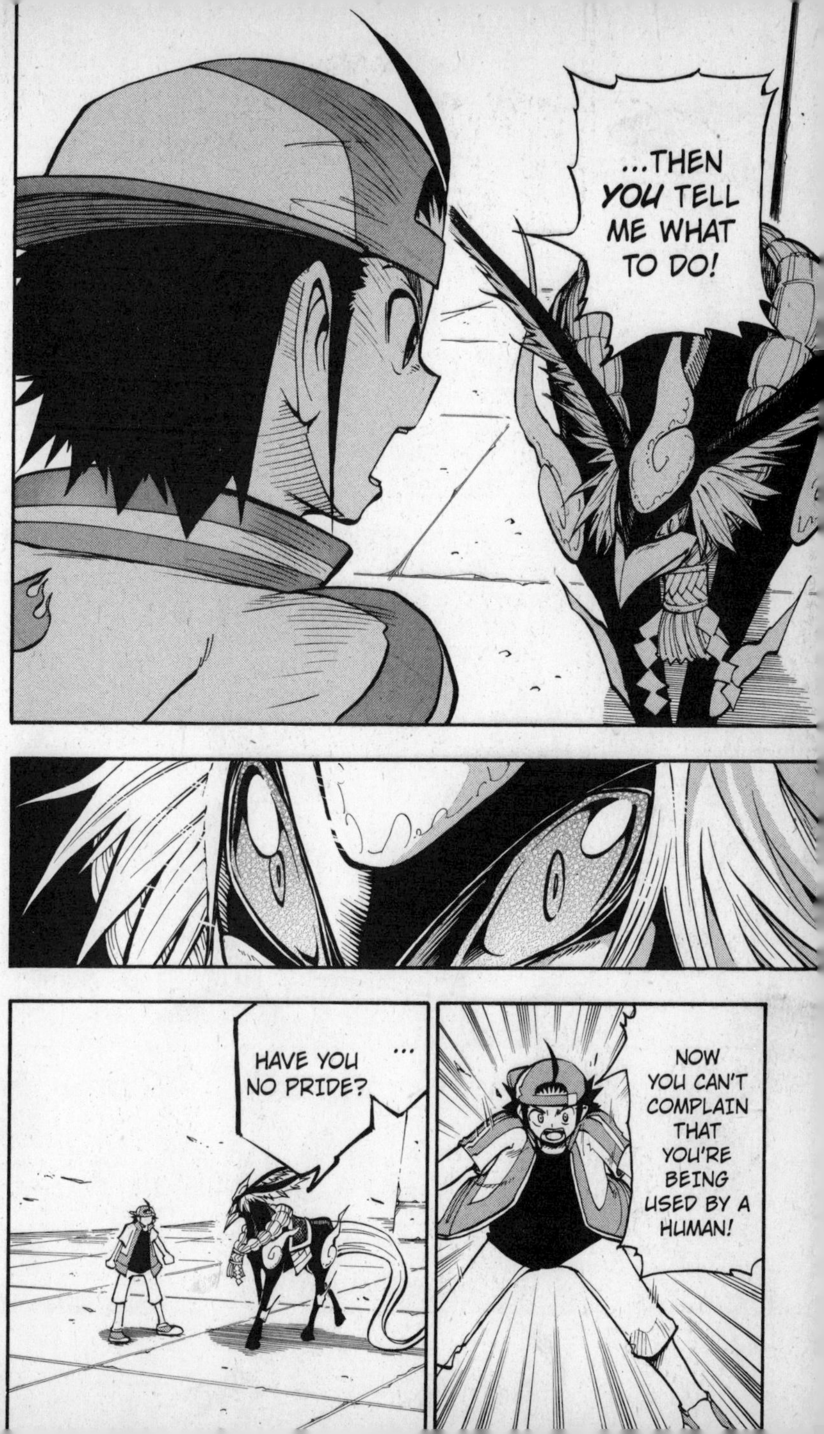
...THEN YOU TELL ME WHAT TO DO!
NOW YOU CAN'T COMPLAIN THAT YOU'RE BEING USED BY A HUMAN!
...
HAVE YOU NO PRIDE?

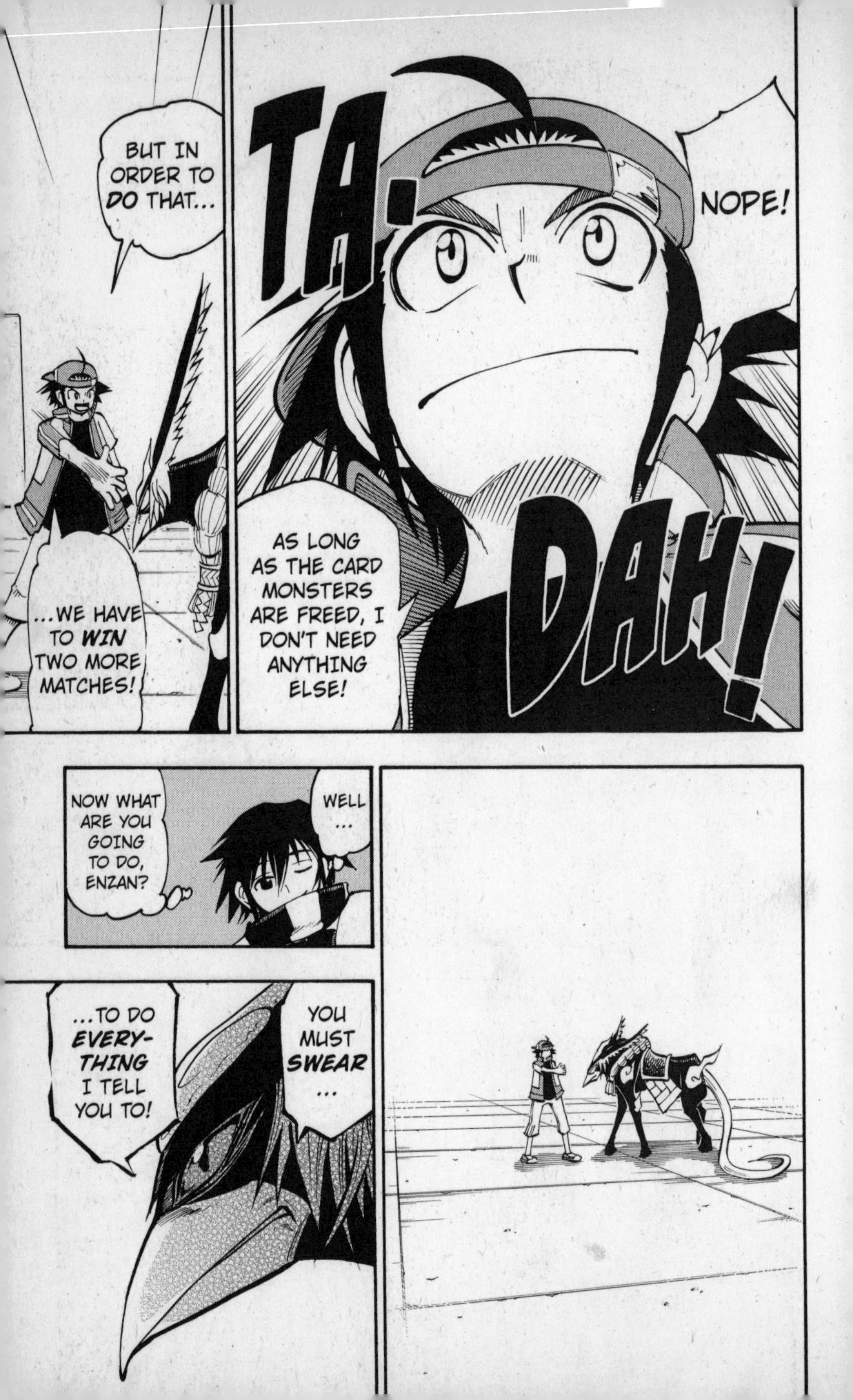
NOPE!
TA-
DAH!
AS LONG AS THE CARD MONSTERS ARE FREED, I DON'T NEED ANYTHING ELSE!
BUT IN ORDER TO DO THAT...
...WE HAVE TO WIN TWO MORE MATCHES!
WELL...
NOW WHAT ARE YOU GOING TO DO, ENZAN?
YOU MUST SWEAR...
...TO DO EVERYTHING I TELL YOU TO!

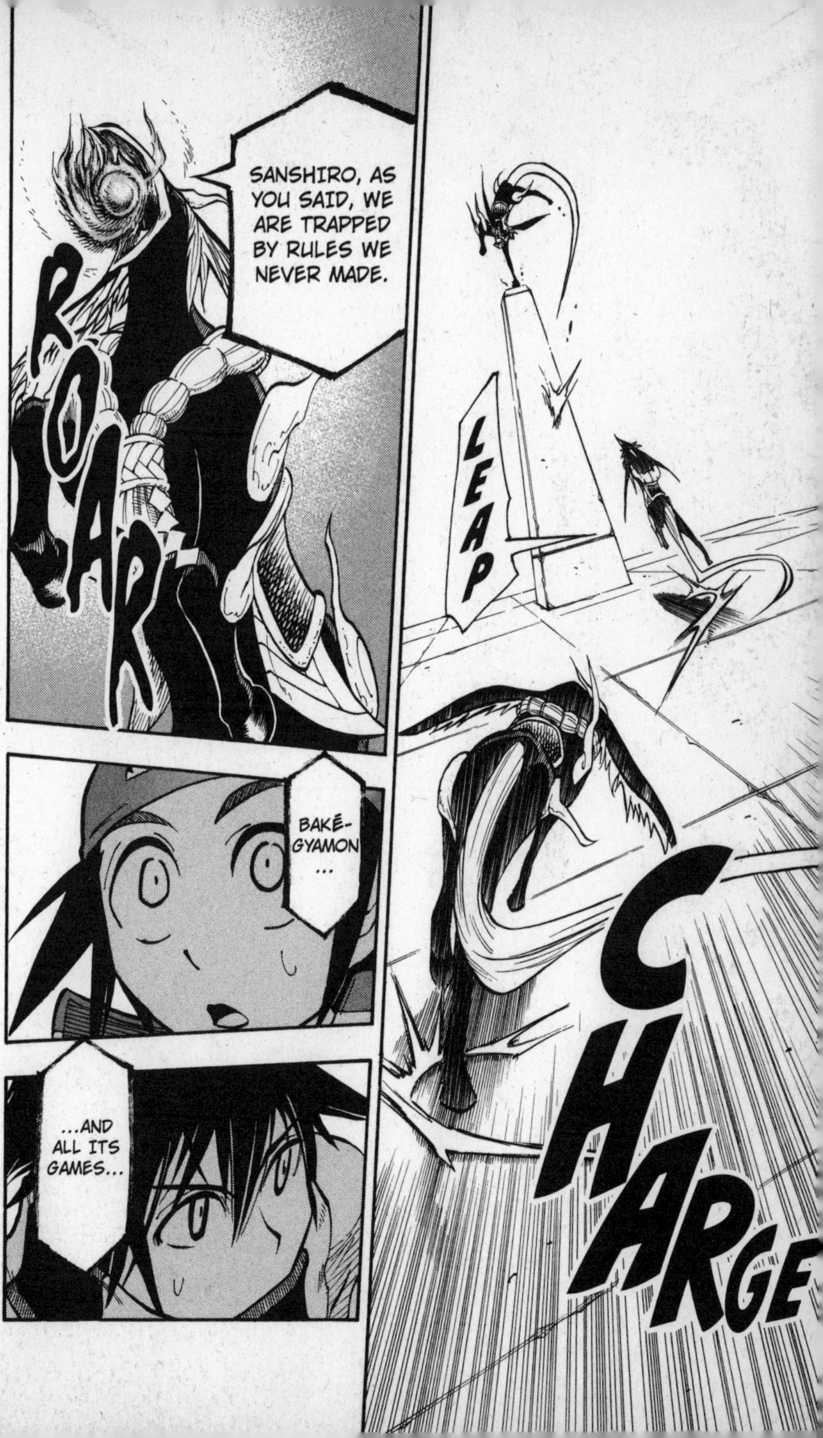

LEAP
CHARGE
SANSHIRO, AS YOU SAID, WE ARE TRAPPED BY RULES WE NEVER MADE.
ROAR
BAKÉ-GYAMON...
...AND ALL ITS GAMES...

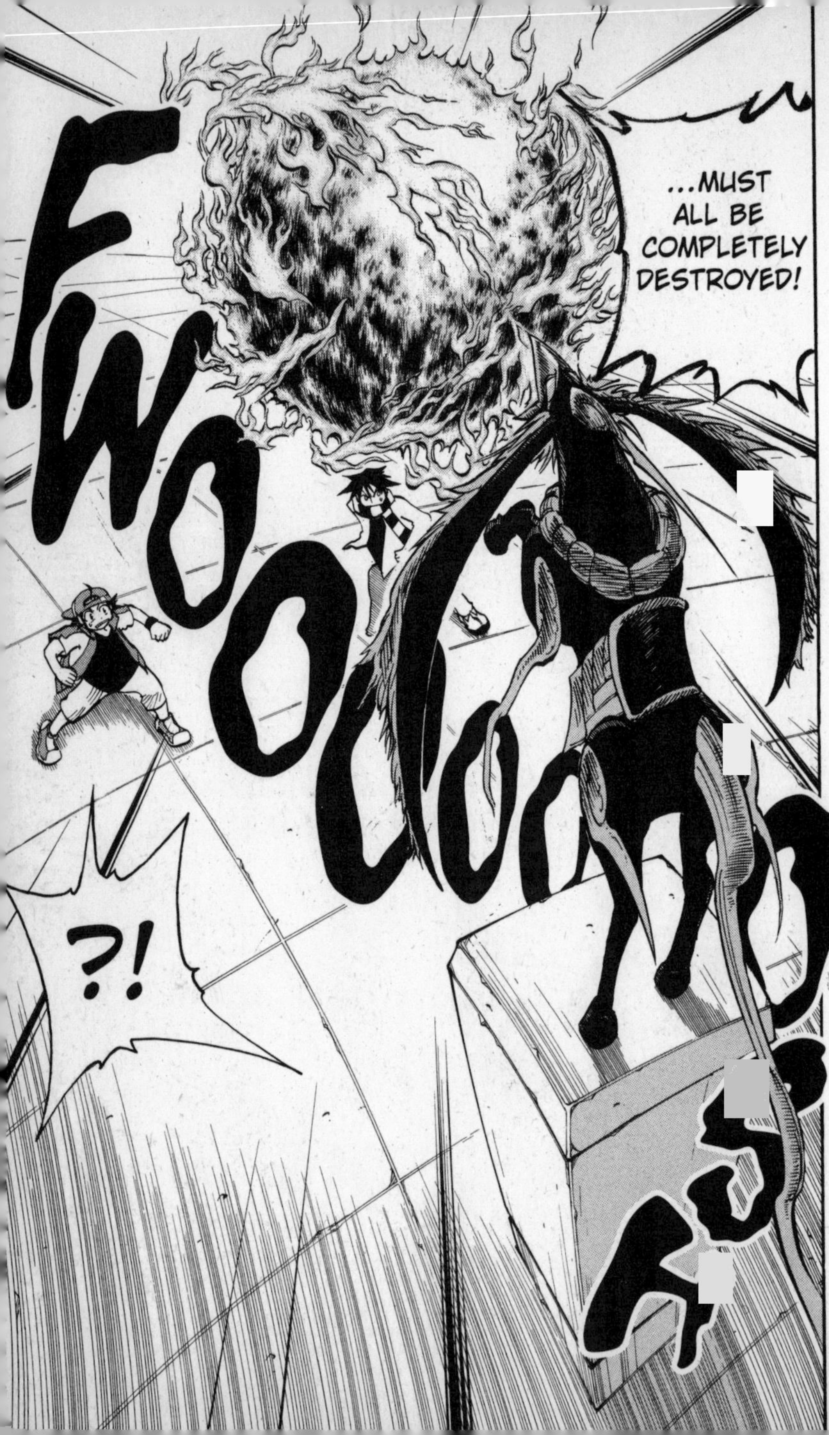
...MUST ALL BE COMPLETELY DESTROYED!
?!

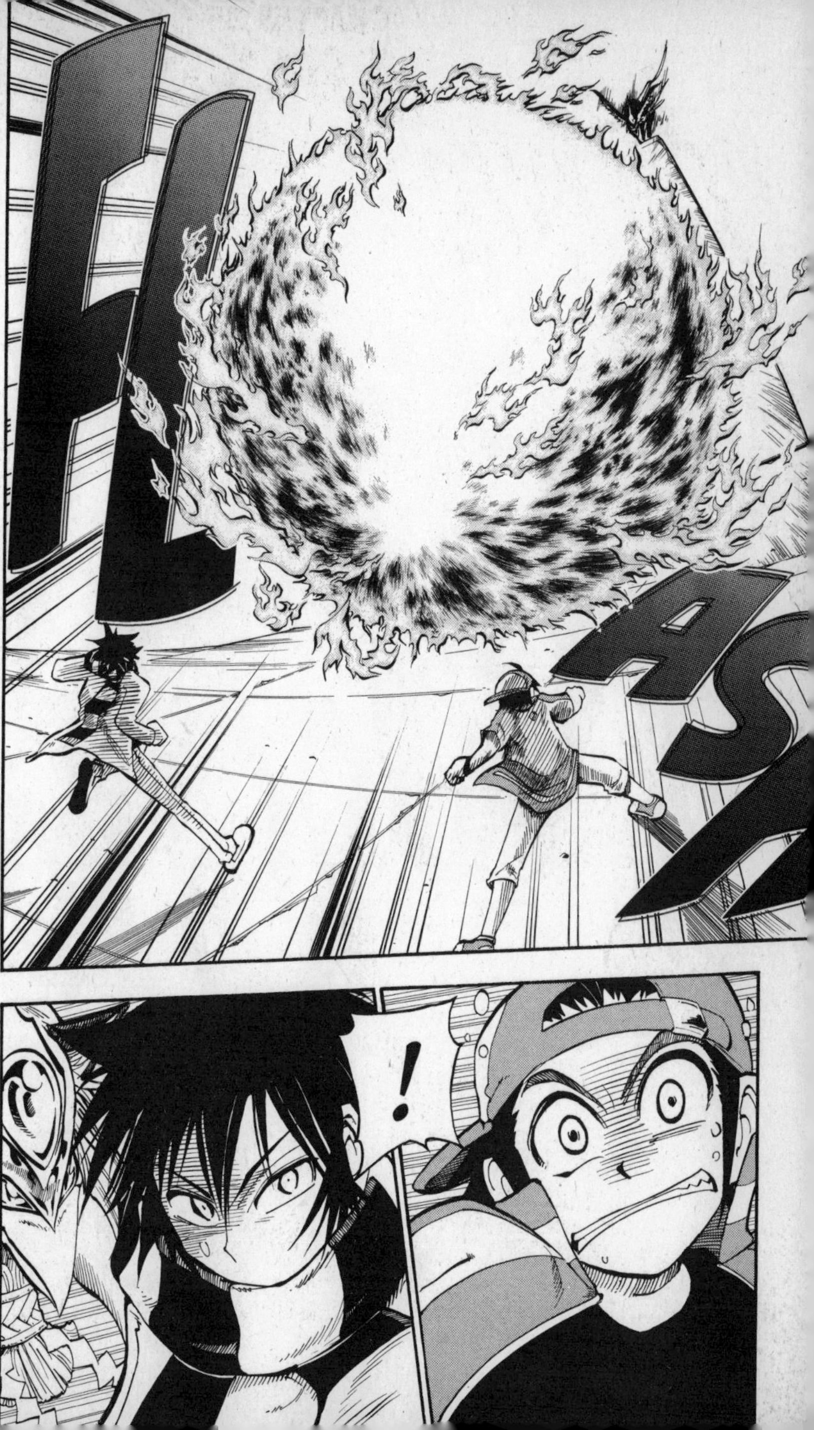
!

CHAPTER 35
I AM SUPERIOR

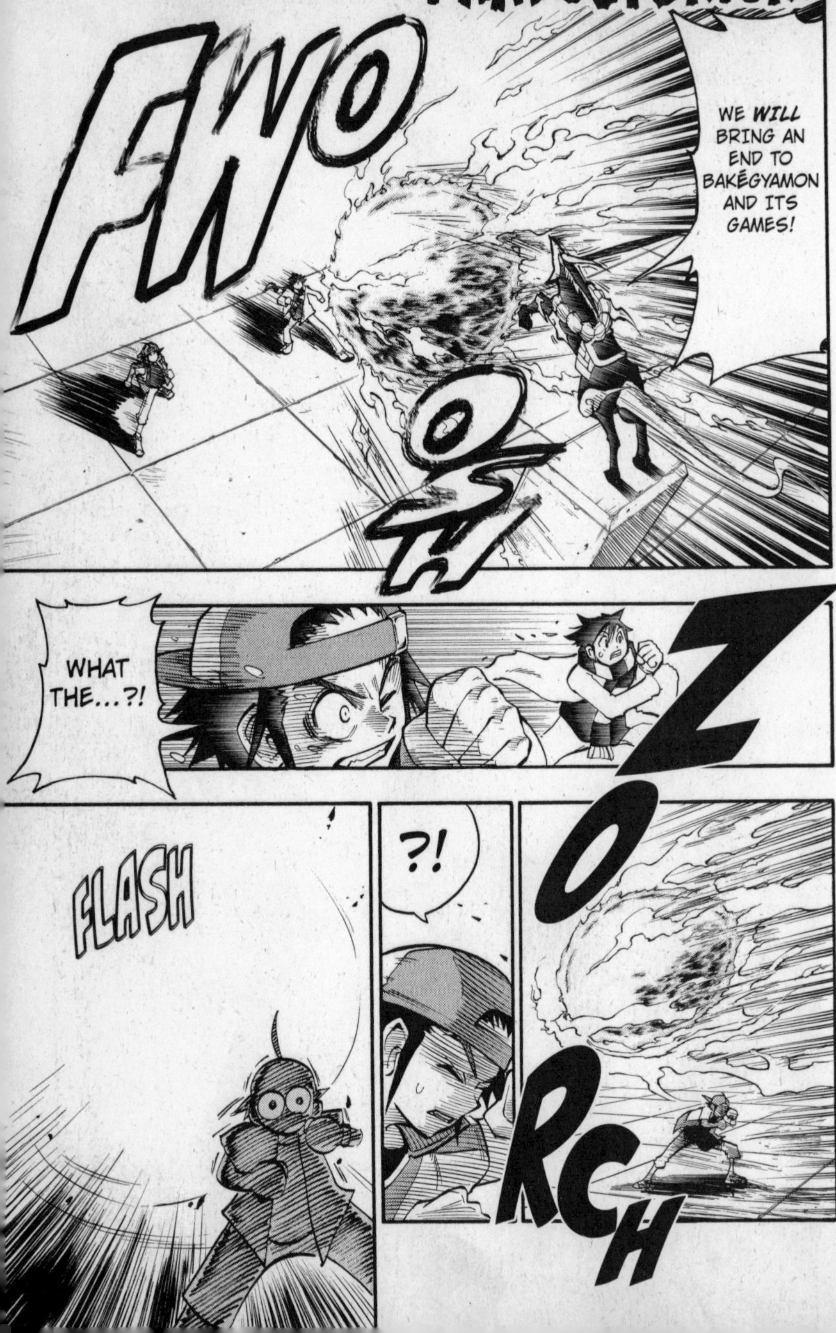

WE WILL BRING AN END TO BAKÉGYAMON AND ITS GAMES!
FWOOSH
WHAT THE...?!
ZORCH
?!
FLASH

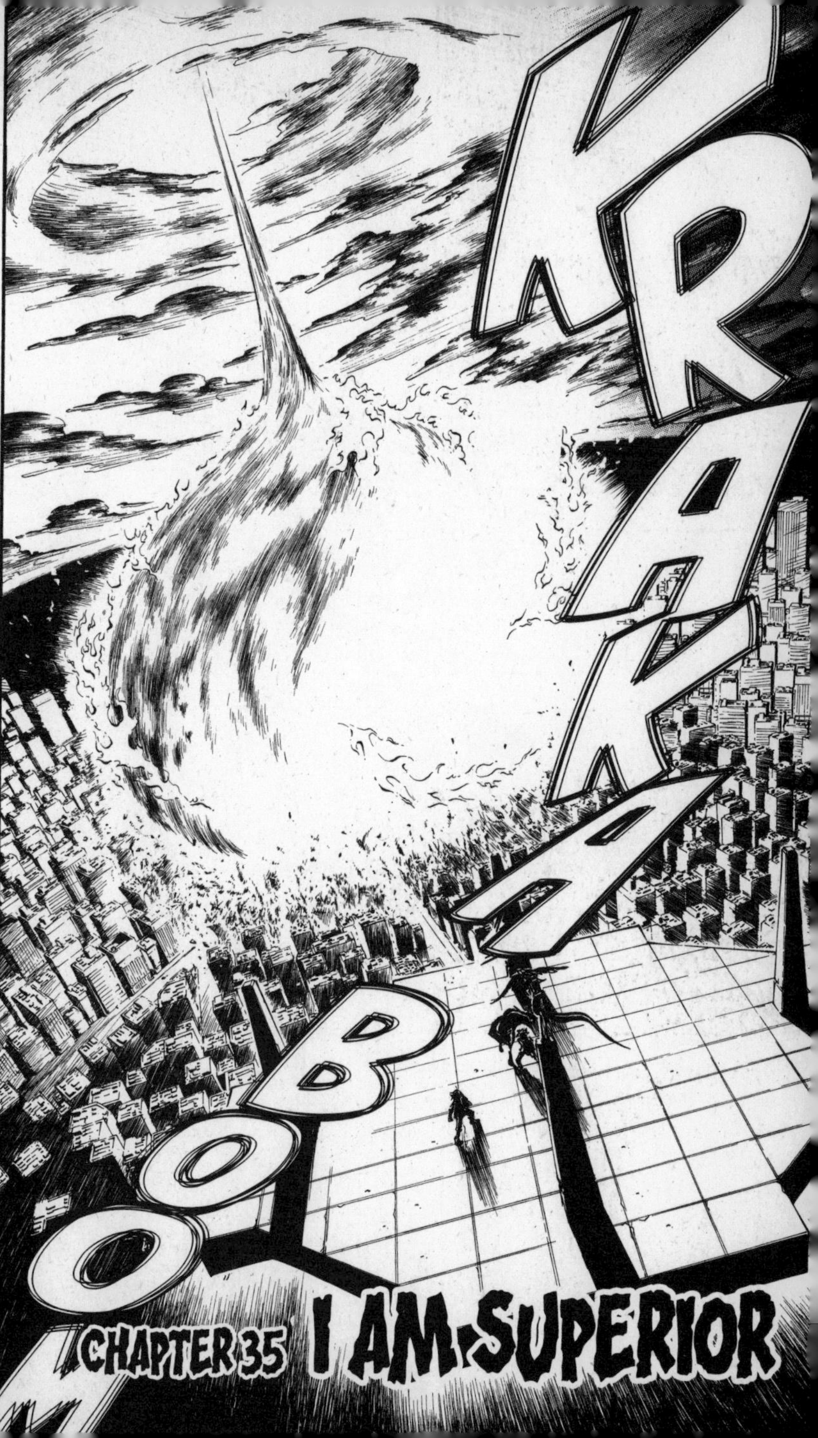
KRAKABOOM

CHAPTER 35 I AM SUPERIOR

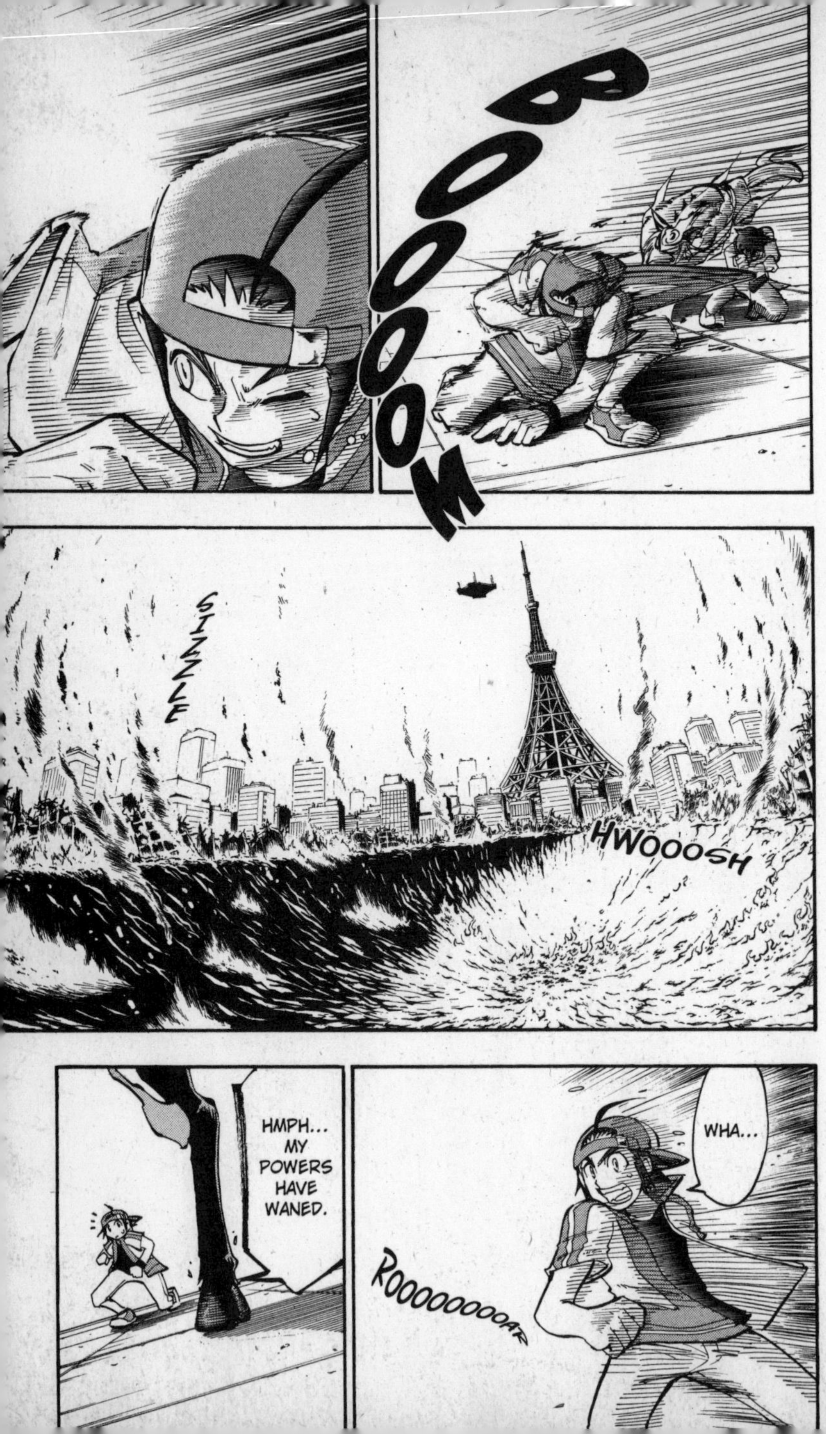
BOOOOOOM
SIZZLE
HWOOOSH
WHA...
ROOOOOOOOAR
HMPH... MY POWERS HAVE WANED.

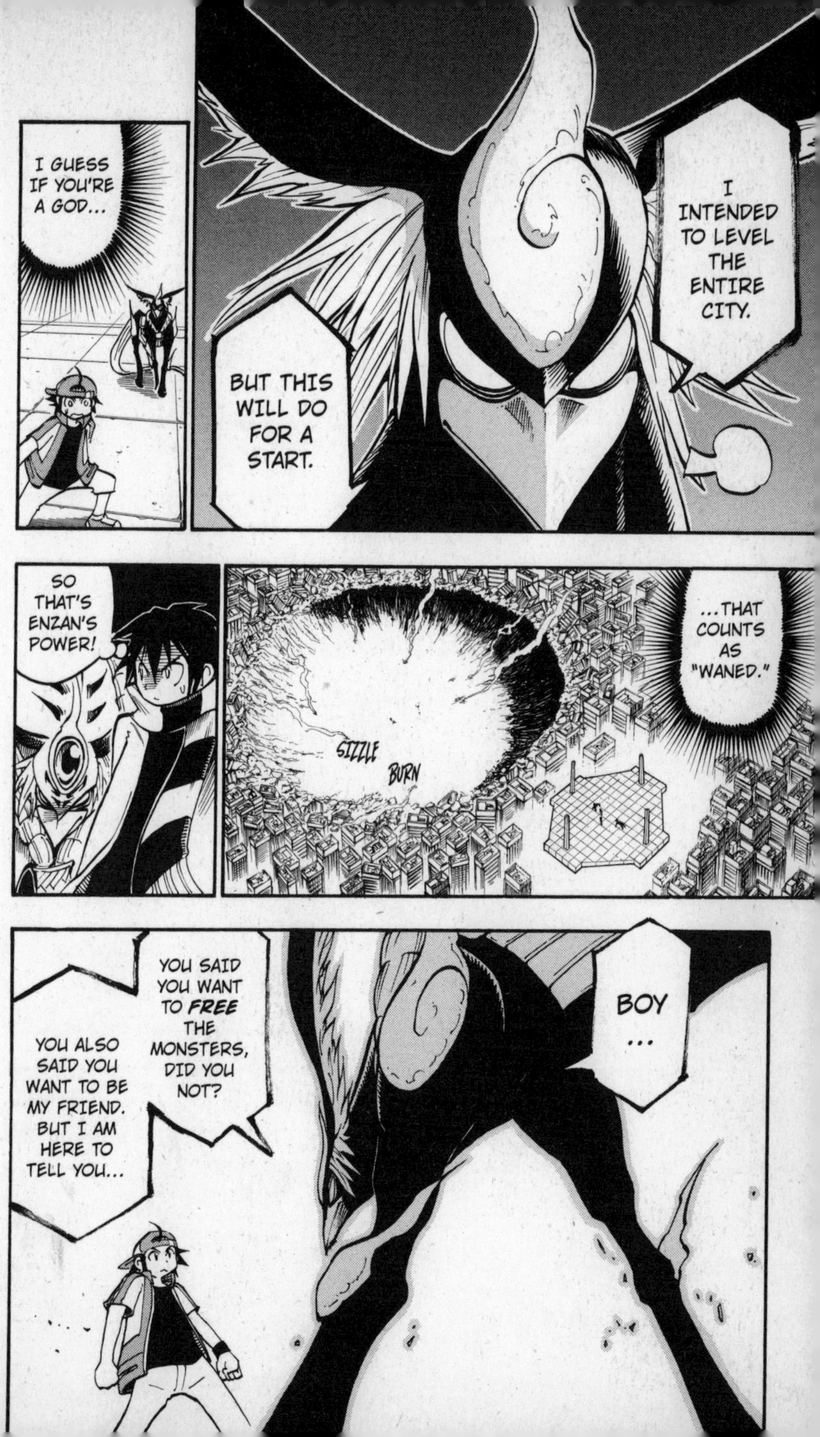
I INTENDED TO LEVEL THE ENTIRE CITY.
BUT THIS WILL DO FOR A START.
I GUESS IF YOU'RE A GOD...
...THAT COUNTS AS "WANED."
SIZZLE
BURN
SO THAT'S ENZAN'S POWER!
BOY ...
YOU SAID YOU WANT TO ***FREE*** THE MONSTERS, DID YOU NOT?
YOU ALSO SAID YOU WANT TO BE MY FRIEND. BUT I AM HERE TO TELL YOU...
...

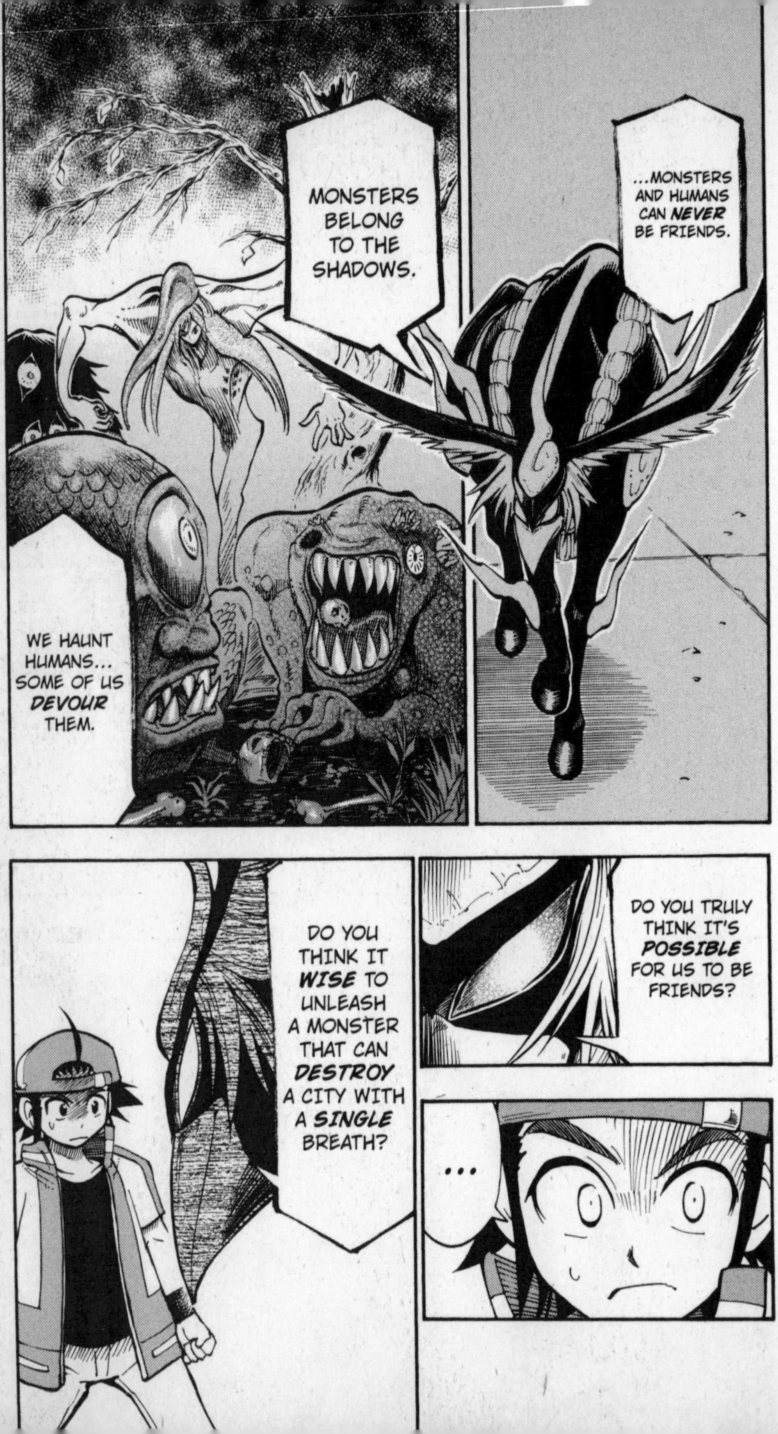
...MONSTERS AND HUMANS CAN ***NEVER*** BE FRIENDS.
MONSTERS BELONG TO THE SHADOWS.
WE HAUNT HUMANS... SOME OF US ***DEVOUR*** THEM.
DO YOU TRULY THINK IT'S ***POSSIBLE*** FOR US TO BE FRIENDS?
...
DO YOU THINK IT ***WISE*** TO UNLEASH A MONSTER THAT CAN ***DESTROY*** A CITY WITH A ***SINGLE*** BREATH?

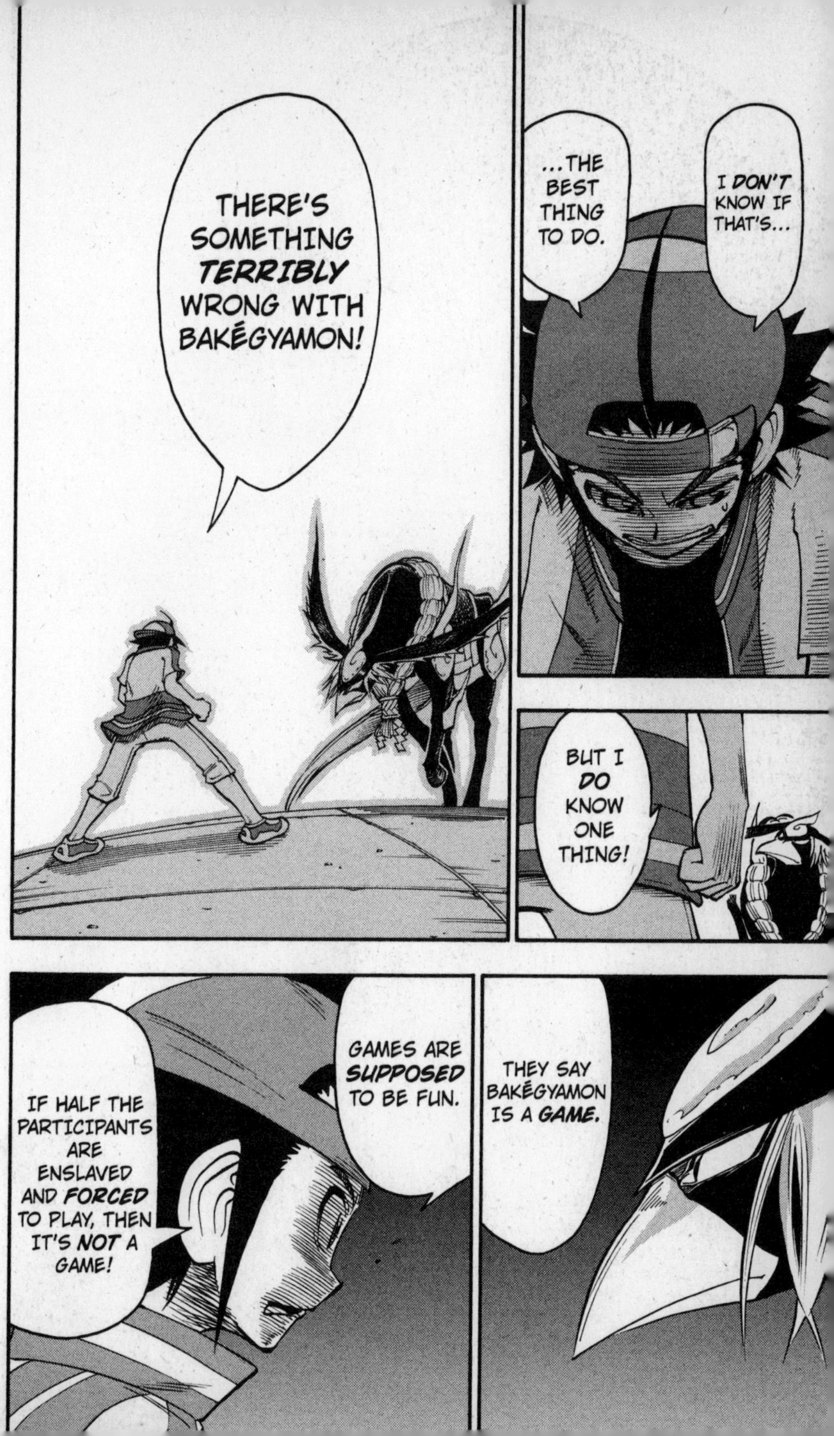
I *DON'T* KNOW IF THAT'S...
...THE BEST THING TO DO.
BUT I *DO* KNOW ONE THING!
THERE'S SOMETHING *TERRIBLY* WRONG WITH BAKĒGYAMON!
THEY SAY BAKĒGYAMON IS A *GAME.*
GAMES ARE *SUPPOSED* TO BE FUN.
IF HALF THE PARTICIPANTS ARE ENSLAVED AND *FORCED* TO PLAY, THEN IT'S *NOT* A GAME!

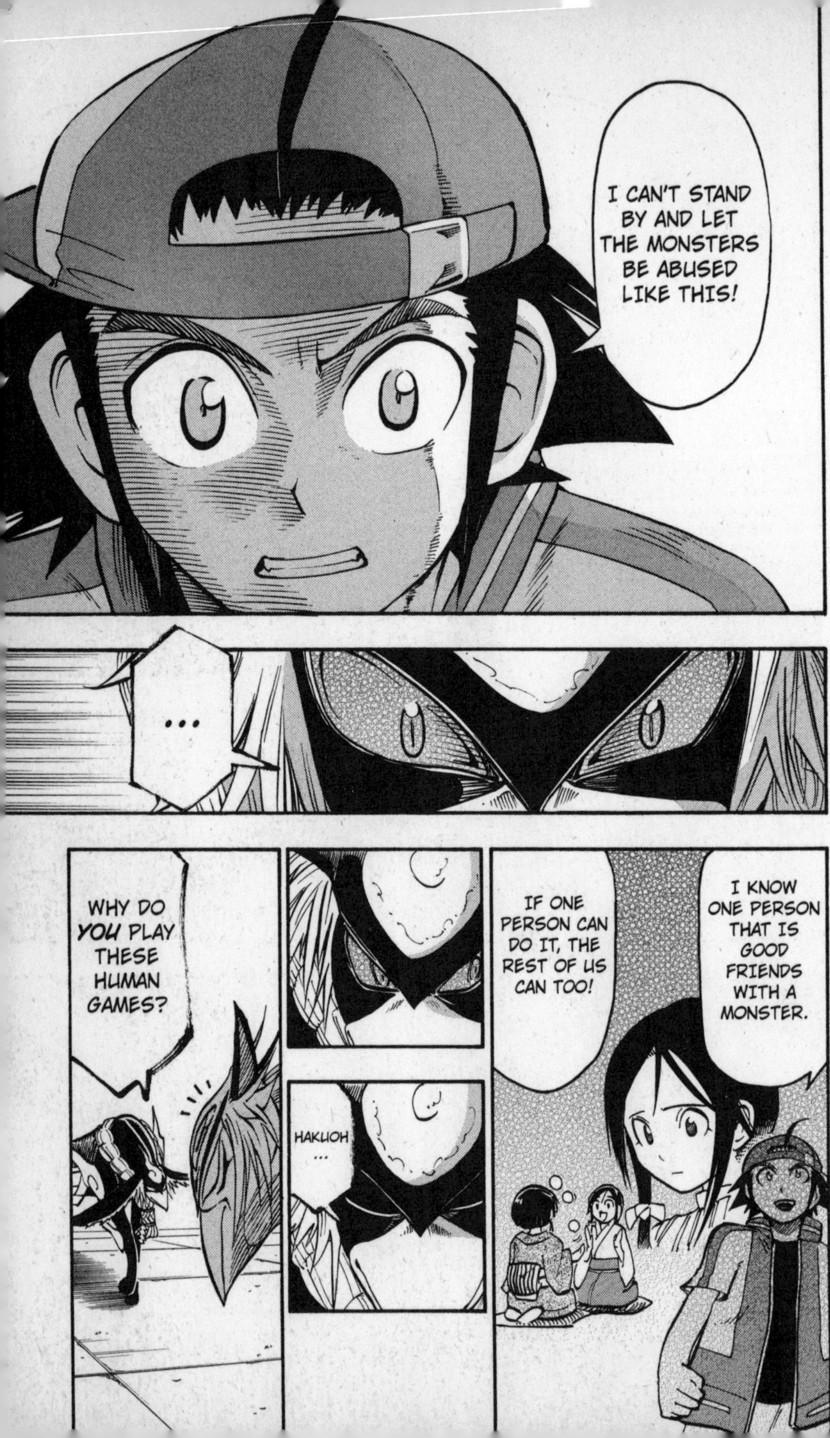

I CAN'T STAND BY AND LET THE MONSTERS BE ABUSED LIKE THIS!
...
I KNOW ONE PERSON THAT IS GOOD FRIENDS WITH A MONSTER.
IF ONE PERSON CAN DO IT, THE REST OF US CAN TOO!
HAKUOH ...
WHY DO YOU PLAY THESE HUMAN GAMES?

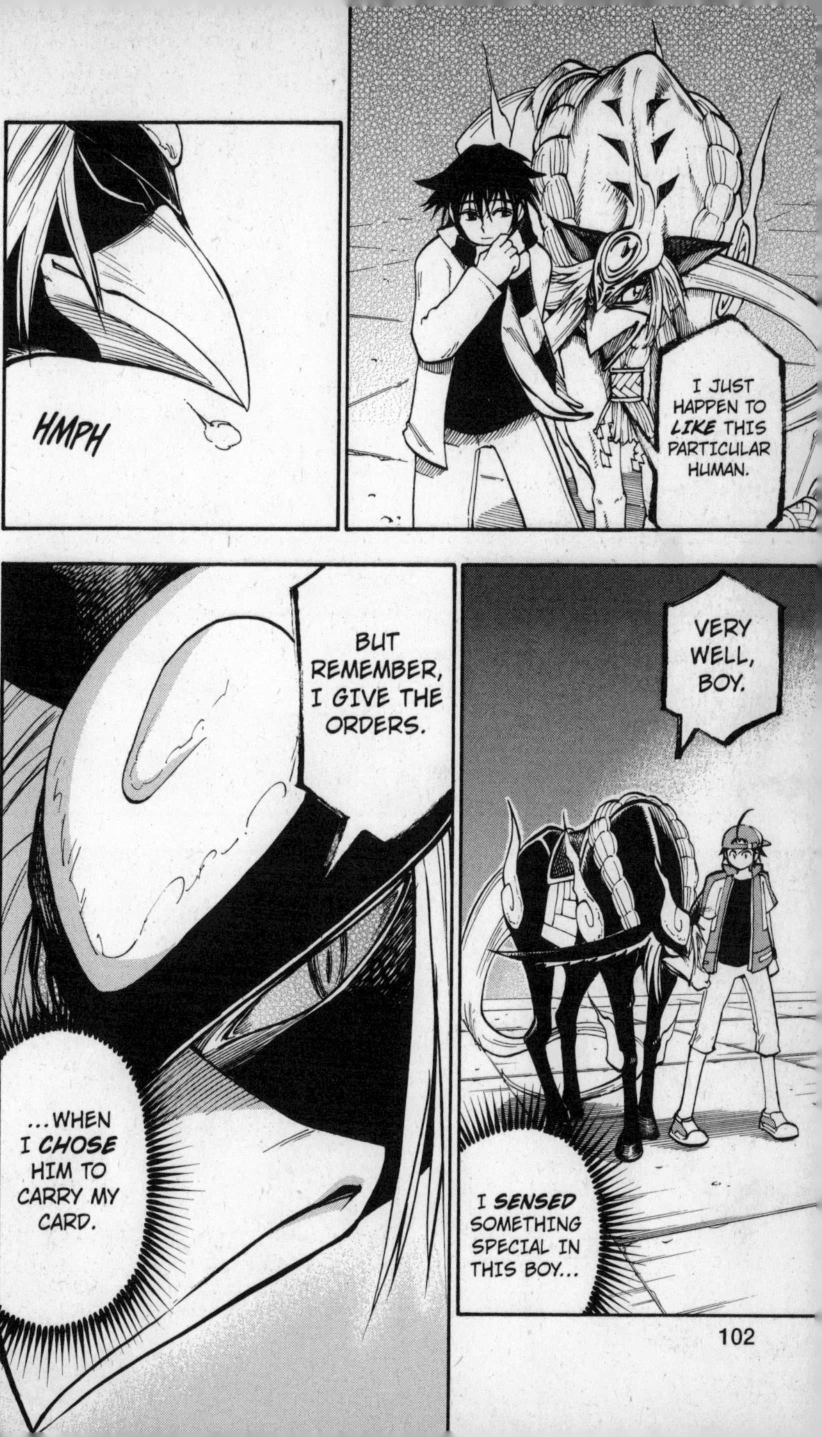
I JUST HAPPEN TO LIKE THIS PARTICULAR HUMAN.
HMPH
VERY WELL, BOY.
I SENSED SOMETHING SPECIAL IN THIS BOY...
BUT REMEMBER, I GIVE THE ORDERS.
...WHEN I CHOSE HIM TO CARRY MY CARD.

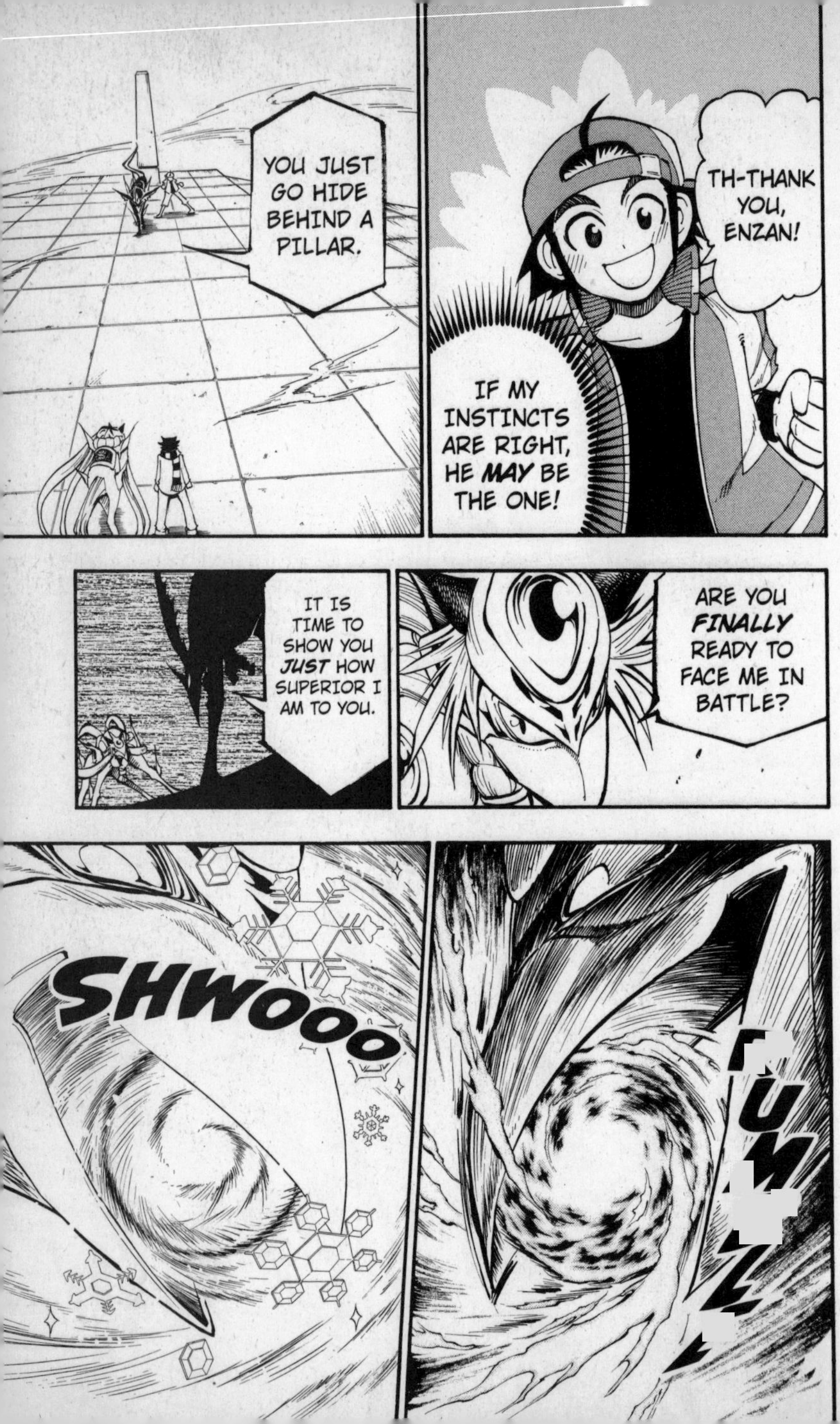
TH-THANK YOU, ENZAN!
IF MY INSTINCTS ARE RIGHT, HE MAY BE THE ONE!
YOU JUST GO HIDE BEHIND A PILLAR.
ARE YOU FINALLY READY TO FACE ME IN BATTLE?
IT IS TIME TO SHOW YOU JUST HOW SUPERIOR I AM TO YOU.
SHWOOO

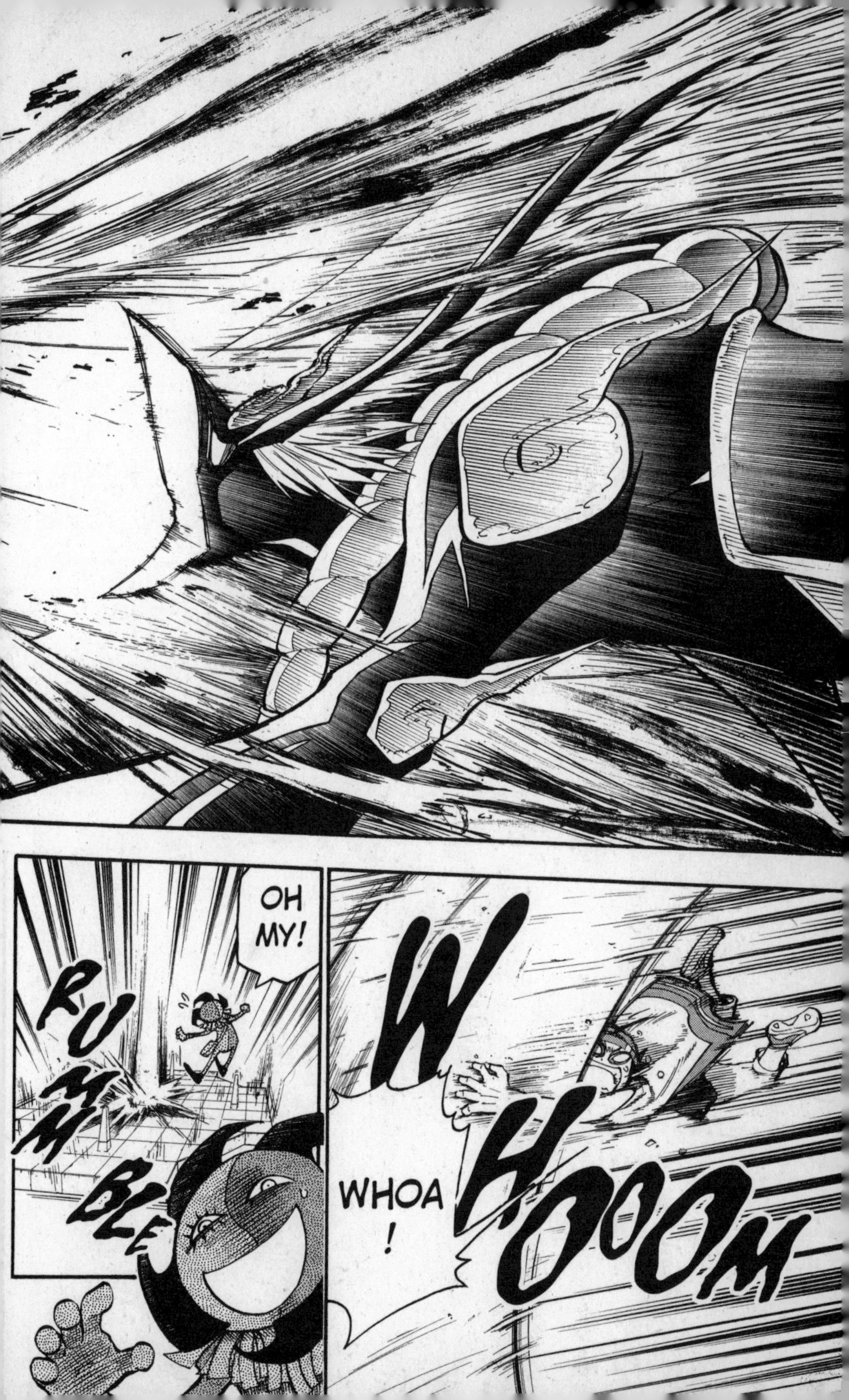
WHOOM
WHOA!
OH MY!
RUMMBLE

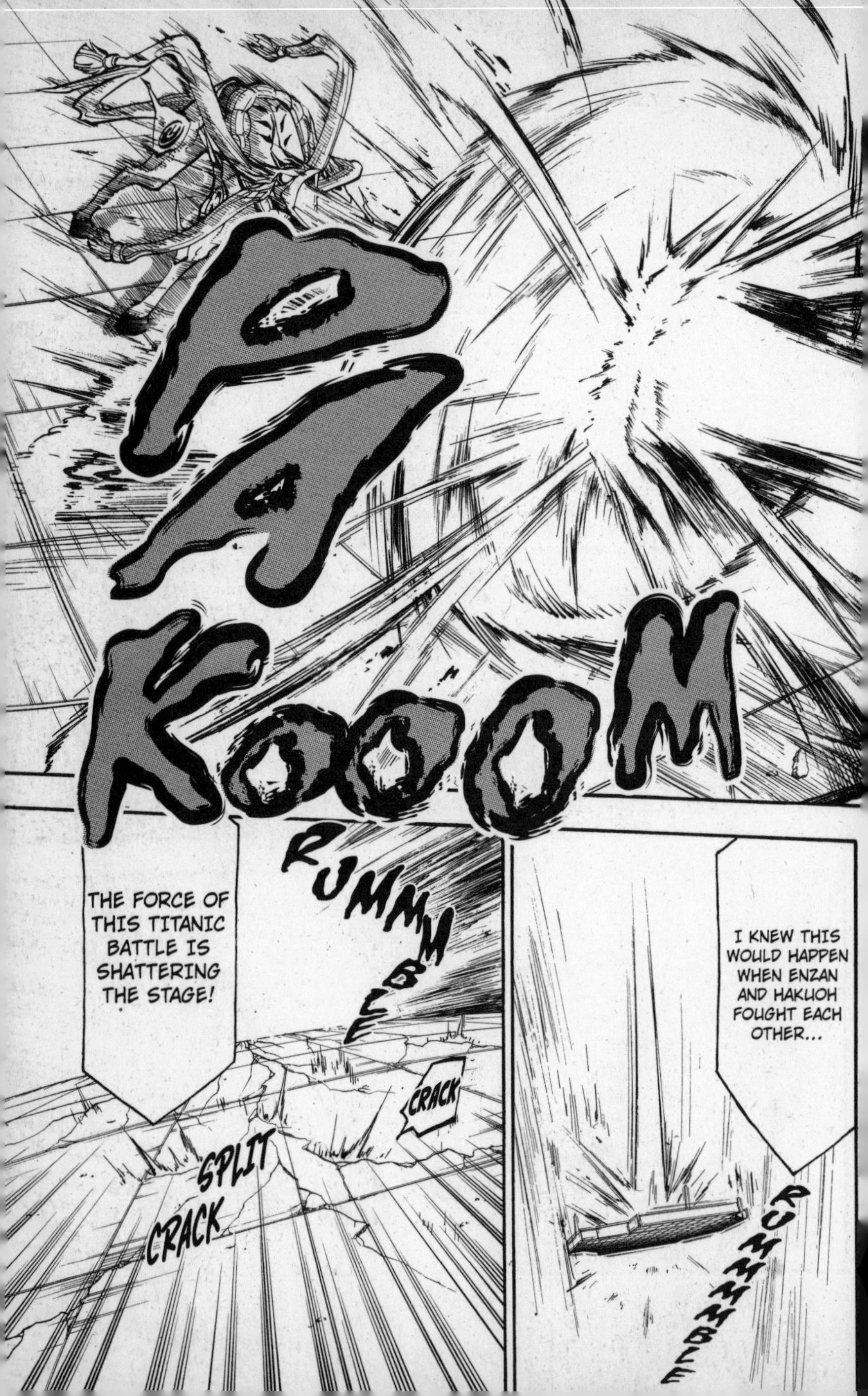
KOOOM
I KNEW THIS WOULD HAPPEN WHEN ENZAN AND HAKUOH FOUGHT EACH OTHER...
RUMMMMBLE
THE FORCE OF THIS TITANIC BATTLE IS SHATTERING THE STAGE!
RUMMMBLE
CRACK
SPLIT
CRACK

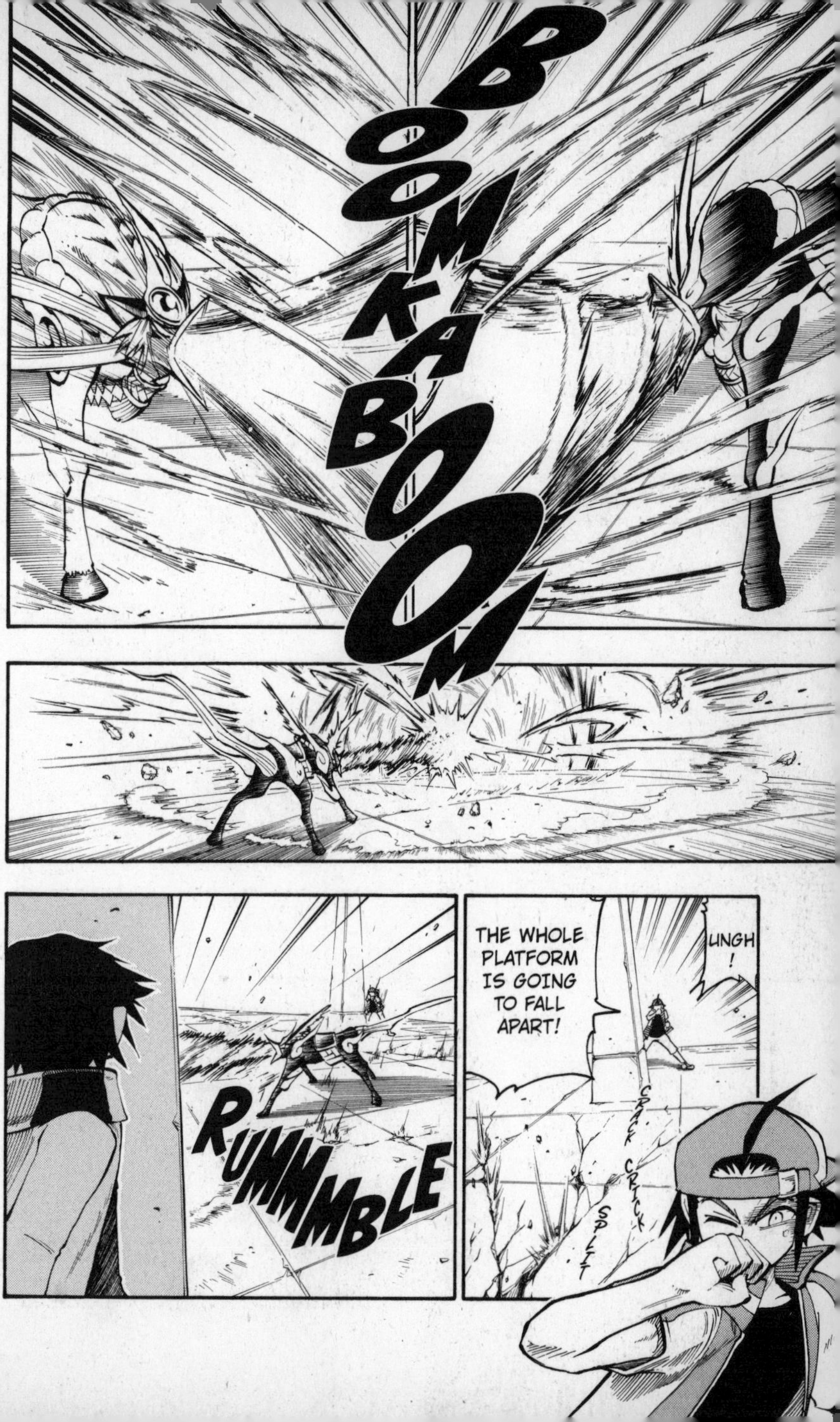
BOOMKABOOOM
UNGH!
THE WHOLE PLATFORM IS GOING TO FALL APART!
CRACK CRACK
SPLIT
RUMMMBLE

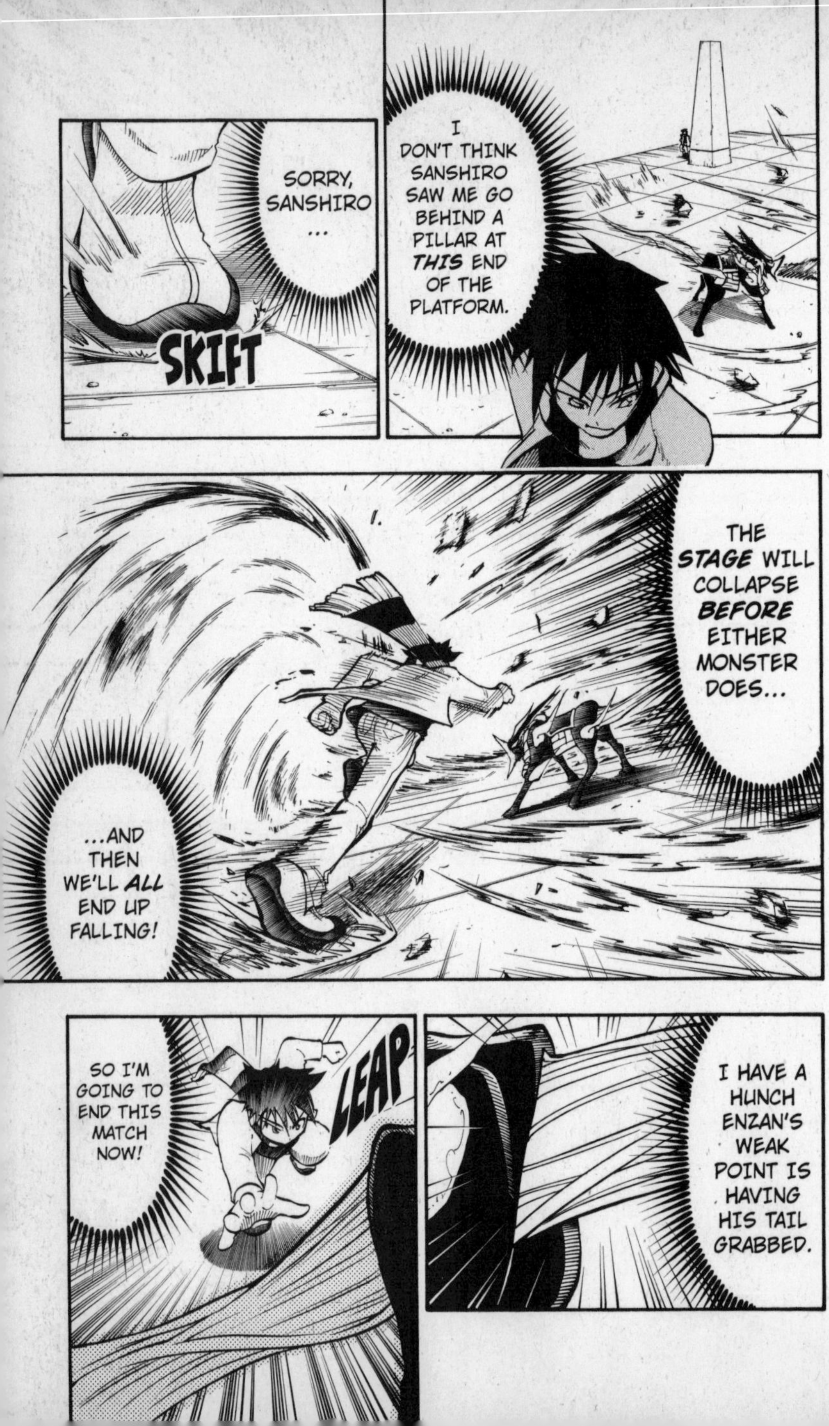
I DON'T THINK SANSHIRO SAW ME GO BEHIND A PILLAR AT THIS END OF THE PLATFORM.
SORRY, SANSHIRO...
SKIFT
THE STAGE WILL COLLAPSE BEFORE EITHER MONSTER DOES...
...AND THEN WE'LL ALL END UP FALLING!
I HAVE A HUNCH ENZAN'S WEAK POINT IS HAVING HIS TAIL GRABBED.
SO I'M GOING TO END THIS MATCH NOW!
LEAP

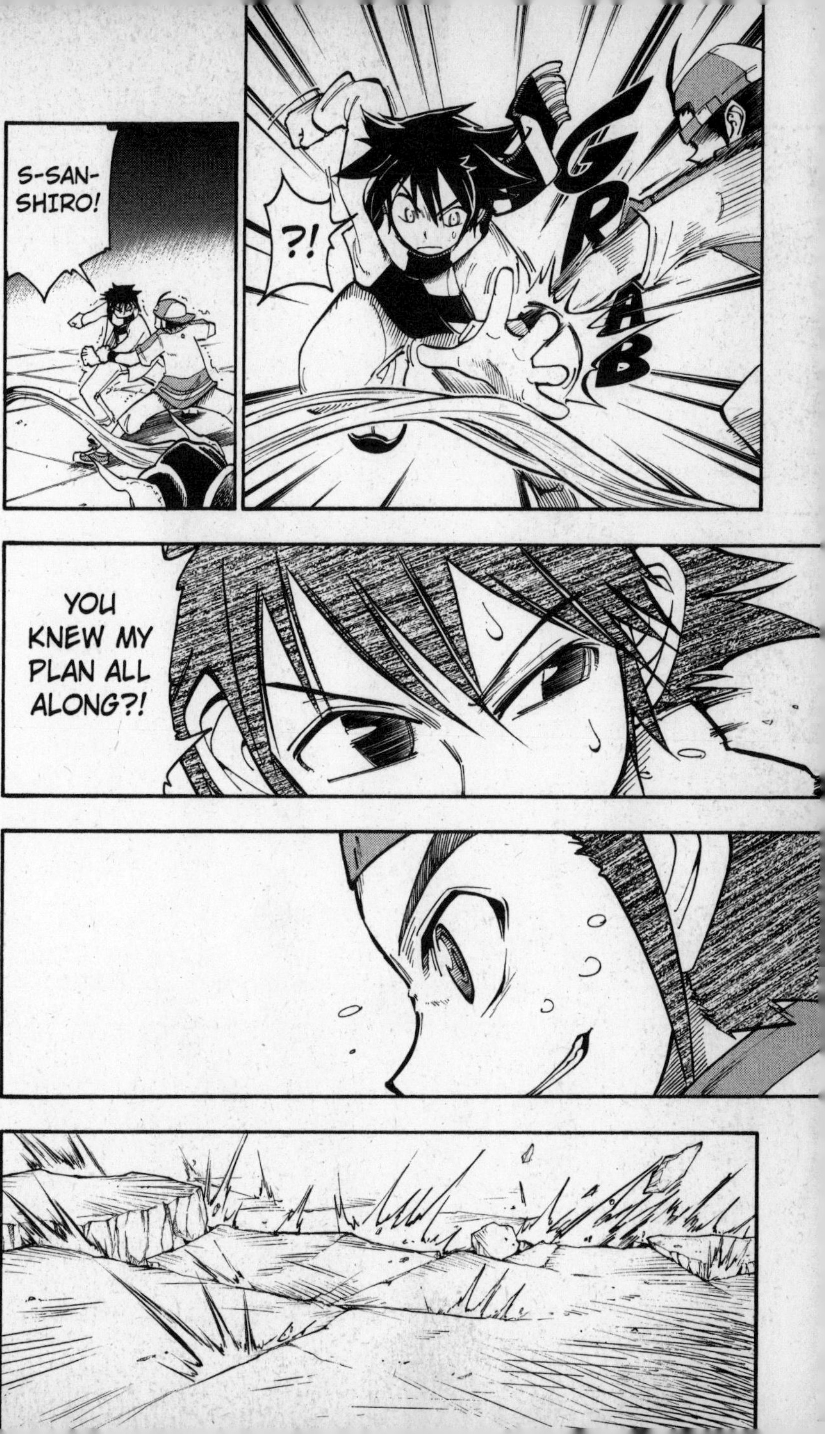
GRAB
?!
S-SAN-SHIRO!
YOU KNEW MY PLAN ALL ALONG?!

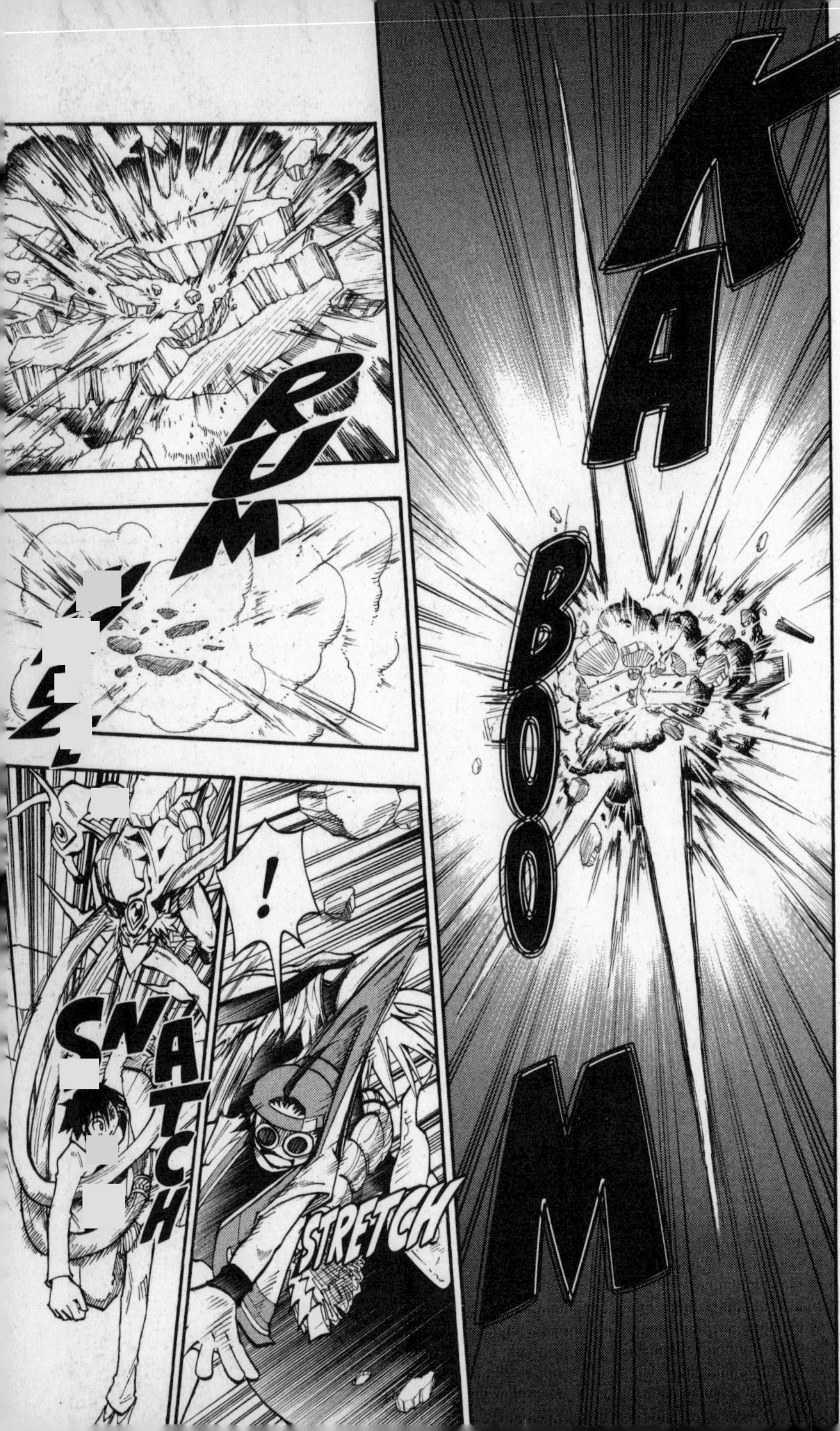
KABOOOM
RUM
!
STRETCH
SNATCH

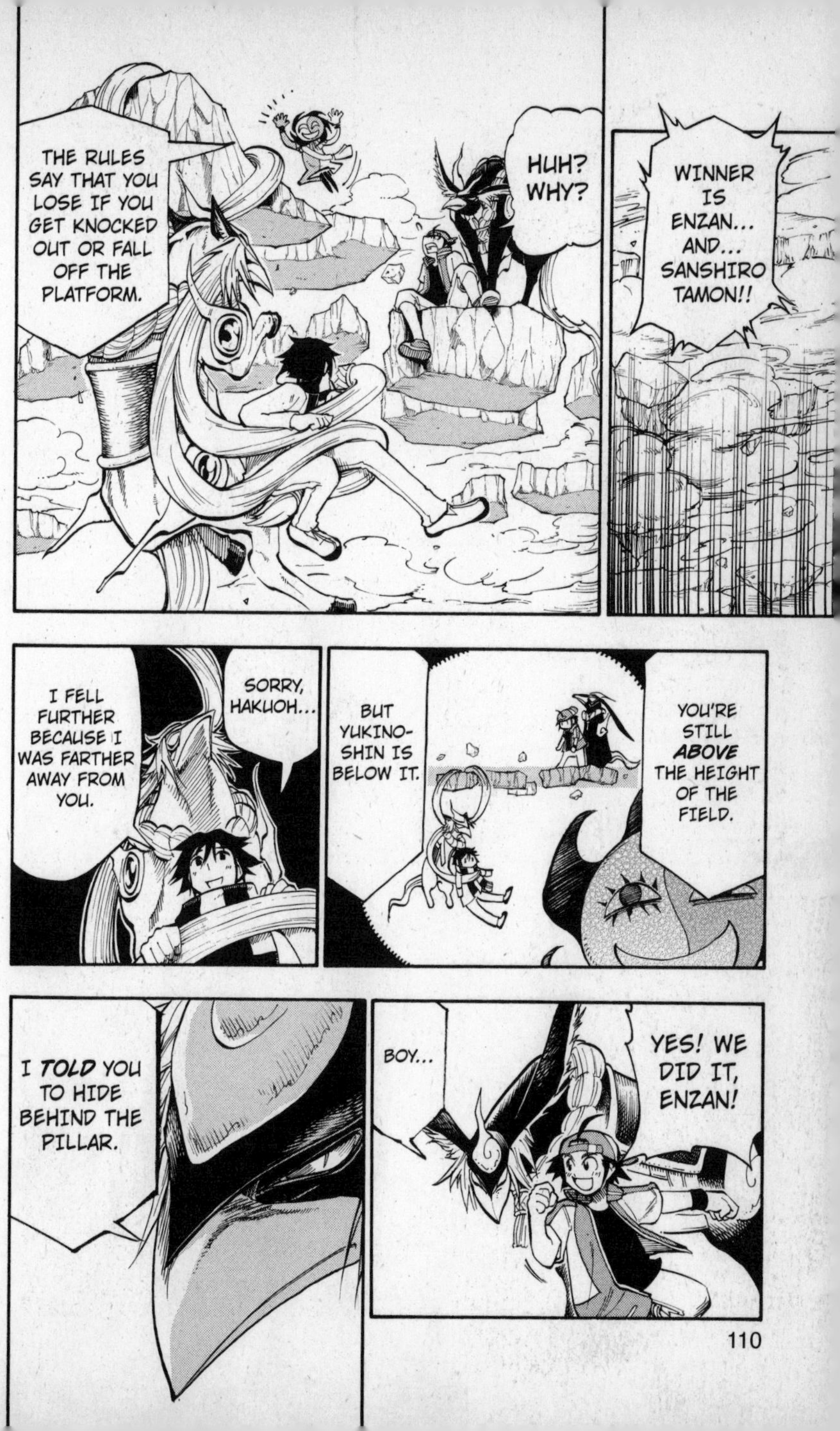
WINNER IS ENZAN... AND... SANSHIRO TAMON!!
HUH? WHY?
THE RULES SAY THAT YOU LOSE IF YOU GET KNOCKED OUT OR FALL OFF THE PLATFORM.
YOU'RE STILL *ABOVE* THE HEIGHT OF THE FIELD.
BUT YUKINO-SHIN IS BELOW IT.
SORRY, HAKUOH...
I FELL FURTHER BECAUSE I WAS FARTHER AWAY FROM YOU.
YES! WE DID IT, ENZAN!
BOY...
I *TOLD* YOU TO HIDE BEHIND THE PILLAR.

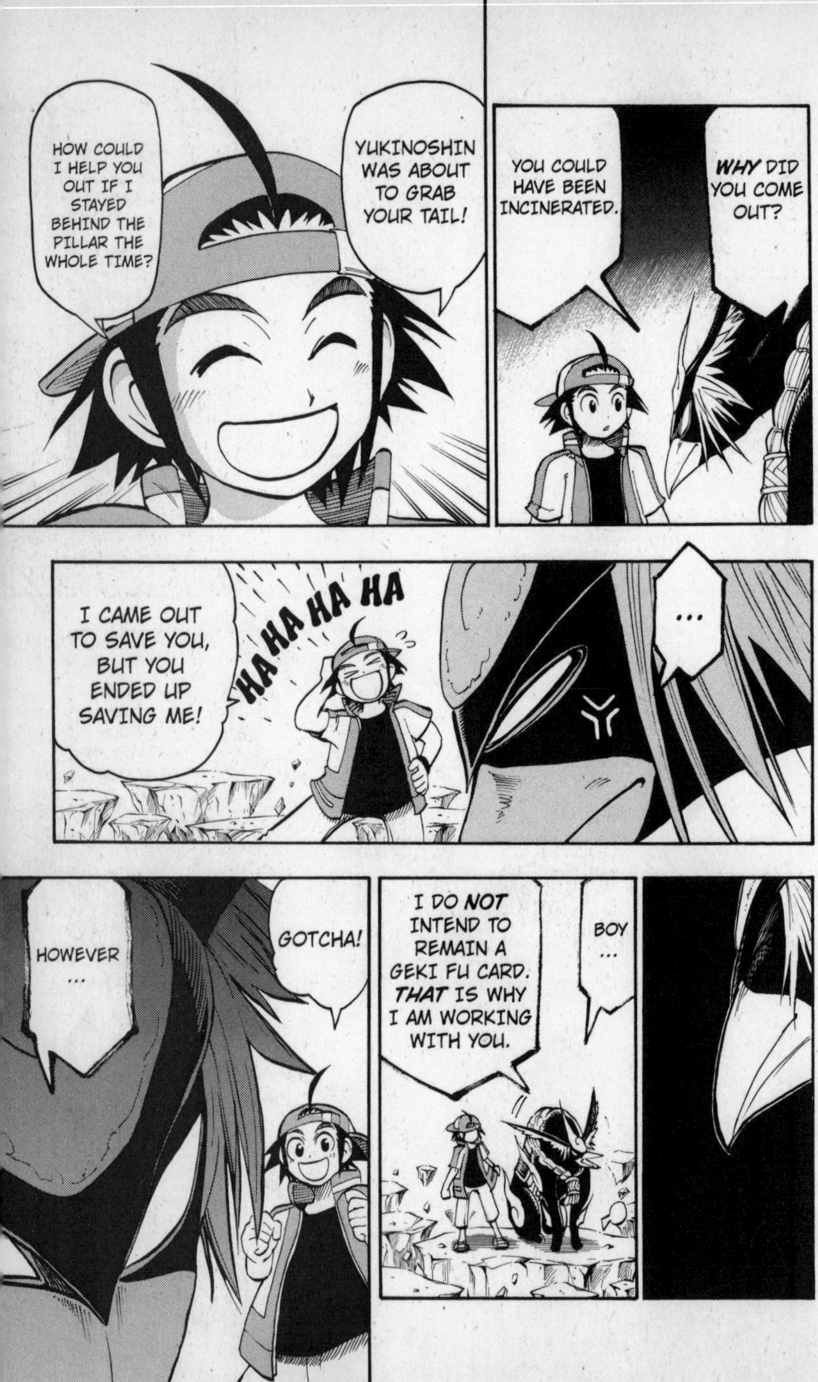
WHY DID YOU COME OUT?
YOU COULD HAVE BEEN INCINERATED.
YUKINOSHIN WAS ABOUT TO GRAB YOUR TAIL!
HOW COULD I HELP YOU OUT IF I STAYED BEHIND THE PILLAR THE WHOLE TIME?
...
HA HA HA HA HA
I CAME OUT TO SAVE YOU, BUT YOU ENDED UP SAVING ME!
BOY ...
I DO NOT INTEND TO REMAIN A GEKI FU CARD. THAT IS WHY I AM WORKING WITH YOU.
GOTCHA!
HOWEVER ...

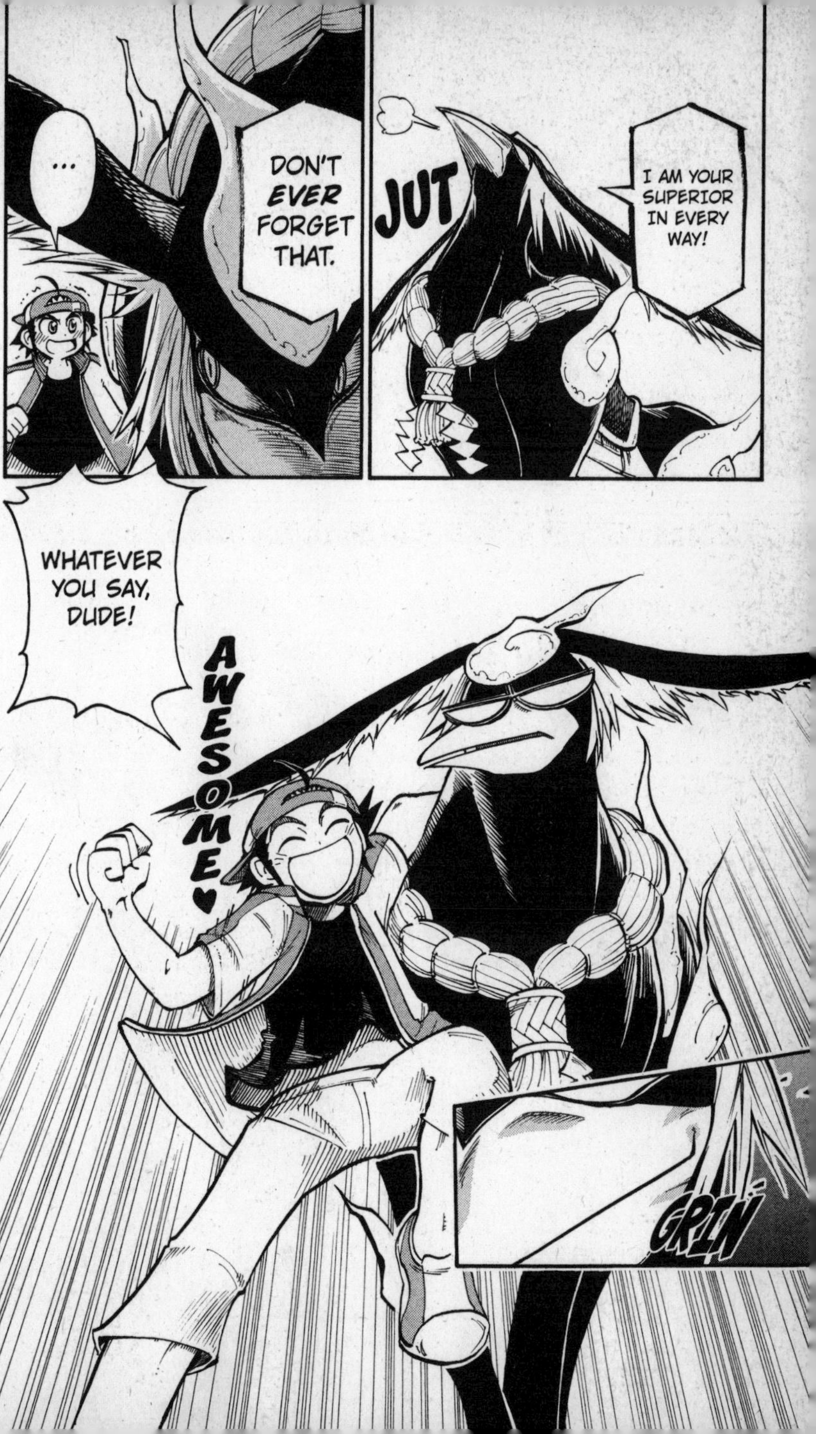
I AM YOUR SUPERIOR IN EVERY WAY!
JUT
DON'T EVER FORGET THAT.
...
WHATEVER YOU SAY, DUDE!
AWESOME
GRIN

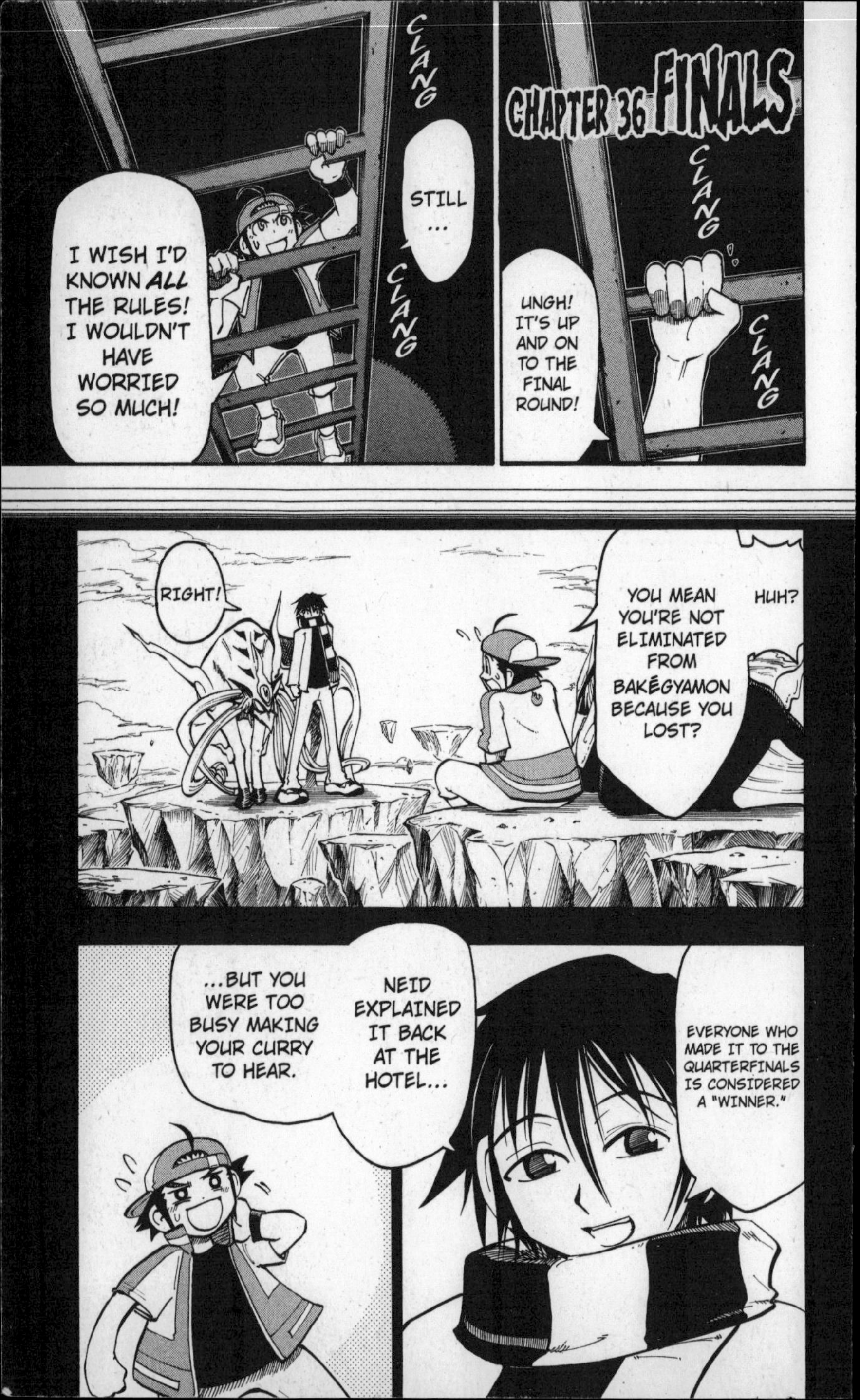
CHAPTER 36 FINALS
CLANG
CLANG
UNGH! IT'S UP AND ON TO THE FINAL ROUND!
CLANG
STILL...
CLANG
I WISH I'D KNOWN ALL THE RULES! I WOULDN'T HAVE WORRIED SO MUCH!
HUH?
YOU MEAN YOU'RE NOT ELIMINATED FROM BAKÉGYAMON BECAUSE YOU LOST?
RIGHT!
EVERYONE WHO MADE IT TO THE QUARTERFINALS IS CONSIDERED A "WINNER."
NEID EXPLAINED IT BACK AT THE HOTEL...
...BUT YOU WERE TOO BUSY MAKING YOUR CURRY TO HEAR.

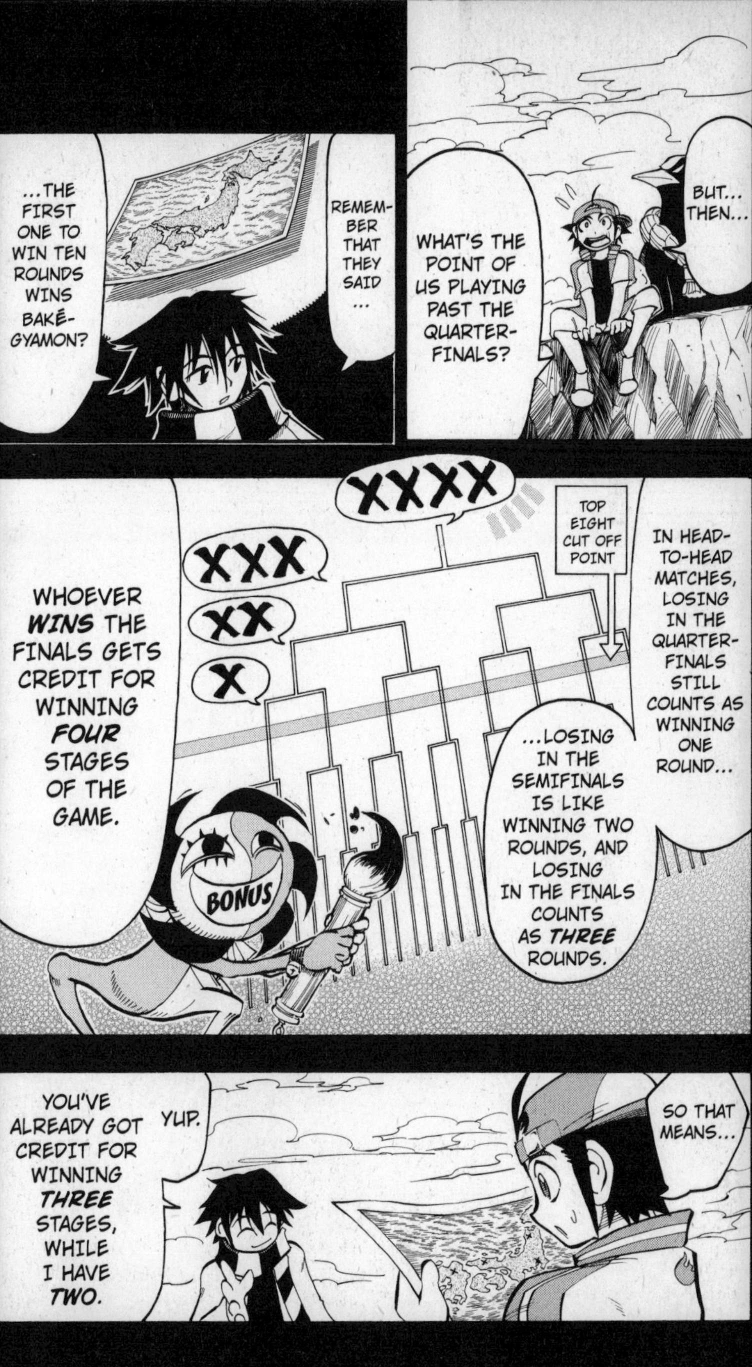
BUT... THEN...
WHAT'S THE POINT OF US PLAYING PAST THE QUARTER-FINALS?
REMEMBER THAT THEY SAID ...
...THE FIRST ONE TO WIN TEN ROUNDS WINS BAKÉ-GYAMON?
IN HEAD-TO-HEAD MATCHES, LOSING IN THE QUARTER-FINALS STILL COUNTS AS WINNING ONE ROUND...
TOP EIGHT CUT OFF POINT
XXXX
...LOSING IN THE SEMIFINALS IS LIKE WINNING TWO ROUNDS, AND LOSING IN THE FINALS COUNTS AS ***THREE*** ROUNDS.
XXX
XX
X
WHOEVER ***WINS*** THE FINALS GETS CREDIT FOR WINNING ***FOUR*** STAGES OF THE GAME.
BONUS
SO THAT MEANS...
YUP.
YOU'VE ALREADY GOT CREDIT FOR WINNING ***THREE*** STAGES, WHILE I HAVE ***TWO***.

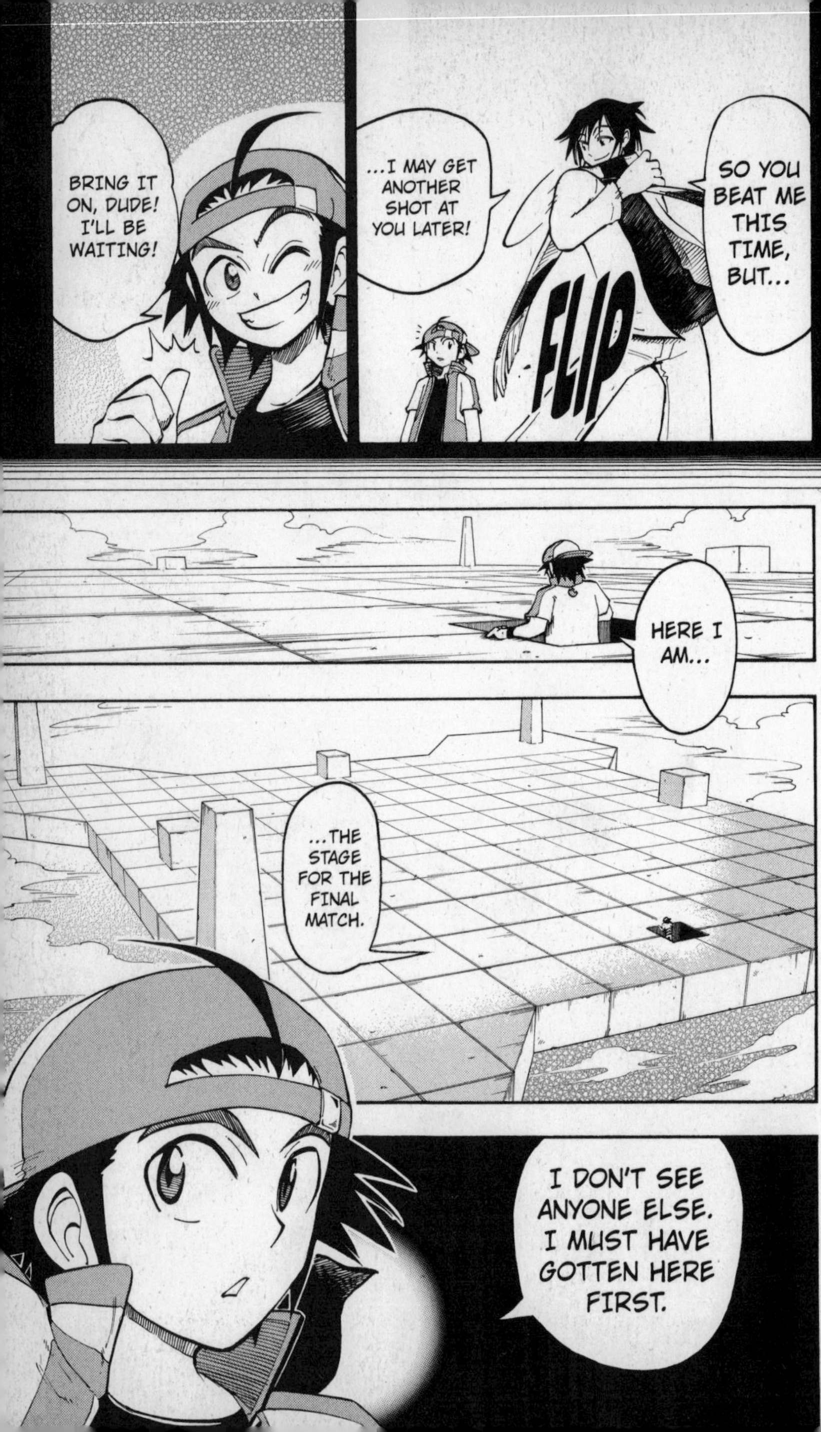
SO YOU BEAT ME THIS TIME, BUT...
...I MAY GET ANOTHER SHOT AT YOU LATER!
FLIP
BRING IT ON, DUDE! I'LL BE WAITING!
HERE I AM...
...THE STAGE FOR THE FINAL MATCH.
I DON'T SEE ANYONE ELSE. I MUST HAVE GOTTEN HERE FIRST.

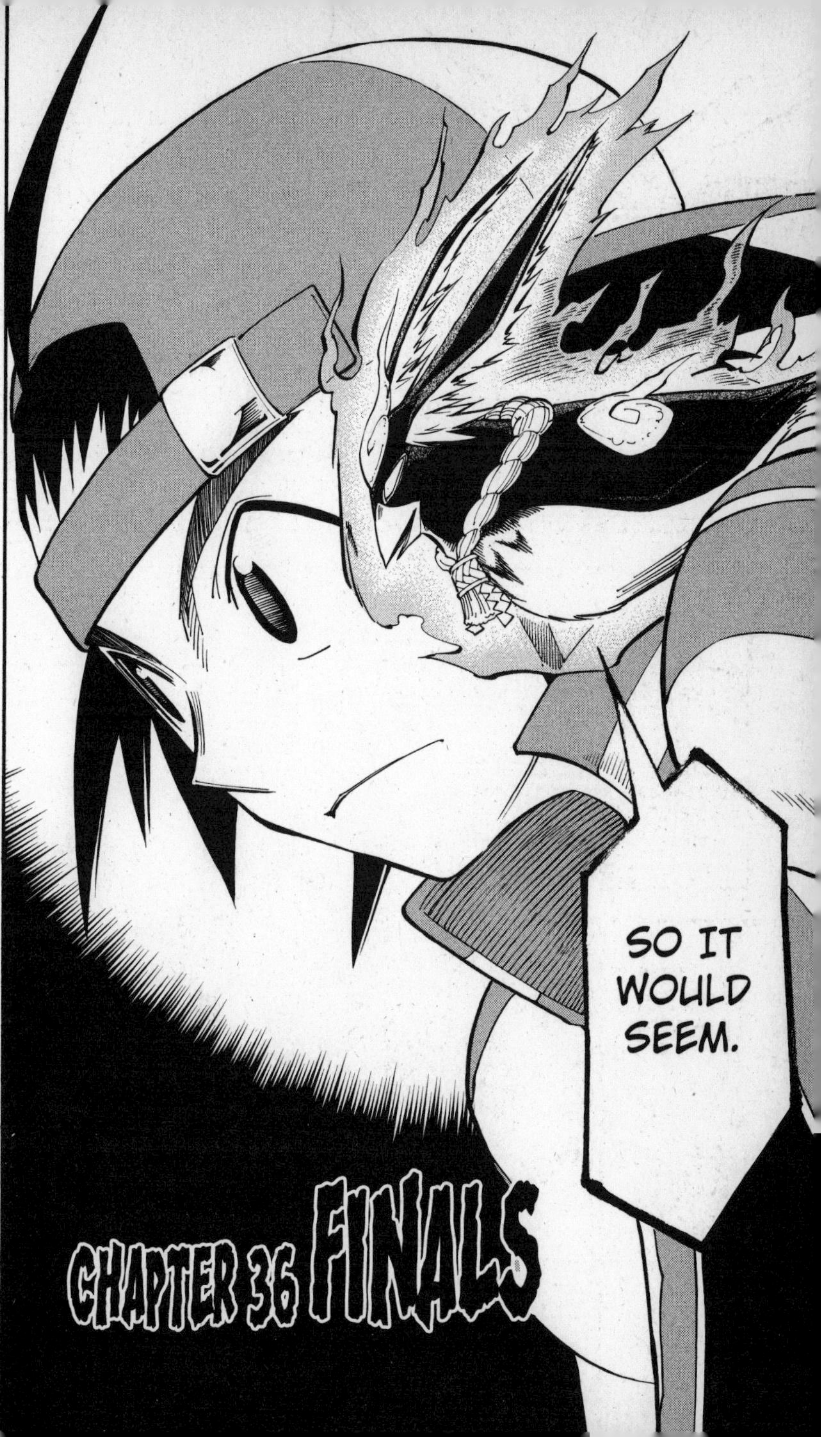
SO IT WOULD SEEM.
CHAPTER 36 FINALS

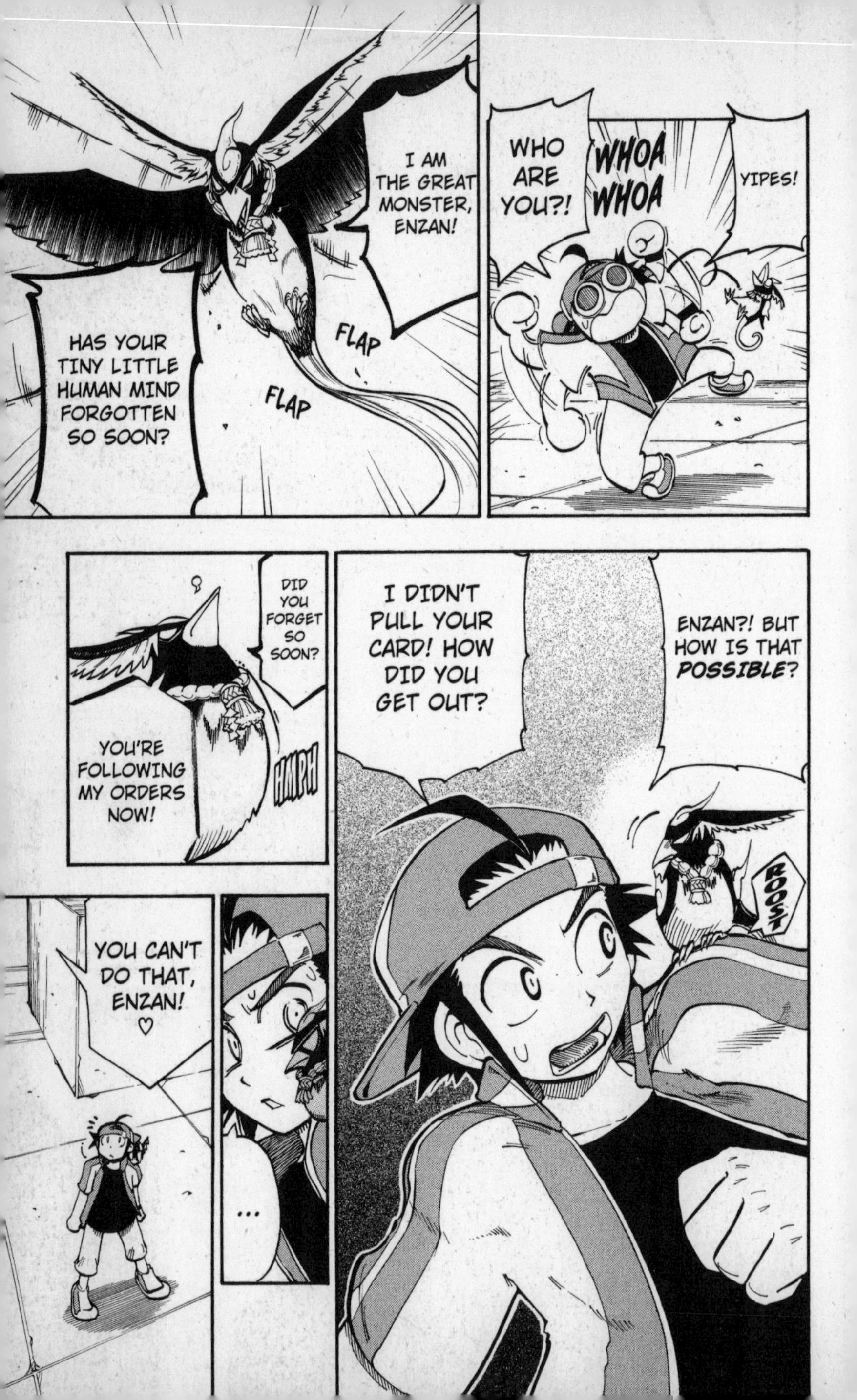
YIPES!
WHOA WHOA
WHO ARE YOU?!
I AM THE GREAT MONSTER, ENZAN!
FLAP
FLAP
HAS YOUR TINY LITTLE HUMAN MIND FORGOTTEN SO SOON?
ENZAN?! BUT HOW IS THAT *POSSIBLE*?
I DIDN'T PULL YOUR CARD! HOW DID YOU GET OUT?
ROOST
DID YOU FORGET SO SOON?
HMPH
YOU'RE FOLLOWING MY ORDERS NOW!
...
YOU CAN'T DO THAT, ENZAN! ♡

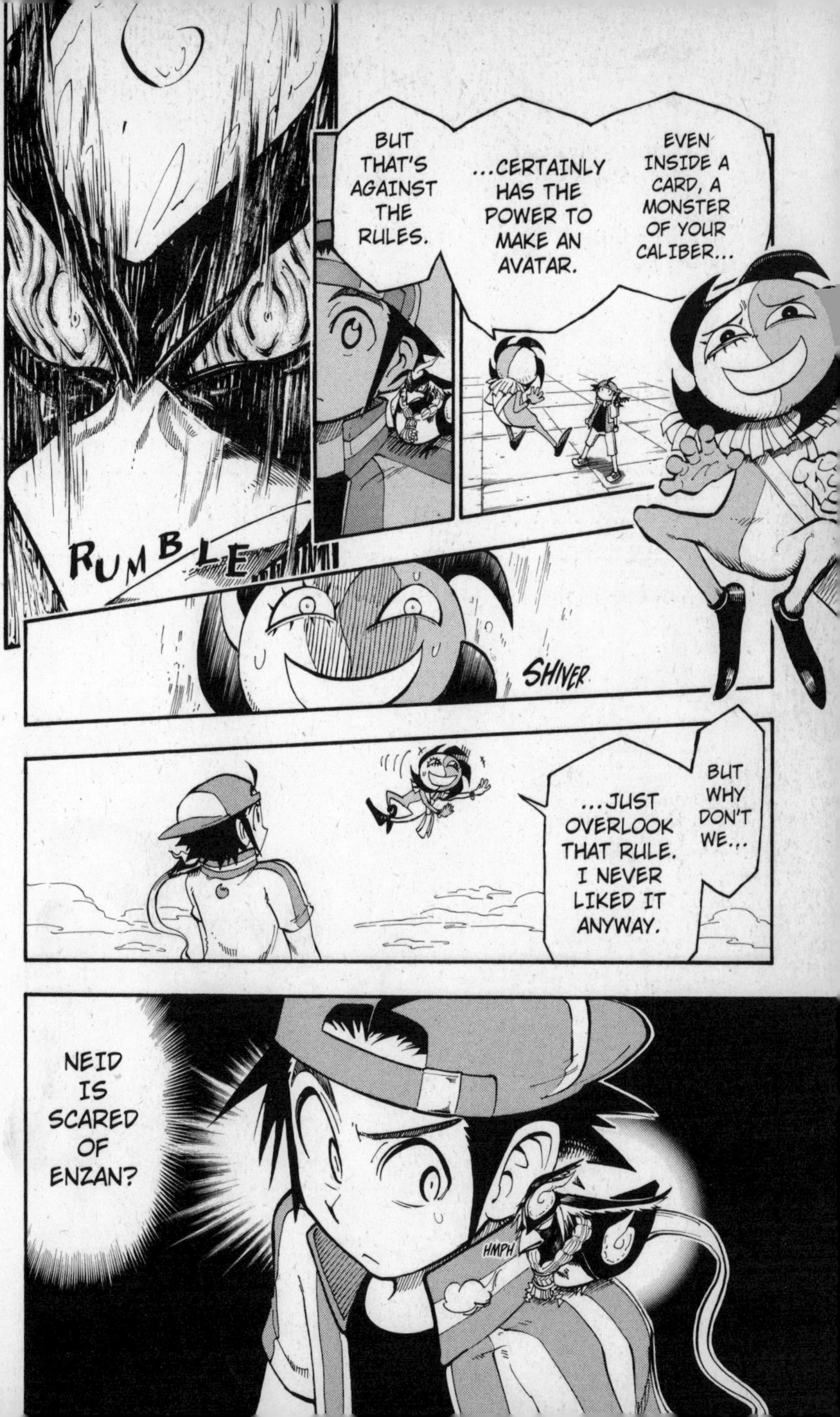
EVEN INSIDE A CARD, A MONSTER OF YOUR CALIBER...
...CERTAINLY HAS THE POWER TO MAKE AN AVATAR.
BUT THAT'S AGAINST THE RULES.
RUMBLE
SHIVER
BUT WHY DON'T WE...
...JUST OVERLOOK THAT RULE. I NEVER LIKED IT ANYWAY.
NEID IS SCARED OF ENZAN?
HMPH

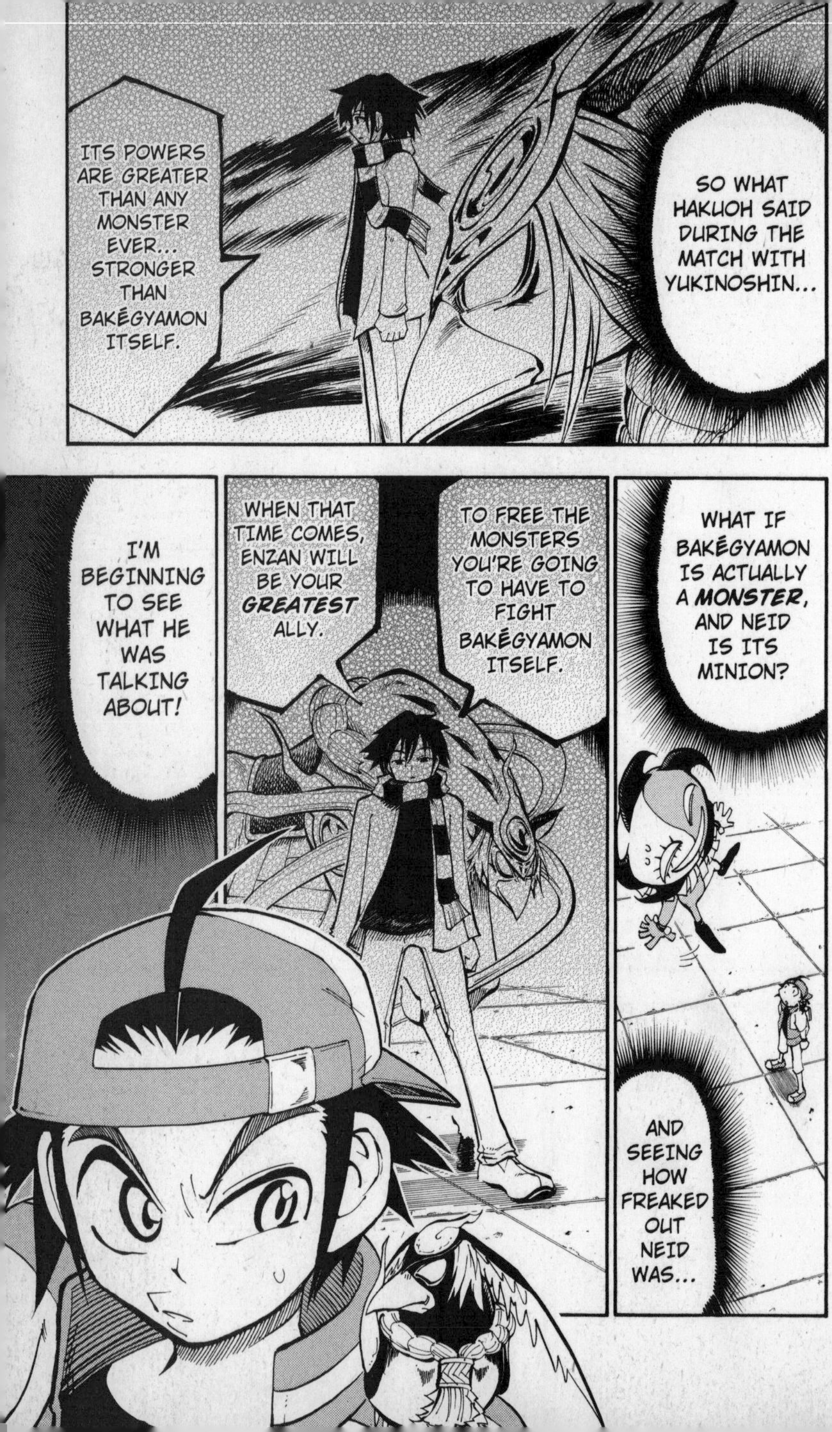
SO WHAT HAKUOH SAID DURING THE MATCH WITH YUKINOSHIN...
ITS POWERS ARE GREATER THAN ANY MONSTER EVER... STRONGER THAN BAKÉGYAMON ITSELF.
WHAT IF BAKÉGYAMON IS ACTUALLY A **MONSTER**, AND NEID IS ITS MINION?
AND SEEING HOW FREAKED OUT NEID WAS...
TO FREE THE MONSTERS YOU'RE GOING TO HAVE TO FIGHT BAKÉGYAMON ITSELF.
WHEN THAT TIME COMES, ENZAN WILL BE YOUR **GREATEST** ALLY.
I'M BEGINNING TO SEE WHAT HE WAS TALKING ABOUT!

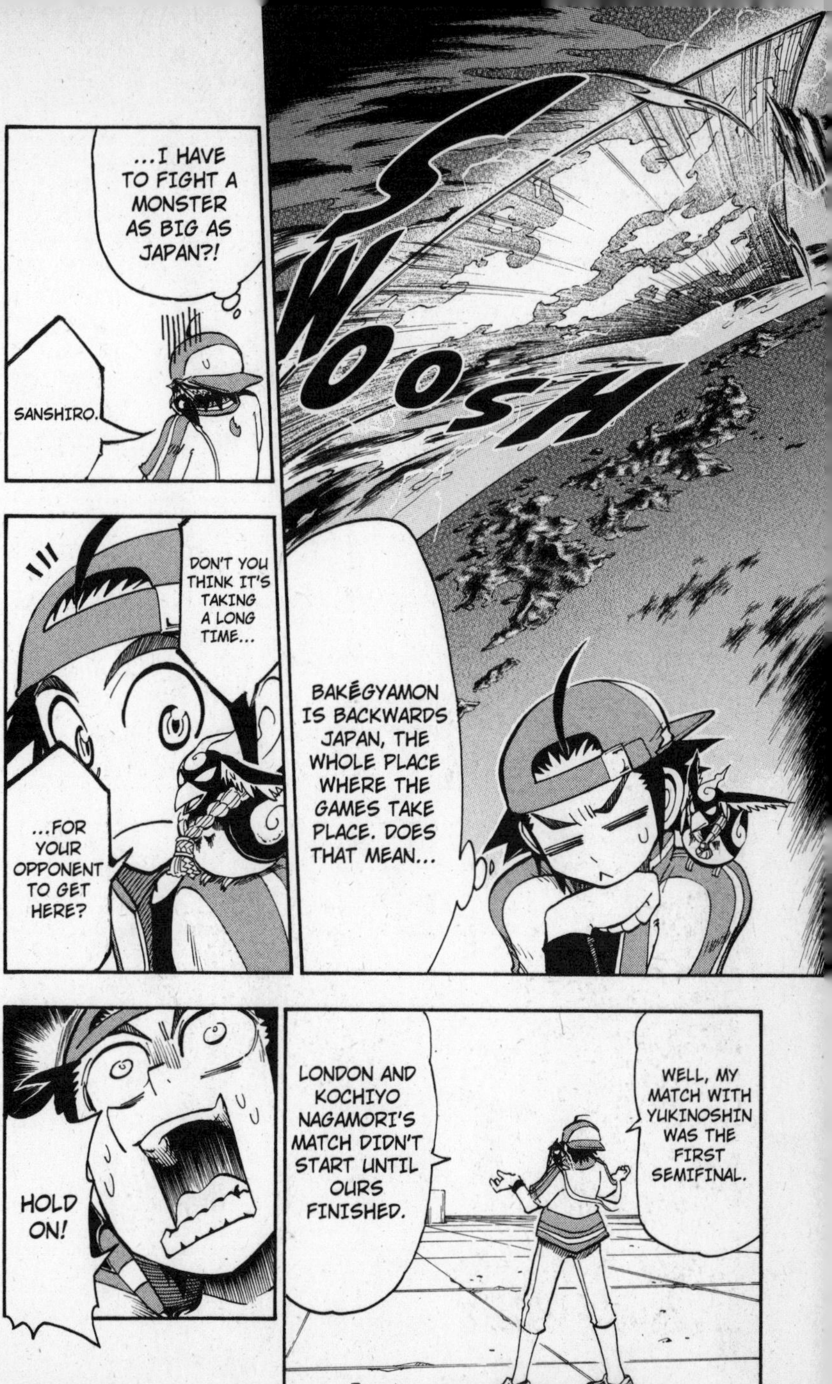
WOOSH
BAKĒGYAMON IS BACKWARDS JAPAN, THE WHOLE PLACE WHERE THE GAMES TAKE PLACE. DOES THAT MEAN...
...I HAVE TO FIGHT A MONSTER AS BIG AS JAPAN?!
SANSHIRO.
DON'T YOU THINK IT'S TAKING A LONG TIME...
...FOR YOUR OPPONENT TO GET HERE?
WELL, MY MATCH WITH YUKINOSHIN WAS THE FIRST SEMIFINAL.
LONDON AND KOCHIYO NAGAMORI'S MATCH DIDN'T START UNTIL OURS FINISHED.
HOLD ON!

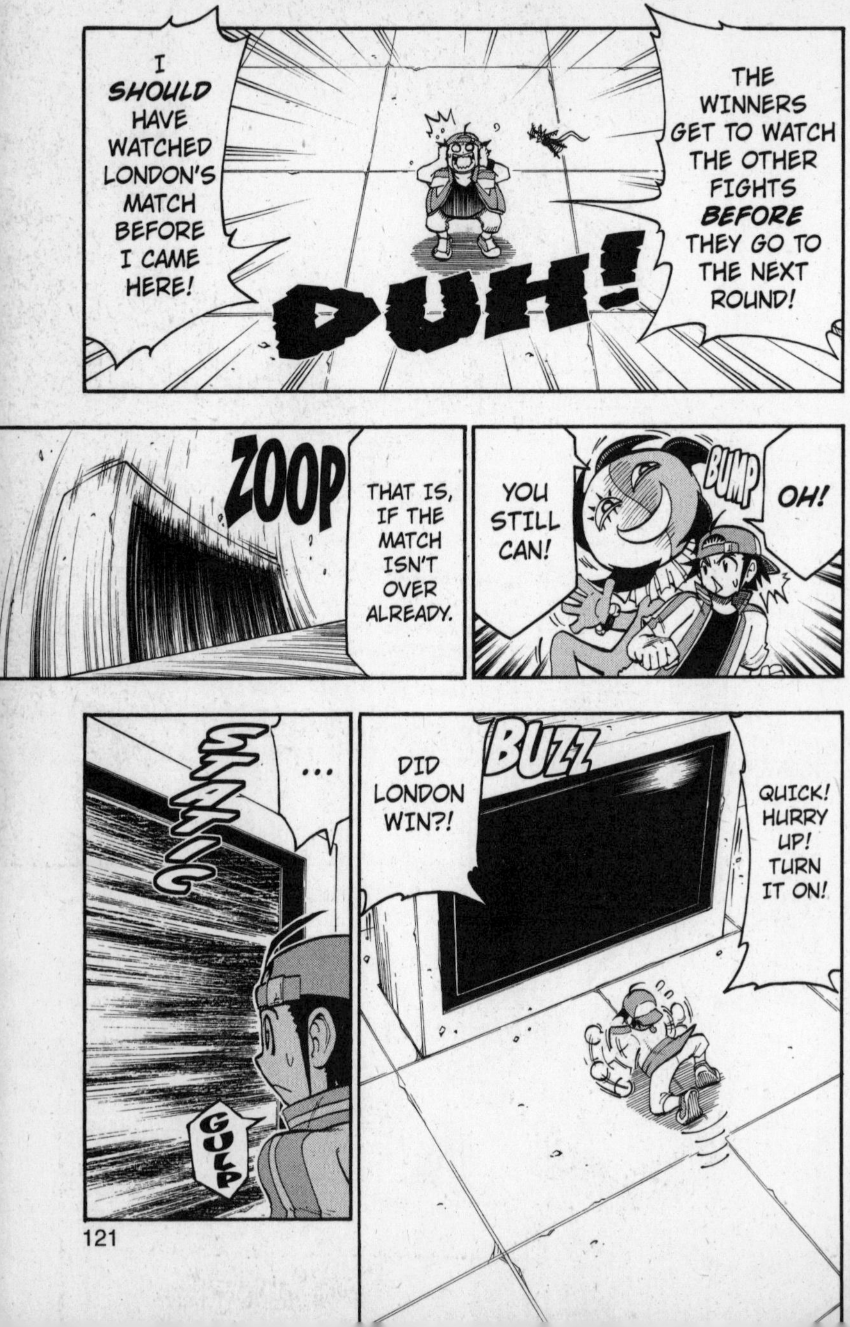
THE WINNERS GET TO WATCH THE OTHER FIGHTS *BEFORE* THEY GO TO THE NEXT ROUND!
I *SHOULD* HAVE WATCHED LONDON'S MATCH BEFORE I CAME HERE!
DUH!
OH!
BUMP
YOU STILL CAN!
THAT IS, IF THE MATCH ISN'T OVER ALREADY.
ZOOP
QUICK! HURRY UP! TURN IT ON!
BUZZ
DID LONDON WIN?!
...
STATIC
GULP

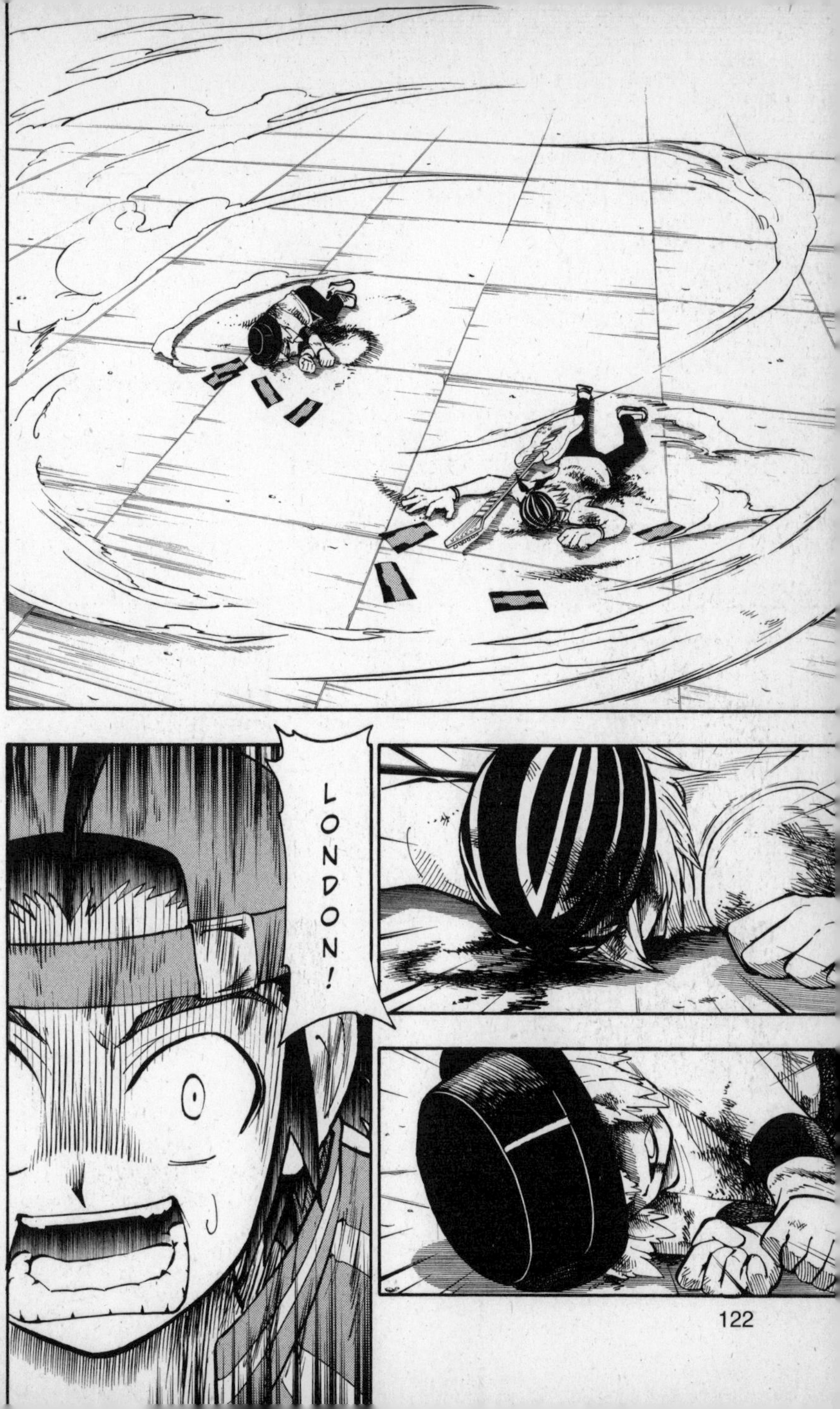
LONDON!

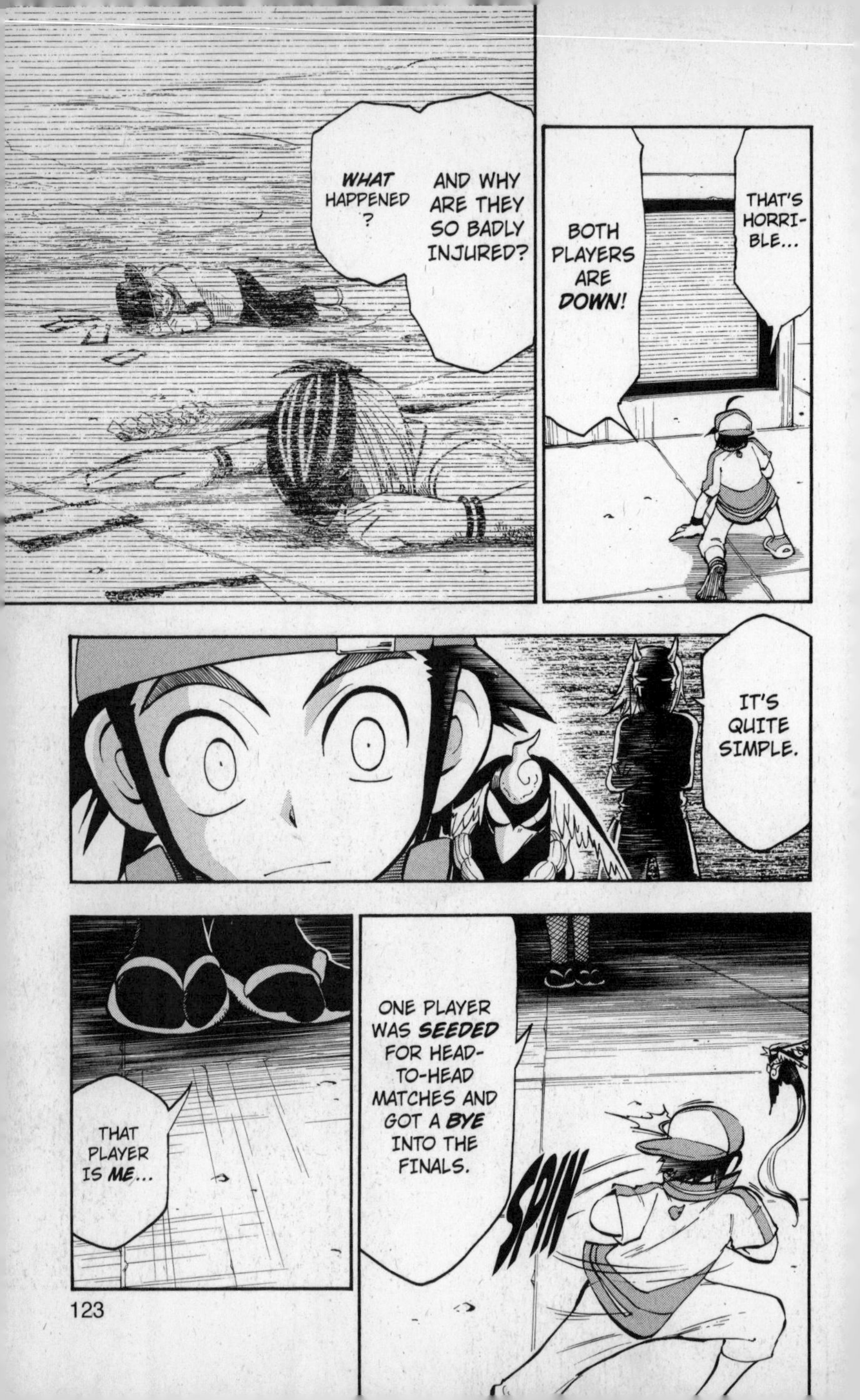
THAT'S HORRI-BLE...
BOTH PLAYERS ARE *DOWN*!
WHAT HAPPENED?
AND WHY ARE THEY SO BADLY INJURED?
IT'S QUITE SIMPLE.
ONE PLAYER WAS *SEEDED* FOR HEAD-TO-HEAD MATCHES AND GOT A *BYE* INTO THE FINALS.
SPIN
THAT PLAYER IS *ME*...

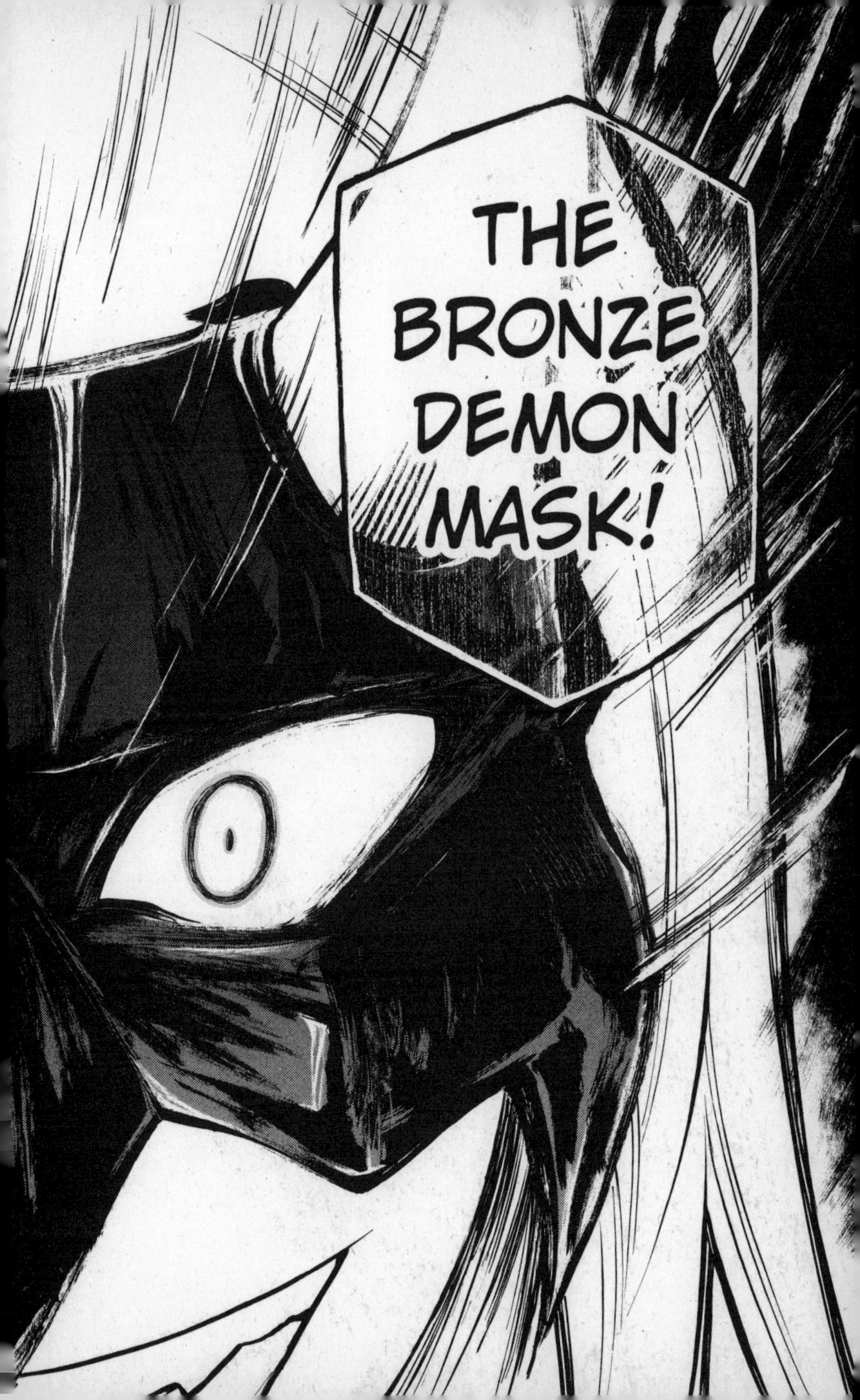
THE BRONZE DEMON MASK!

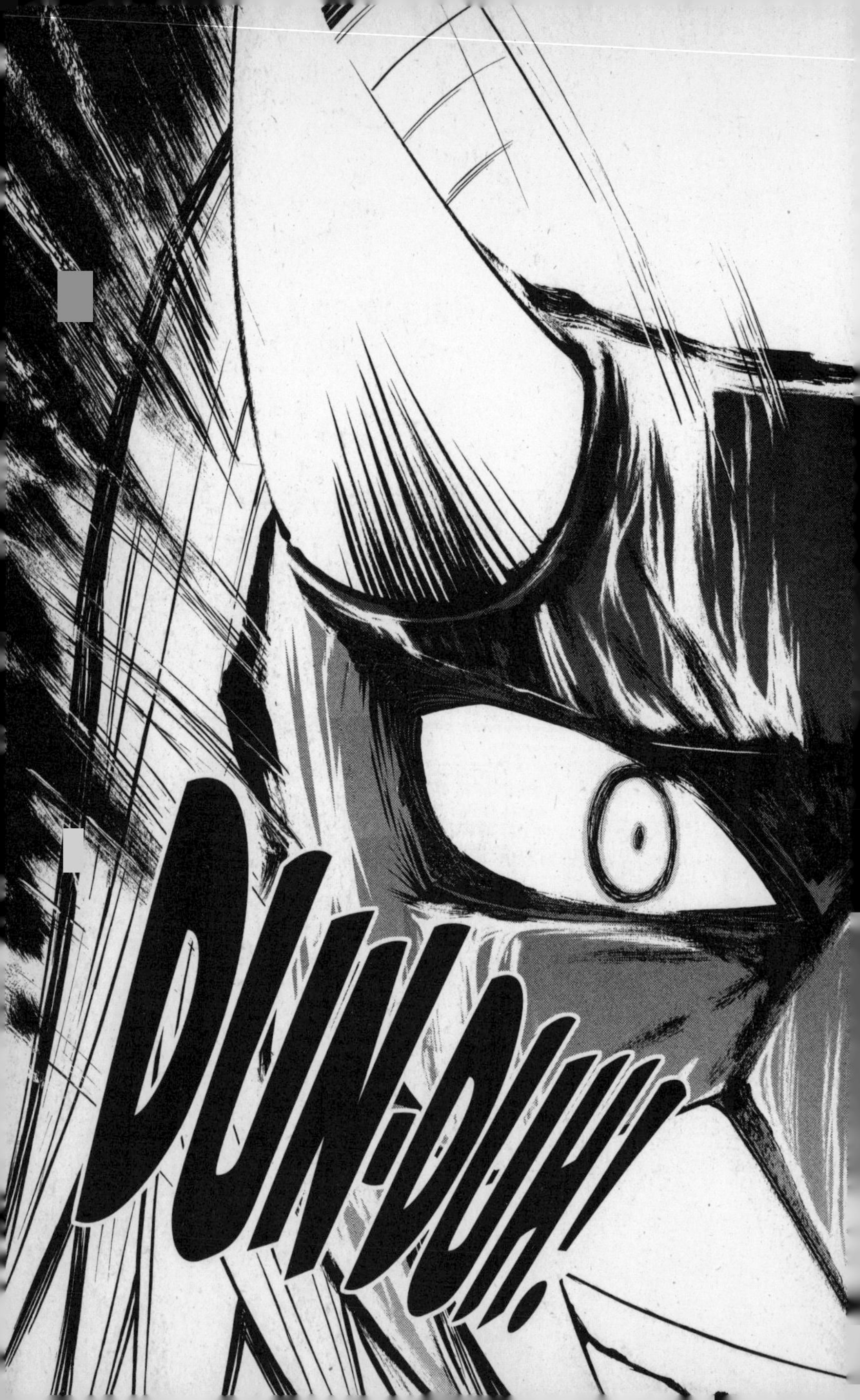

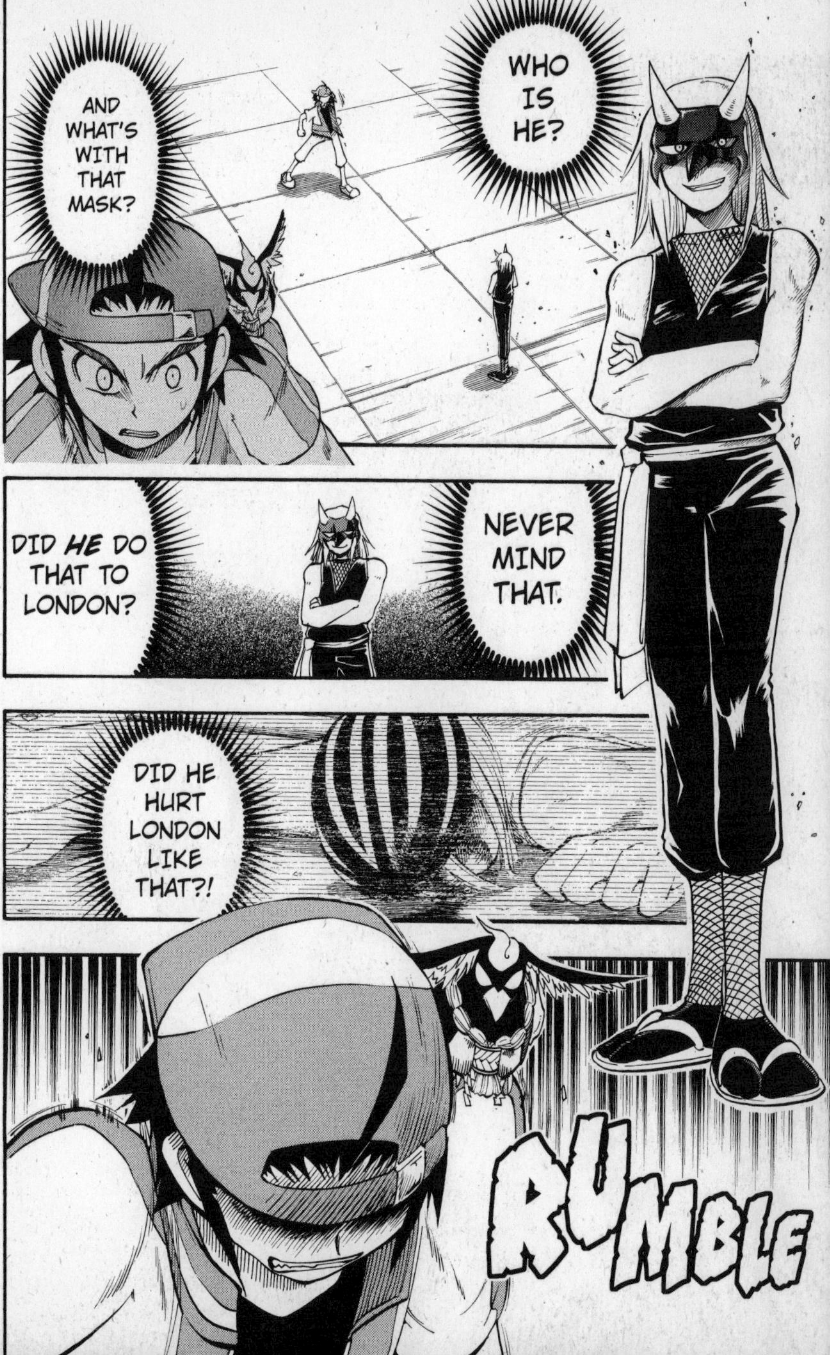
WHO IS HE?
AND WHAT'S WITH THAT MASK?
NEVER MIND THAT.
DID *HE* DO THAT TO LONDON?
DID HE HURT LONDON LIKE THAT?!
RUMBLE

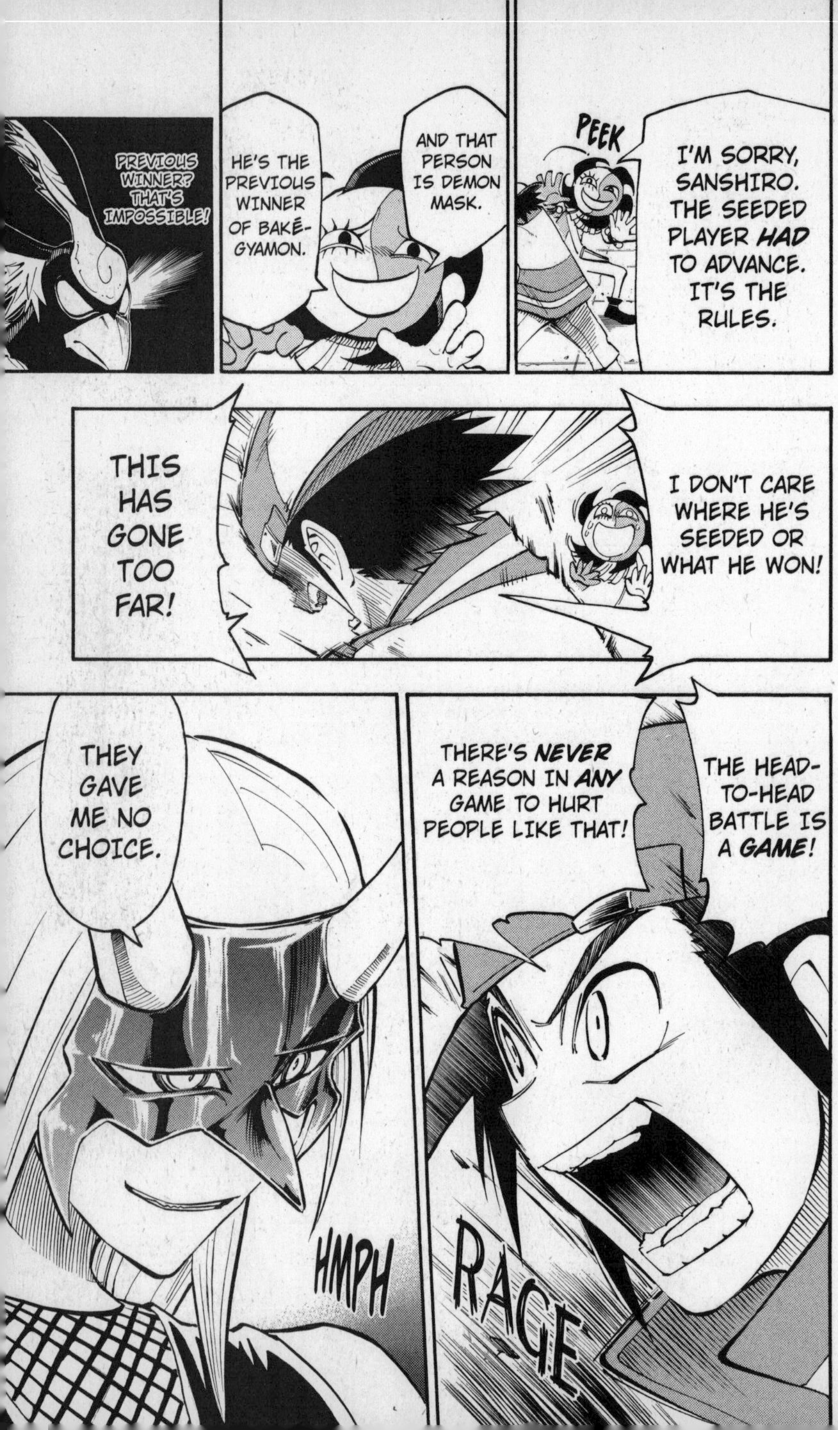
PEEK
I'M SORRY, SANSHIRO. THE SEEDED PLAYER *HAD* TO ADVANCE. IT'S THE RULES.
AND THAT PERSON IS DEMON MASK.
HE'S THE PREVIOUS WINNER OF BAKÉ-GYAMON.
PREVIOUS WINNER? THAT'S IMPOSSIBLE!
I DON'T CARE WHERE HE'S SEEDED OR WHAT HE WON!
THIS HAS GONE TOO FAR!
THE HEAD-TO-HEAD BATTLE IS A *GAME*!
THERE'S *NEVER* A REASON IN *ANY* GAME TO HURT PEOPLE LIKE THAT!
RAGE
THEY GAVE ME NO CHOICE.
HMPH

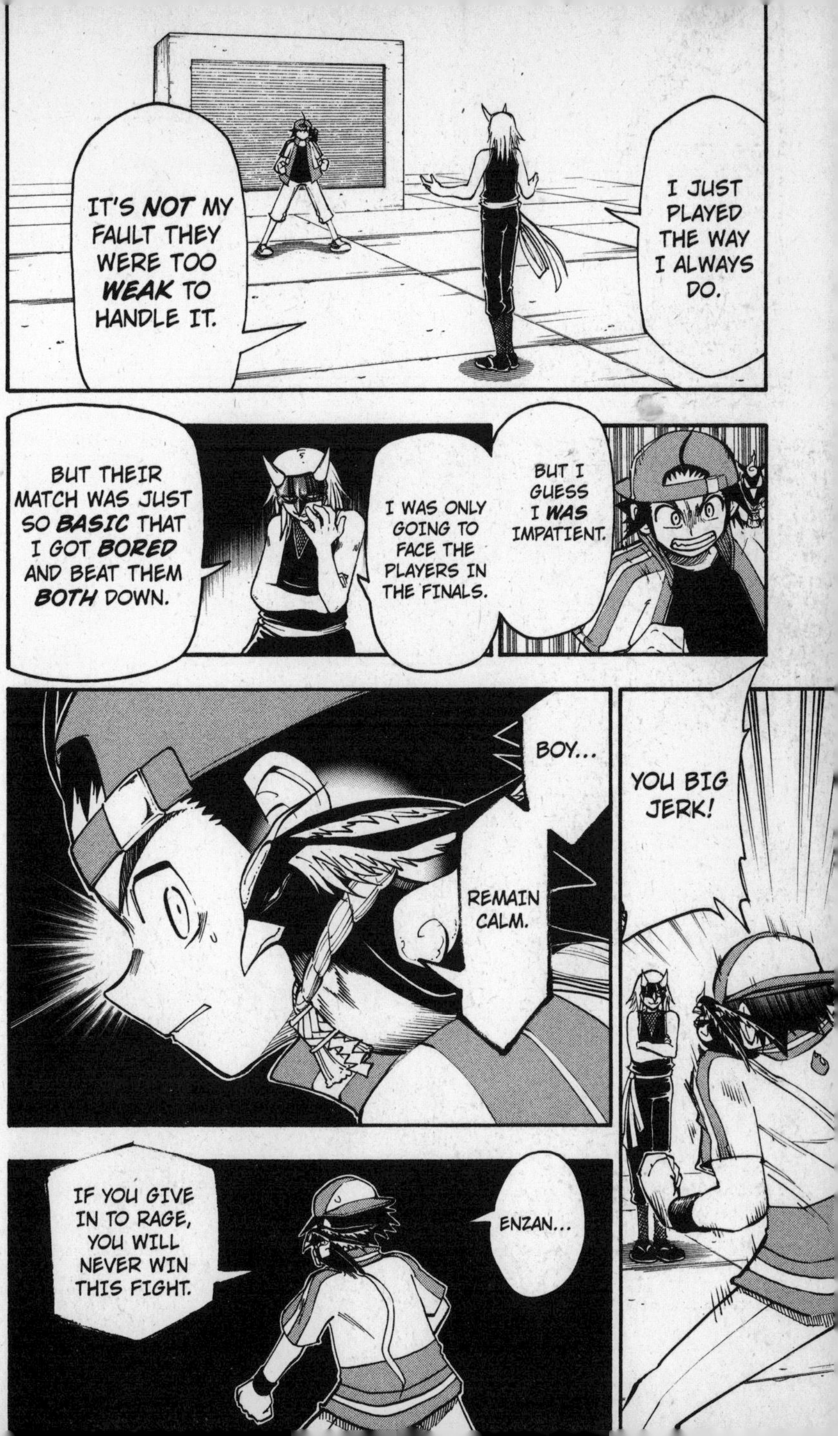
I JUST PLAYED THE WAY I ALWAYS DO.
IT'S **NOT** MY FAULT THEY WERE TOO **WEAK** TO HANDLE IT.
BUT I GUESS I **WAS** IMPATIENT.
I WAS ONLY GOING TO FACE THE PLAYERS IN THE FINALS.
BUT THEIR MATCH WAS JUST SO **BASIC** THAT I GOT **BORED** AND BEAT THEM **BOTH** DOWN.
YOU BIG JERK!
BOY...
REMAIN CALM.
ENZAN...
IF YOU GIVE IN TO RAGE, YOU WILL NEVER WIN THIS FIGHT.

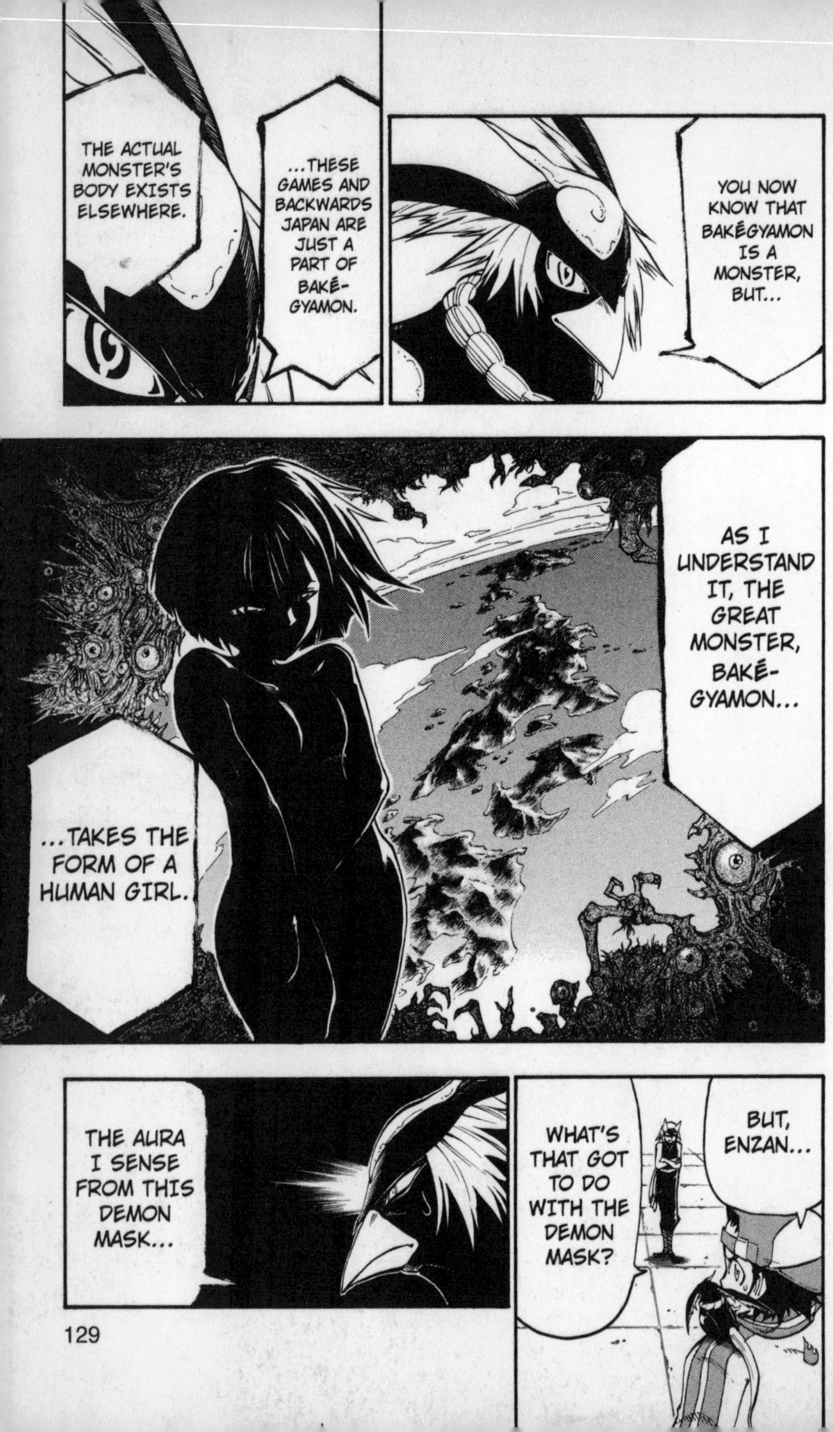
YOU NOW KNOW THAT BAKÉGYAMON IS A MONSTER, BUT...
...THESE GAMES AND BACKWARDS JAPAN ARE JUST A PART OF BAKÉ-GYAMON.
THE ACTUAL MONSTER'S BODY EXISTS ELSEWHERE.
AS I UNDERSTAND IT, THE GREAT MONSTER, BAKÉ-GYAMON...
...TAKES THE FORM OF A HUMAN GIRL.
BUT, ENZAN...
WHAT'S THAT GOT TO DO WITH THE DEMON MASK?
THE AURA I SENSE FROM THIS DEMON MASK...

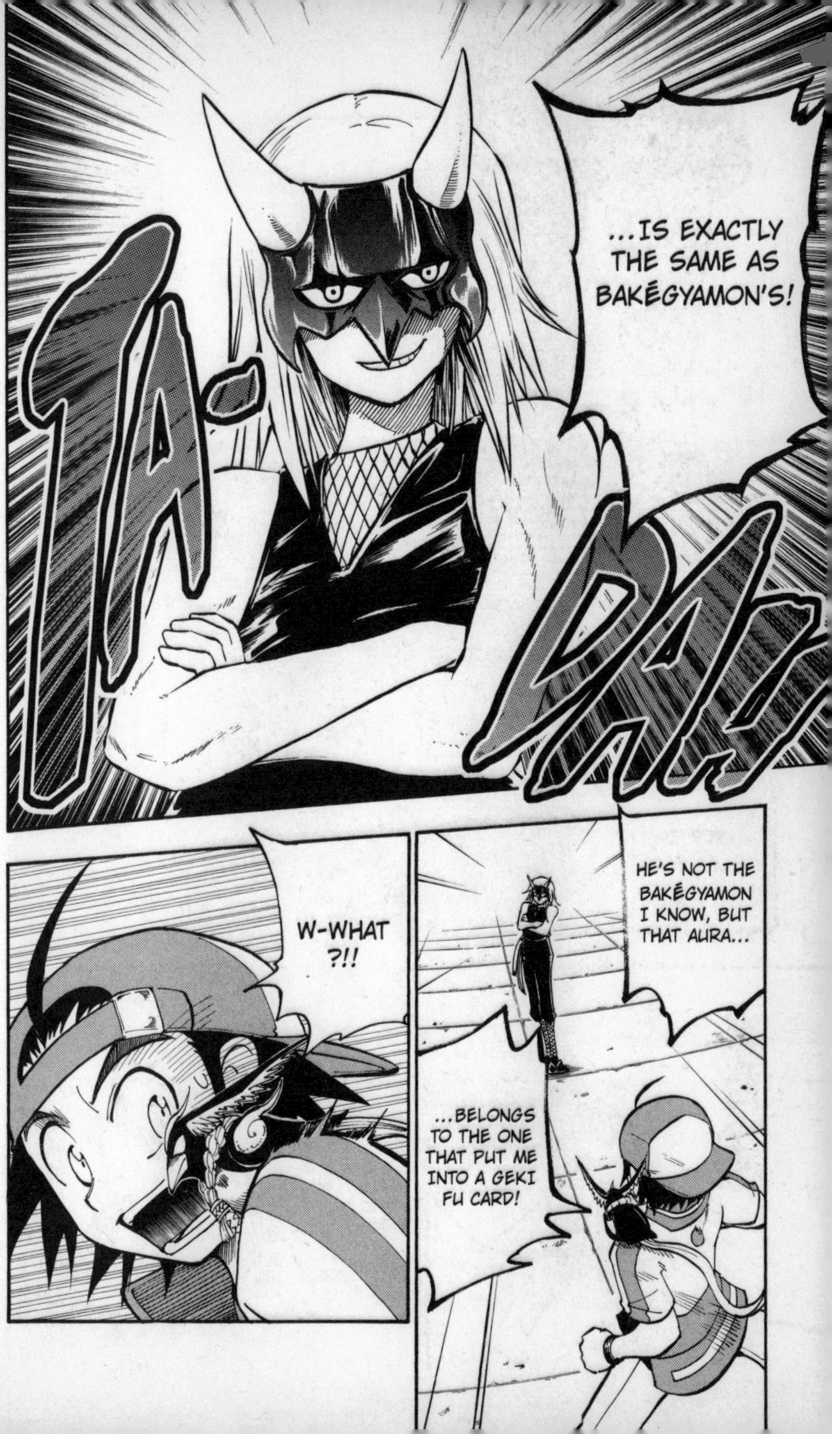
...IS EXACTLY THE SAME AS BAKĒGYAMON'S!
HE'S NOT THE BAKĒGYAMON I KNOW, BUT THAT AURA...
...BELONGS TO THE ONE THAT PUT ME INTO A GEKI FU CARD!
W-WHAT ?!!

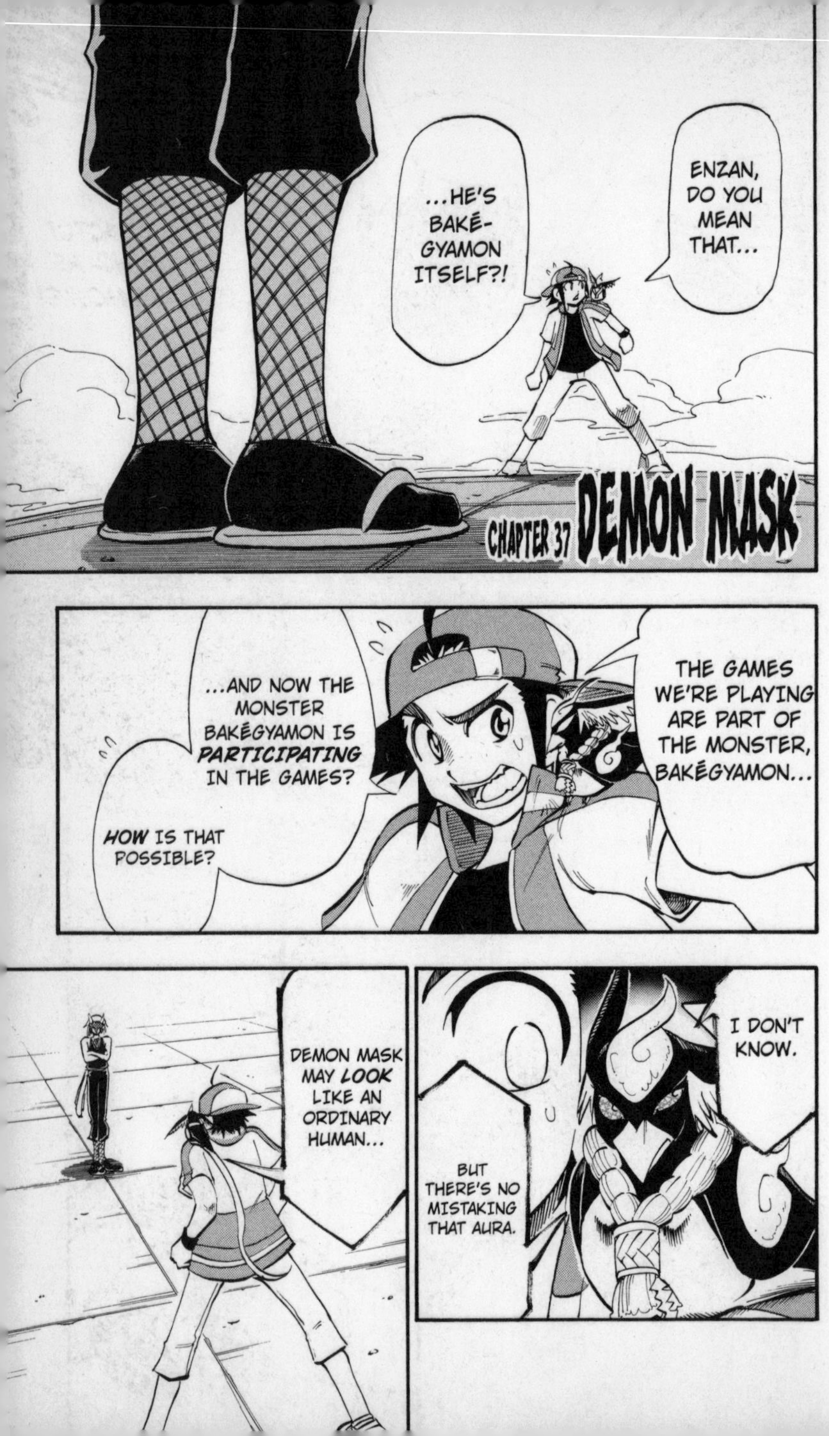
ENZAN, DO YOU MEAN THAT...
...HE'S BAKÉ-GYAMON ITSELF?!
CHAPTER 37 DEMON MASK
THE GAMES WE'RE PLAYING ARE PART OF THE MONSTER, BAKÉGYAMON...
...AND NOW THE MONSTER BAKÉGYAMON IS PARTICIPATING IN THE GAMES?
HOW IS THAT POSSIBLE?
I DON'T KNOW.
BUT THERE'S NO MISTAKING THAT AURA.
DEMON MASK MAY LOOK LIKE AN ORDINARY HUMAN...

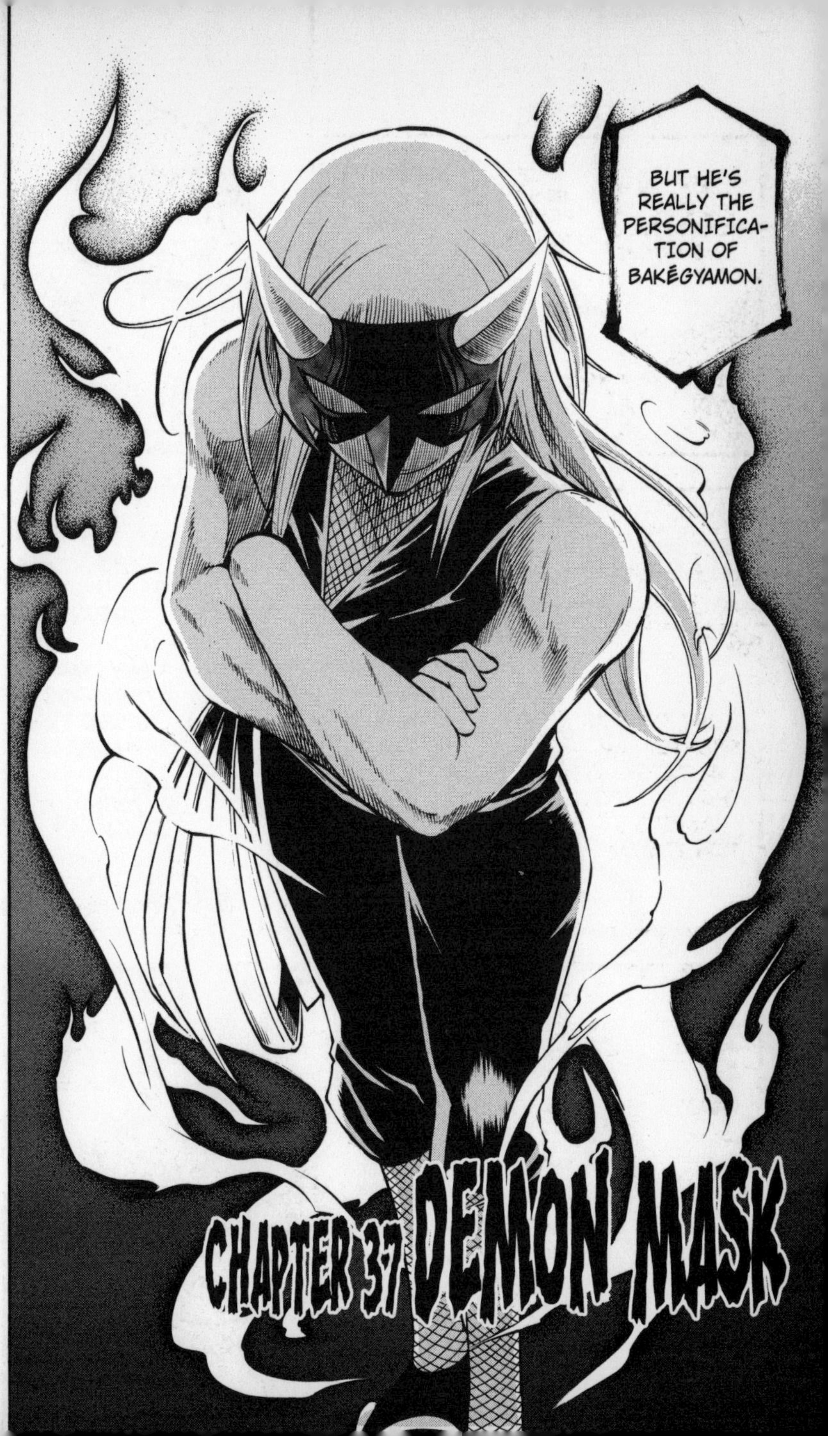
BUT HE'S REALLY THE PERSONIFICATION OF BAKÉGYAMON.
CHAPTER 37 DEMON MASK

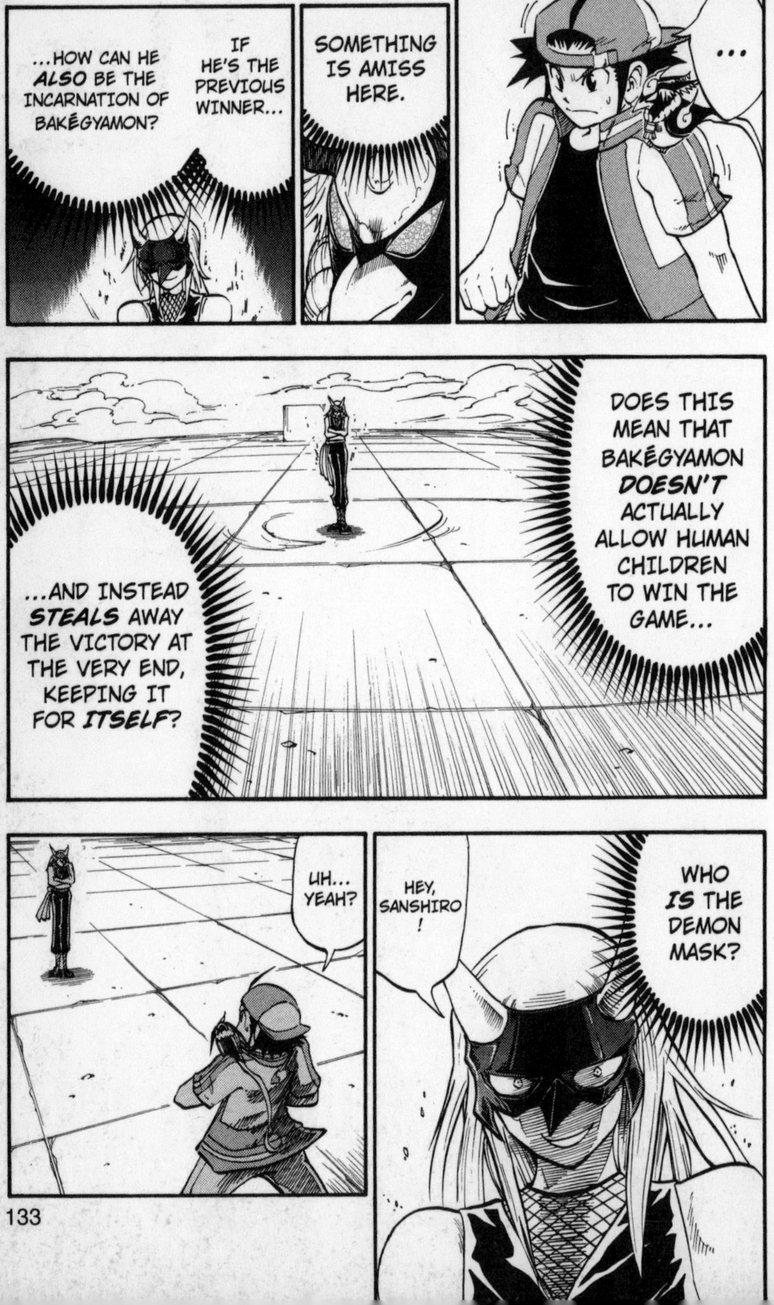
...
SOMETHING IS AMISS HERE.
IF HE'S THE PREVIOUS WINNER...
...HOW CAN HE ALSO BE THE INCARNATION OF BAKÉGYAMON?
DOES THIS MEAN THAT BAKÉGYAMON DOESN'T ACTUALLY ALLOW HUMAN CHILDREN TO WIN THE GAME...
...AND INSTEAD STEALS AWAY THE VICTORY AT THE VERY END, KEEPING IT FOR ITSELF?
WHO IS THE DEMON MASK?
HEY, SANSHIRO!
UH... YEAH?

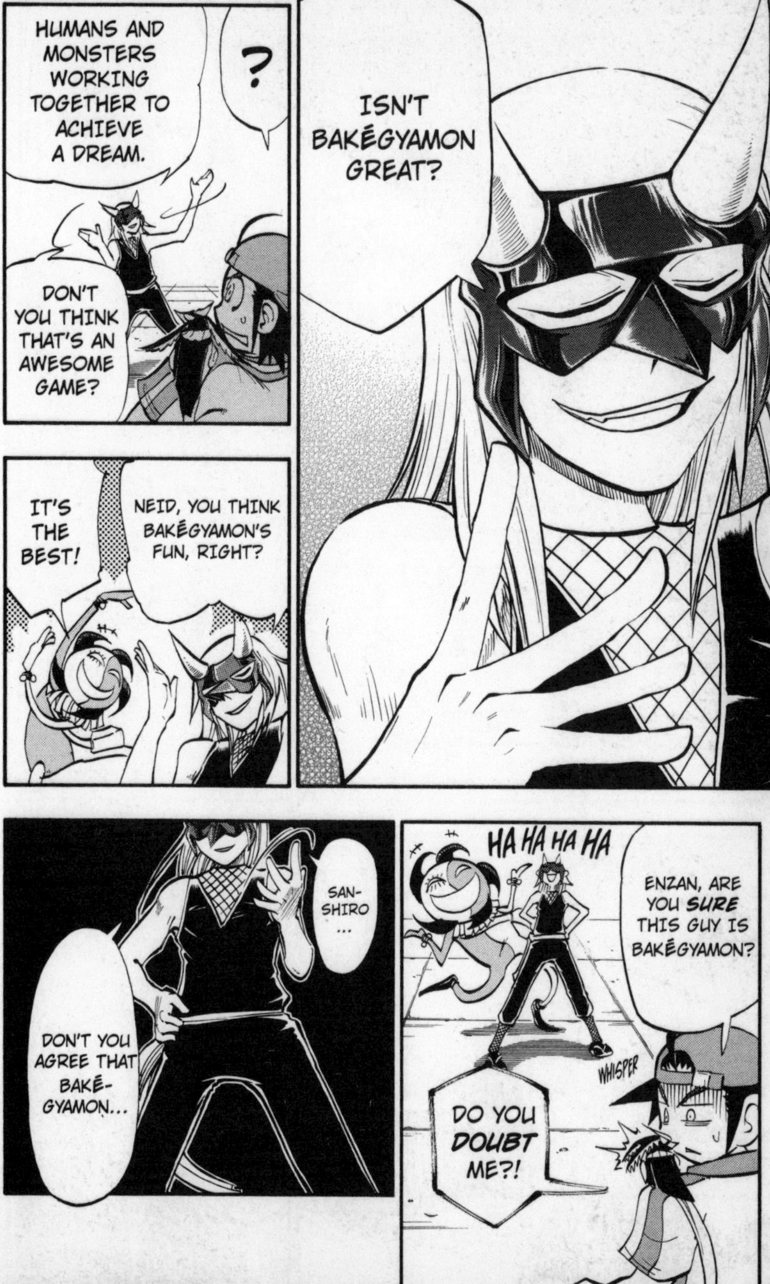
ISN'T BAKĒGYAMON GREAT?
?
HUMANS AND MONSTERS WORKING TOGETHER TO ACHIEVE A DREAM.
DON'T YOU THINK THAT'S AN AWESOME GAME?
NEID, YOU THINK BAKĒGYAMON'S FUN, RIGHT?
IT'S THE BEST!
ENZAN, ARE YOU **SURE** THIS GUY IS BAKĒGYAMON?
HA HA HA HA
WHISPER
DO YOU **DOUBT** ME?!
SAN-SHIRO ...
DON'T YOU AGREE THAT BAKĒ-GYAMON...

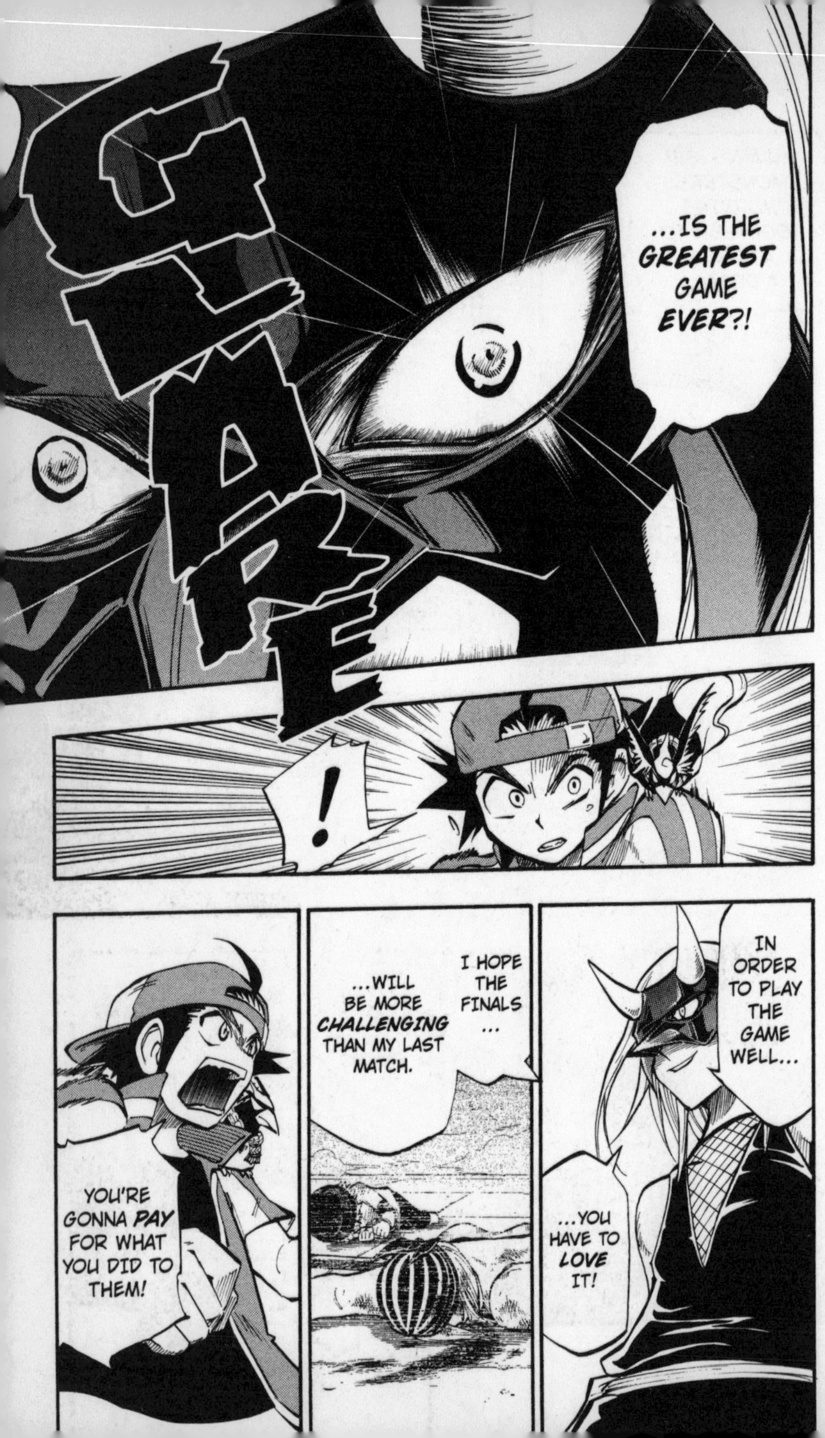
...IS THE GREATEST GAME EVER?!
GLARE
!
IN ORDER TO PLAY THE GAME WELL...
...YOU HAVE TO LOVE IT!
I HOPE THE FINALS...
...WILL BE MORE CHALLENGING THAN MY LAST MATCH.
YOU'RE GONNA PAY FOR WHAT YOU DID TO THEM!

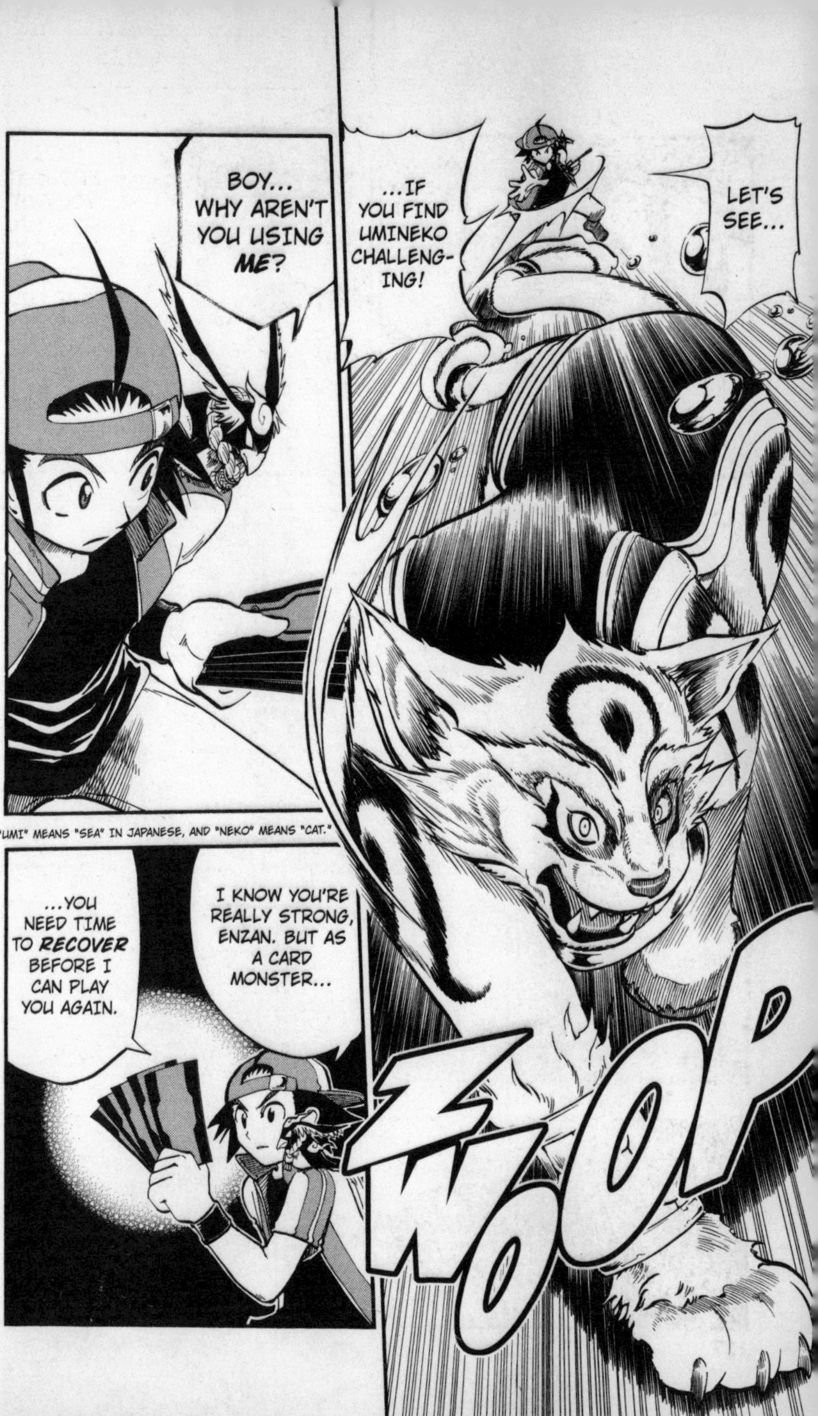
LET'S SEE...
...IF YOU FIND UMINEKO CHALLENGING!
ZWOOP
BOY... WHY AREN'T YOU USING *ME*?
I KNOW YOU'RE REALLY STRONG, ENZAN. BUT AS A CARD MONSTER...
...YOU NEED TIME TO *RECOVER* BEFORE I CAN PLAY YOU AGAIN.

"UMI" MEANS "SEA" IN JAPANESE, AND "NEKO" MEANS "CAT."

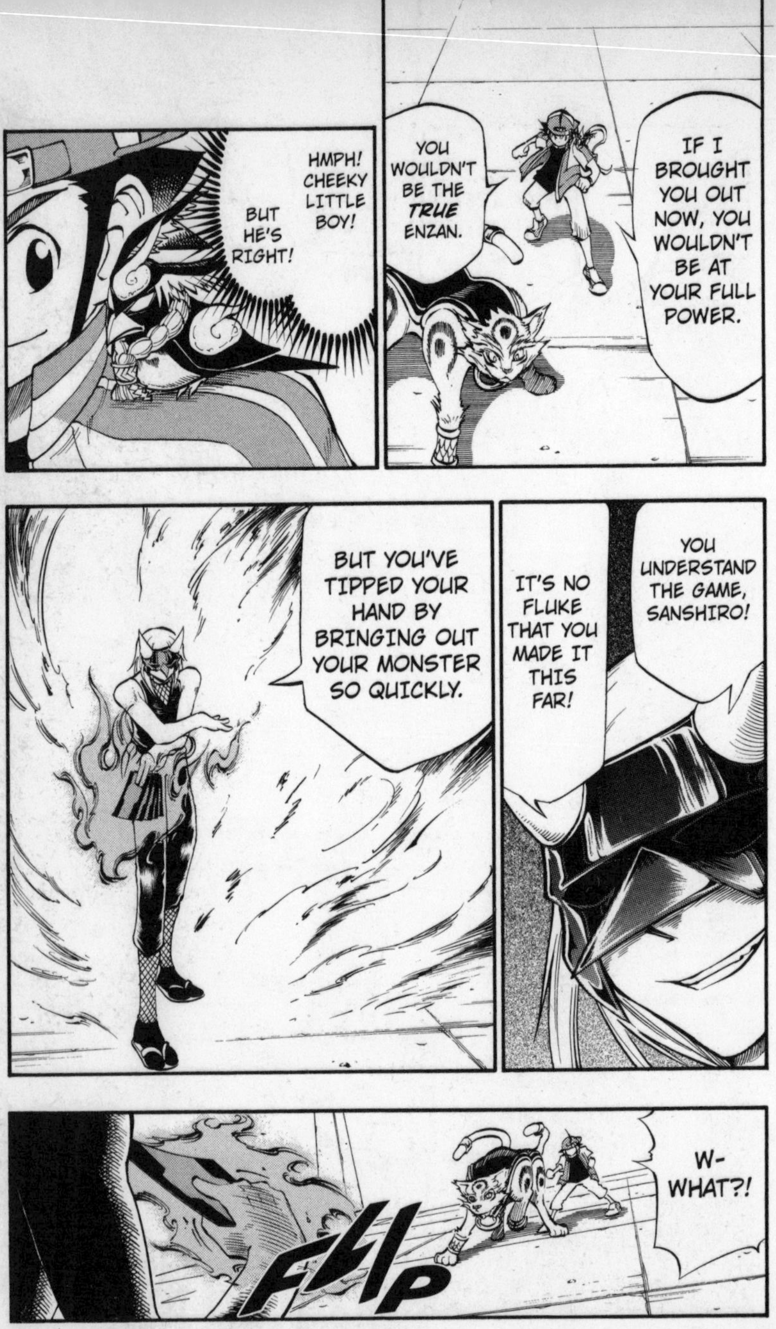
IF I BROUGHT YOU OUT NOW, YOU WOULDN'T BE AT YOUR FULL POWER.
YOU WOULDN'T BE THE TRUE ENZAN.
HMPH! CHEEKY LITTLE BOY!
BUT HE'S RIGHT!
YOU UNDERSTAND THE GAME, SANSHIRO!
IT'S NO FLUKE THAT YOU MADE IT THIS FAR!
BUT YOU'VE TIPPED YOUR HAND BY BRINGING OUT YOUR MONSTER SO QUICKLY.
W-WHAT?!
FLIP

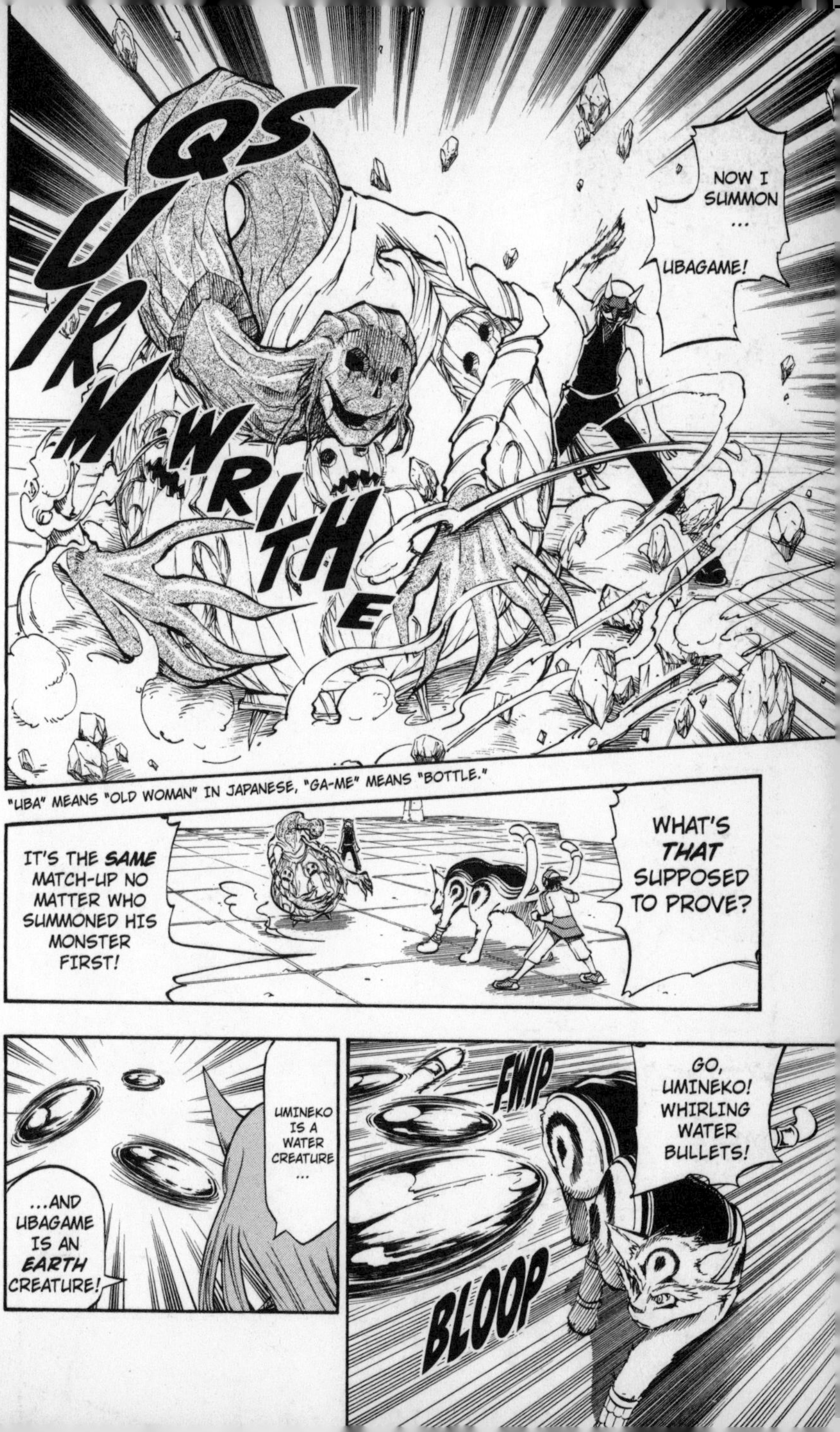
NOW I SUMMON ... UBAGAME!
SQUIRM
WRITHE
"UBA" MEANS "OLD WOMAN" IN JAPANESE, "GA-ME" MEANS "BOTTLE."
WHAT'S *THAT* SUPPOSED TO PROVE?
IT'S THE *SAME* MATCH-UP NO MATTER WHO SUMMONED HIS MONSTER FIRST!
FWIP
GO, UMINEKO! WHIRLING WATER BULLETS!
BLOOP
UMINEKO IS A WATER CREATURE ...
...AND UBAGAME IS AN *EARTH* CREATURE!

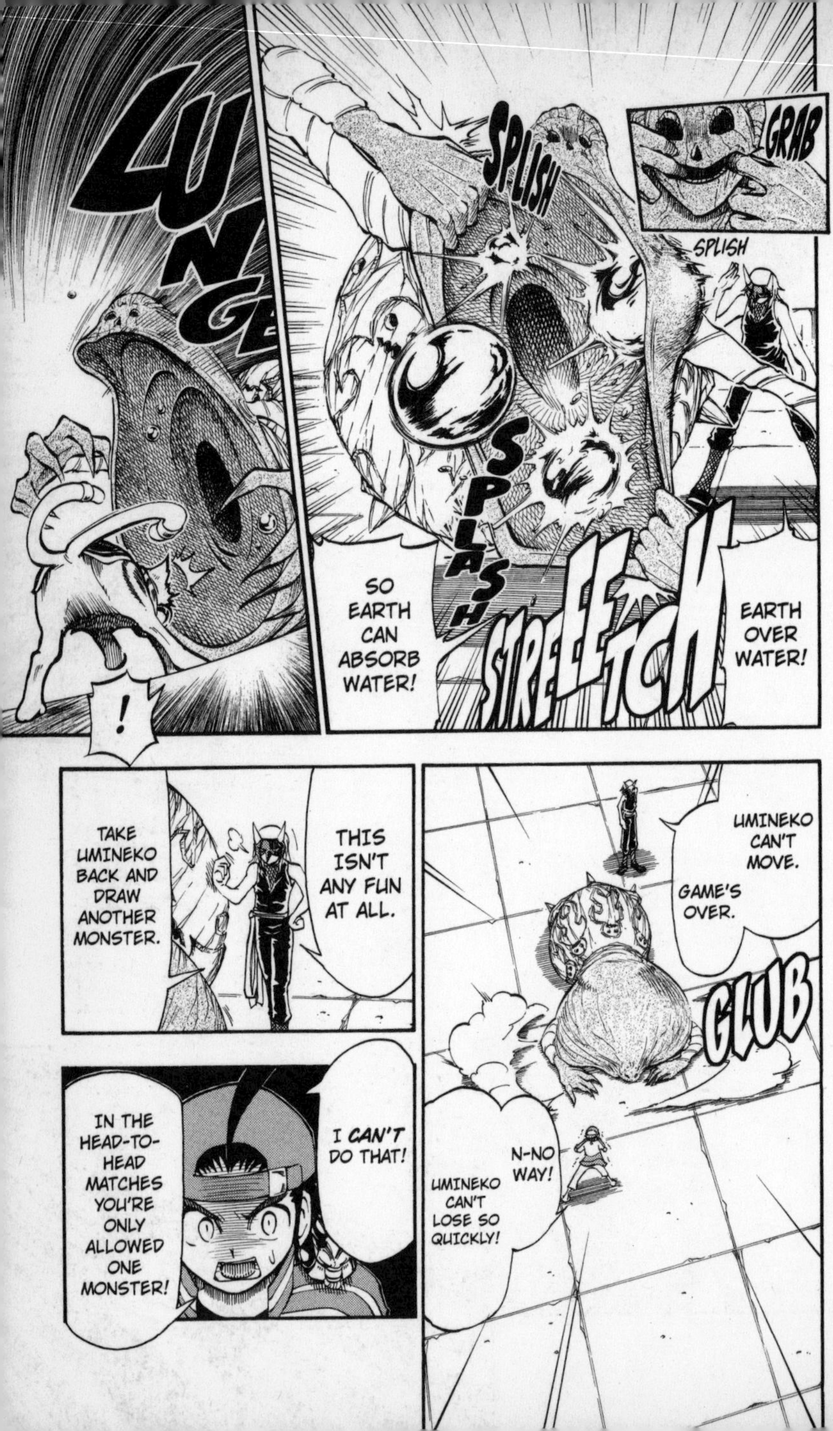
GRAB
SPLISH
SPLISH
SPLASH
EARTH OVER WATER!
STREEETCH
SO EARTH CAN ABSORB WATER!
LUNGE
!
UMINEKO CAN'T MOVE.
GAME'S OVER.
CLUB
N-NO WAY!
UMINEKO CAN'T LOSE SO QUICKLY!
THIS ISN'T ANY FUN AT ALL.
TAKE UMINEKO BACK AND DRAW ANOTHER MONSTER.
I *CAN'T* DO THAT!
IN THE HEAD-TO-HEAD MATCHES YOU'RE ONLY ALLOWED ONE MONSTER!

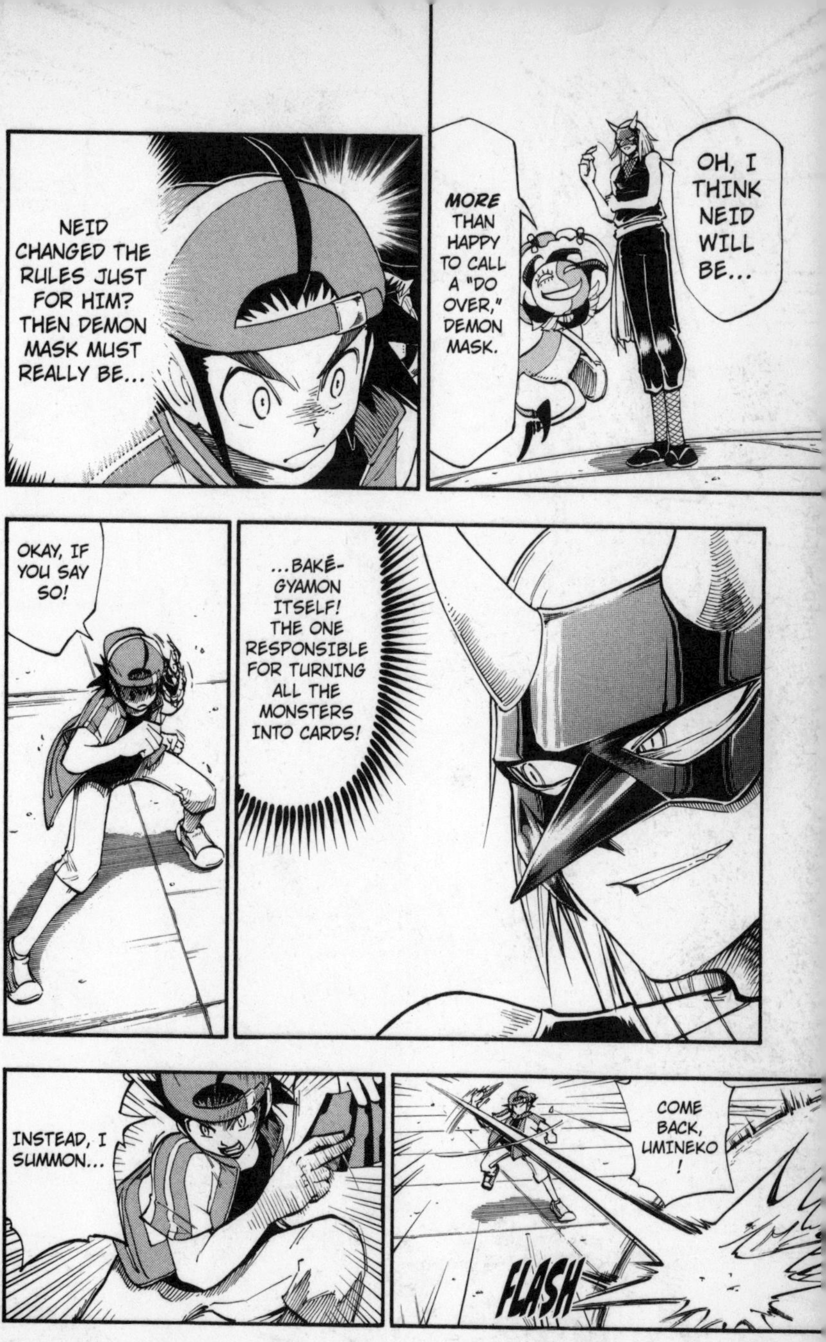
OH, I THINK NEID WILL BE...
MORE THAN HAPPY TO CALL A "DO OVER," DEMON MASK.
NEID CHANGED THE RULES JUST FOR HIM? THEN DEMON MASK MUST REALLY BE...
...BAKÉ-GYAMON ITSELF! THE ONE RESPONSIBLE FOR TURNING ALL THE MONSTERS INTO CARDS!
OKAY, IF YOU SAY SO!
COME BACK, UMINEKO!
FLASH
INSTEAD, I SUMMON...

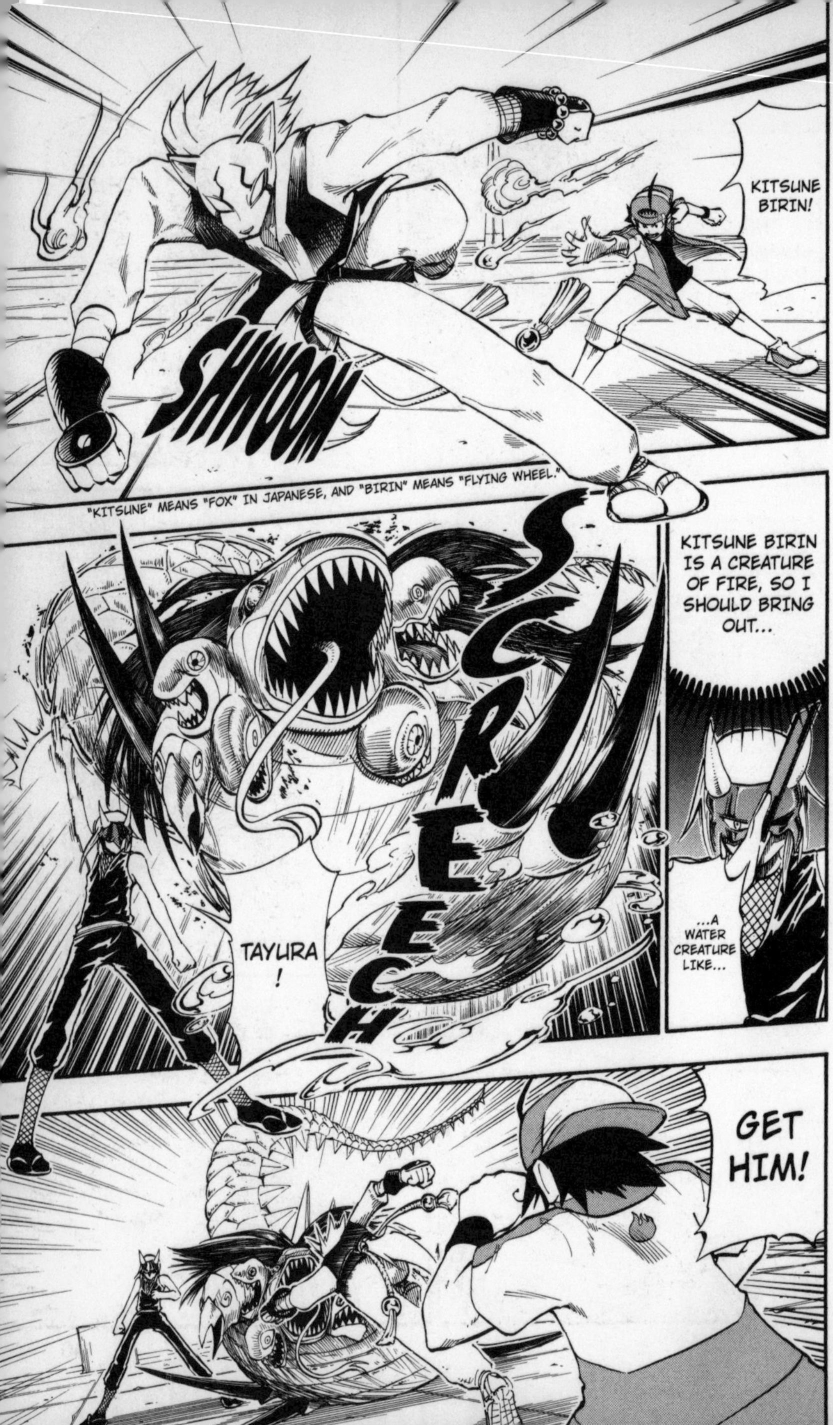
KITSUNE BIRIN!
SHWOOM
"KITSUNE" MEANS "FOX" IN JAPANESE, AND "BIRIN" MEANS "FLYING WHEEL."
KITSUNE BIRIN IS A CREATURE OF FIRE, SO I SHOULD BRING OUT...
...A WATER CREATURE LIKE...
TAYURA!
SCREEECH
GET HIM!

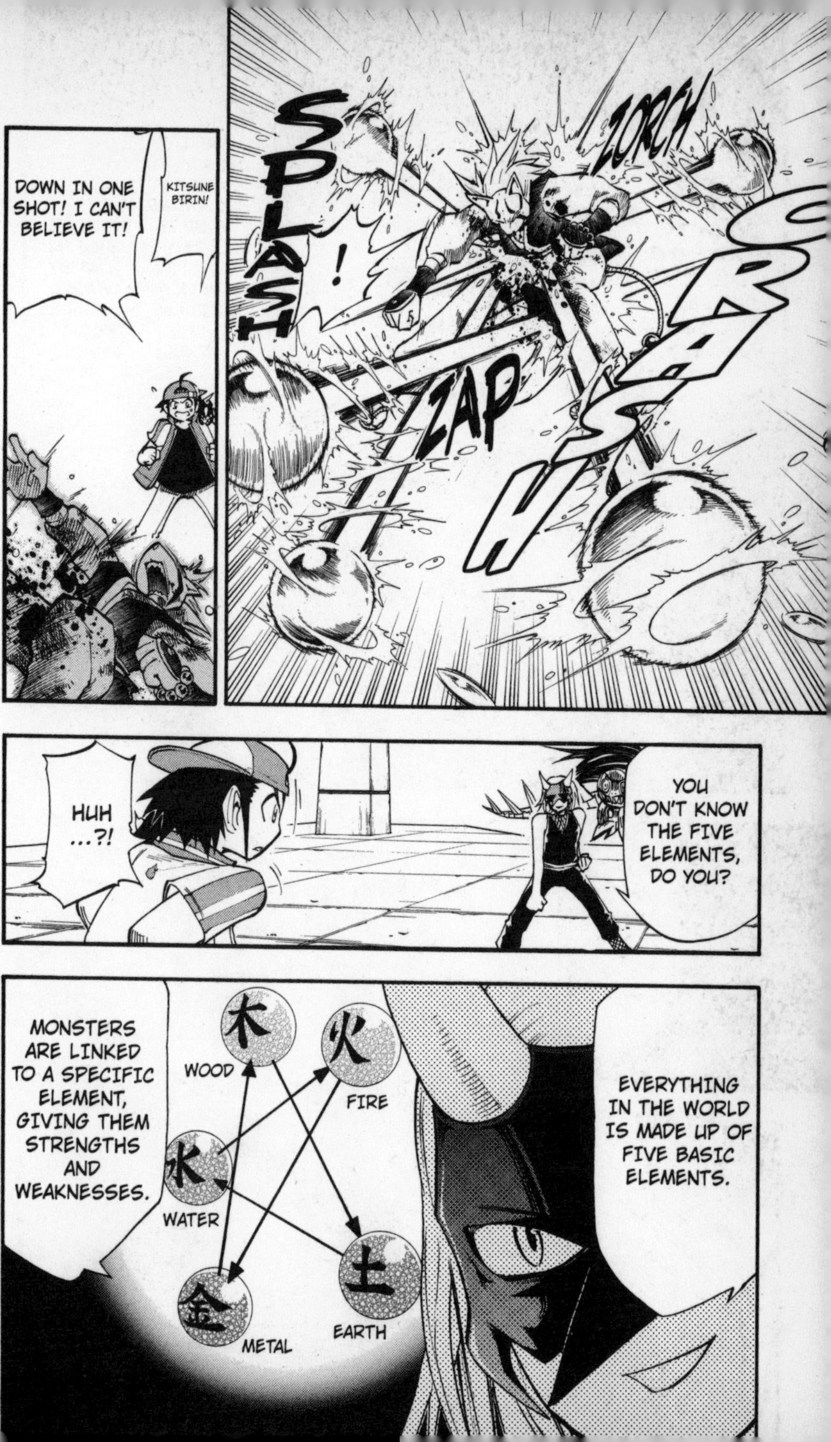
ZORCH
CRASH
SPLASH
!
ZAP
KITSUNE BIRIN!
DOWN IN ONE SHOT! I CAN'T BELIEVE IT!
YOU DON'T KNOW THE FIVE ELEMENTS, DO YOU?
HUH ...?!
EVERYTHING IN THE WORLD IS MADE UP OF FIVE BASIC ELEMENTS.
木
WOOD
火
FIRE
水
WATER
土
EARTH
金
METAL
MONSTERS ARE LINKED TO A SPECIFIC ELEMENT, GIVING THEM STRENGTHS AND WEAKNESSES.

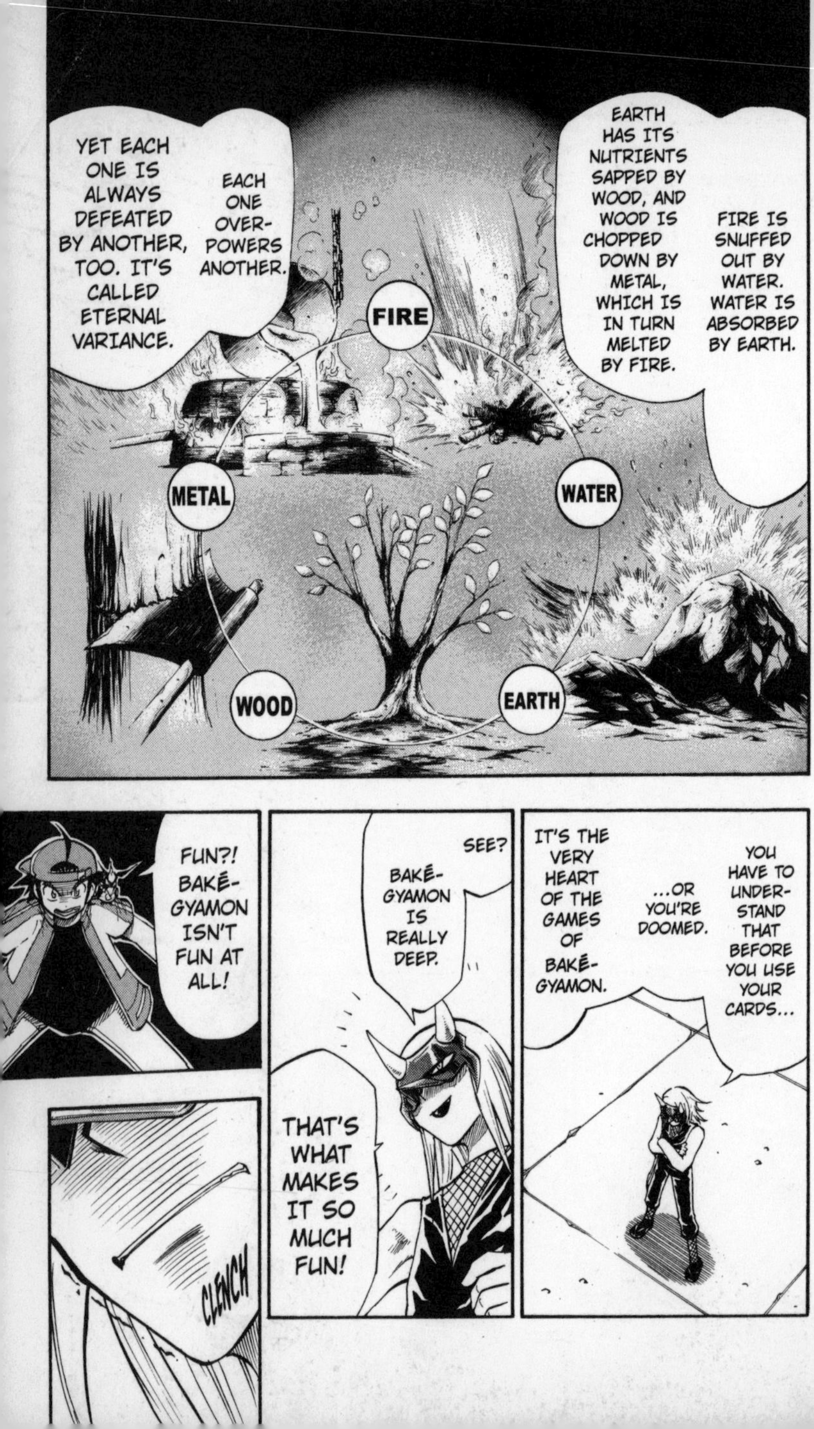
FIRE IS SNUFFED OUT BY WATER. WATER IS ABSORBED BY EARTH.
EARTH HAS ITS NUTRIENTS SAPPED BY WOOD, AND WOOD IS CHOPPED DOWN BY METAL, WHICH IS IN TURN MELTED BY FIRE.
EACH ONE OVER-POWERS ANOTHER.
YET EACH ONE IS ALWAYS DEFEATED BY ANOTHER, TOO. IT'S CALLED ETERNAL VARIANCE.
FIRE
WATER
EARTH
WOOD
METAL
YOU HAVE TO UNDER-STAND THAT BEFORE YOU USE YOUR CARDS...
...OR YOU'RE DOOMED.
IT'S THE VERY HEART OF THE GAMES OF BAKÉ-GYAMON.
SEE?
BAKÉ-GYAMON IS REALLY DEEP.
THAT'S WHAT MAKES IT SO MUCH FUN!
FUN?! BAKÉ-GYAMON ISN'T FUN AT ALL!
CLENCH

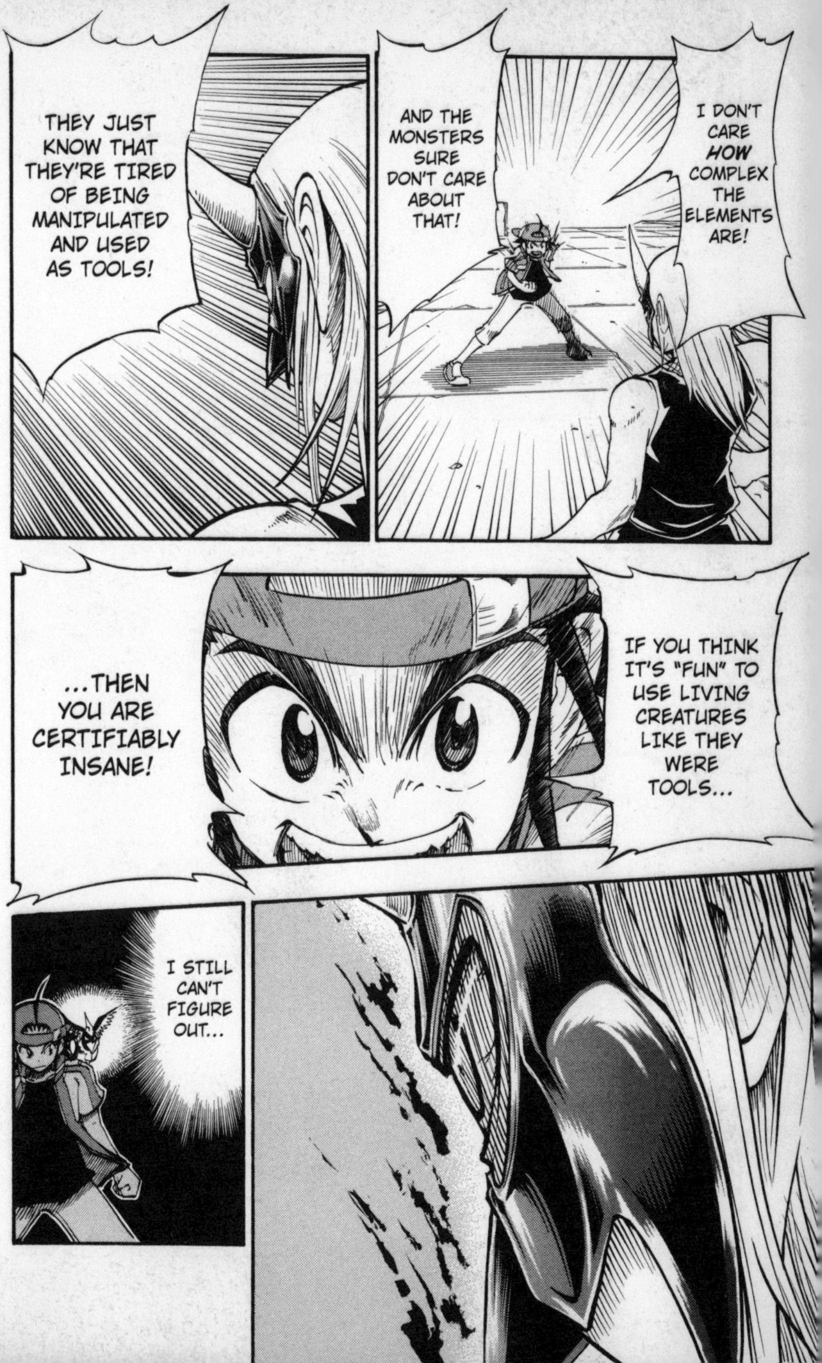
I DON'T CARE *HOW* COMPLEX THE ELEMENTS ARE!
AND THE MONSTERS SURE DON'T CARE ABOUT THAT!
THEY JUST KNOW THAT THEY'RE TIRED OF BEING MANIPULATED AND USED AS TOOLS!
IF YOU THINK IT'S "FUN" TO USE LIVING CREATURES LIKE THEY WERE TOOLS...
...THEN YOU ARE CERTIFIABLY INSANE!
I STILL CAN'T FIGURE OUT...

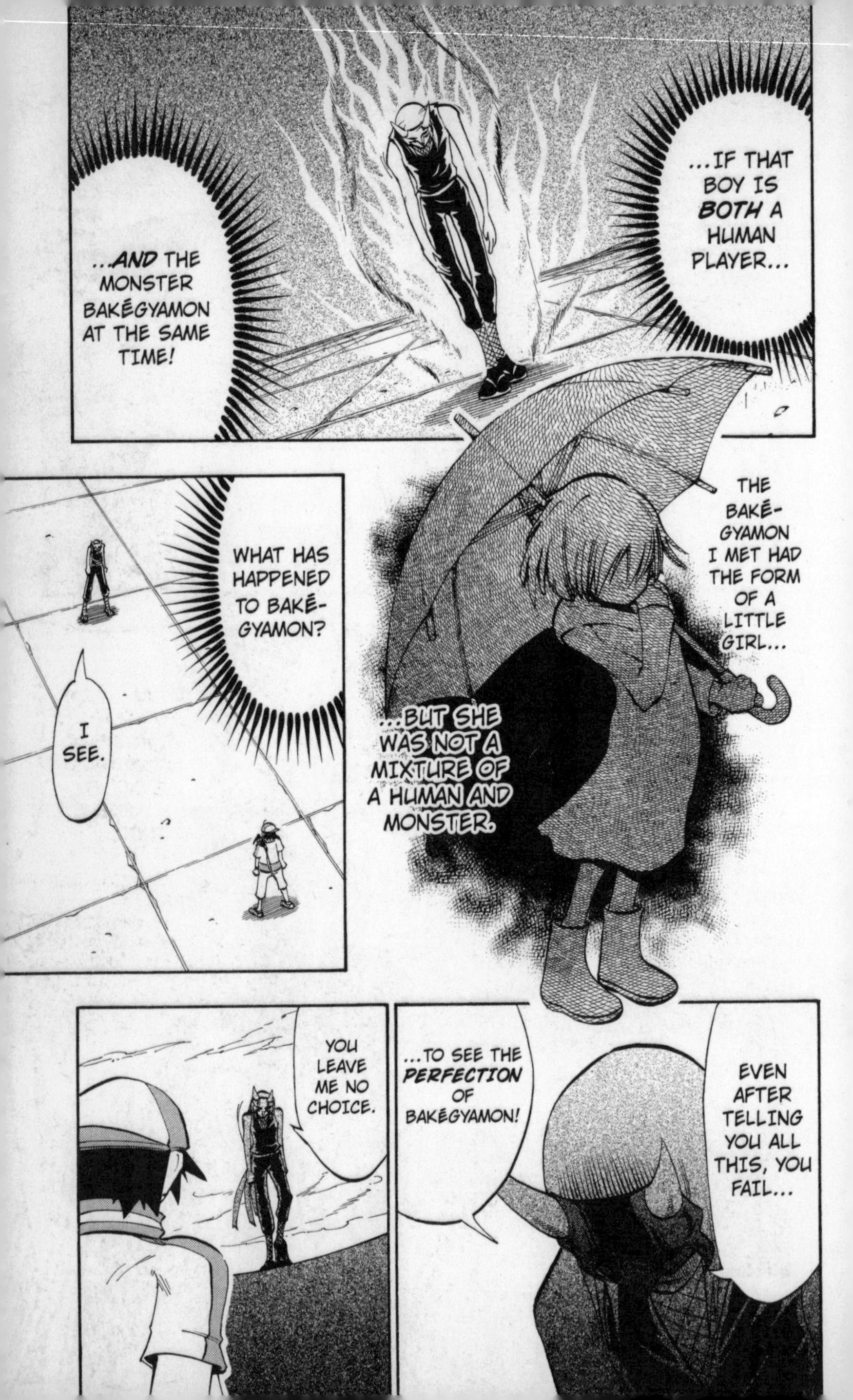
...IF THAT BOY IS *BOTH* A HUMAN PLAYER...
...*AND* THE MONSTER BAKÉGYAMON AT THE SAME TIME!
THE BAKÉ-GYAMON I MET HAD THE FORM OF A LITTLE GIRL...
...BUT SHE WAS NOT A MIXTURE OF A HUMAN AND MONSTER.
WHAT HAS HAPPENED TO BAKÉ-GYAMON?
I SEE.
EVEN AFTER TELLING YOU ALL THIS, YOU FAIL...
...TO SEE THE *PERFECTION* OF BAKÉGYAMON!
YOU LEAVE ME NO CHOICE.

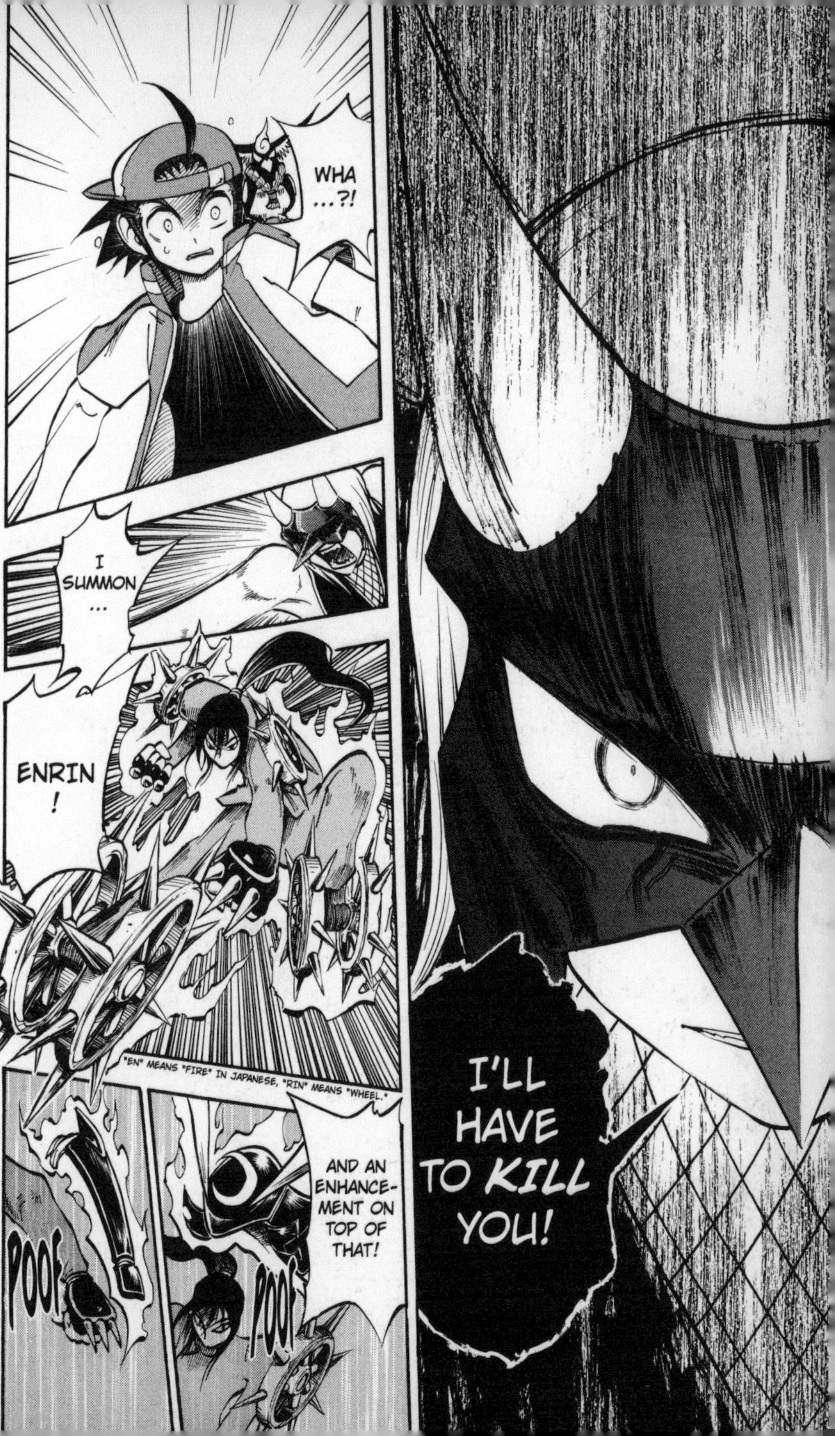
I'LL HAVE TO KILL YOU!
WHA ...?!
I SUMMON ...
ENRIN !
"EN" MEANS "FIRE" IN JAPANESE, "RIN" MEANS "WHEEL."
AND AN ENHANCEMENT ON TOP OF THAT!
POOF
POOF

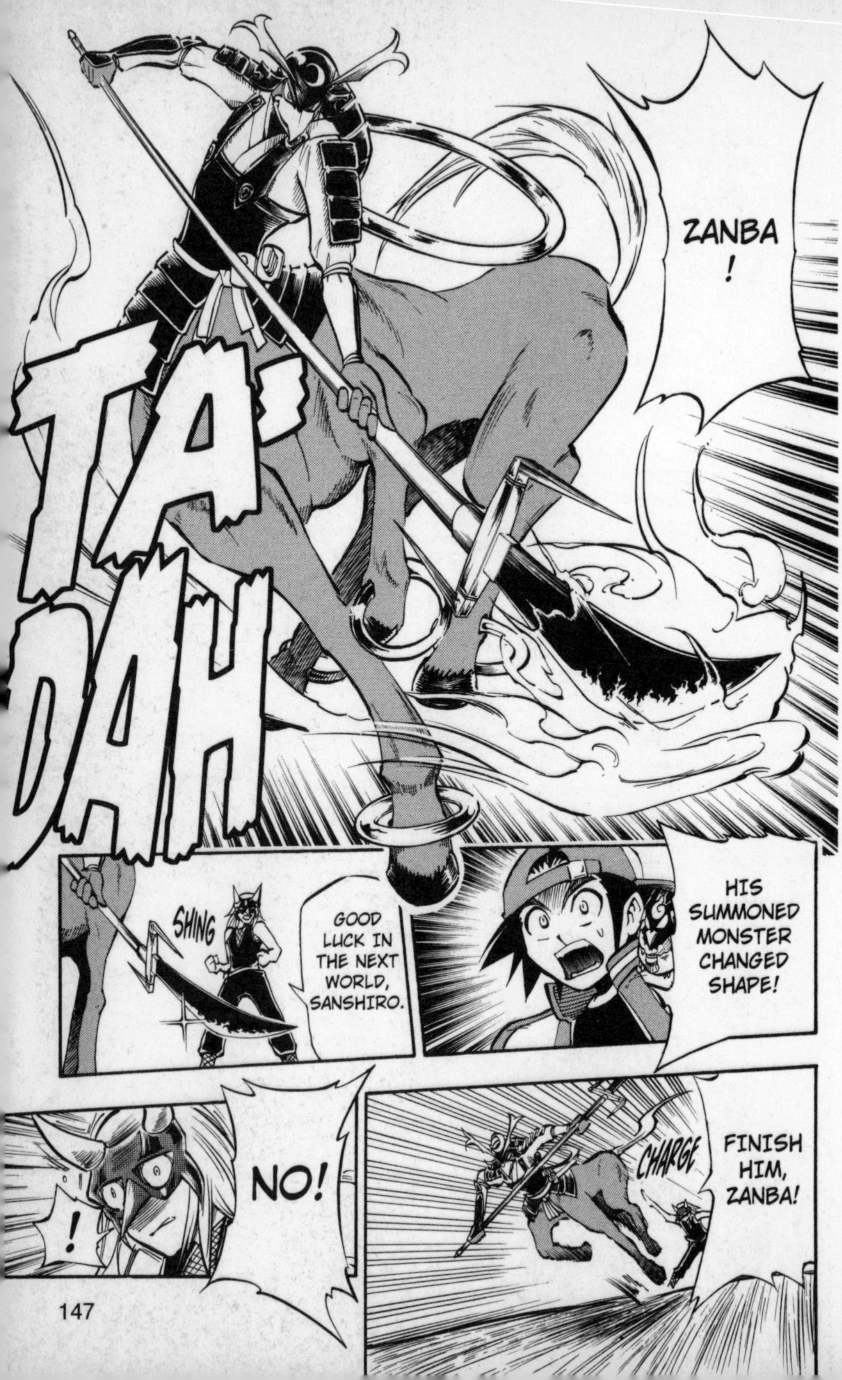
ZANBA
!
TA DAH
HIS SUMMONED MONSTER CHANGED SHAPE!
GOOD LUCK IN THE NEXT WORLD, SANSHIRO.
SHING
FINISH HIM, ZANBA!
CHARGE
NO!
!

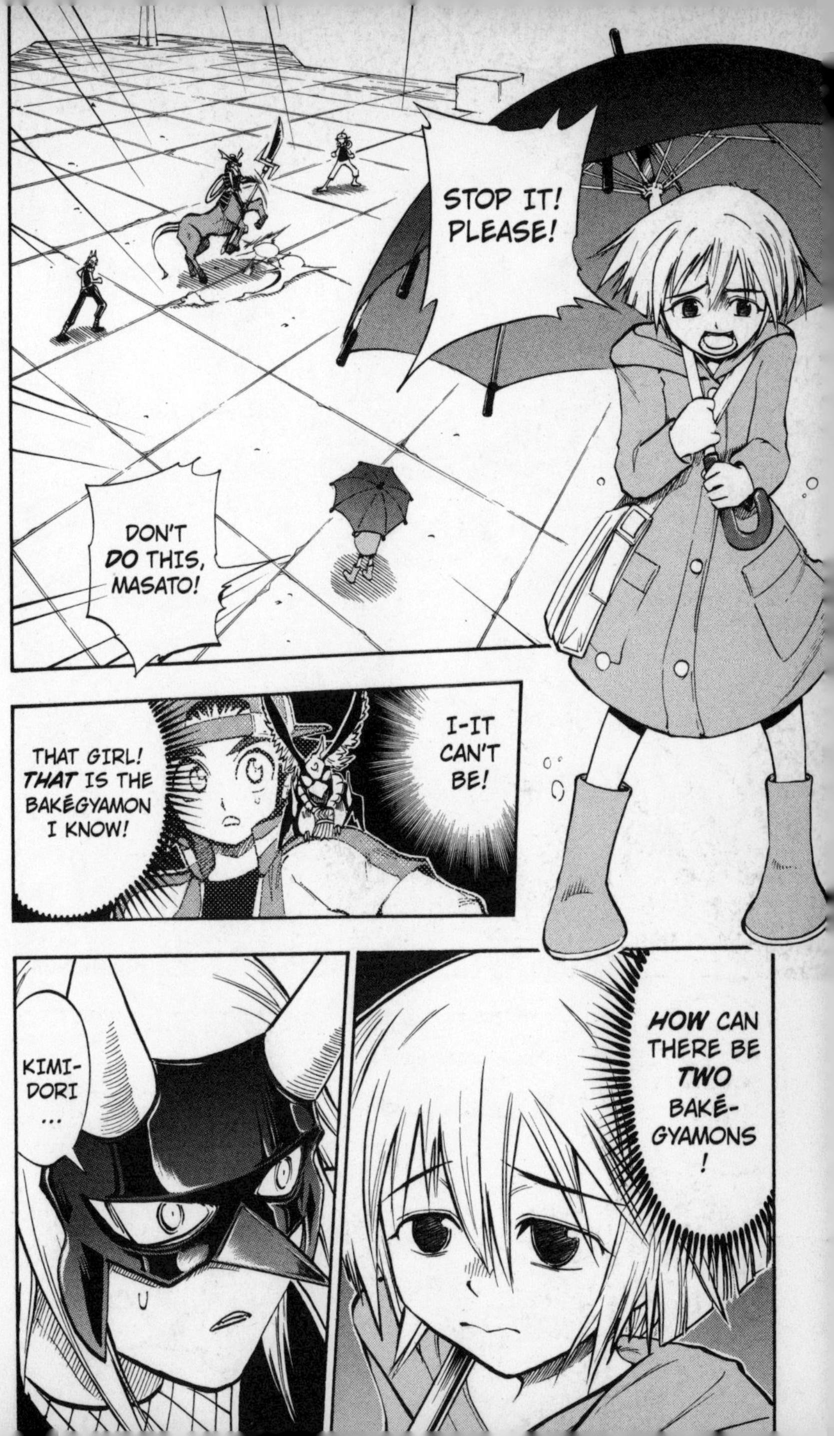
STOP IT! PLEASE!
DON'T DO THIS, MASATO!
I-IT CAN'T BE!
THAT GIRL! THAT IS THE BAKÉGYAMON I KNOW!
HOW CAN THERE BE TWO BAKÉ-GYAMONS!
KIMI-DORI ...

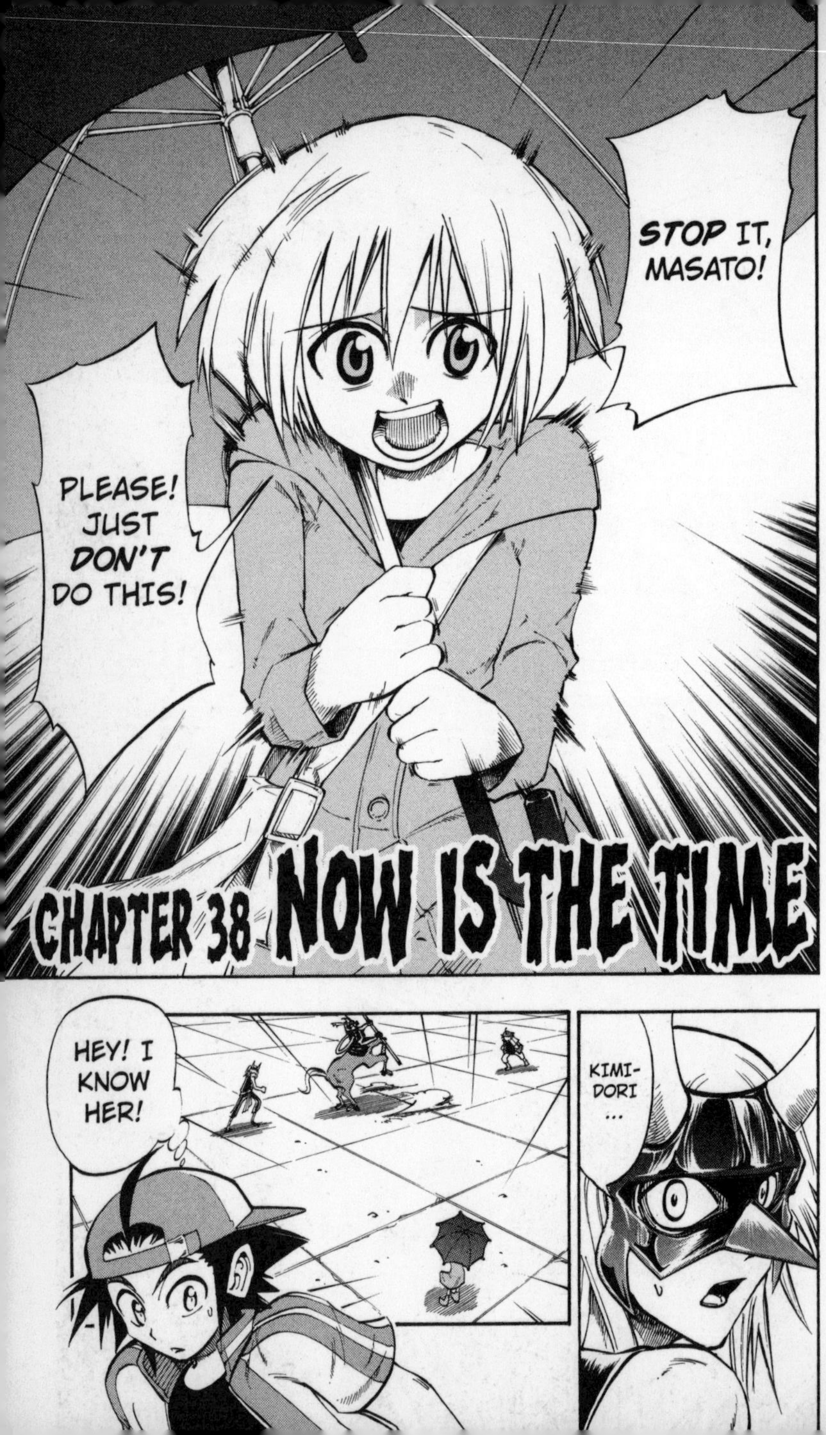
STOP IT, MASATO!
PLEASE! JUST DON'T DO THIS!
CHAPTER 38 NOW IS THE TIME
KIMI-DORI ...
HEY! I KNOW HER!

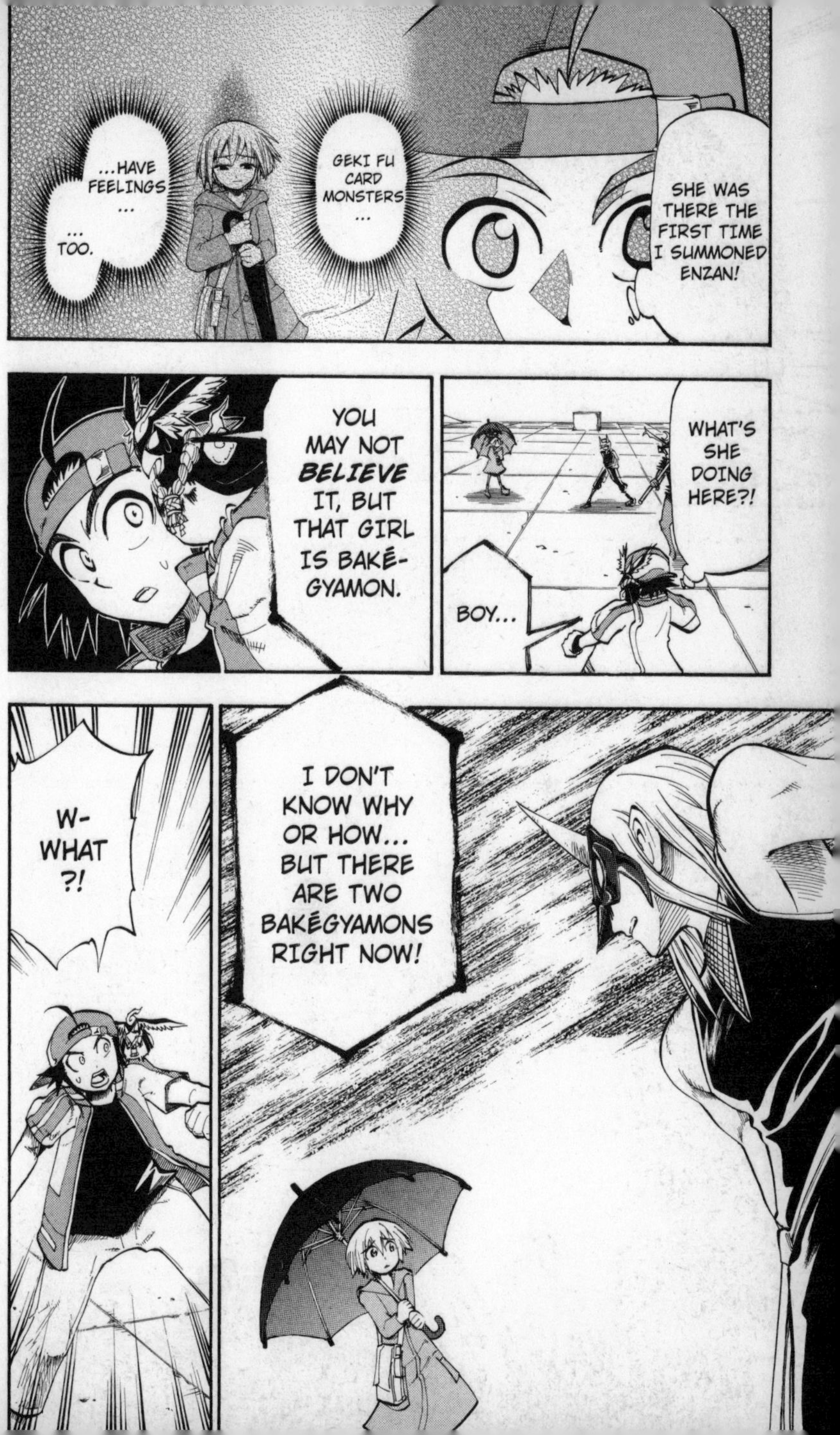
SHE WAS THERE THE FIRST TIME I SUMMONED ENZAN!
GEKI FU CARD MONSTERS ...
...HAVE FEELINGS ...
... TOO.
WHAT'S SHE DOING HERE?!
BOY...
YOU MAY NOT BELIEVE IT, BUT THAT GIRL IS BAKÉ-GYAMON.
I DON'T KNOW WHY OR HOW... BUT THERE ARE TWO BAKÉGYAMONS RIGHT NOW!
W-WHAT?!

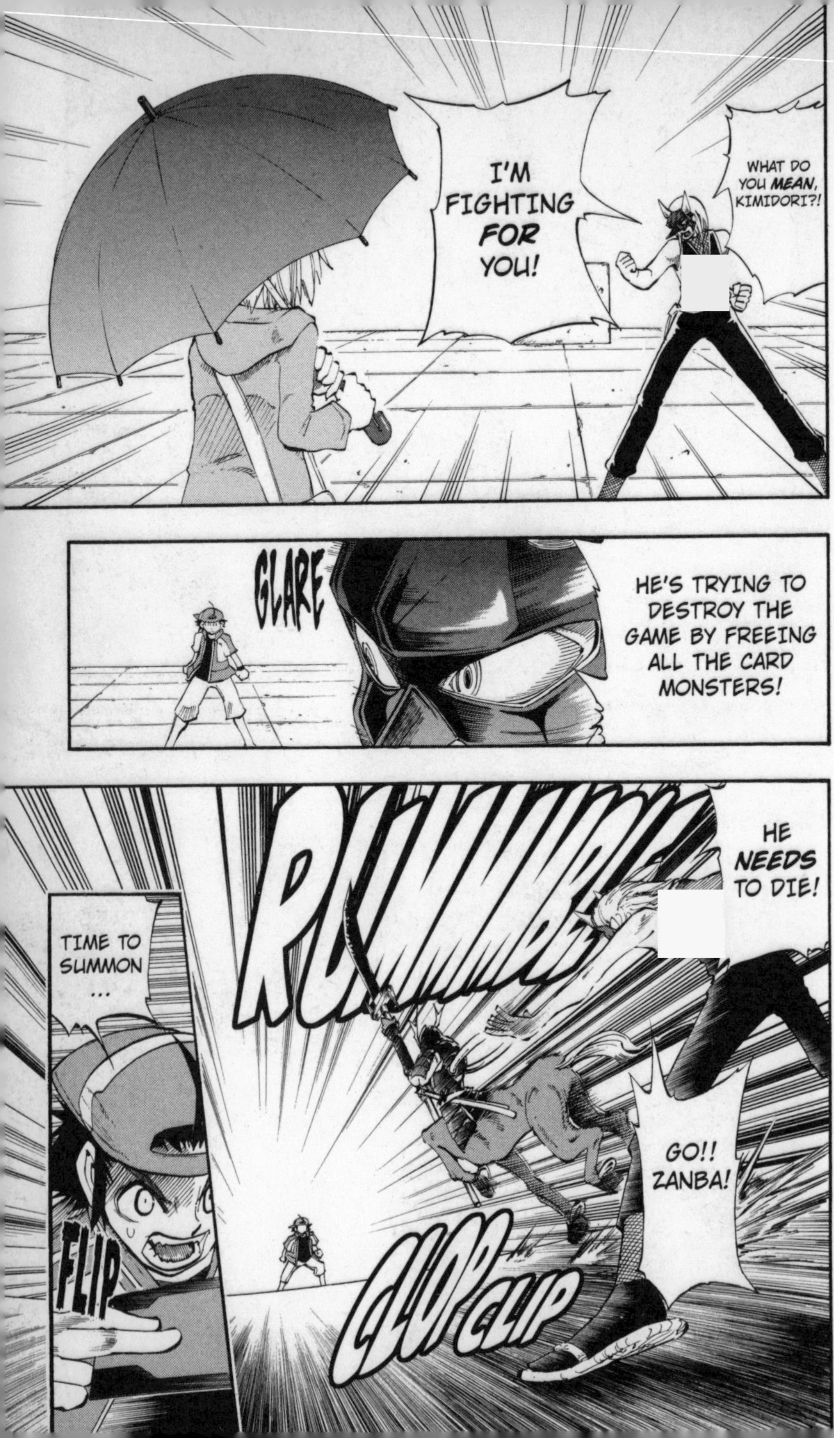
WHAT DO YOU MEAN, KIMIDORI?!
I'M FIGHTING FOR YOU!
HE'S TRYING TO DESTROY THE GAME BY FREEING ALL THE CARD MONSTERS!
GLARE
HE NEEDS TO DIE!
GO!! ZANBA!
CLOP CLIP
TIME TO SUMMON ...
FLIP

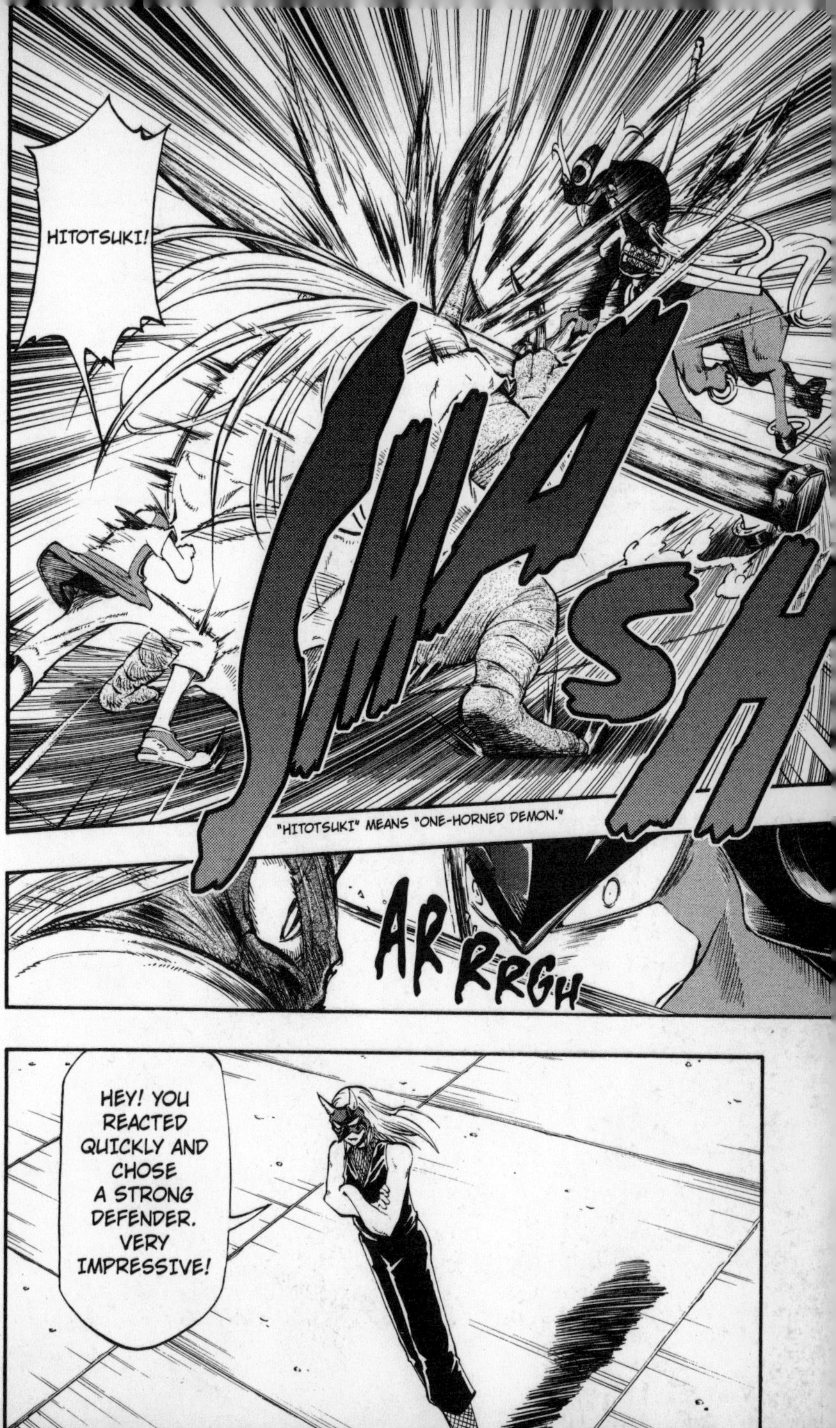
HITOTSUKI!
SMASH
"HITOTSUKI" MEANS "ONE-HORNED DEMON."
ARRRGH
HEY! YOU REACTED QUICKLY AND CHOSE A STRONG DEFENDER. VERY IMPRESSIVE!

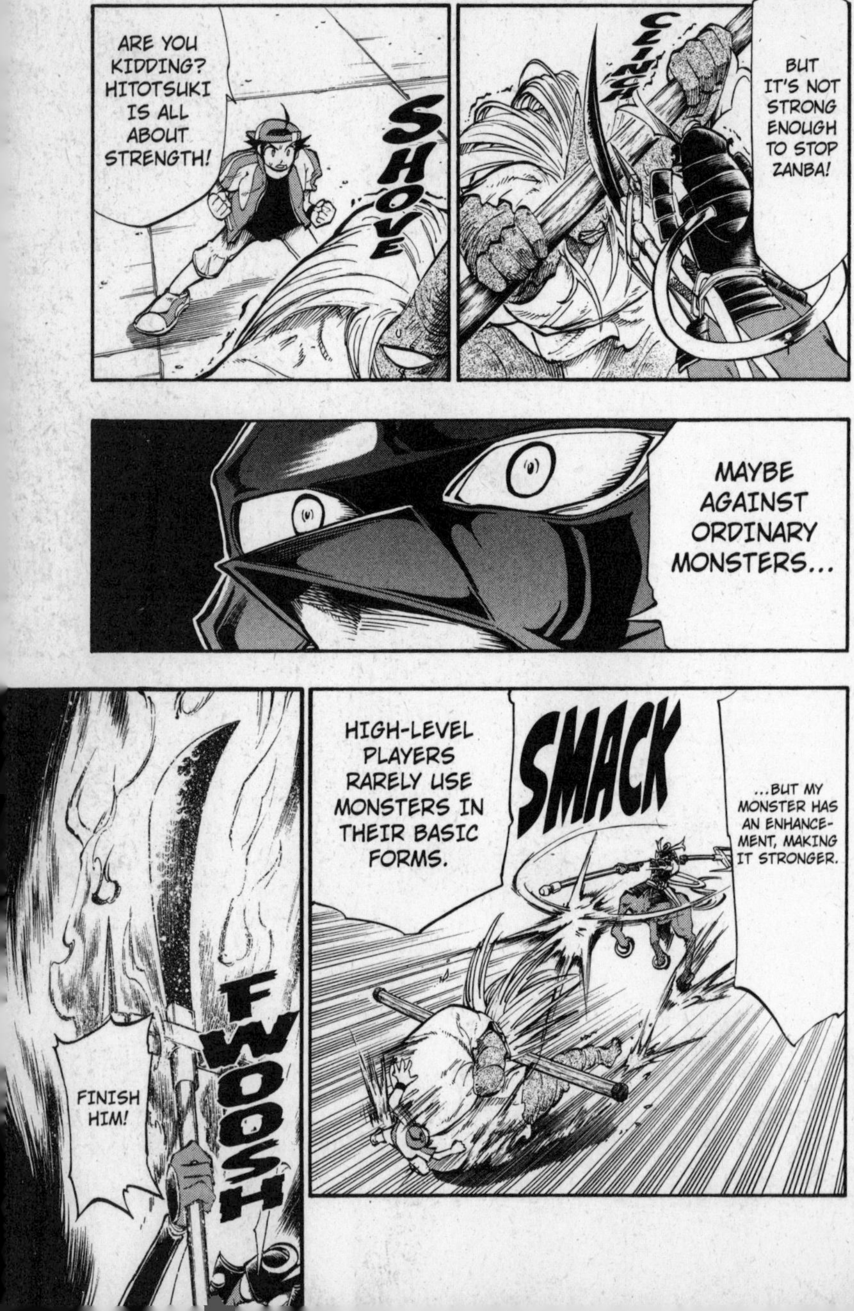
CLINCH
BUT IT'S NOT STRONG ENOUGH TO STOP ZANBA!
SHOVE
ARE YOU KIDDING? HITOTSUKI IS ALL ABOUT STRENGTH!
MAYBE AGAINST ORDINARY MONSTERS...
SMACK
...BUT MY MONSTER HAS AN ENHANCEMENT, MAKING IT STRONGER.
HIGH-LEVEL PLAYERS RARELY USE MONSTERS IN THEIR BASIC FORMS.
FWOOSH
FINISH HIM!

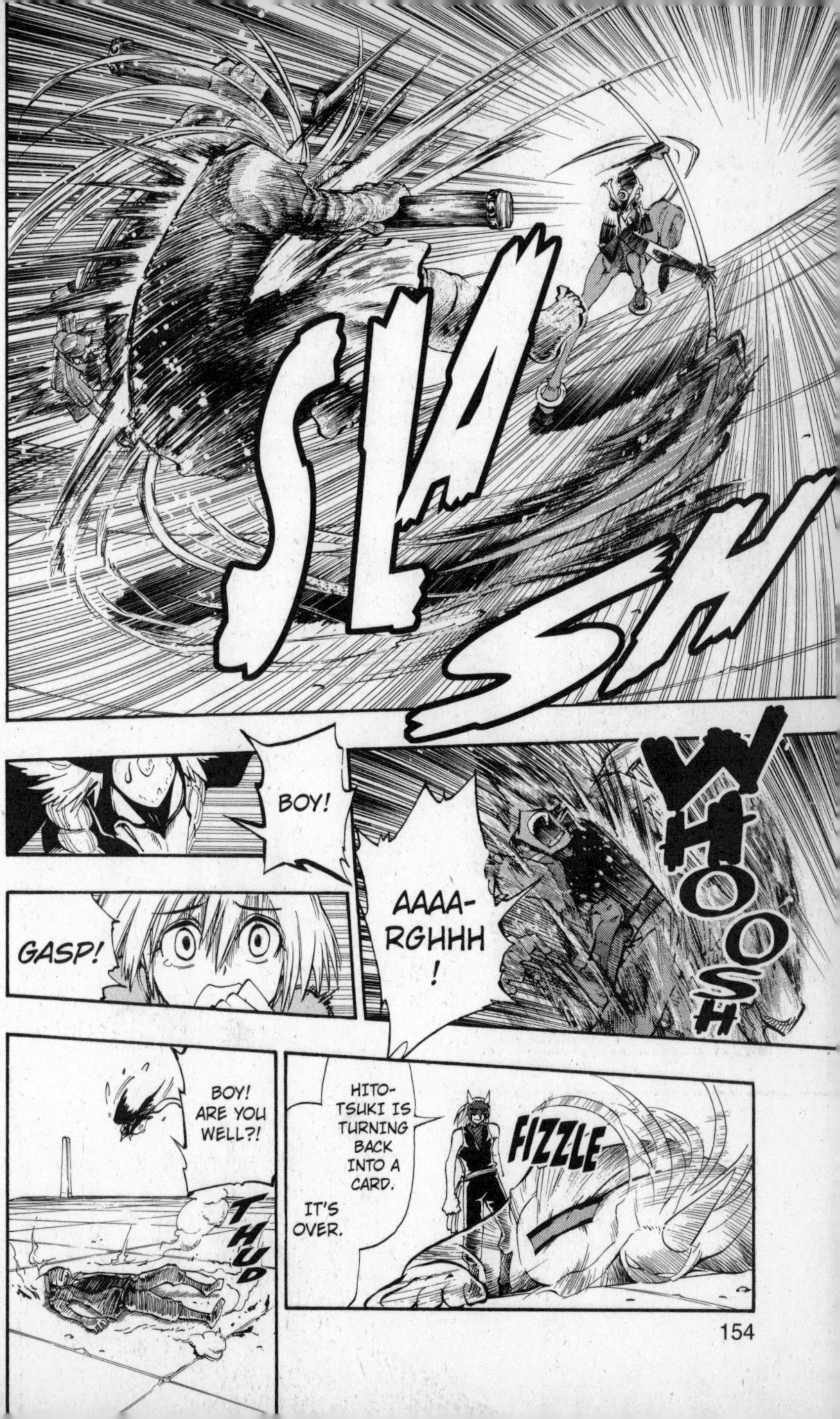
SLASH
WHOOSH
AAAA-RGHHH!
BOY!
GASP!
HITO-TSUKI IS TURNING BACK INTO A CARD.
IT'S OVER.
FIZZLE
BOY! ARE YOU WELL?!
THUD

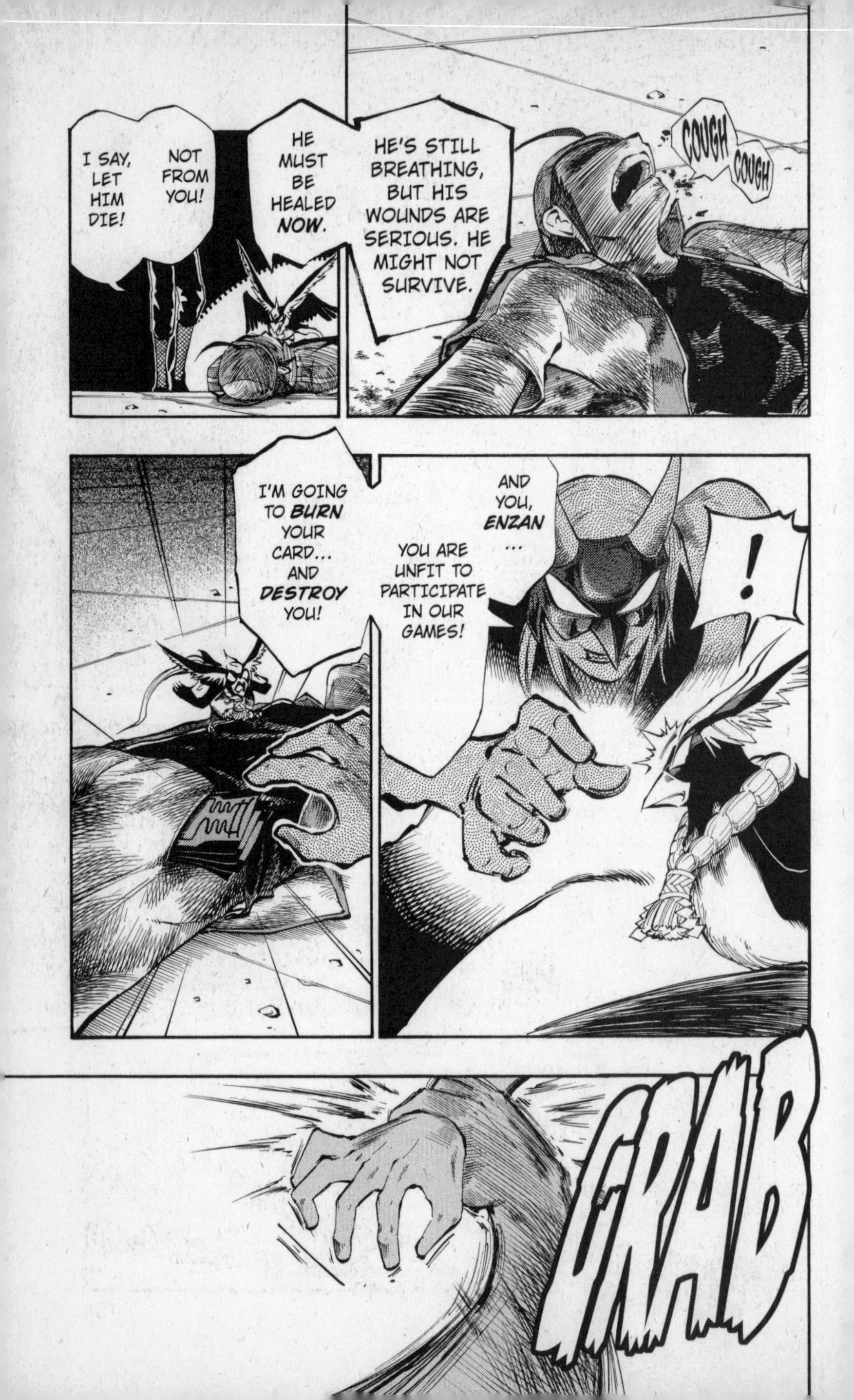
COUGH
COUGH
HE'S STILL BREATHING, BUT HIS WOUNDS ARE SERIOUS. HE MIGHT NOT SURVIVE.
HE MUST BE HEALED *NOW*.
NOT FROM YOU!
I SAY, LET HIM DIE!
AND YOU, *ENZAN*...
YOU ARE UNFIT TO PARTICIPATE IN OUR GAMES!
!
I'M GOING TO *BURN* YOUR CARD... AND *DESTROY* YOU!
GRAB

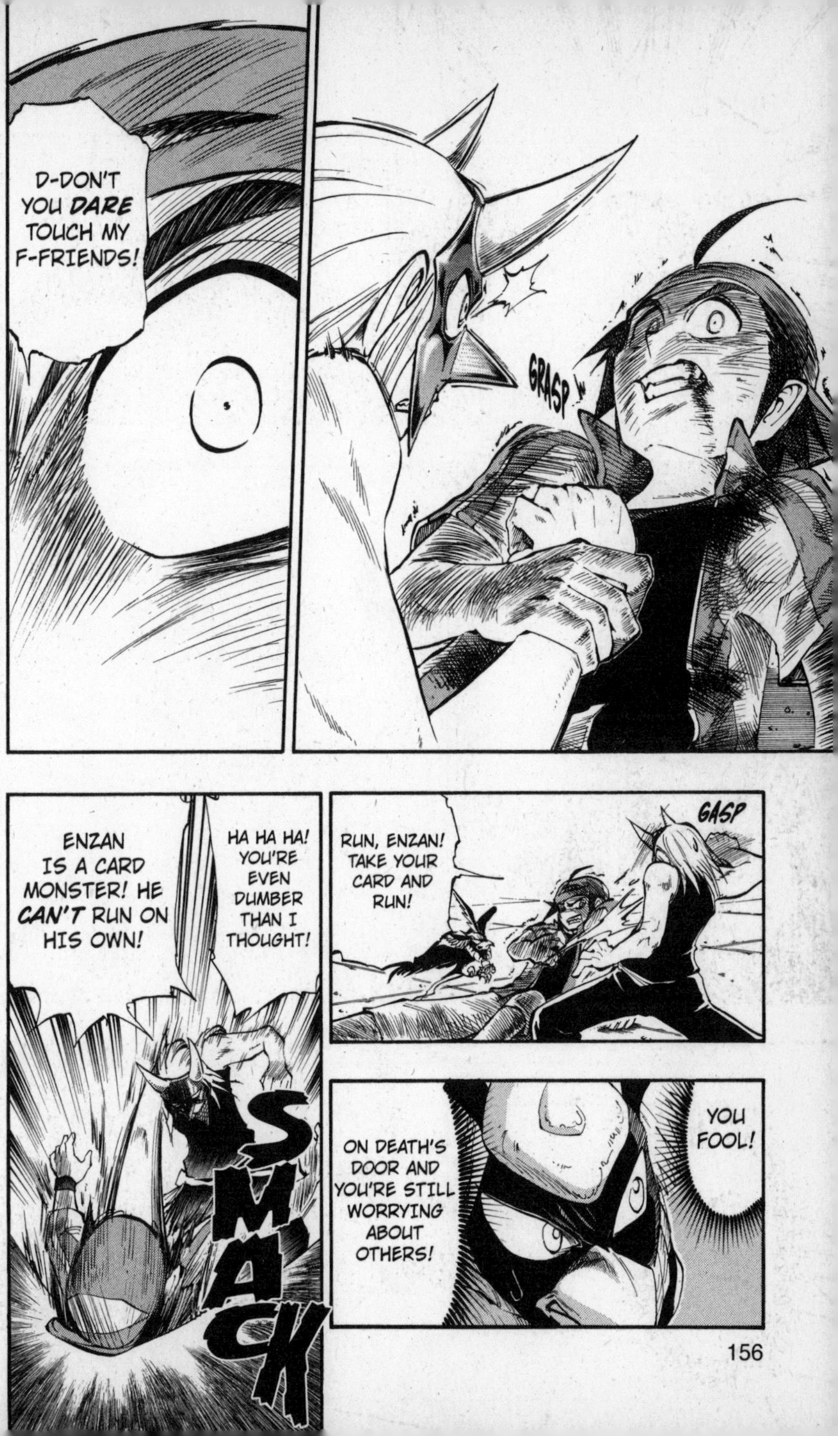
GRASP
D-DON'T YOU DARE TOUCH MY F-FRIENDS!
GASP
RUN, ENZAN! TAKE YOUR CARD AND RUN!
YOU FOOL!
ON DEATH'S DOOR AND YOU'RE STILL WORRYING ABOUT OTHERS!
HA HA HA! YOU'RE EVEN DUMBER THAN I THOUGHT!
ENZAN IS A CARD MONSTER! HE CAN'T RUN ON HIS OWN!
SMACK

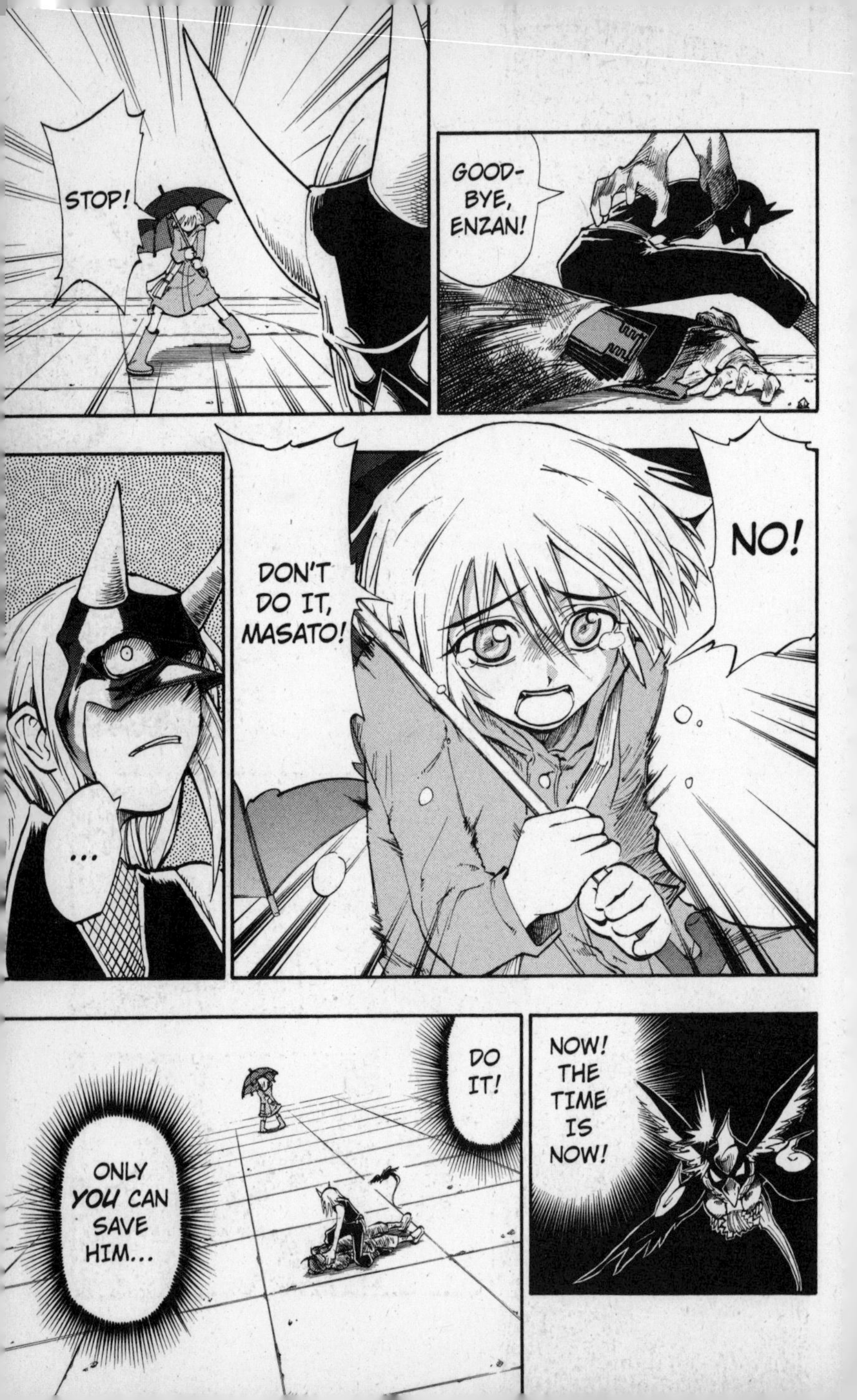
GOOD-BYE, ENZAN!
STOP!
NO!
DON'T DO IT, MASATO!
...
NOW! THE TIME IS NOW!
DO IT!
ONLY *YOU* CAN SAVE HIM...

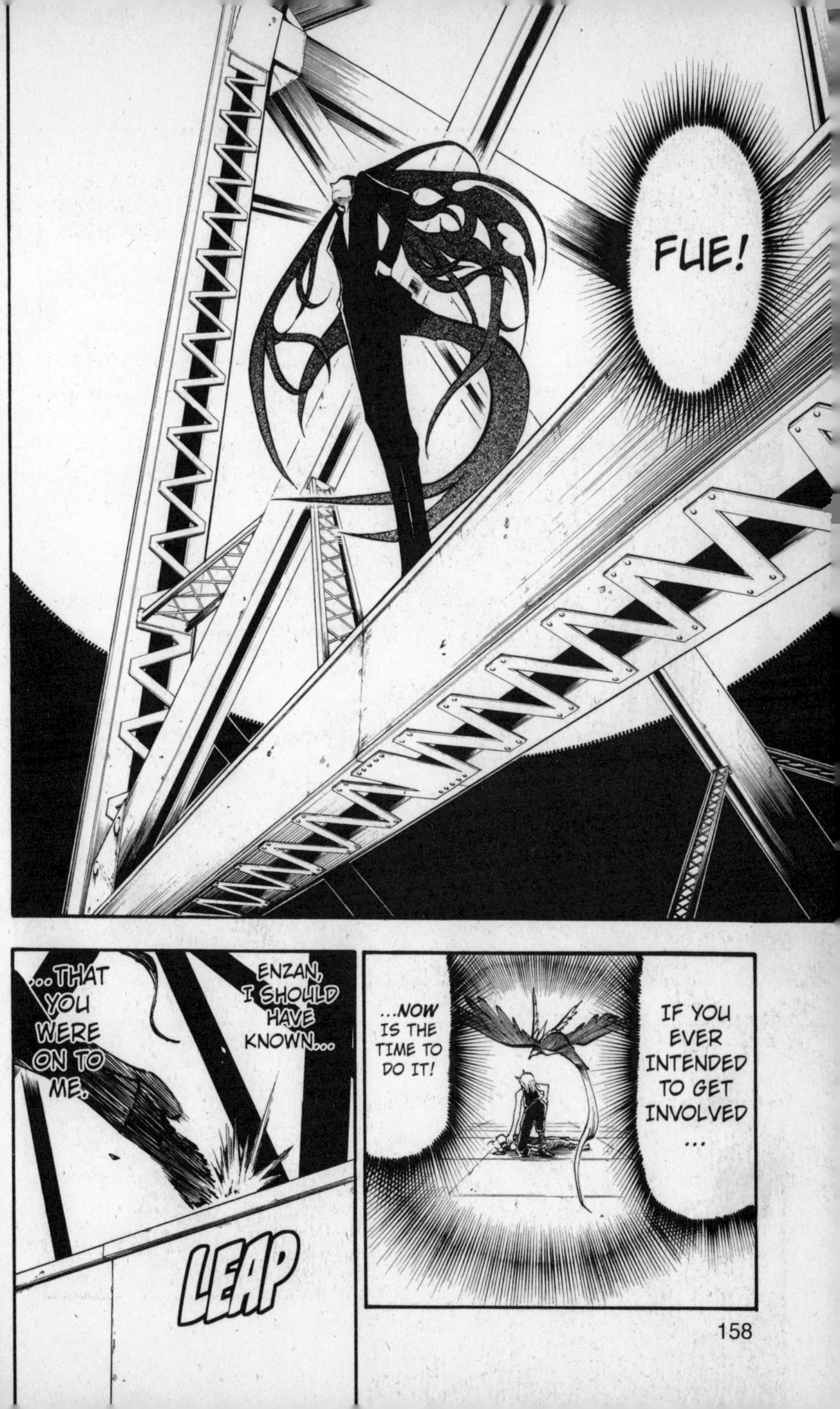
FUE!
IF YOU EVER INTENDED TO GET INVOLVED ...
...NOW IS THE TIME TO DO IT!
ENZAN, I SHOULD HAVE KNOWN...
...THAT YOU WERE ON TO ME.
LEAP

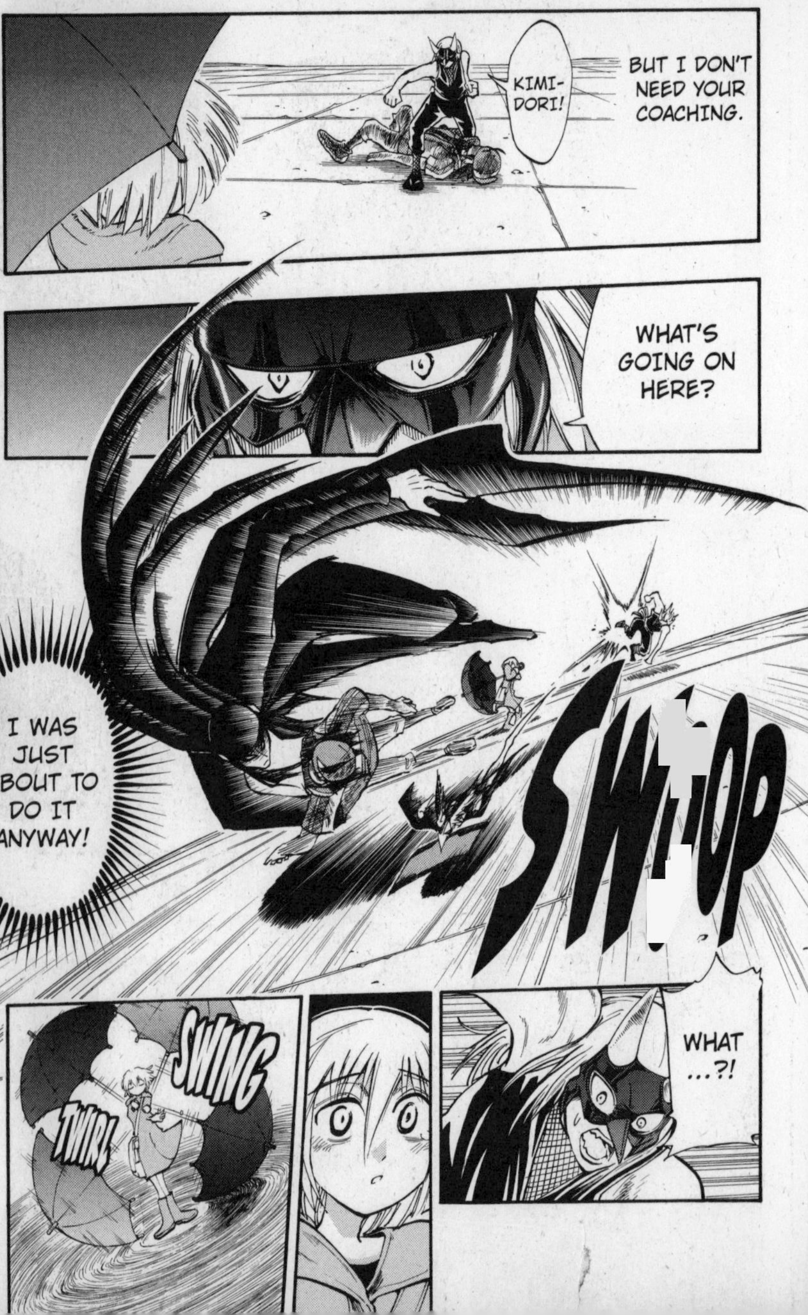
BUT I DON'T NEED YOUR COACHING.
KIMI-DORI!
WHAT'S GOING ON HERE?
I WAS JUST ABOUT TO DO IT ANYWAY!
WHAT ...?!
SWING
TWIRL

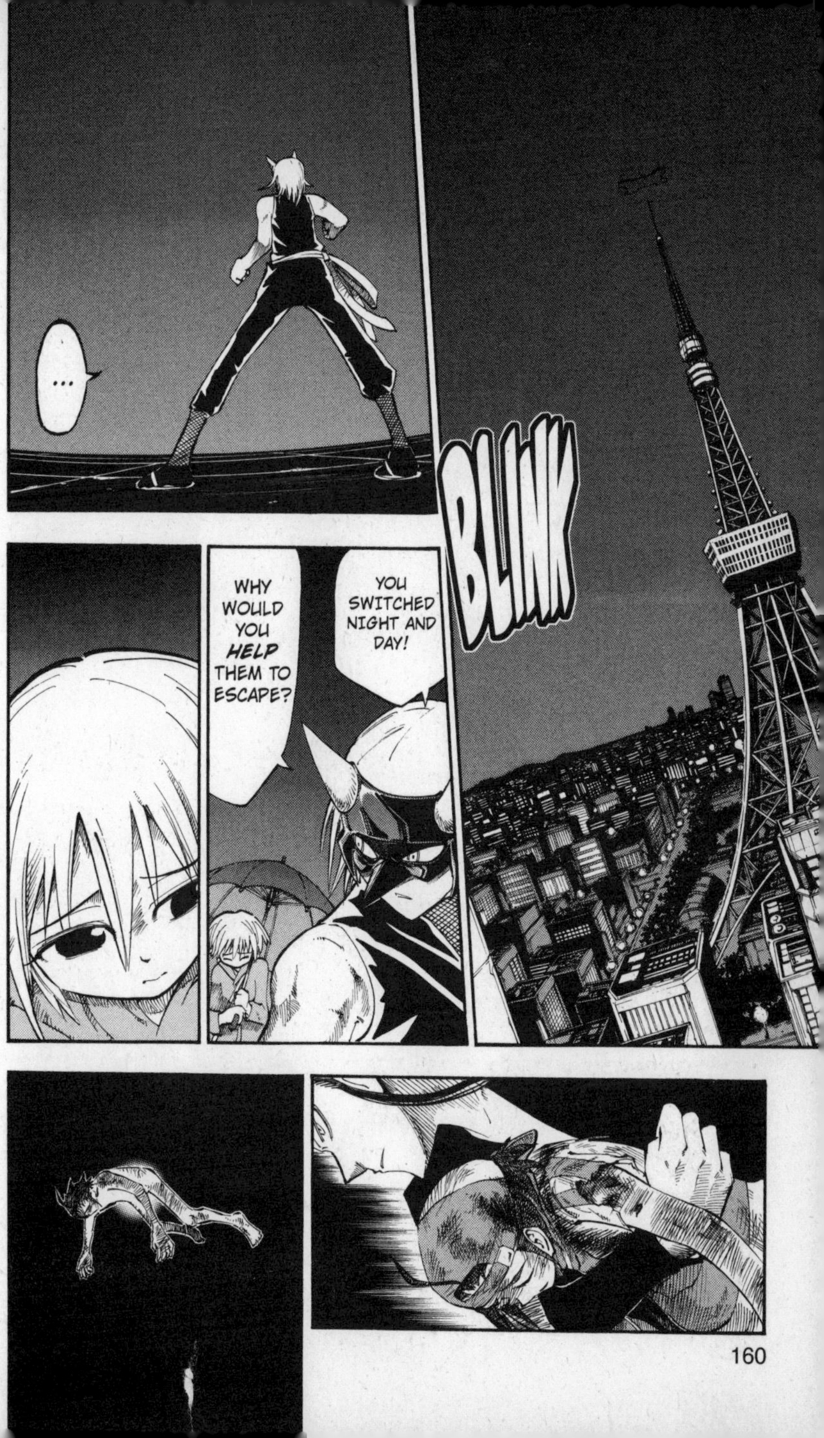
BLINK
...
YOU SWITCHED NIGHT AND DAY!
WHY WOULD YOU HELP THEM TO ESCAPE?

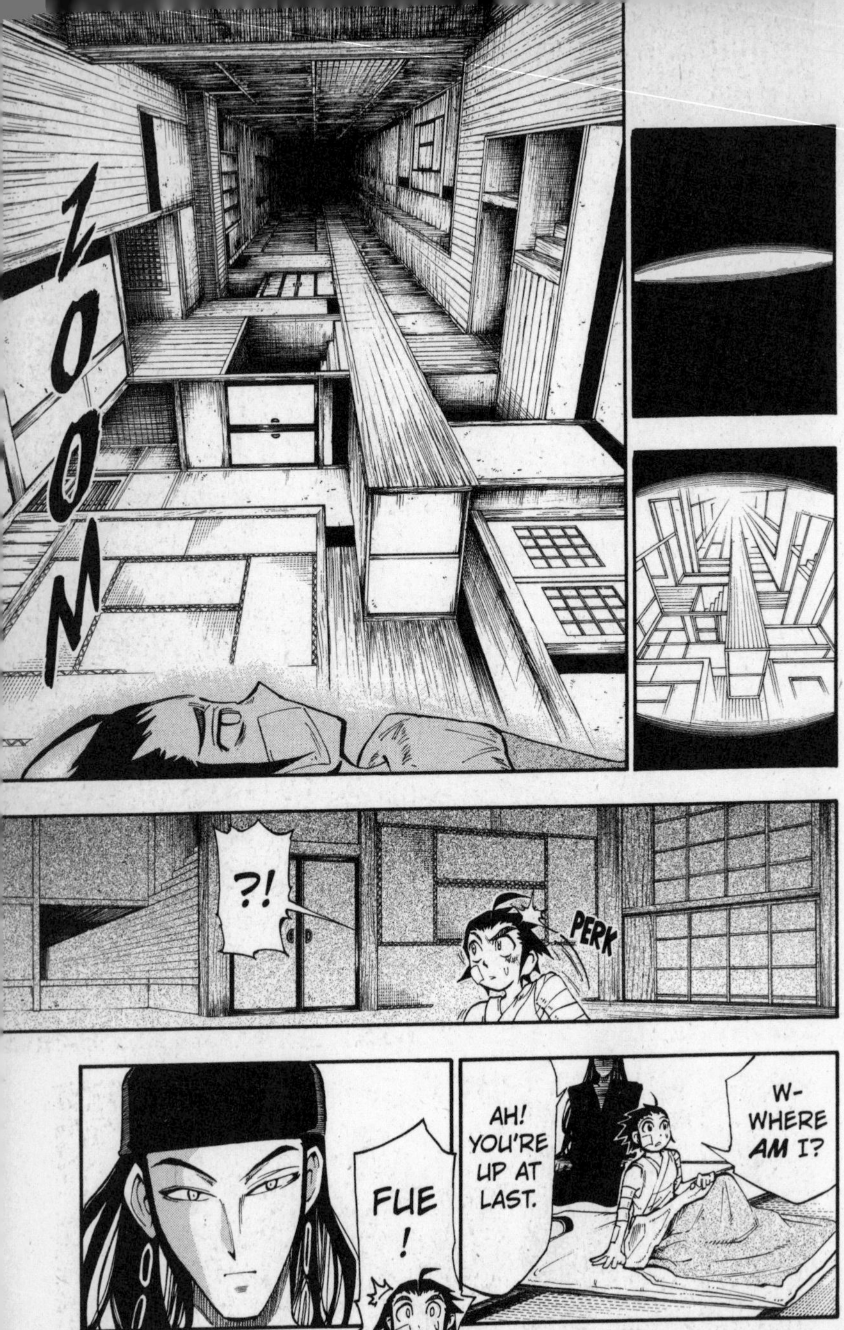
ZOOM
?!
PERK
W-WHERE AM I?
AH! YOU'RE UP AT LAST.
FUE!

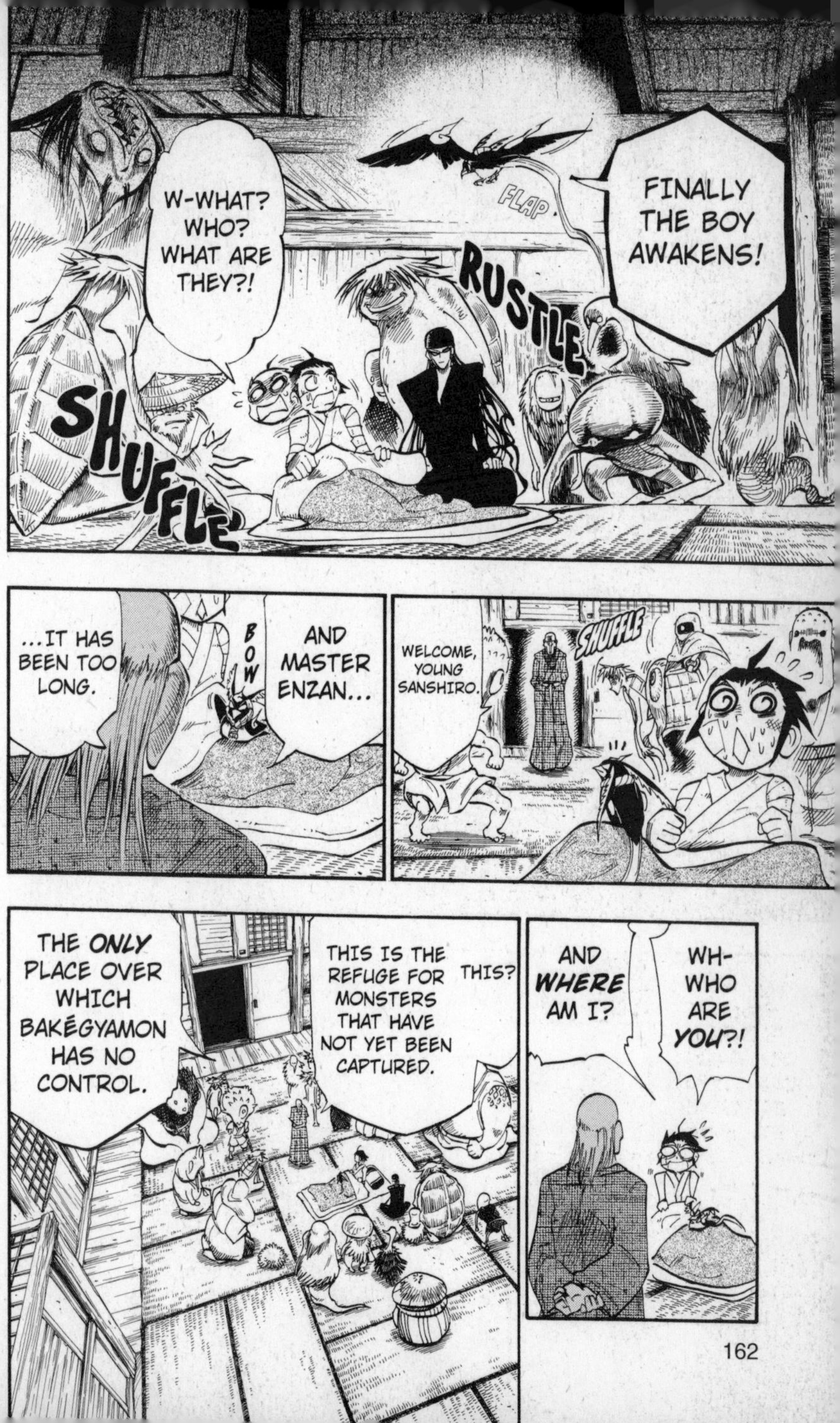
FINALLY THE BOY AWAKENS!
FLAP
RUSTLE
W-WHAT? WHO? WHAT ARE THEY?!
SHUFFLE
SHUFFLE
WELCOME, YOUNG SANSHIRO.
AND MASTER ENZAN...
BOW
...IT HAS BEEN TOO LONG.
WH-WHO ARE YOU?!
AND WHERE AM I?
THIS?
THIS IS THE REFUGE FOR MONSTERS THAT HAVE NOT YET BEEN CAPTURED.
THE ONLY PLACE OVER WHICH BAKÉGYAMON HAS NO CONTROL.

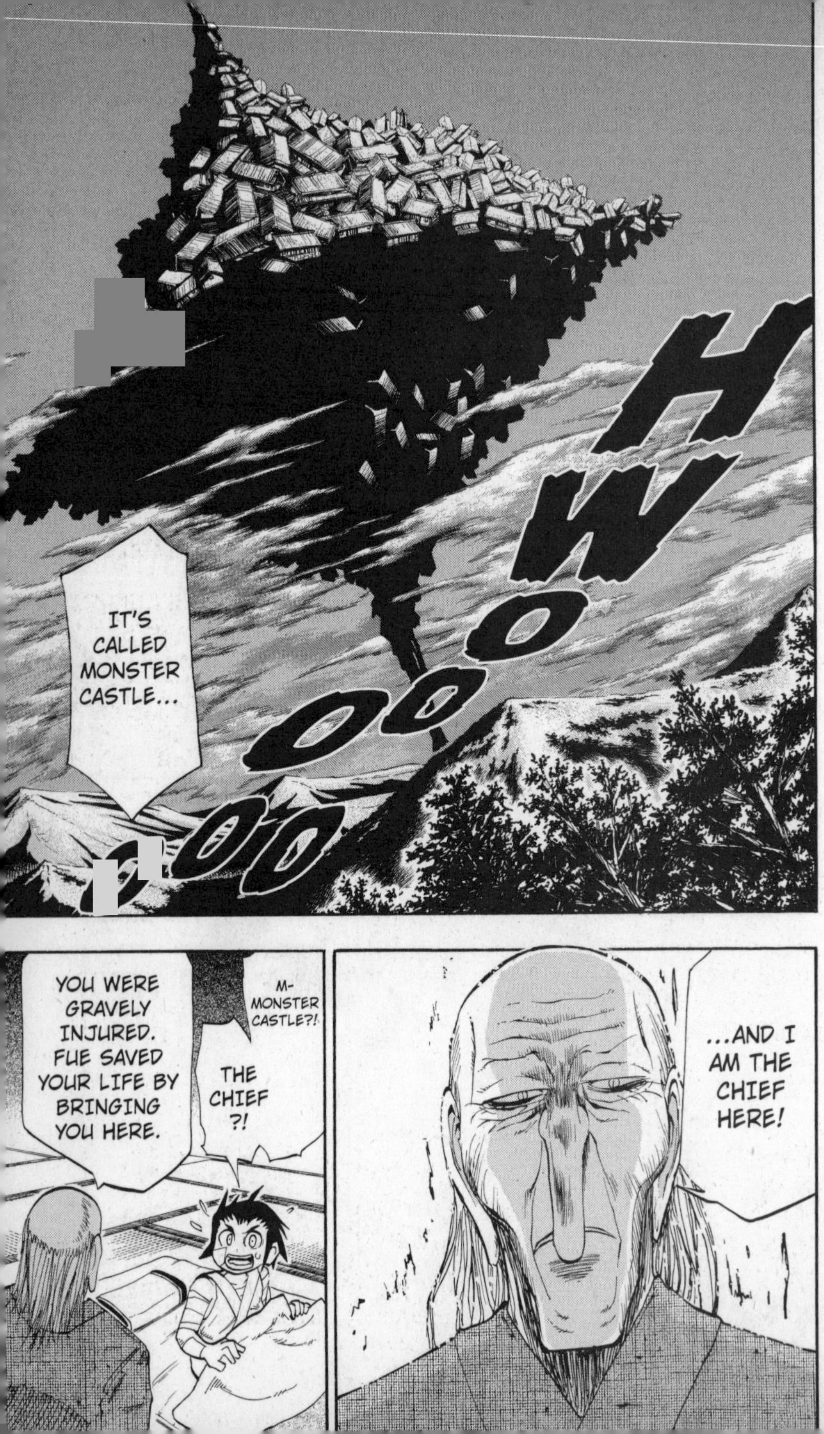
HWOOOOOO
IT'S CALLED MONSTER CASTLE...
...AND I AM THE CHIEF HERE!
M-MONSTER CASTLE?!
YOU WERE GRAVELY INJURED. FUE SAVED YOUR LIFE BY BRINGING YOU HERE.
THE CHIEF ?!

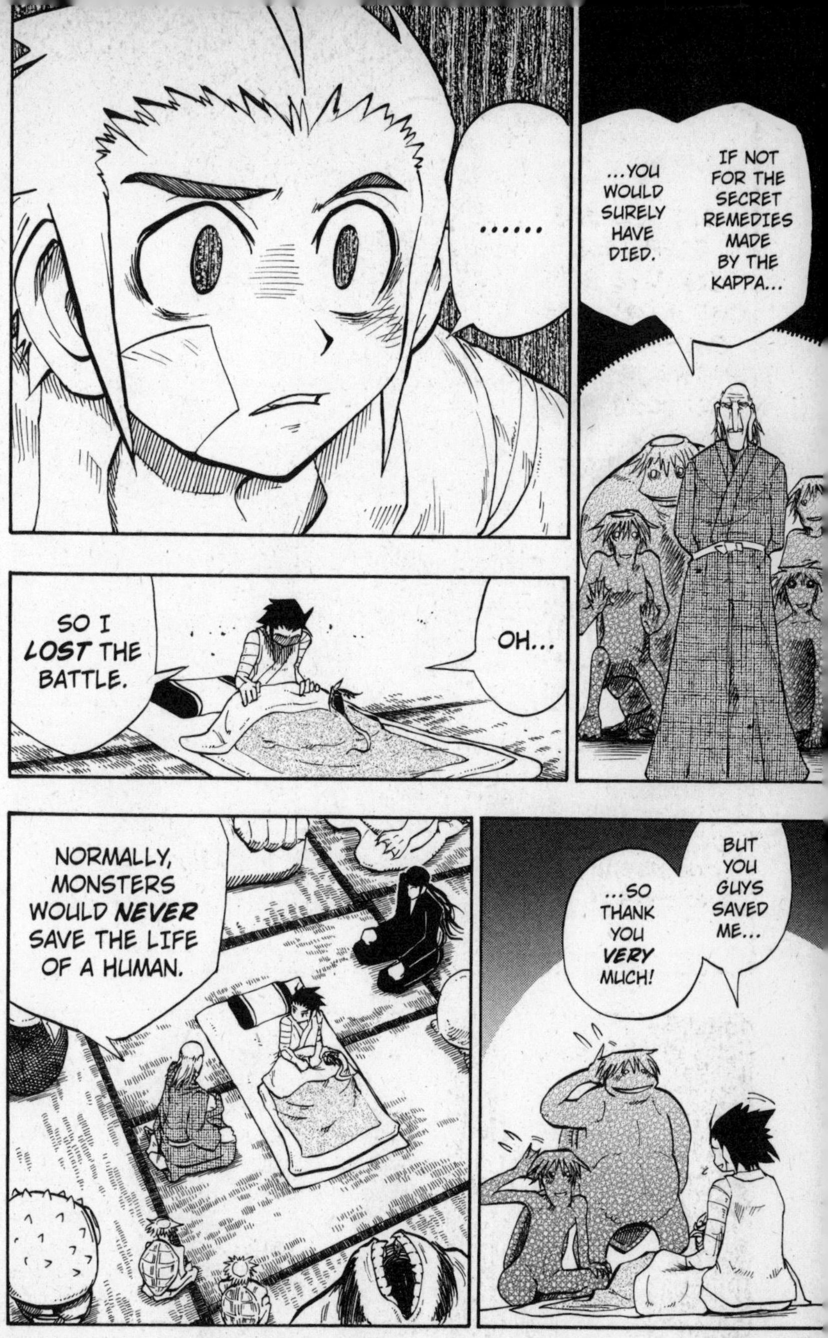
IF NOT FOR THE SECRET REMEDIES MADE BY THE KAPPA...
...YOU WOULD SURELY HAVE DIED.
......
OH...
SO I **LOST** THE BATTLE.
BUT YOU GUYS SAVED ME...
...SO THANK YOU **VERY** MUCH!
NORMALLY, MONSTERS WOULD **NEVER** SAVE THE LIFE OF A HUMAN.

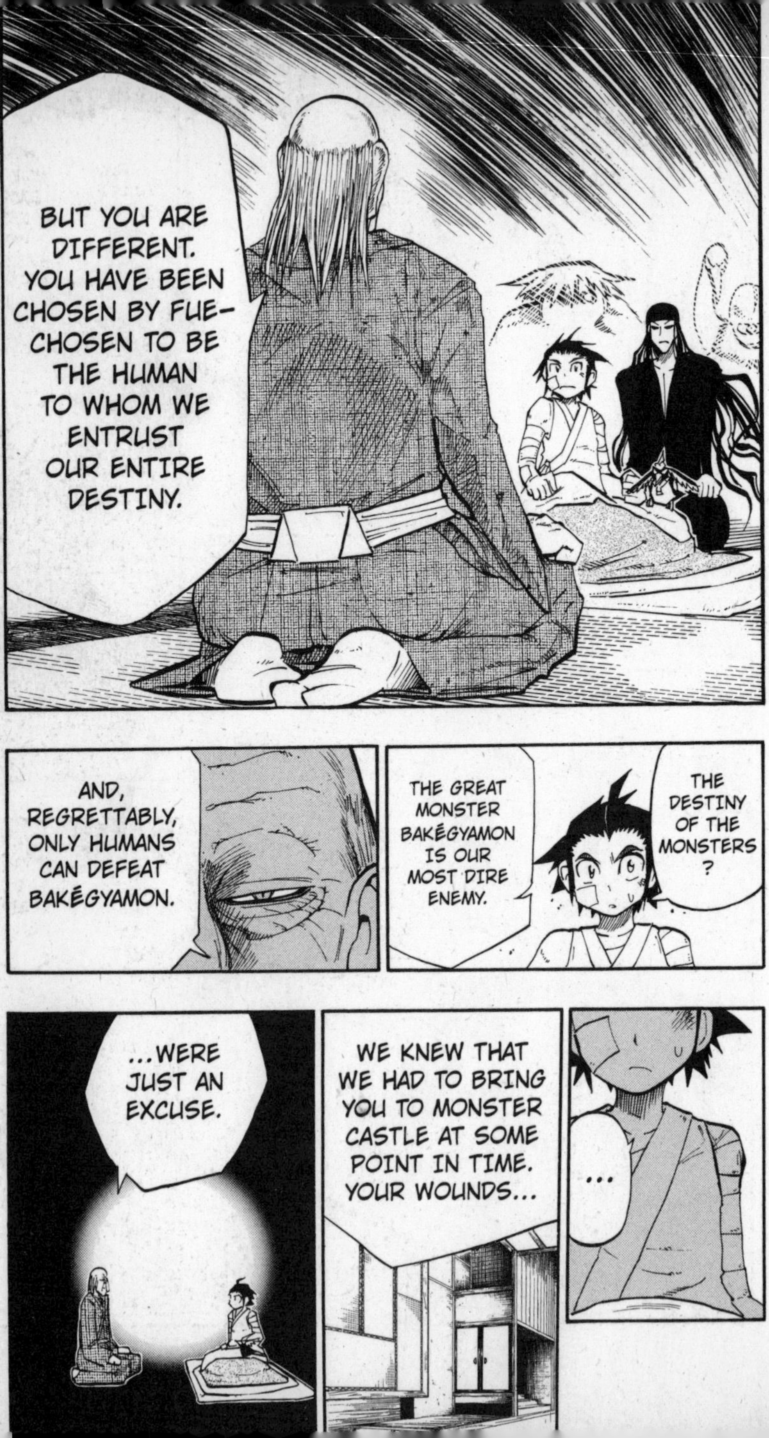
BUT YOU ARE DIFFERENT. YOU HAVE BEEN CHOSEN BY FUE-CHOSEN TO BE THE HUMAN TO WHOM WE ENTRUST OUR ENTIRE DESTINY.
THE DESTINY OF THE MONSTERS?
THE GREAT MONSTER BAKÉGYAMON IS OUR MOST DIRE ENEMY.
AND, REGRETTABLY, ONLY HUMANS CAN DEFEAT BAKÉGYAMON.
...
WE KNEW THAT WE HAD TO BRING YOU TO MONSTER CASTLE AT SOME POINT IN TIME. YOUR WOUNDS...
...WERE JUST AN EXCUSE.

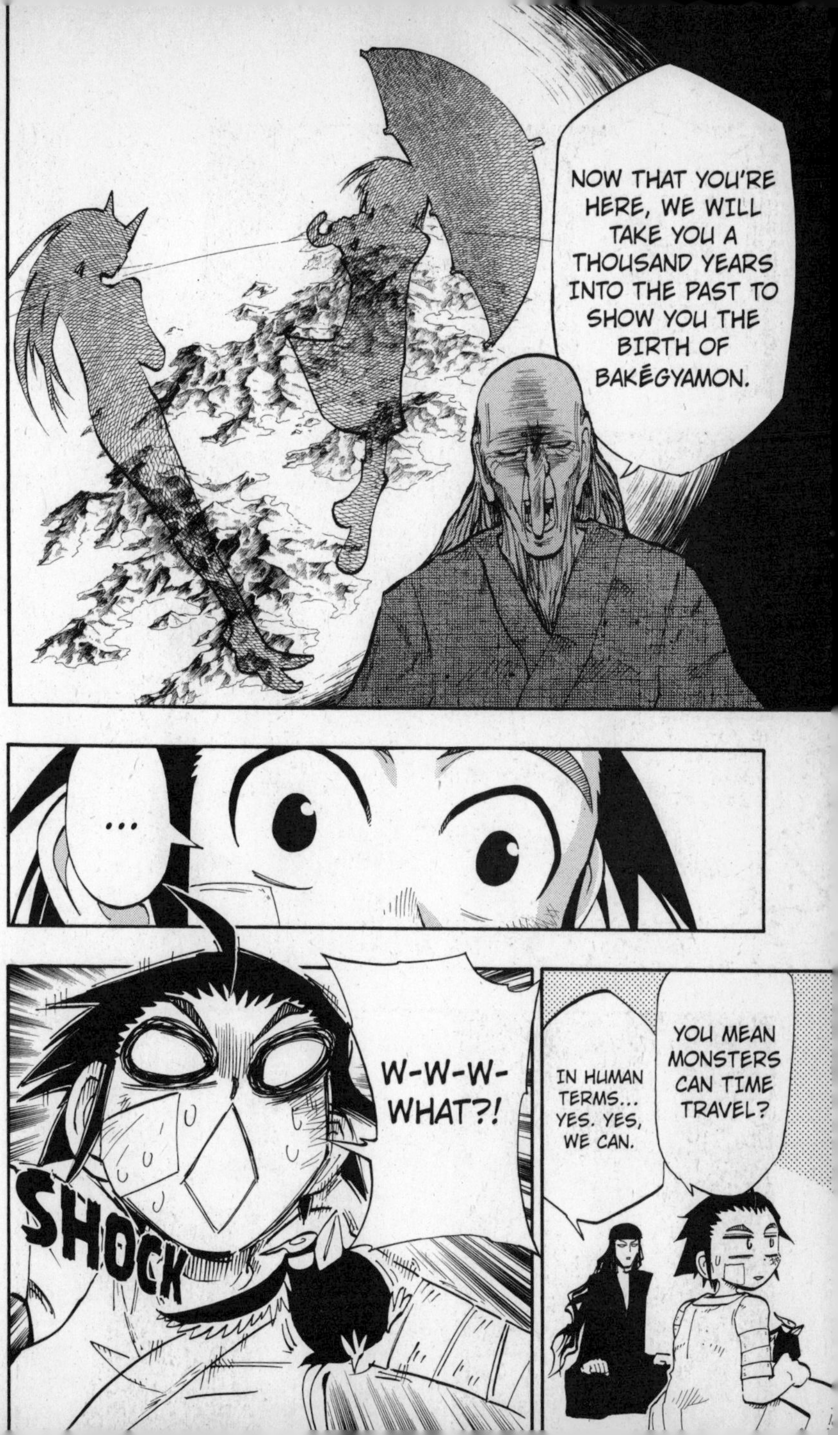
NOW THAT YOU'RE HERE, WE WILL TAKE YOU A THOUSAND YEARS INTO THE PAST TO SHOW YOU THE BIRTH OF BAKĒGYAMON.
...
YOU MEAN MONSTERS CAN TIME TRAVEL?
IN HUMAN TERMS... YES. YES, WE CAN.
W-W-W-WHAT?!
SHOCK

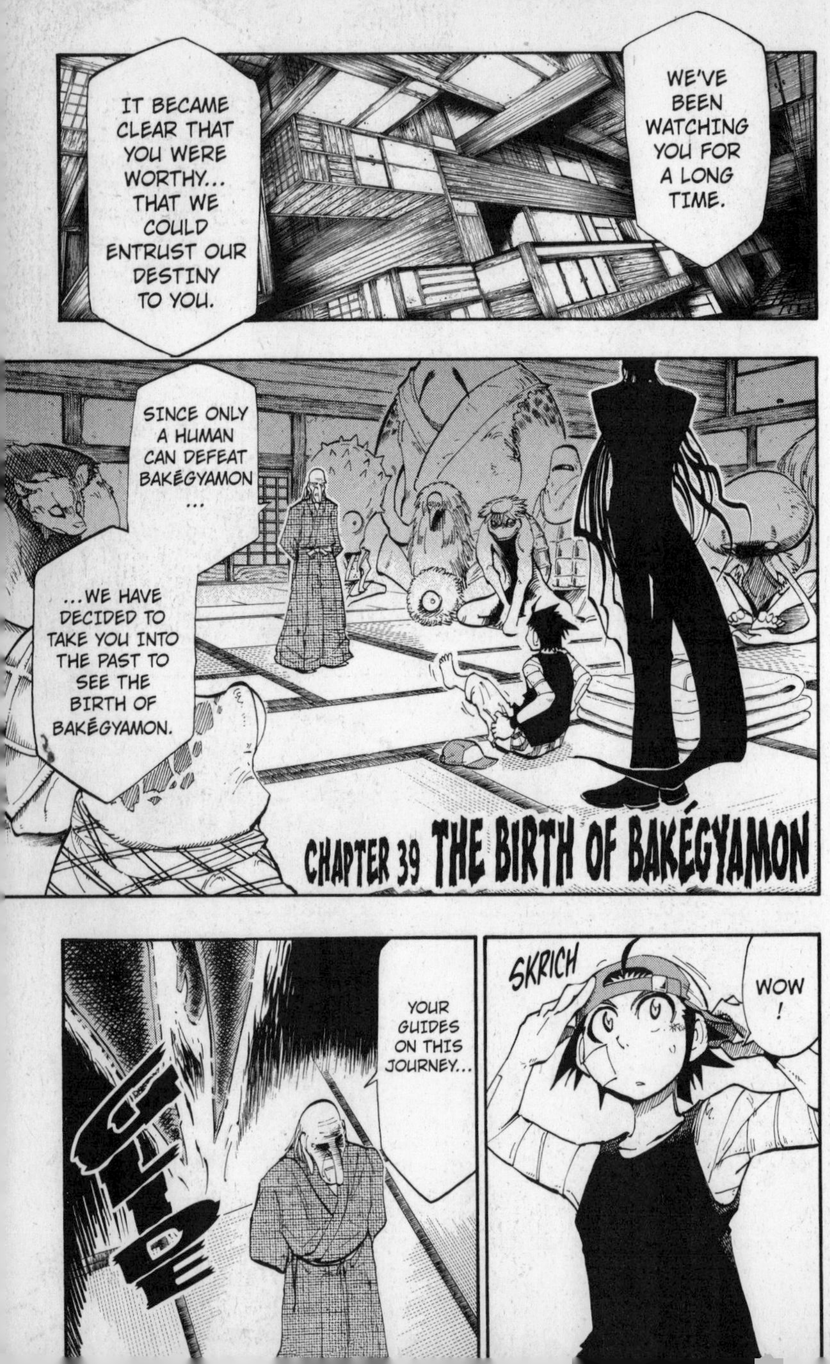
WE'VE BEEN WATCHING YOU FOR A LONG TIME.
IT BECAME CLEAR THAT YOU WERE WORTHY... THAT WE COULD ENTRUST OUR DESTINY TO YOU.
SINCE ONLY A HUMAN CAN DEFEAT BAKÉGYAMON...
...WE HAVE DECIDED TO TAKE YOU INTO THE PAST TO SEE THE BIRTH OF BAKÉGYAMON.
CHAPTER 39 THE BIRTH OF BAKÉGYAMON
SKRICH
WOW!
YOUR GUIDES ON THIS JOURNEY...

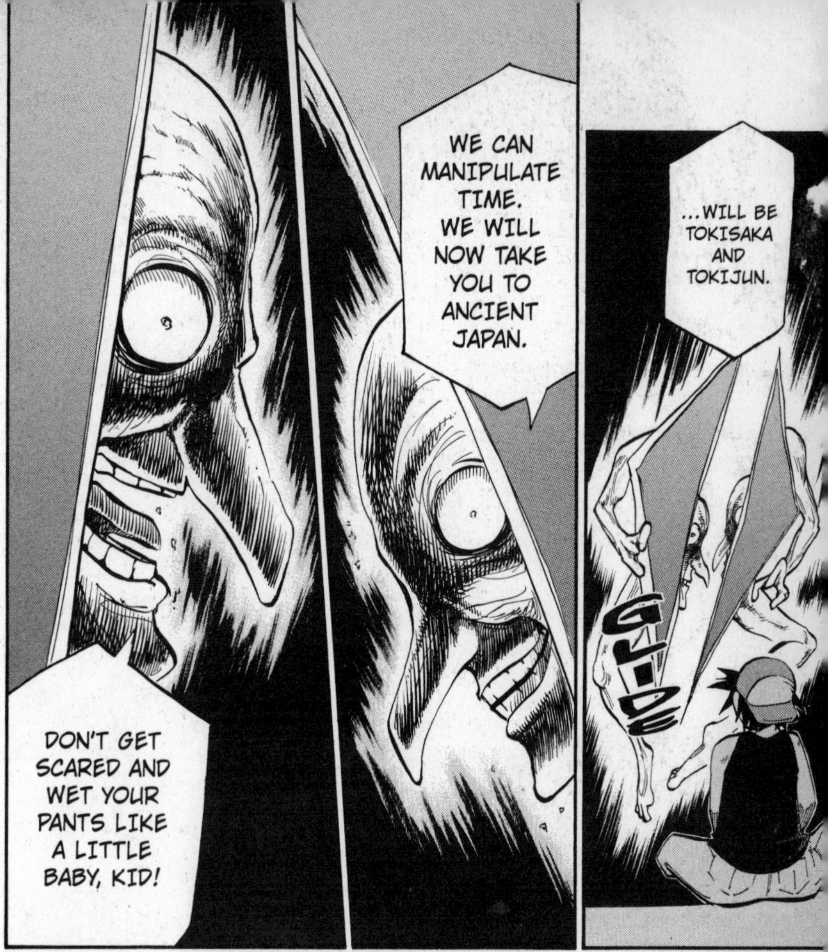
...WILL BE TOKISAKA AND TOKIJUN.
GLIDE
WE CAN MANIPULATE TIME. WE WILL NOW TAKE YOU TO ANCIENT JAPAN.
DON'T GET SCARED AND WET YOUR PANTS LIKE A LITTLE BABY, KID!

"TOKI" MEANS "TIME" IN JAPANESE, "SAKA" MEANS "REVERSE," AND "JUN" MEANS "ORDER."

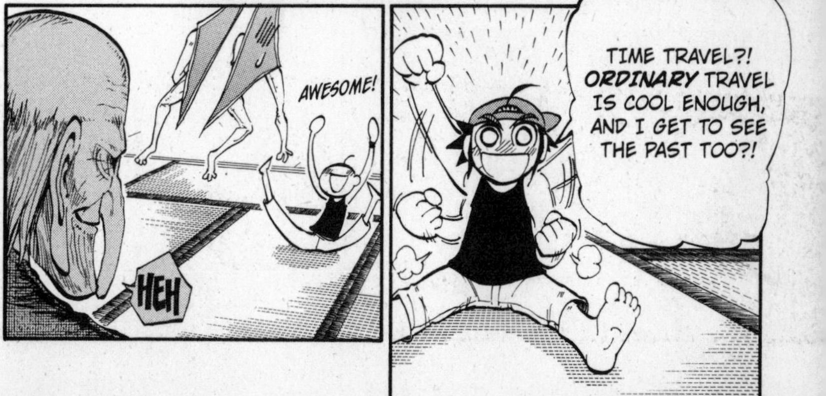
TIME TRAVEL?! ***ORDINARY*** TRAVEL IS COOL ENOUGH, AND I GET TO SEE THE PAST TOO?!
AWESOME!
HEH

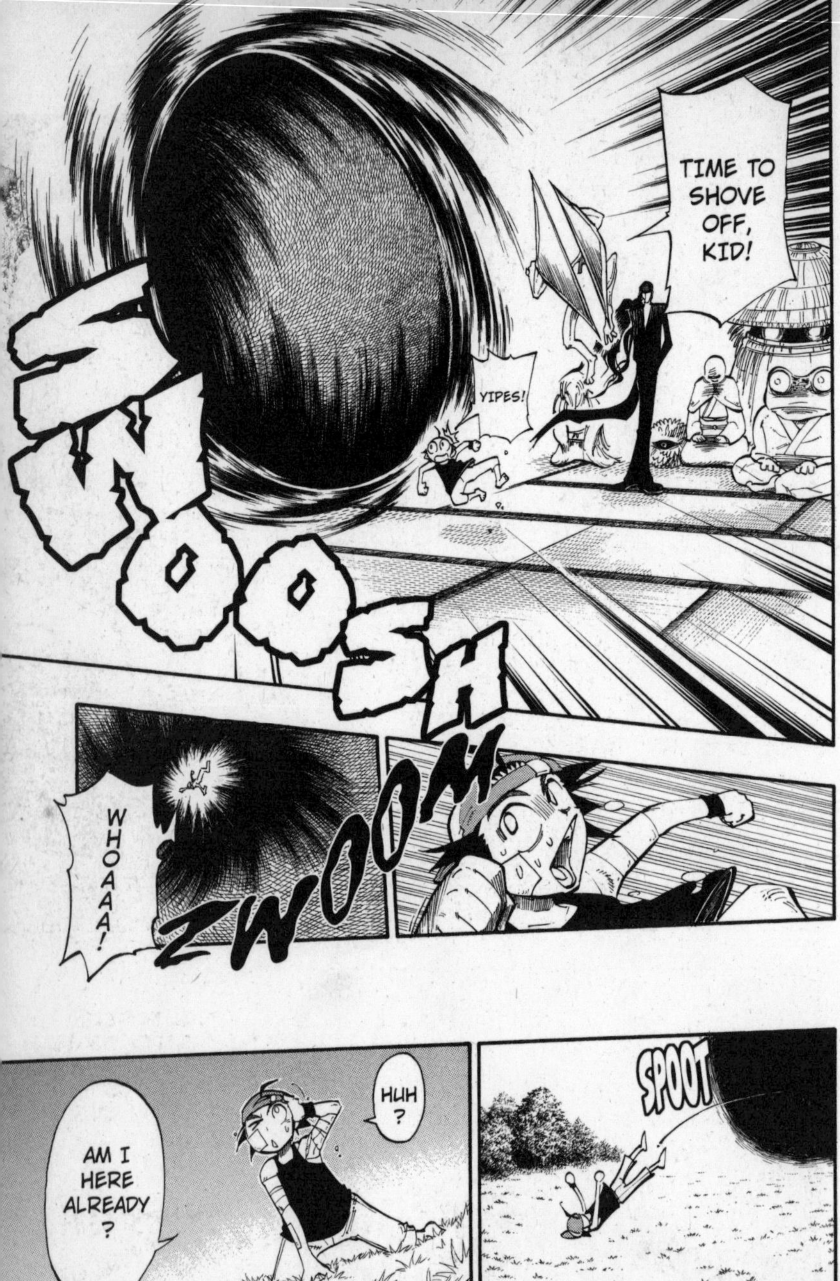
TIME TO SHOVE OFF, KID!
YIPES!
ZOOOSH
ZWOOM
WHOAAAA!
SPOOT
HUH?
AM I HERE ALREADY?

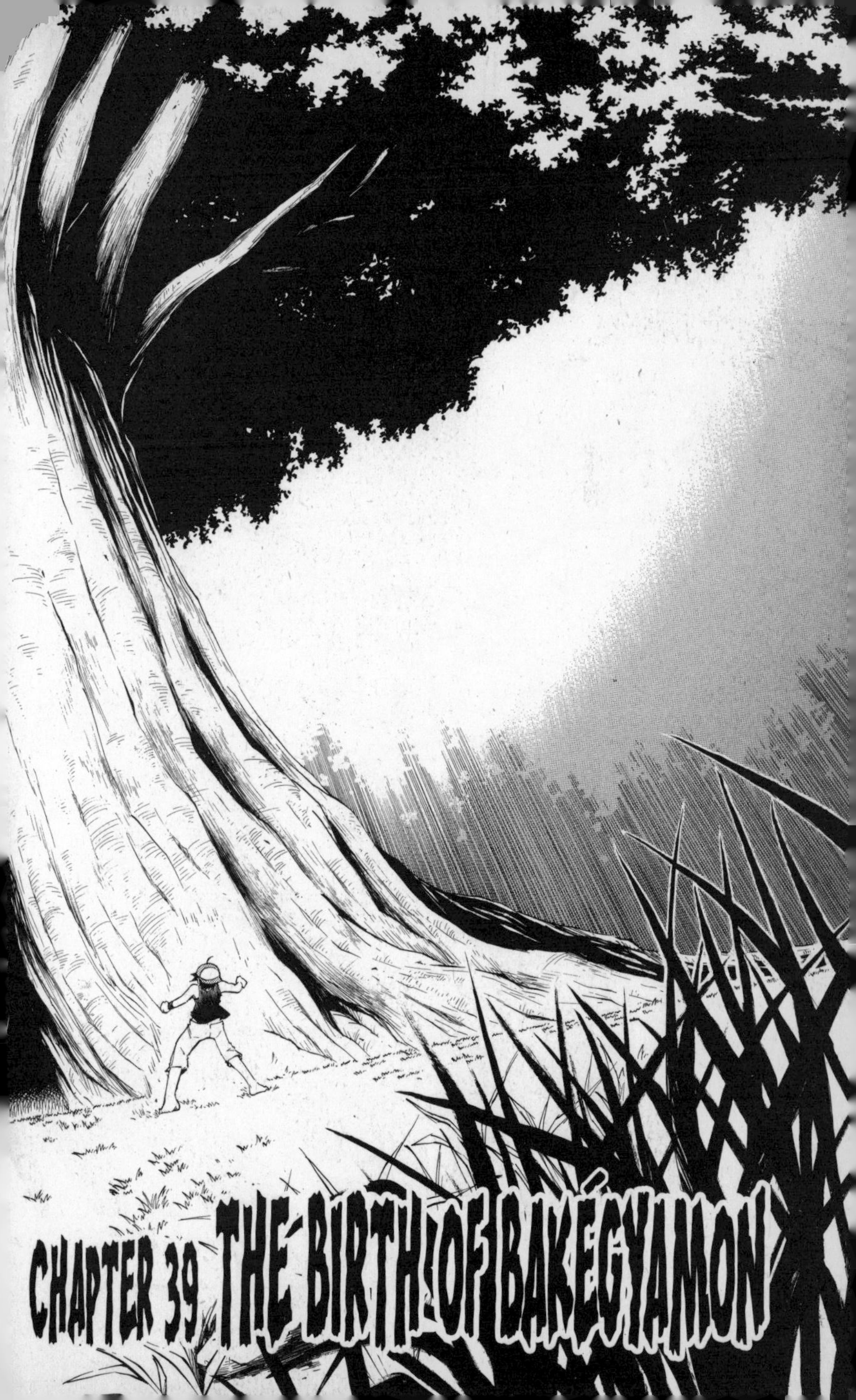
CHAPTER 39 THE BIRTH OF BAKÉGYAMON

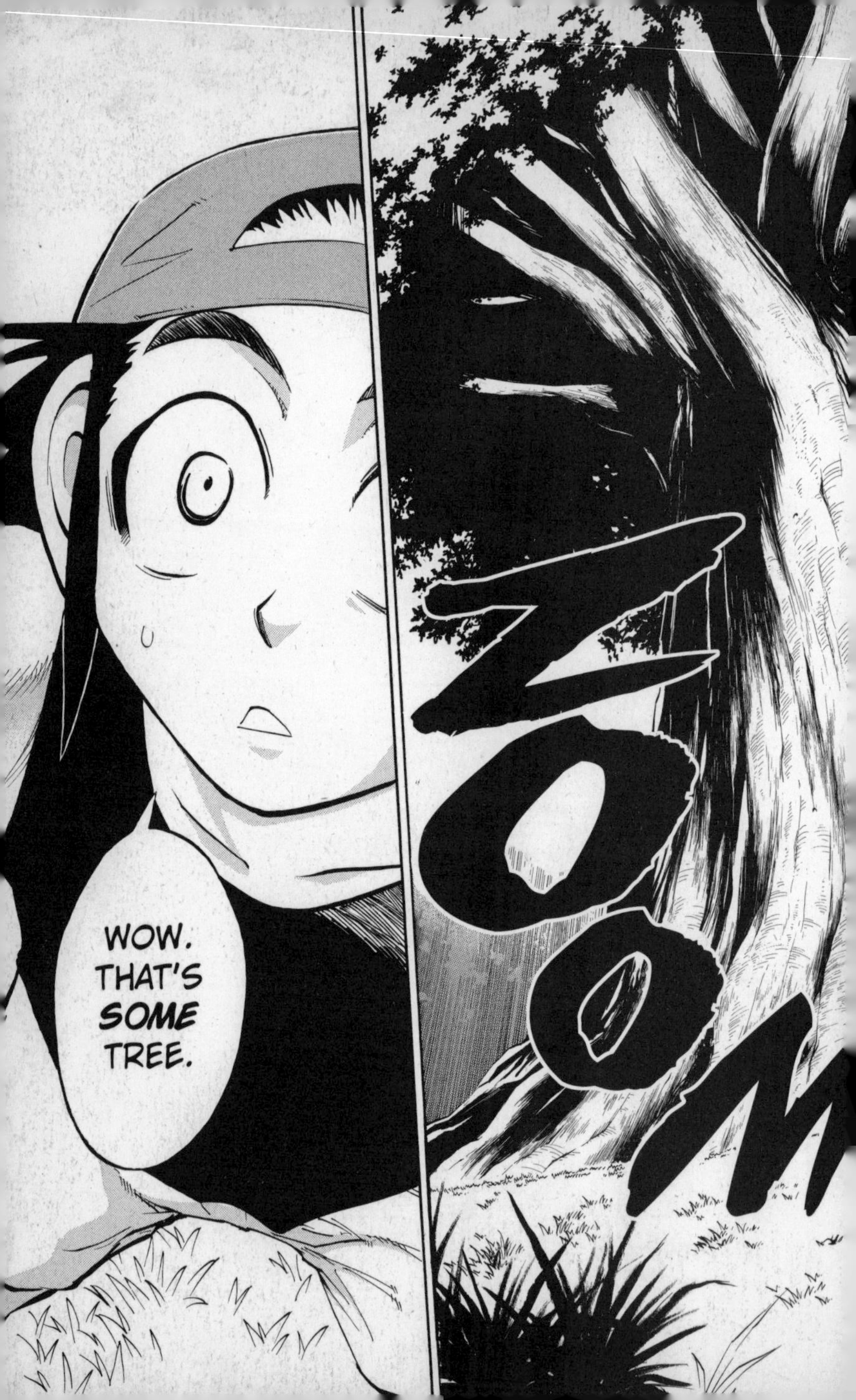
ZOOM
WOW. THAT'S **SOME** TREE.

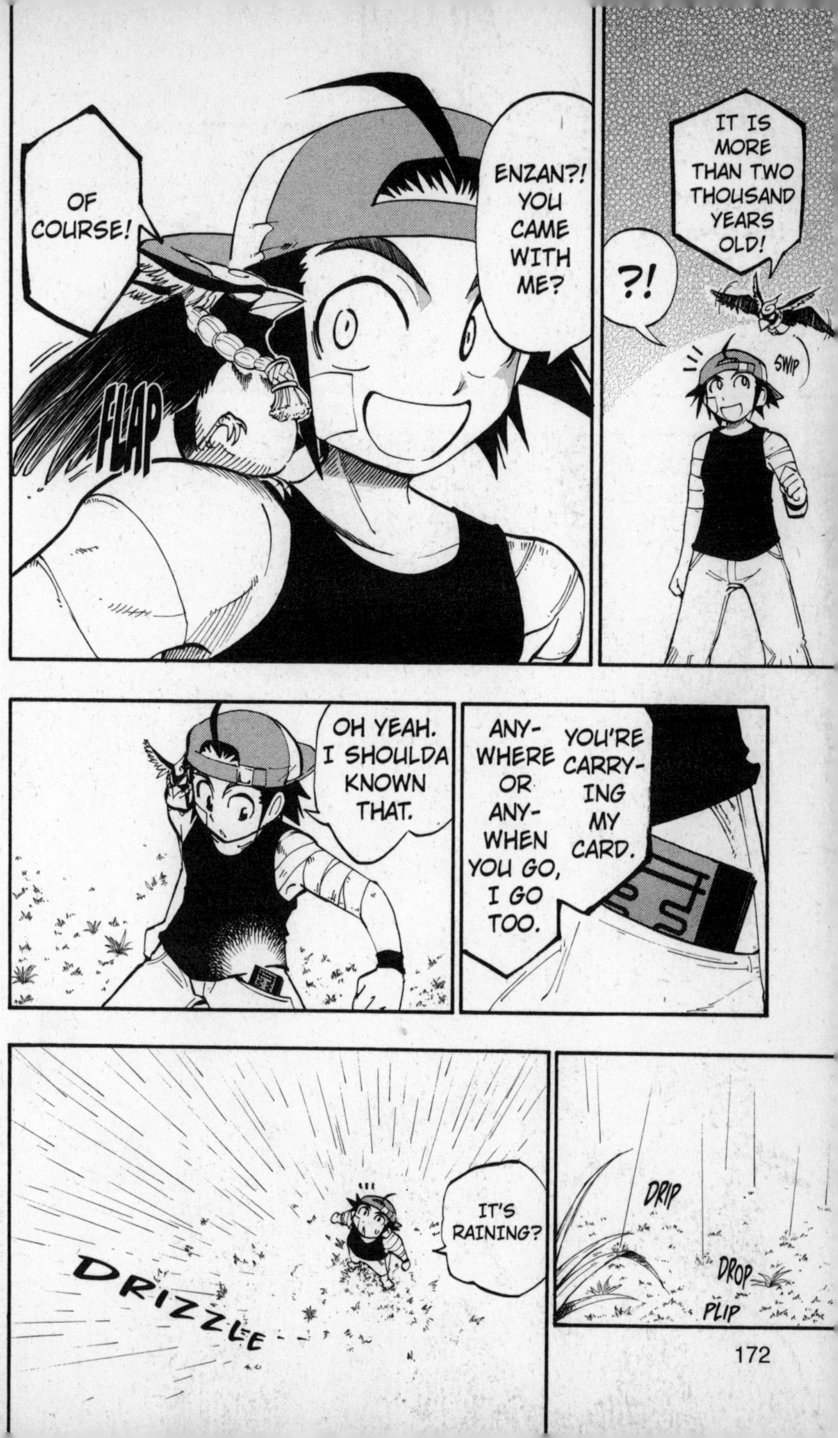
IT IS MORE THAN TWO THOUSAND YEARS OLD!
?!
SWIP
ENZAN?! YOU CAME WITH ME?
OF COURSE!
FLAP
YOU'RE CARRY-ING MY CARD.
ANY-WHERE OR ANY-WHEN YOU GO, I GO TOO.
OH YEAH. I SHOULDA KNOWN THAT.
DRIP
DROP
PLIP
IT'S RAINING?
DRIZZLEE

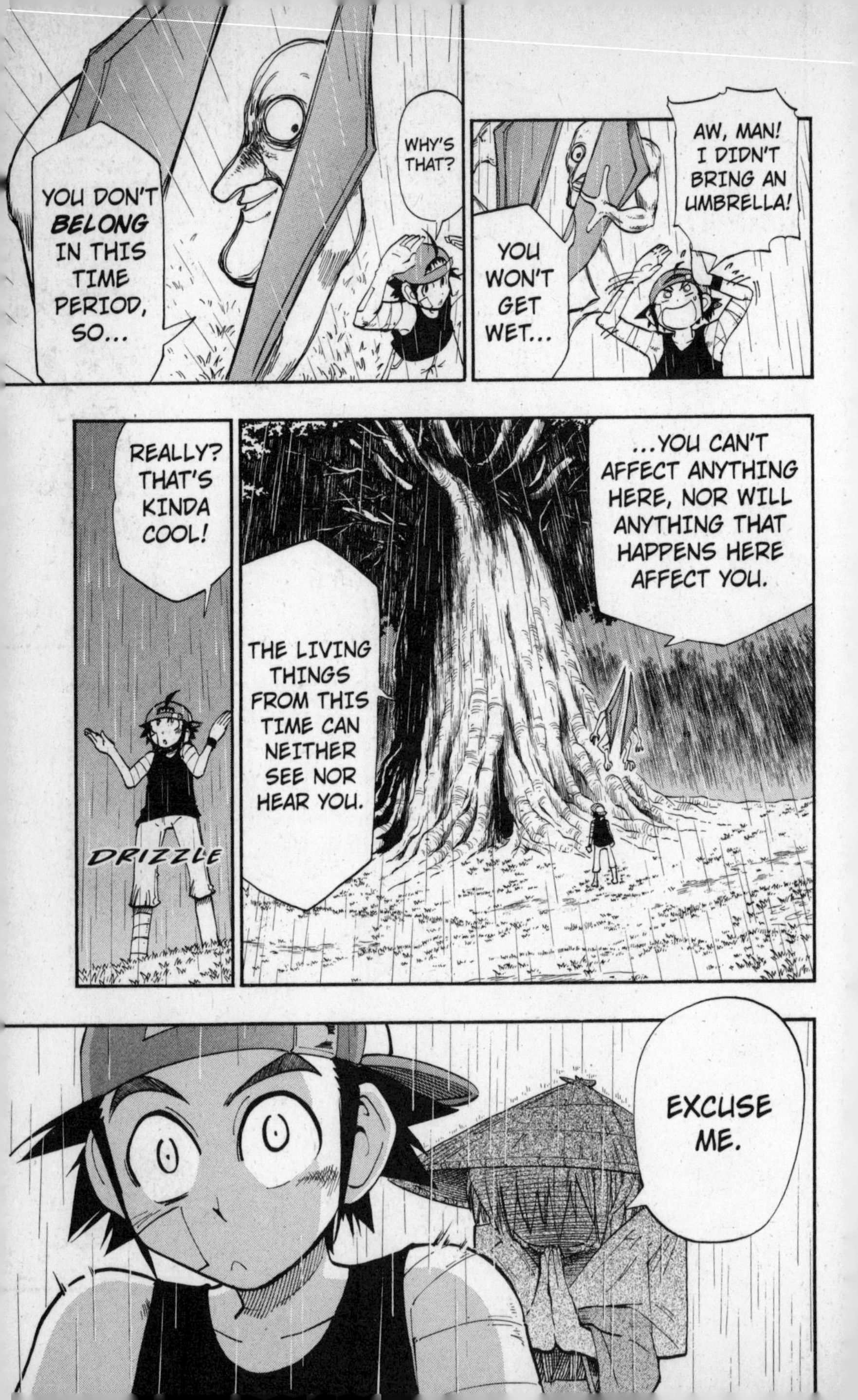
AW, MAN! I DIDN'T BRING AN UMBRELLA!
YOU WON'T GET WET...
WHY'S THAT?
YOU DON'T **BELONG** IN THIS TIME PERIOD, SO...
...YOU CAN'T AFFECT ANYTHING HERE, NOR WILL ANYTHING THAT HAPPENS HERE AFFECT YOU.
THE LIVING THINGS FROM THIS TIME CAN NEITHER SEE NOR HEAR YOU.
REALLY? THAT'S KINDA COOL!
DRIZZLE
EXCUSE ME.

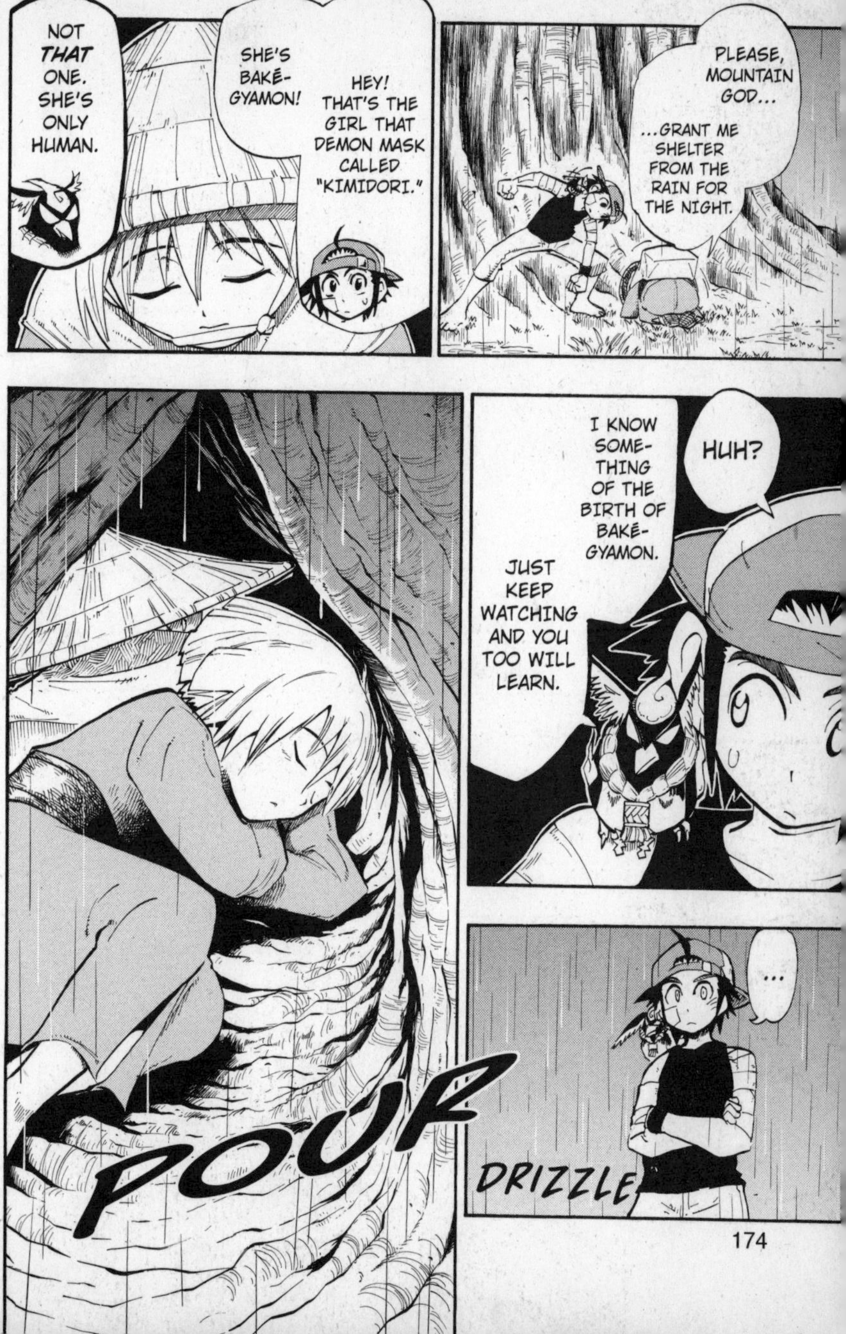
PLEASE, MOUNTAIN GOD...
...GRANT ME SHELTER FROM THE RAIN FOR THE NIGHT.
HEY! THAT'S THE GIRL THAT DEMON MASK CALLED "KIMIDORI."
SHE'S BAKÉ-GYAMON!
NOT THAT ONE. SHE'S ONLY HUMAN.
HUH?
I KNOW SOMETHING OF THE BIRTH OF BAKÉ-GYAMON.
JUST KEEP WATCHING AND YOU TOO WILL LEARN.
...
DRIZZLE
POUR

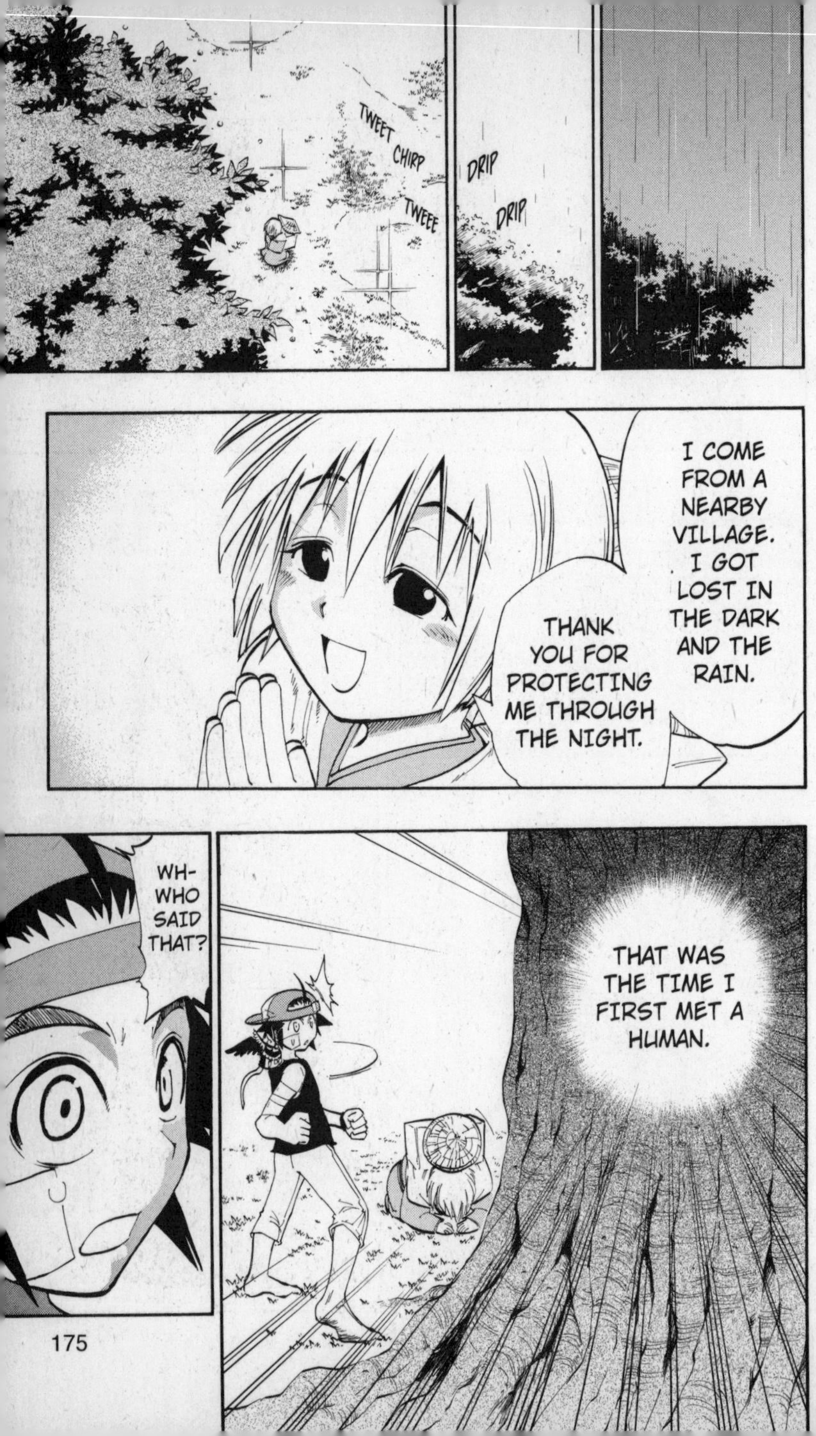
DRIP
DRIP
TWEET
CHIRP
TWEEE
I COME FROM A NEARBY VILLAGE. I GOT LOST IN THE DARK AND THE RAIN.
THANK YOU FOR PROTECTING ME THROUGH THE NIGHT.
THAT WAS THE TIME I FIRST MET A HUMAN.
WH- WHO SAID THAT?

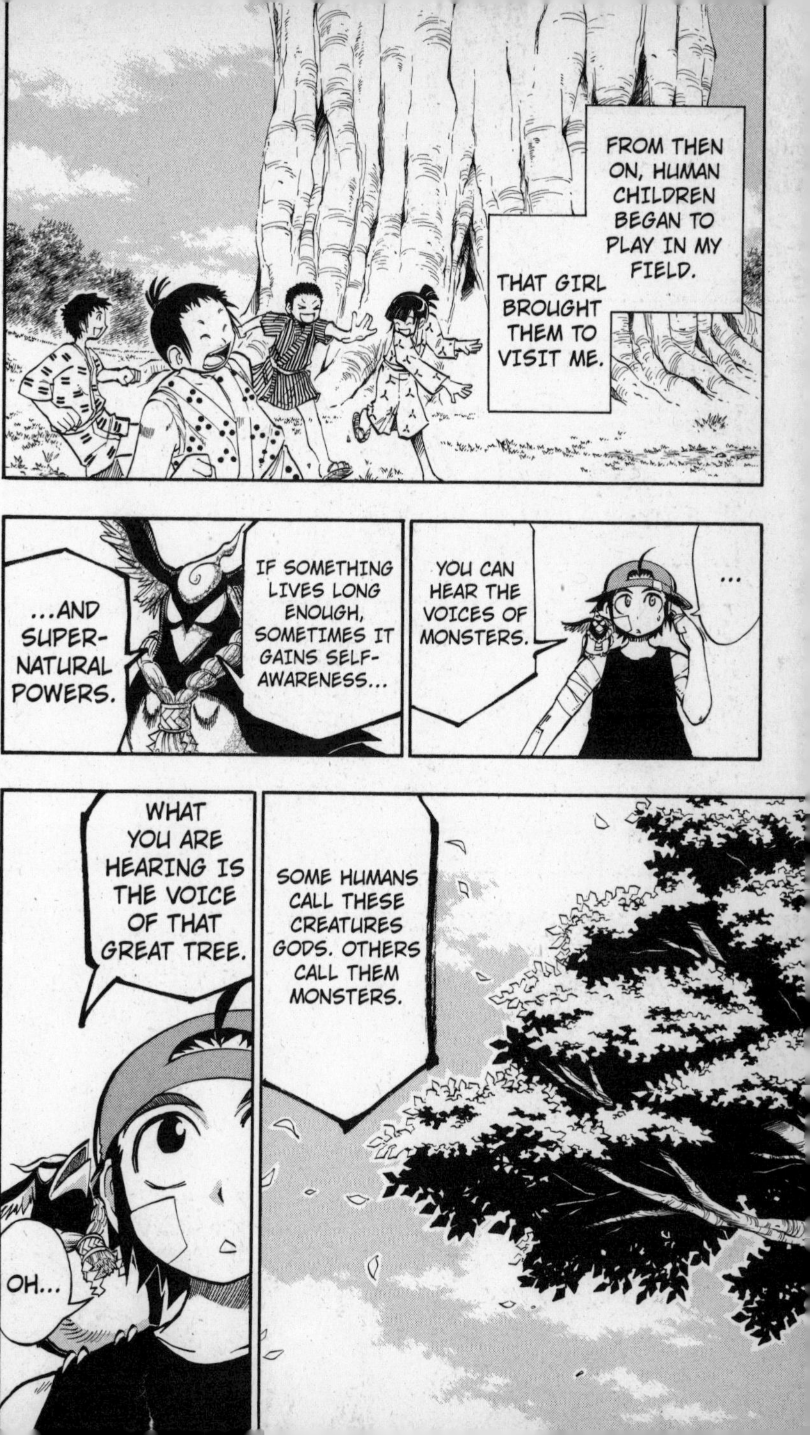
FROM THEN ON, HUMAN CHILDREN BEGAN TO PLAY IN MY FIELD.
THAT GIRL BROUGHT THEM TO VISIT ME.
...
YOU CAN HEAR THE VOICES OF MONSTERS.
IF SOMETHING LIVES LONG ENOUGH, SOMETIMES IT GAINS SELF-AWARENESS...
...AND SUPER-NATURAL POWERS.
SOME HUMANS CALL THESE CREATURES GODS. OTHERS CALL THEM MONSTERS.
WHAT YOU ARE HEARING IS THE VOICE OF THAT GREAT TREE.
OH...

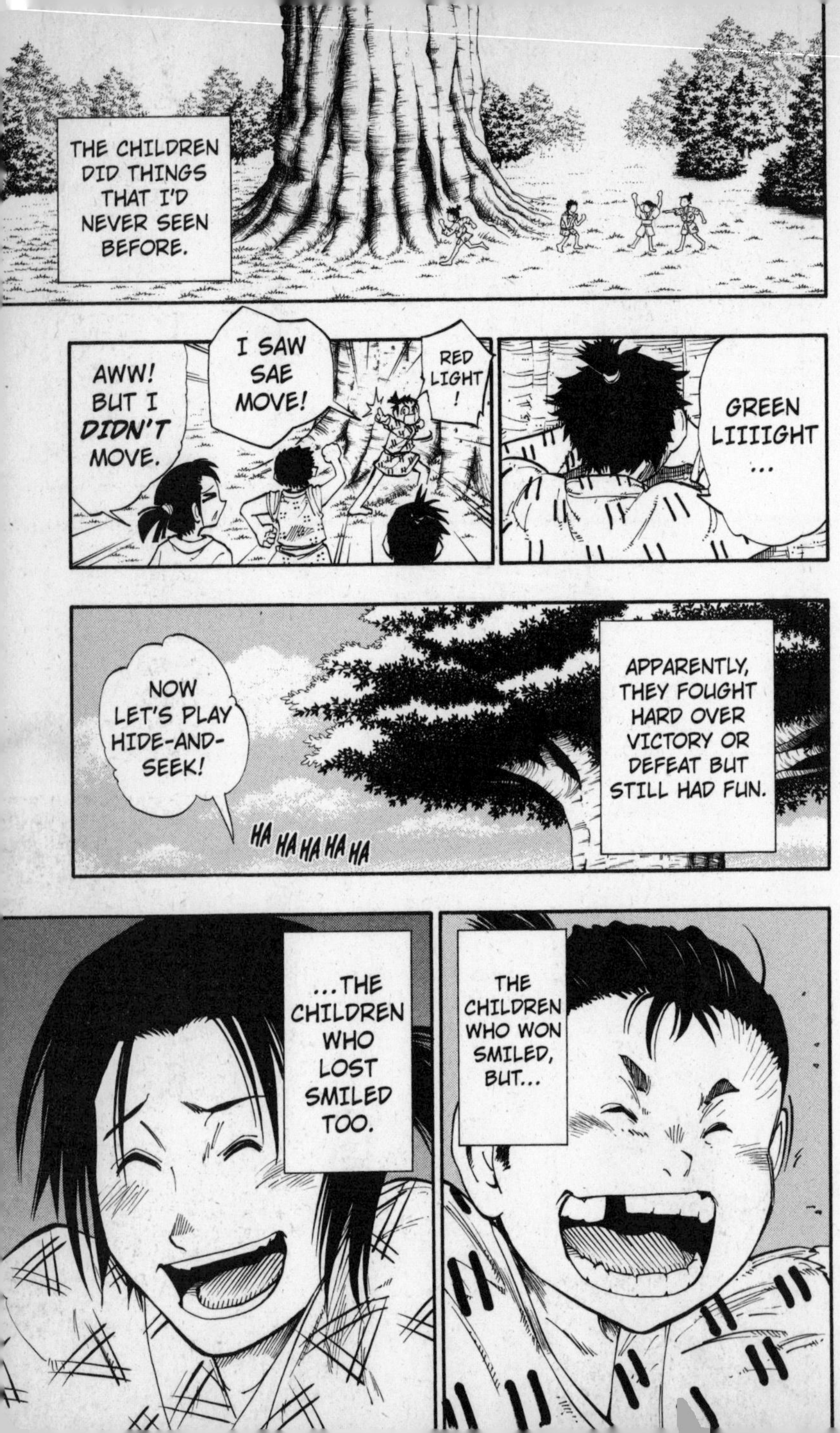
THE CHILDREN DID THINGS THAT I'D NEVER SEEN BEFORE.
GREEN LIIIIGHT...
RED LIGHT!
I SAW SAE MOVE!
AWW! BUT I DIDN'T MOVE.
APPARENTLY, THEY FOUGHT HARD OVER VICTORY OR DEFEAT BUT STILL HAD FUN.
NOW LET'S PLAY HIDE-AND-SEEK!
HA HA HA HA HA
THE CHILDREN WHO WON SMILED, BUT...
...THE CHILDREN WHO LOST SMILED TOO.

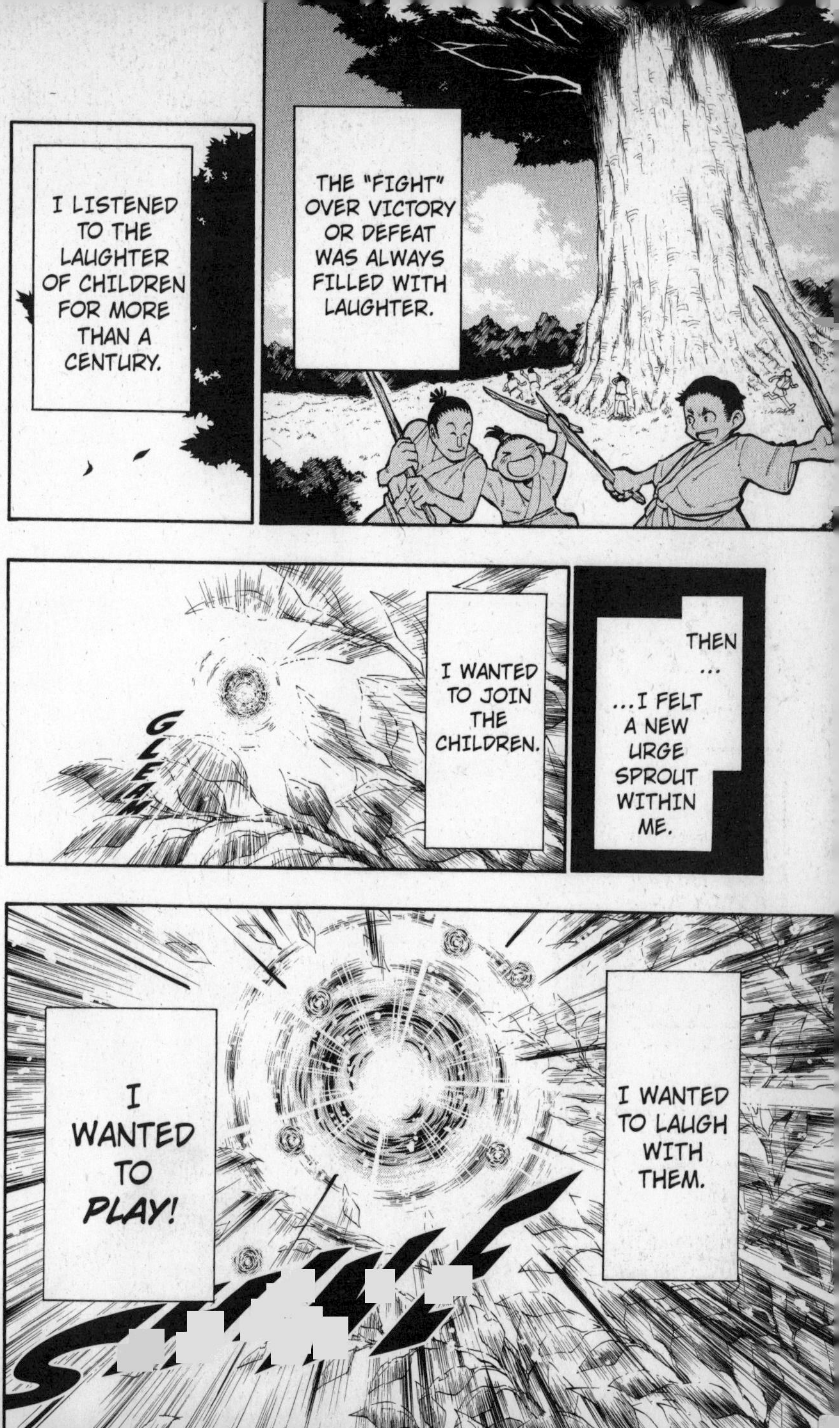
THE "FIGHT" OVER VICTORY OR DEFEAT WAS ALWAYS FILLED WITH LAUGHTER.
I LISTENED TO THE LAUGHTER OF CHILDREN FOR MORE THAN A CENTURY.
THEN...
...I FELT A NEW URGE SPROUT WITHIN ME.
I WANTED TO JOIN THE CHILDREN.
GLEAM
I WANTED TO LAUGH WITH THEM.
I WANTED TO PLAY!

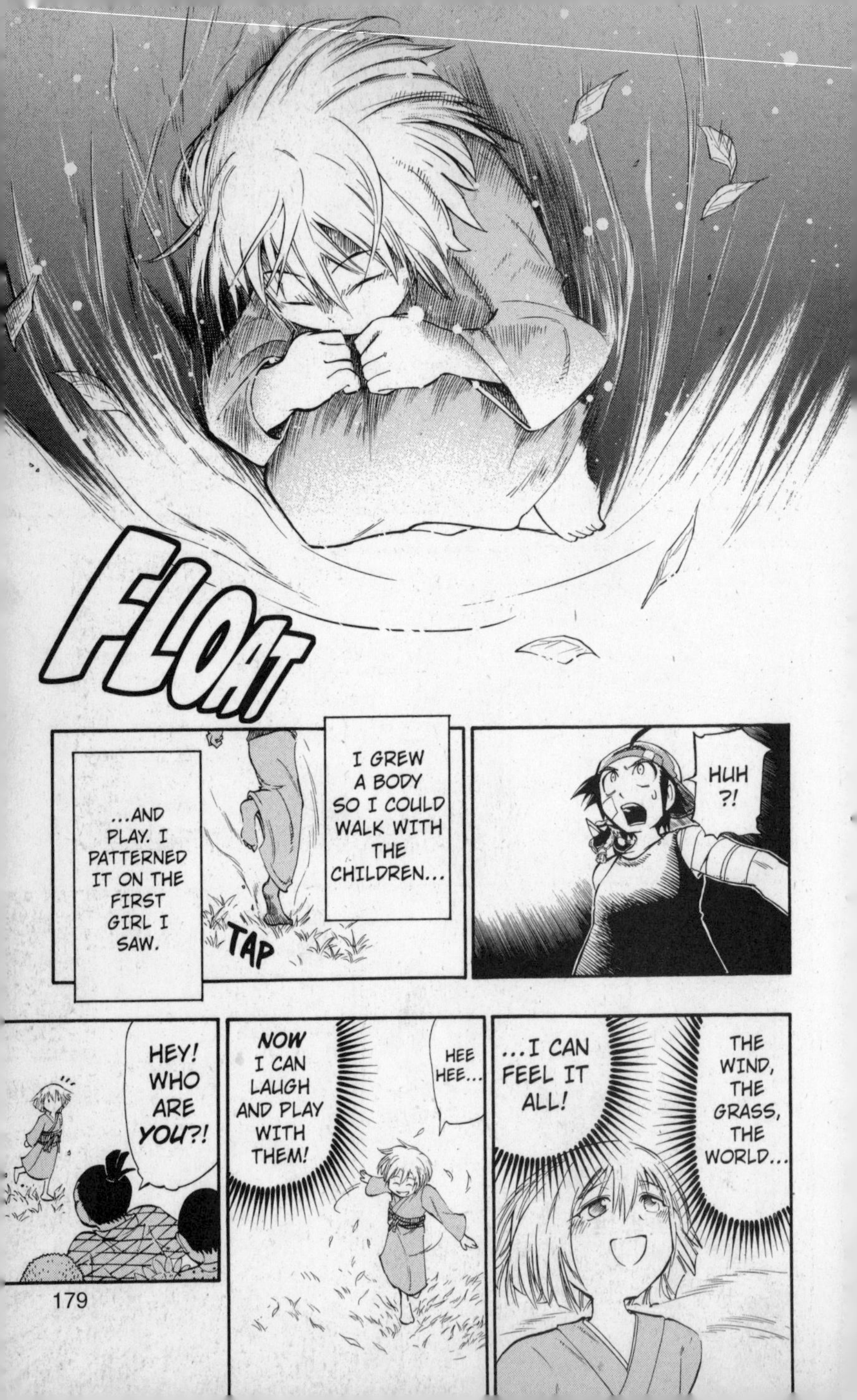
FLOAT
HUH ?!
I GREW A BODY SO I COULD WALK WITH THE CHILDREN...
...AND PLAY. I PATTERNED IT ON THE FIRST GIRL I SAW.
TAP
THE WIND, THE GRASS, THE WORLD...
...I CAN FEEL IT ALL!
HEE HEE...
NOW I CAN LAUGH AND PLAY WITH THEM!
HEY! WHO ARE YOU?!

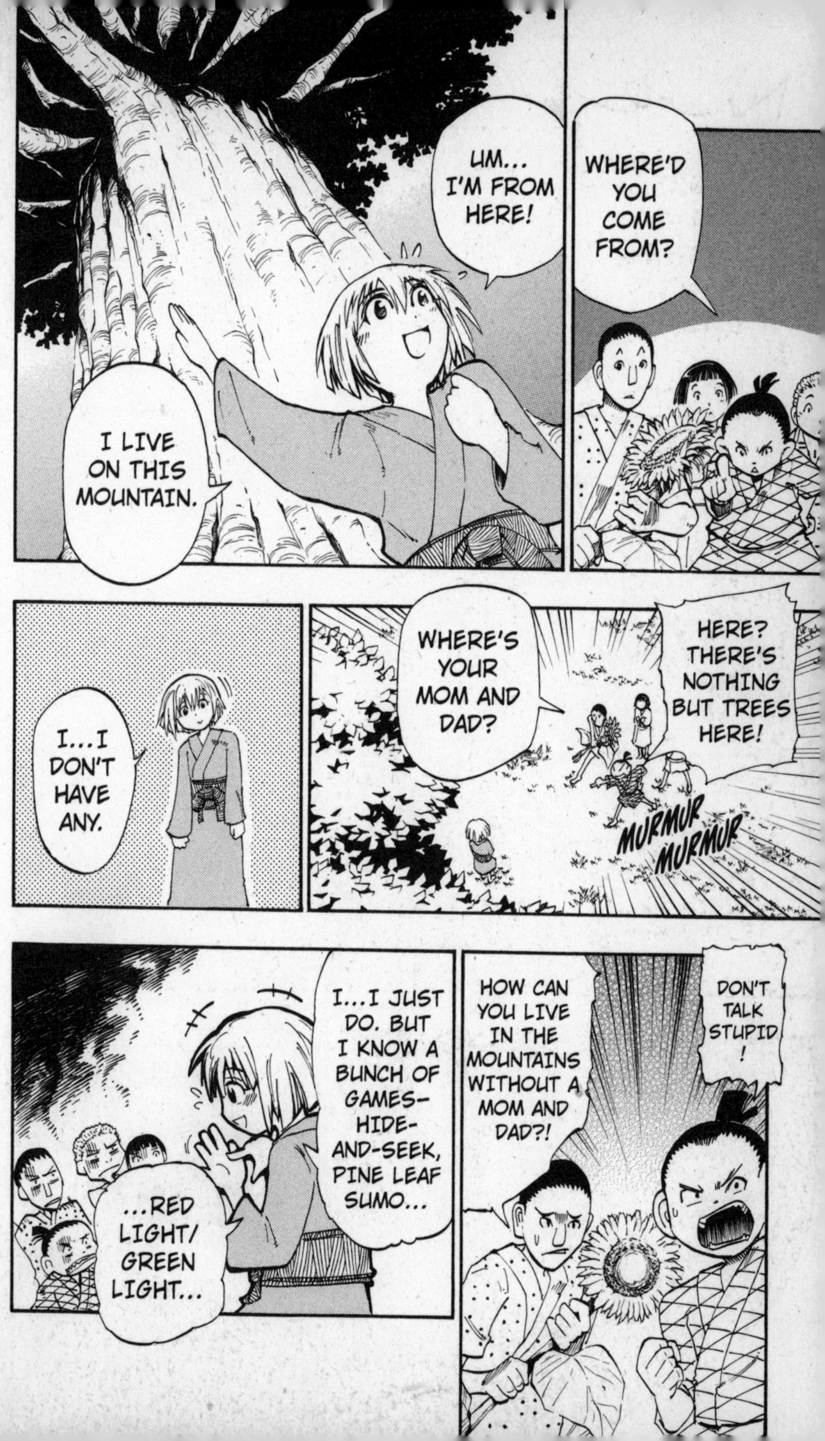
WHERE'D YOU COME FROM?
UM... I'M FROM HERE!
I LIVE ON THIS MOUNTAIN.
HERE? THERE'S NOTHING BUT TREES HERE!
WHERE'S YOUR MOM AND DAD?
MURMUR MURMUR
I...I DON'T HAVE ANY.
DON'T TALK STUPID!
HOW CAN YOU LIVE IN THE MOUNTAINS WITHOUT A MOM AND DAD?!
I...I JUST DO. BUT I KNOW A BUNCH OF GAMES-HIDE-AND-SEEK, PINE LEAF SUMO...
...RED LIGHT/GREEN LIGHT...

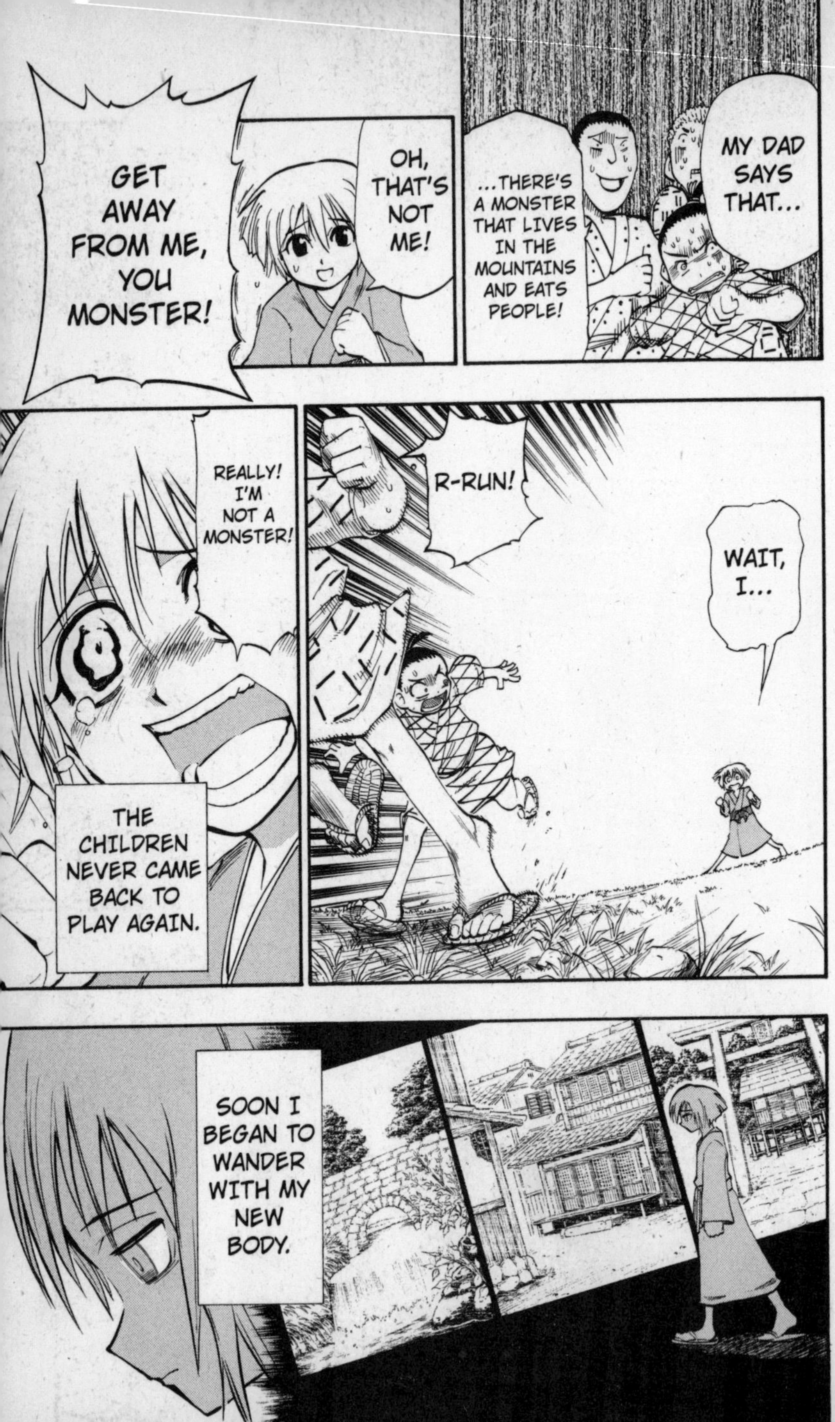
MY DAD SAYS THAT...
...THERE'S A MONSTER THAT LIVES IN THE MOUNTAINS AND EATS PEOPLE!
OH, THAT'S NOT ME!
GET AWAY FROM ME, YOU MONSTER!
R-RUN!
WAIT, I...
REALLY! I'M NOT A MONSTER!
THE CHILDREN NEVER CAME BACK TO PLAY AGAIN.
SOON I BEGAN TO WANDER WITH MY NEW BODY.

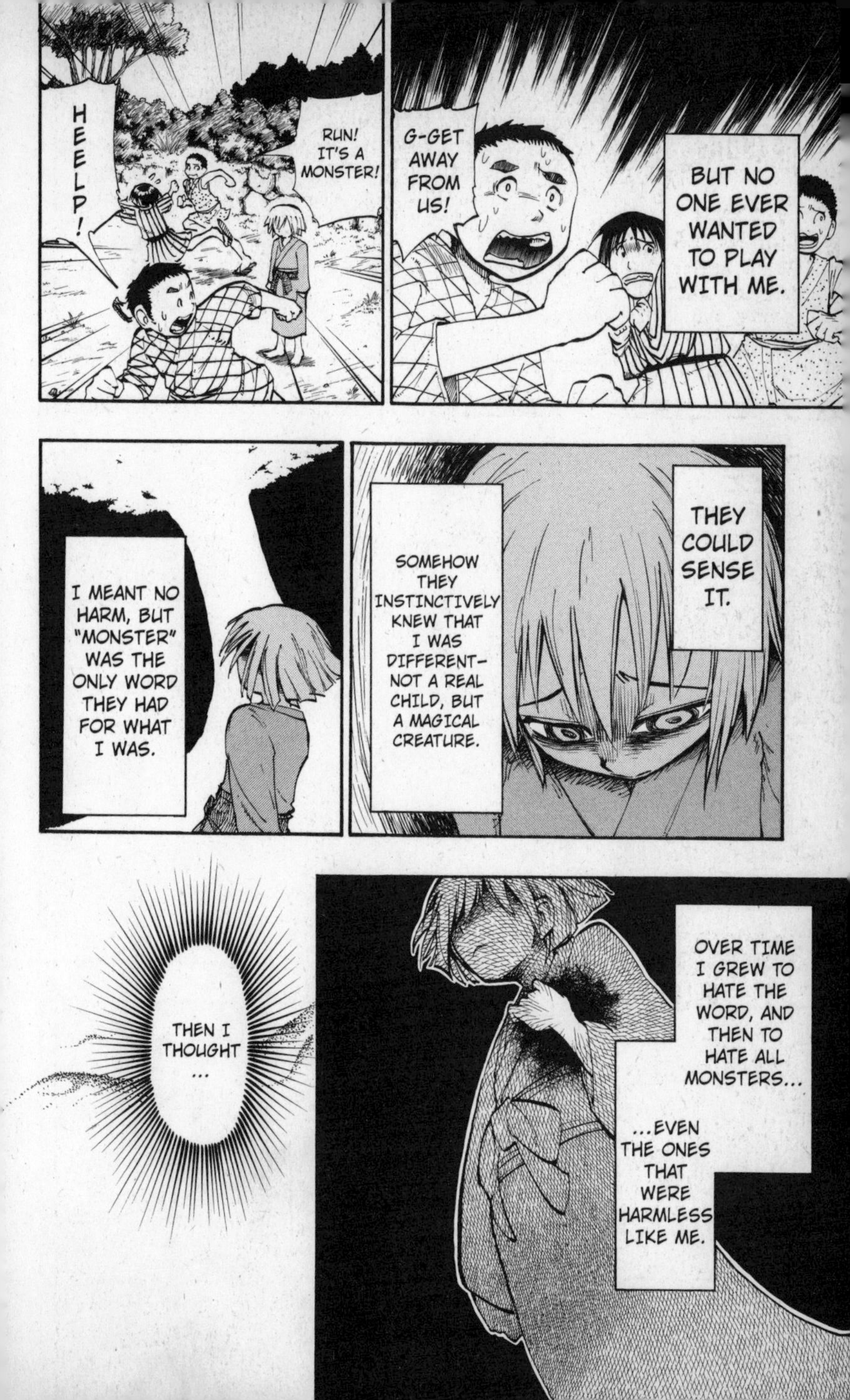
BUT NO ONE EVER WANTED TO PLAY WITH ME.
G-GET AWAY FROM US!
RUN! IT'S A MONSTER!
HEELP!
THEY COULD SENSE IT.
SOMEHOW THEY INSTINCTIVELY KNEW THAT I WAS DIFFERENT– NOT A REAL CHILD, BUT A MAGICAL CREATURE.
I MEANT NO HARM, BUT "MONSTER" WAS THE ONLY WORD THEY HAD FOR WHAT I WAS.
OVER TIME I GREW TO HATE THE WORD, AND THEN TO HATE ALL MONSTERS...
...EVEN THE ONES THAT WERE HARMLESS LIKE ME.
THEN I THOUGHT ...

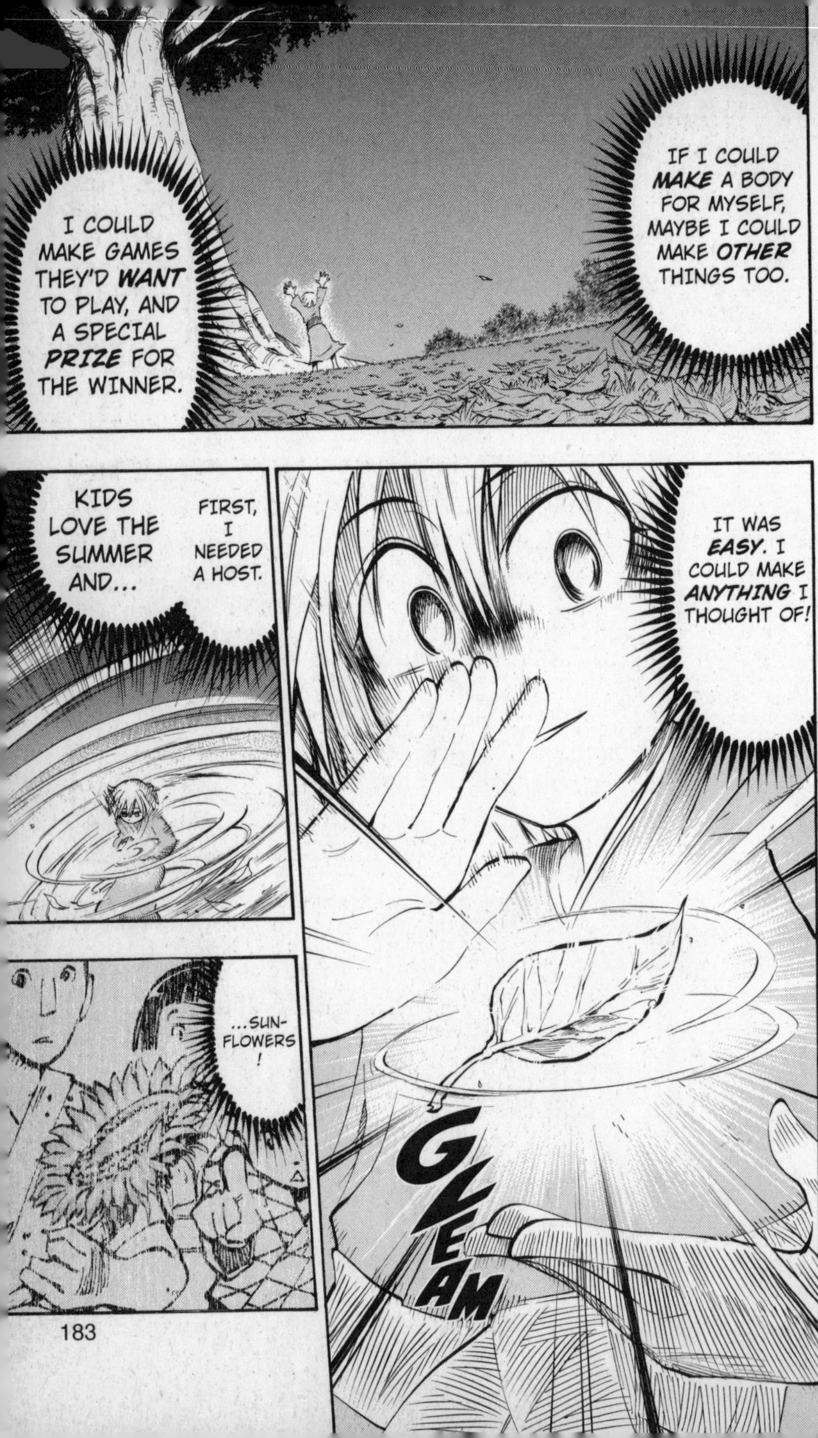
IF I COULD MAKE A BODY FOR MYSELF, MAYBE I COULD MAKE OTHER THINGS TOO.
I COULD MAKE GAMES THEY'D WANT TO PLAY, AND A SPECIAL PRIZE FOR THE WINNER.
IT WAS EASY. I COULD MAKE ANYTHING I THOUGHT OF!
GLEAM
FIRST, I NEEDED A HOST.
KIDS LOVE THE SUMMER AND...
...SUN-FLOWERS!

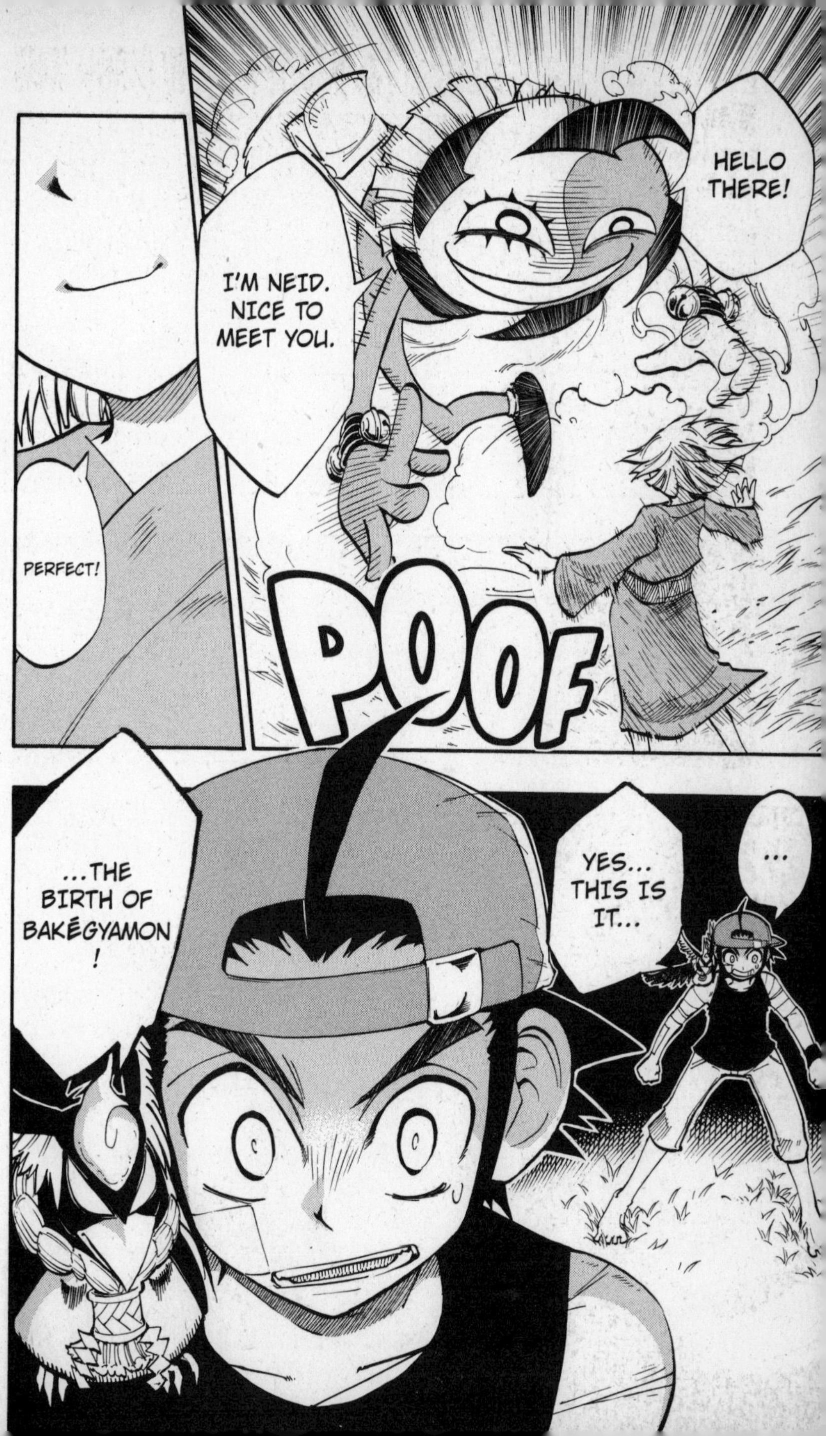
HELLO THERE!
I'M NEID. NICE TO MEET YOU.
POOF
PERFECT!
...
YES... THIS IS IT...
...THE BIRTH OF BAKĒGYAMON!

CHAPTER 40 THE MYSTERY BEHIND DEMON MASK

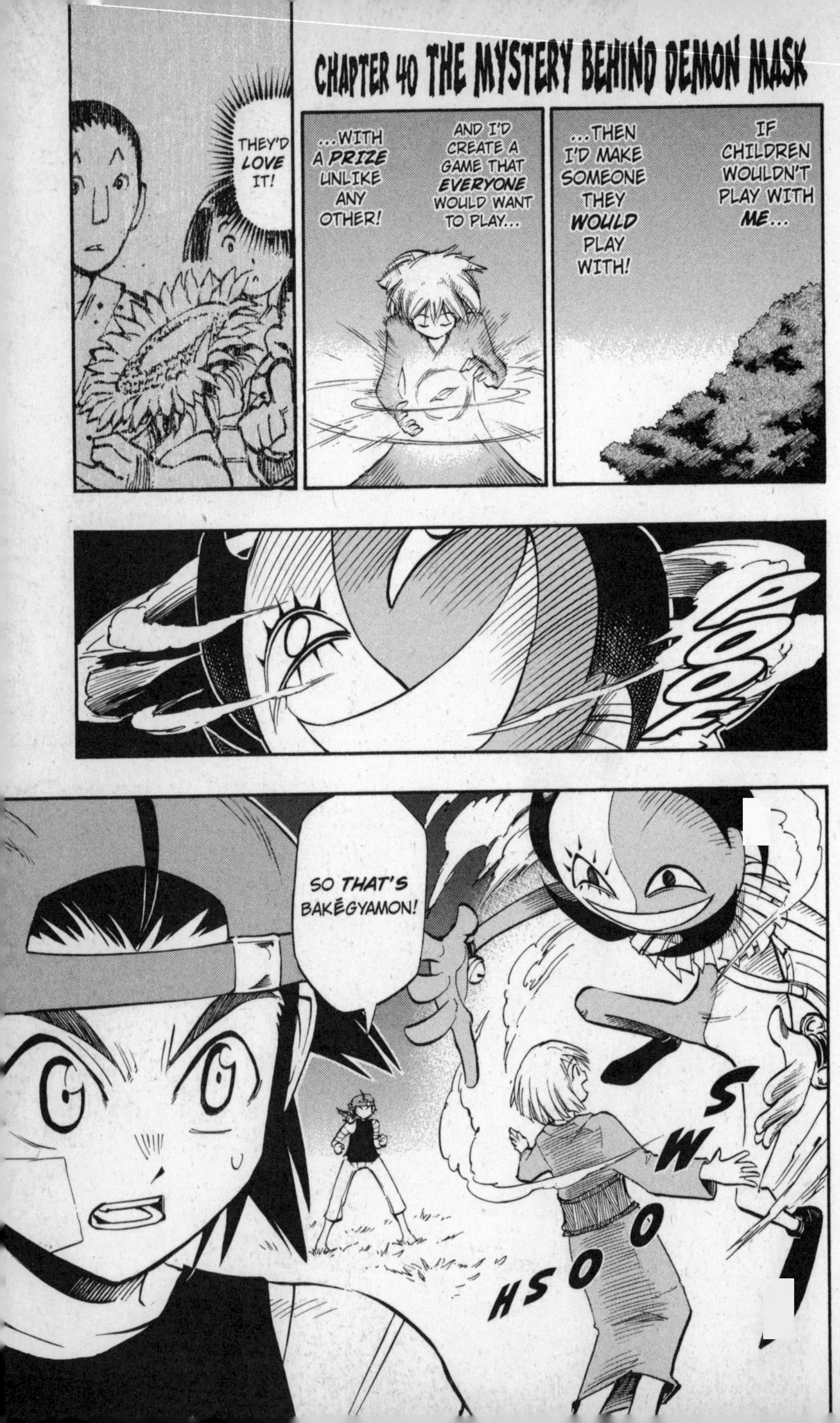
IF CHILDREN WOULDN'T PLAY WITH ME...
...THEN I'D MAKE SOMEONE THEY WOULD PLAY WITH!
AND I'D CREATE A GAME THAT EVERYONE WOULD WANT TO PLAY...
...WITH A PRIZE UNLIKE ANY OTHER!
THEY'D LOVE IT!
SWOOOSH
SO THAT'S BAKĒGYAMON!

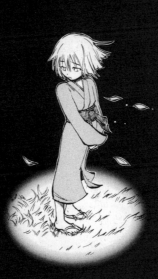

CHAPTER 40 THE MYSTERY BEHIND DEMON MASK

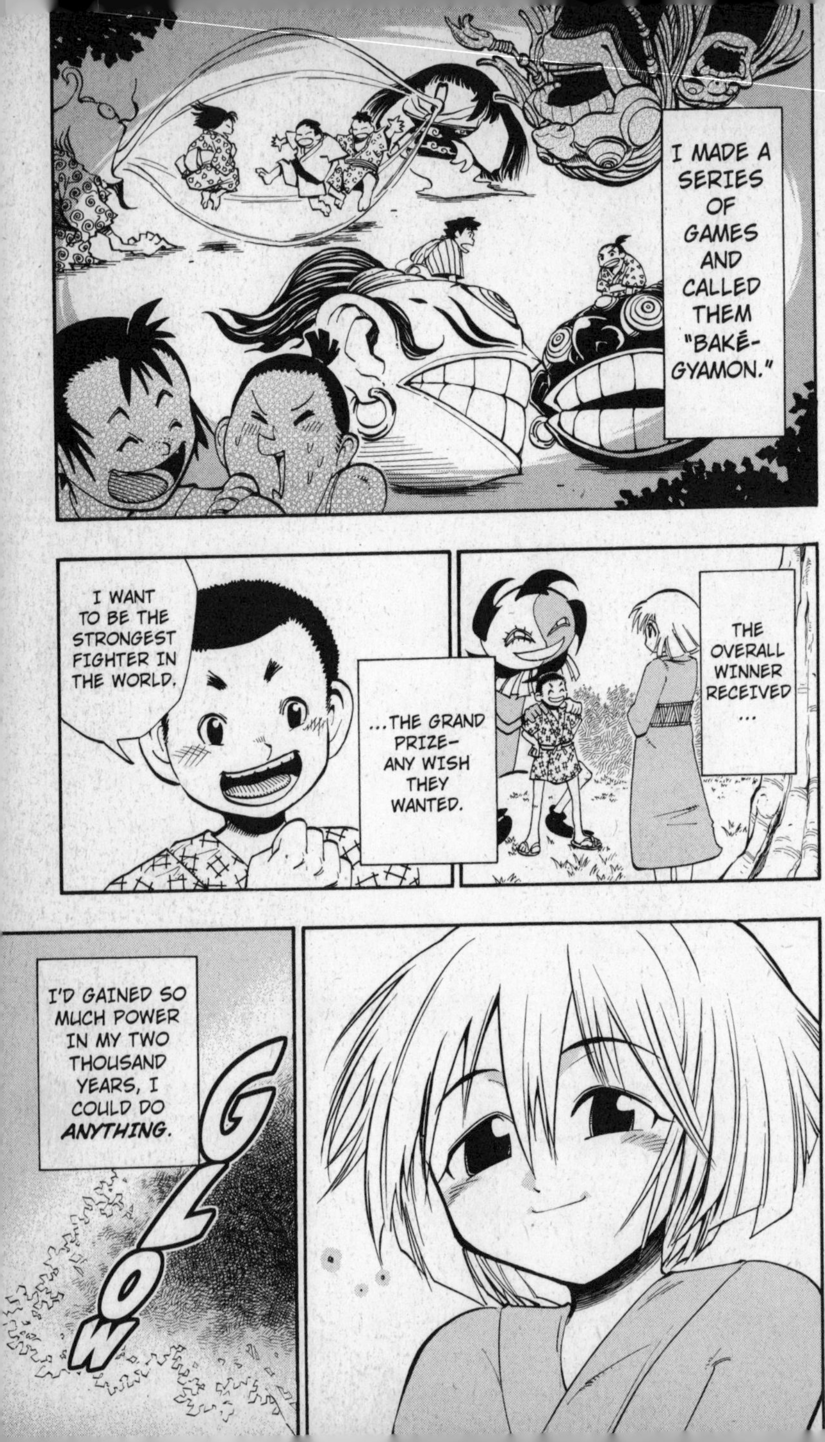
I MADE A SERIES OF GAMES AND CALLED THEM "BAKÉ-GYAMON."
THE OVERALL WINNER RECEIVED ...
...THE GRAND PRIZE-ANY WISH THEY WANTED.
I WANT TO BE THE STRONGEST FIGHTER IN THE WORLD.
I'D GAINED SO MUCH POWER IN MY TWO THOUSAND YEARS, I COULD DO ANYTHING.
GLOW

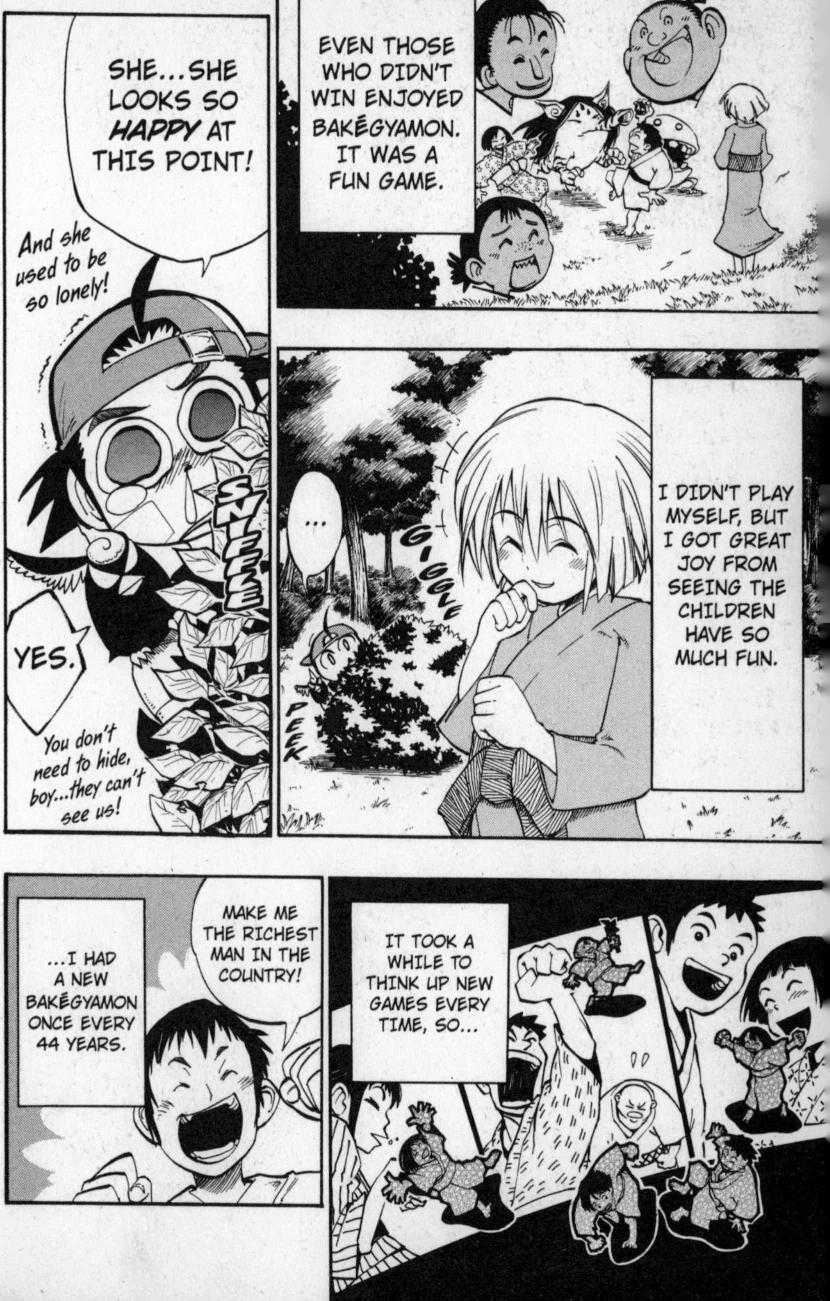

EVEN THOSE WHO DIDN'T WIN ENJOYED BAKÉGYAMON. IT WAS A FUN GAME.
I DIDN'T PLAY MYSELF, BUT I GOT GREAT JOY FROM SEEING THE CHILDREN HAVE SO MUCH FUN.
...
GIGGLE
PEEK
SHE...SHE LOOKS SO *HAPPY* AT THIS POINT!
And she used to be so lonely!
SNIFFLE
YES.
You don't need to hide, boy...they can't see us!
IT TOOK A WHILE TO THINK UP NEW GAMES EVERY TIME, SO...
MAKE ME THE RICHEST MAN IN THE COUNTRY!
...I HAD A NEW BAKÉGYAMON ONCE EVERY 44 YEARS.

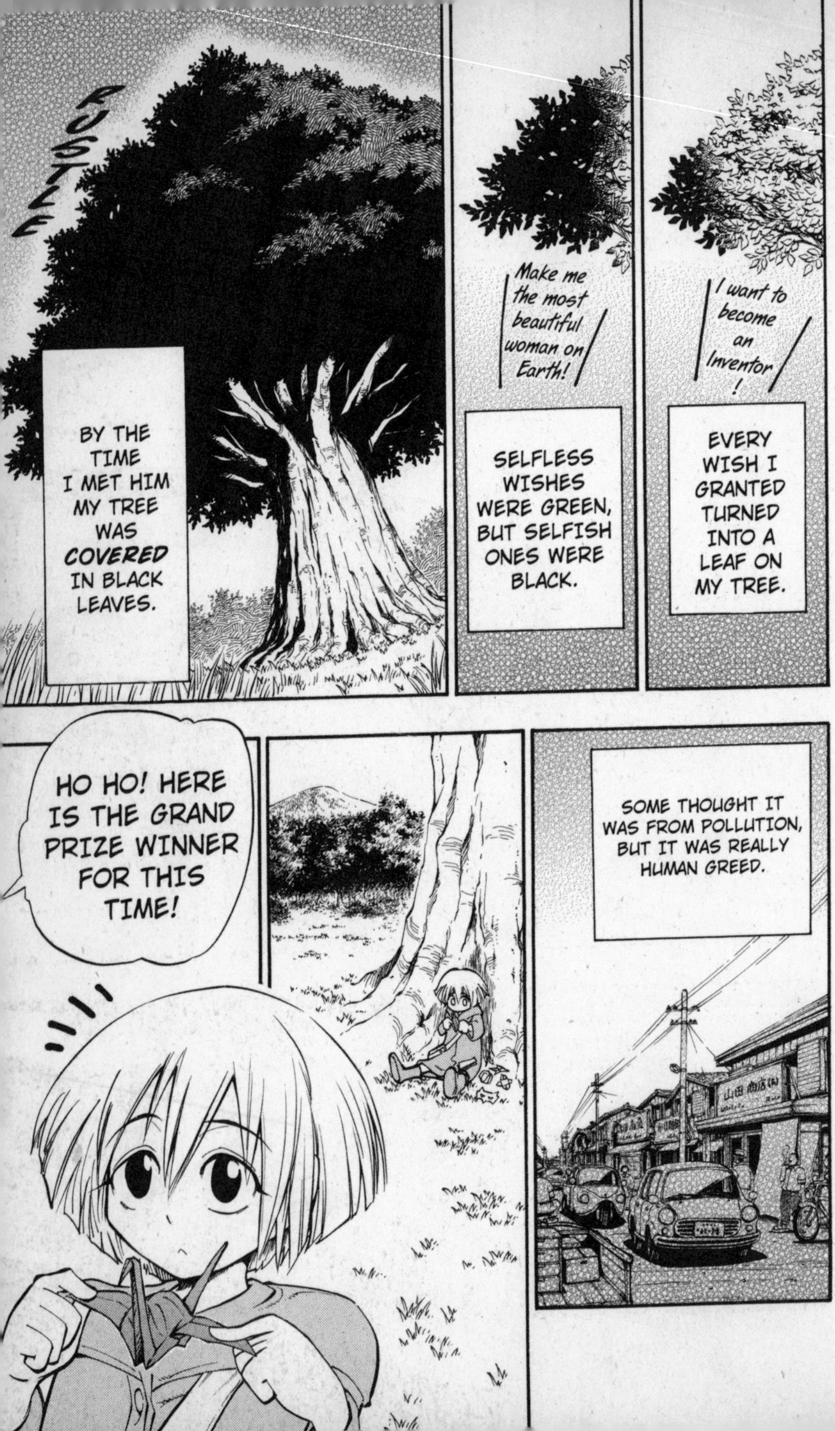
I want to become an Inventor!
EVERY WISH I GRANTED TURNED INTO A LEAF ON MY TREE.
Make me the most beautiful woman on Earth!
SELFLESS WISHES WERE GREEN, BUT SELFISH ONES WERE BLACK.
RUSTLE
BY THE TIME I MET HIM MY TREE WAS COVERED IN BLACK LEAVES.
SOME THOUGHT IT WAS FROM POLLUTION, BUT IT WAS REALLY HUMAN GREED.
HO HO! HERE IS THE GRAND PRIZE WINNER FOR THIS TIME!

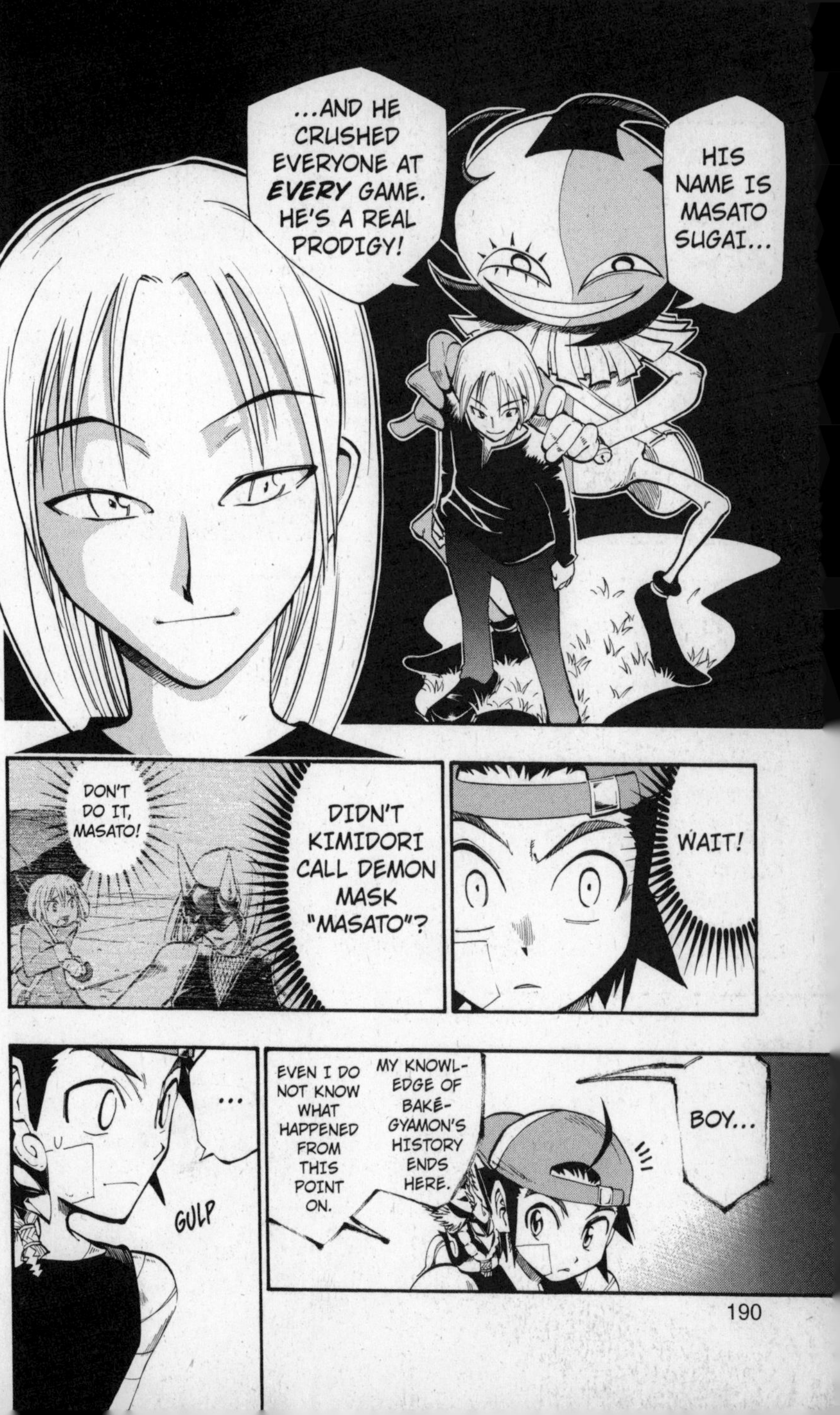
HIS NAME IS MASATO SUGAI...
...AND HE CRUSHED EVERYONE AT *EVERY* GAME. HE'S A REAL PRODIGY!
WAIT!
DIDN'T KIMIDORI CALL DEMON MASK "MASATO"?
DON'T DO IT, MASATO!
BOY...
MY KNOWL-EDGE OF BAKÉ-GYAMON'S HISTORY ENDS HERE.
EVEN I DO NOT KNOW WHAT HAPPENED FROM THIS POINT ON.
...
GULP

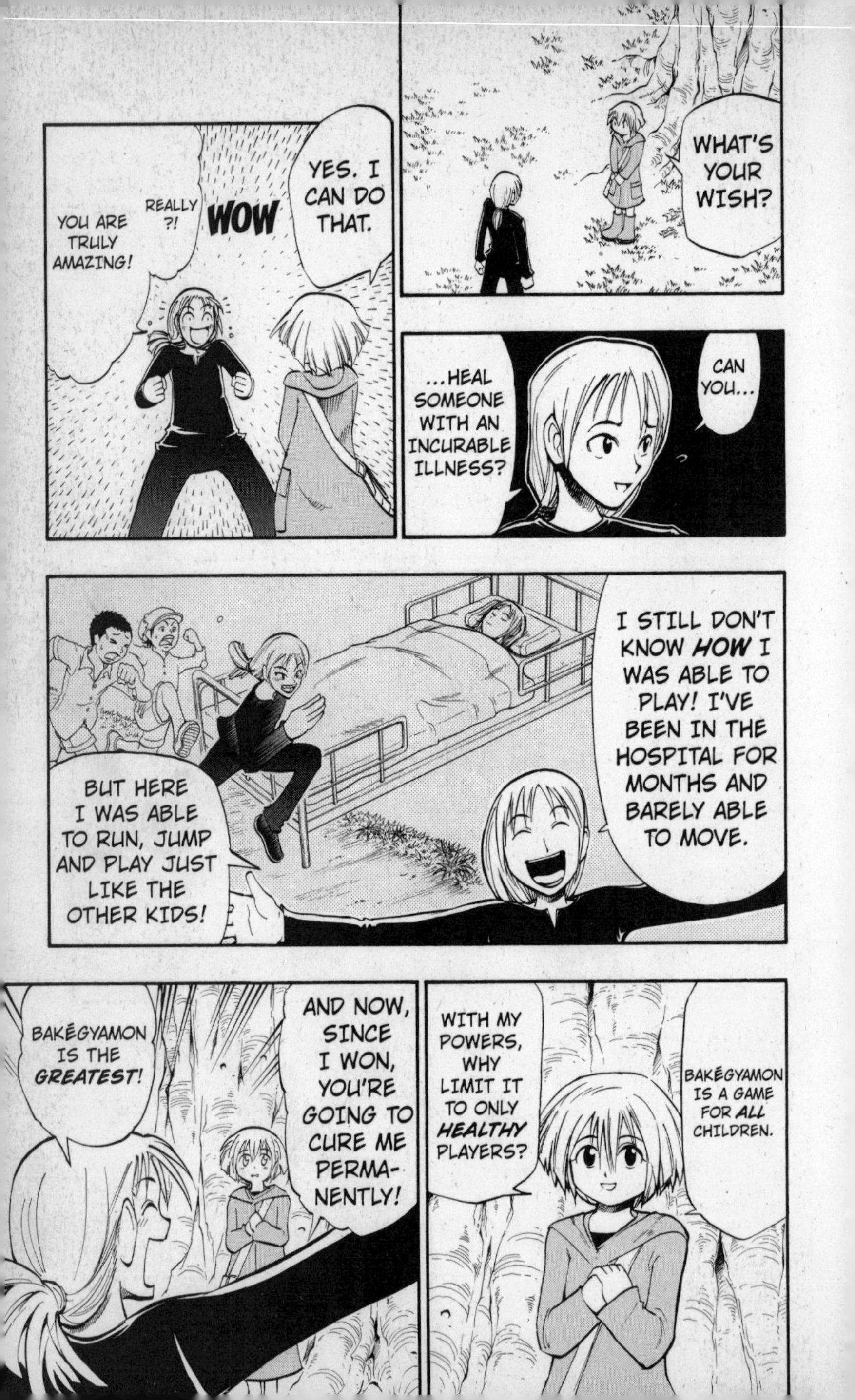

WHAT'S YOUR WISH?
CAN YOU...
...HEAL SOMEONE WITH AN INCURABLE ILLNESS?
YES. I CAN DO THAT.
WOW
REALLY ?!
YOU ARE TRULY AMAZING!
I STILL DON'T KNOW *HOW* I WAS ABLE TO PLAY! I'VE BEEN IN THE HOSPITAL FOR MONTHS AND BARELY ABLE TO MOVE.
BUT HERE I WAS ABLE TO RUN, JUMP AND PLAY JUST LIKE THE OTHER KIDS!
BAKÉGYAMON IS A GAME FOR *ALL* CHILDREN.
WITH MY POWERS, WHY LIMIT IT TO ONLY *HEALTHY* PLAYERS?
AND NOW, SINCE I WON, YOU'RE GOING TO CURE ME PERMA-NENTLY!
BAKÉGYAMON IS THE *GREATEST*!

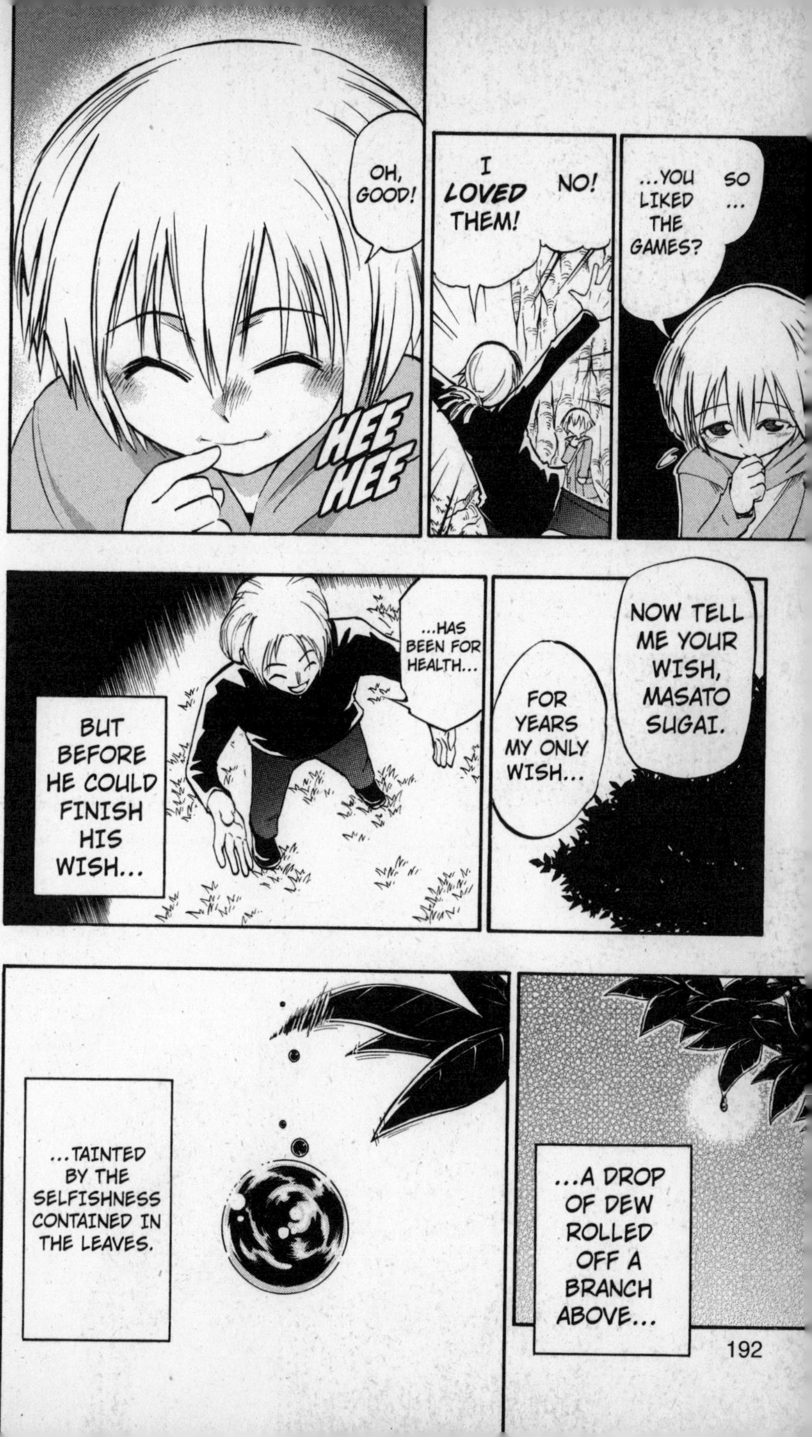
SO ...
...YOU LIKED THE GAMES?
NO!
I **LOVED** THEM!
OH, GOOD!
HEE HEE
NOW TELL ME YOUR WISH, MASATO SUGAI.
FOR YEARS MY ONLY WISH...
...HAS BEEN FOR HEALTH...
BUT BEFORE HE COULD FINISH HIS WISH...
...A DROP OF DEW ROLLED OFF A BRANCH ABOVE...
...TAINTED BY THE SELFISHNESS CONTAINED IN THE LEAVES.

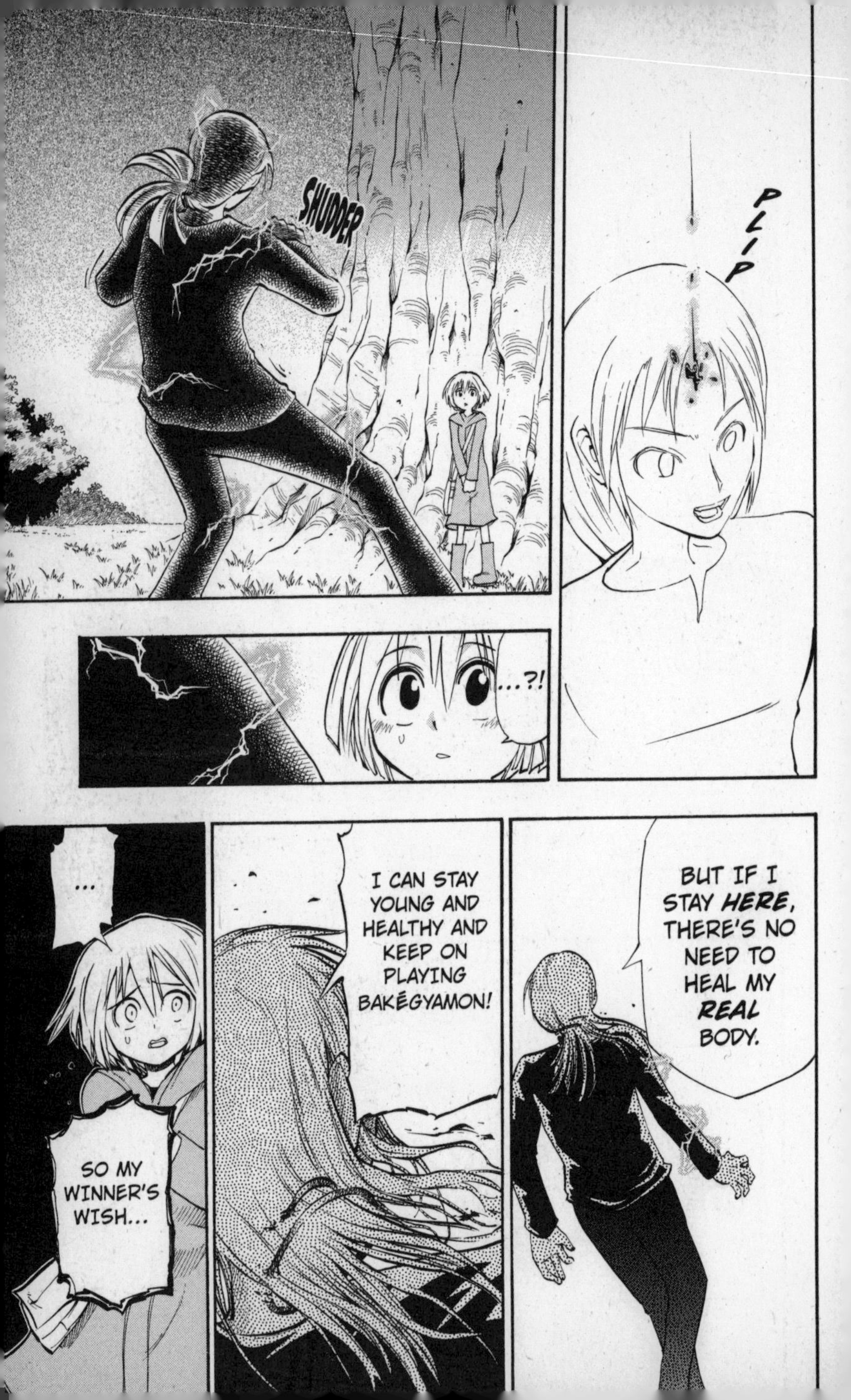
PLIP
SHUDDER
...?!
BUT IF I STAY HERE, THERE'S NO NEED TO HEAL MY REAL BODY.
I CAN STAY YOUNG AND HEALTHY AND KEEP ON PLAYING BAKÉGYAMON!
...
SO MY WINNER'S WISH...

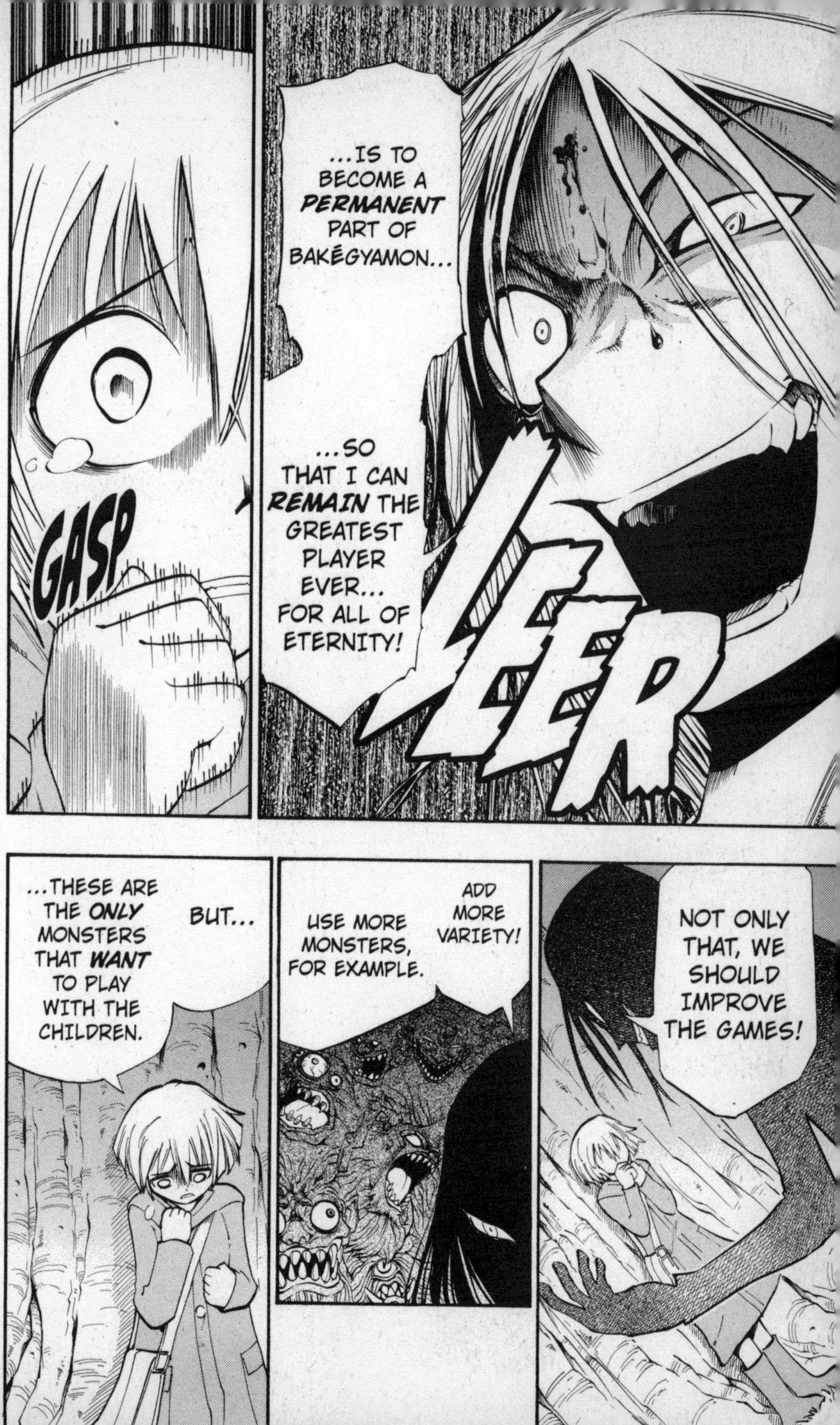
...IS TO BECOME A PERMANENT PART OF BAKÉGYAMON...
...SO THAT I CAN REMAIN THE GREATEST PLAYER EVER... FOR ALL OF ETERNITY!
LEER
GASP
NOT ONLY THAT, WE SHOULD IMPROVE THE GAMES!
ADD MORE VARIETY!
USE MORE MONSTERS, FOR EXAMPLE.
BUT...
...THESE ARE THE ONLY MONSTERS THAT WANT TO PLAY WITH THE CHILDREN.

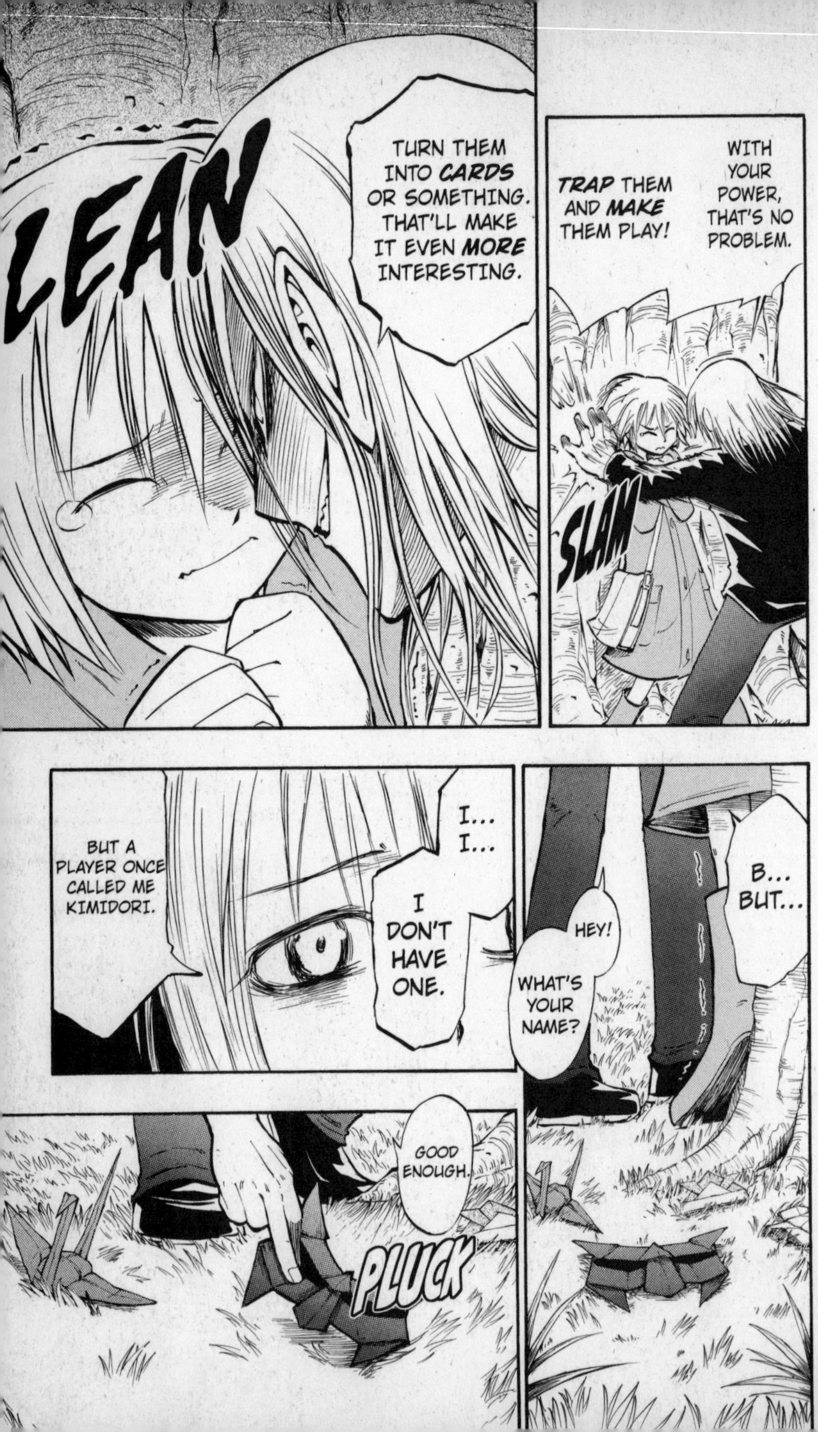
WITH YOUR POWER, THAT'S NO PROBLEM.
TRAP THEM AND MAKE THEM PLAY!
SLAM
TURN THEM INTO CARDS OR SOMETHING. THAT'LL MAKE IT EVEN MORE INTERESTING.
LEAN
B... BUT...
HEY!
WHAT'S YOUR NAME?
I... I...
I DON'T HAVE ONE.
BUT A PLAYER ONCE CALLED ME KIMIDORI.
GOOD ENOUGH.
PLUCK

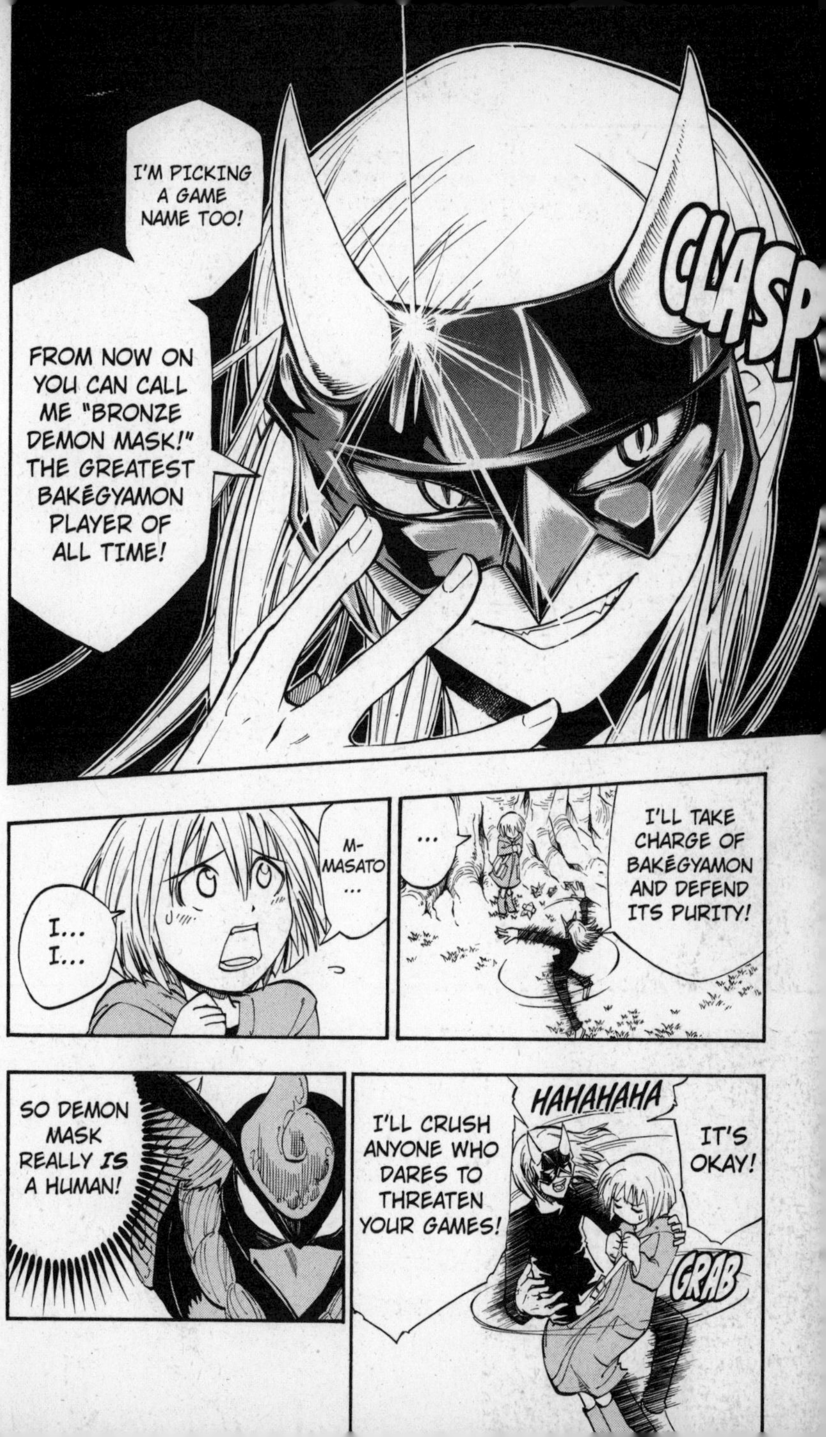

CLASP
I'M PICKING A GAME NAME TOO!
FROM NOW ON YOU CAN CALL ME "BRONZE DEMON MASK!" THE GREATEST BAKÉGYAMON PLAYER OF ALL TIME!
I'LL TAKE CHARGE OF BAKÉGYAMON AND DEFEND ITS PURITY!
...
M-MASATO ...
I... I...
HAHAHAHA
IT'S OKAY!
I'LL CRUSH ANYONE WHO DARES TO THREATEN YOUR GAMES!
GRAB
SO DEMON MASK REALLY *IS* A HUMAN!

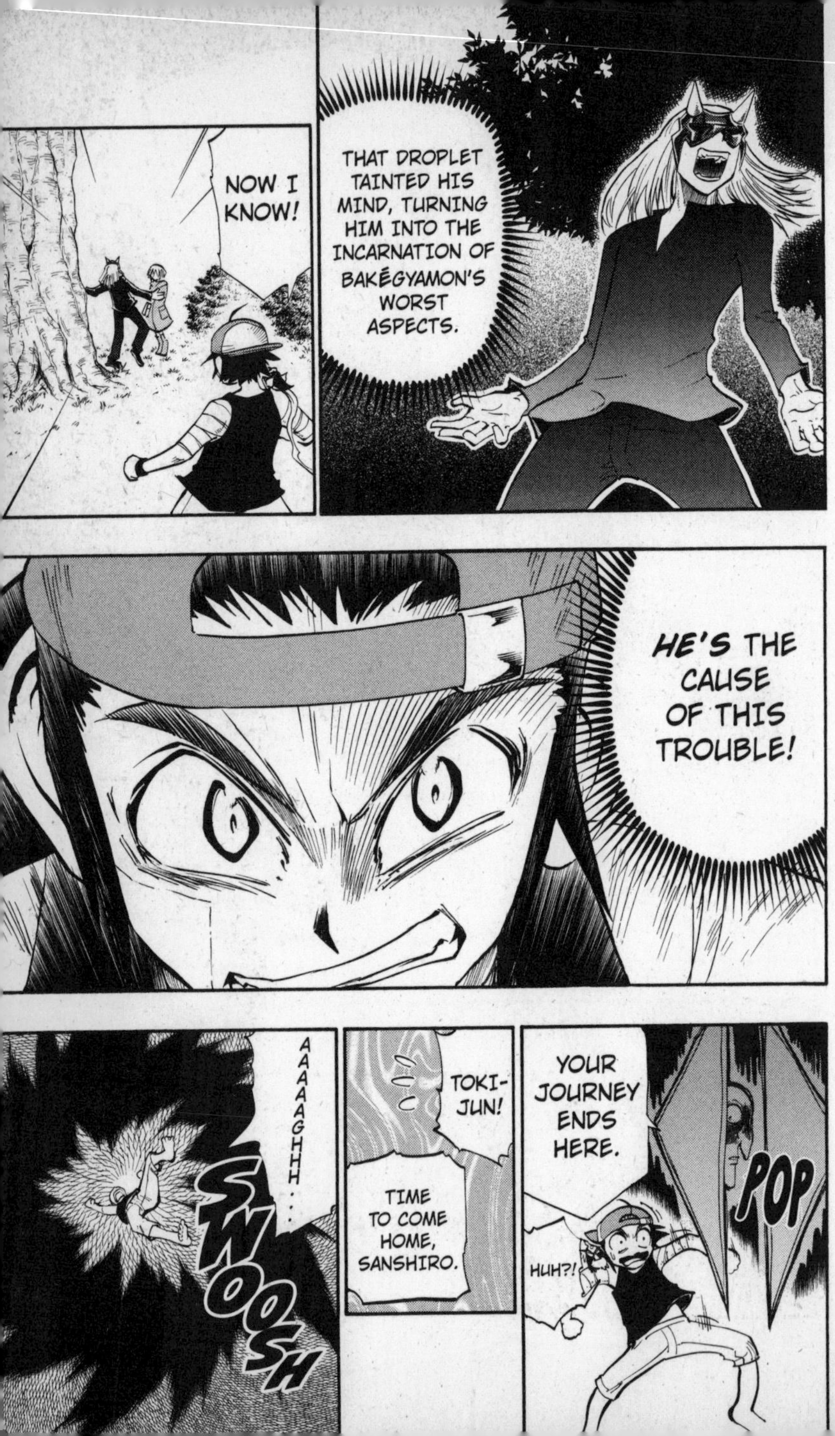
THAT DROPLET TAINTED HIS MIND, TURNING HIM INTO THE INCARNATION OF BAKÉGYAMON'S WORST ASPECTS.
NOW I KNOW!
HE'S THE CAUSE OF THIS TROUBLE!
YOUR JOURNEY ENDS HERE.
POP
HUH?!
TOKI-JUN!
TIME TO COME HOME, SANSHIRO.
AAAAAAGHHH...
SWOOSH

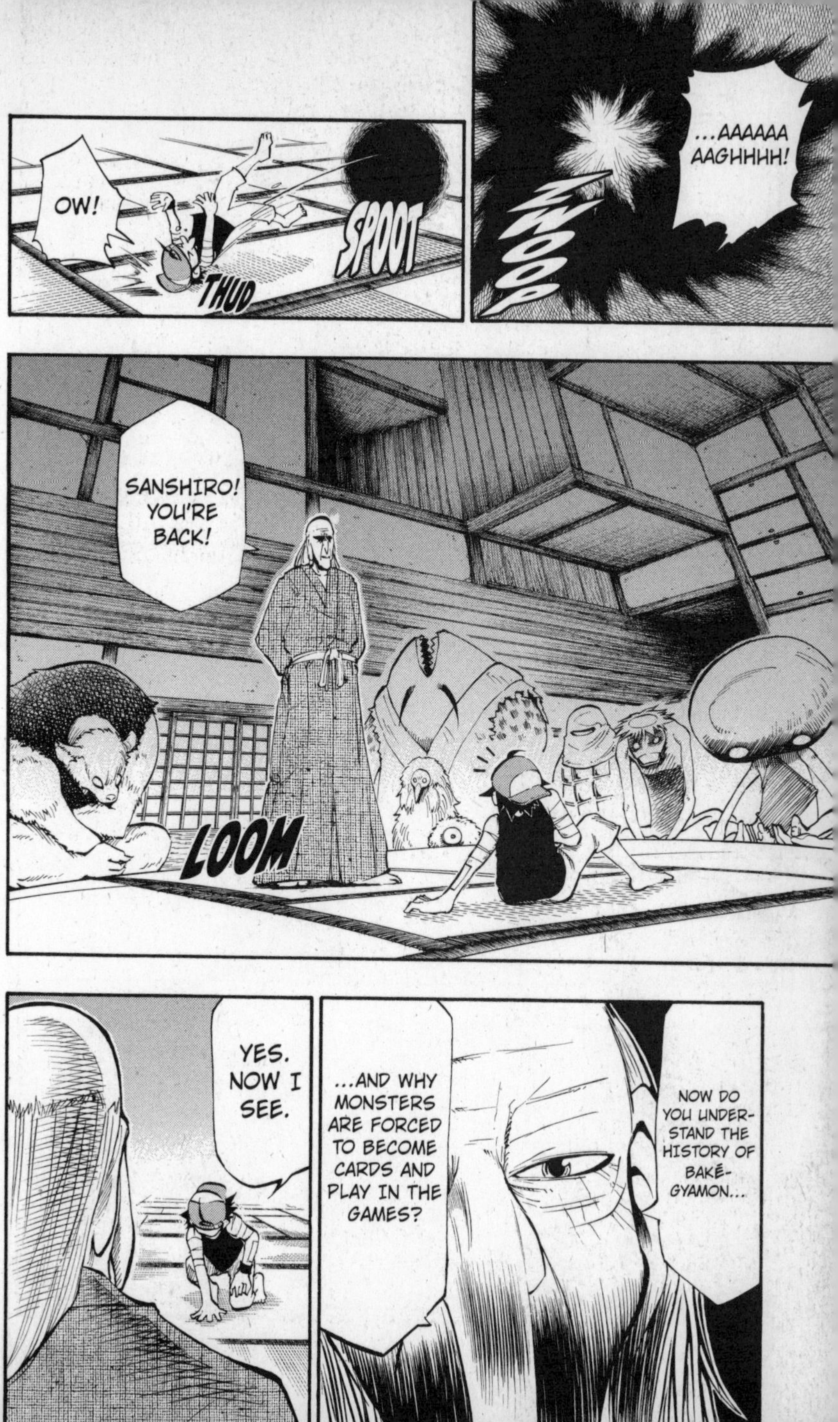
...AAAAAA AAGHHHH!
WHOOOP
SPOOT
OW!
THUD
SANSHIRO! YOU'RE BACK!
LOOM
NOW DO YOU UNDER-STAND THE HISTORY OF BAKÉ-GYAMON...
...AND WHY MONSTERS ARE FORCED TO BECOME CARDS AND PLAY IN THE GAMES?
YES. NOW I SEE.

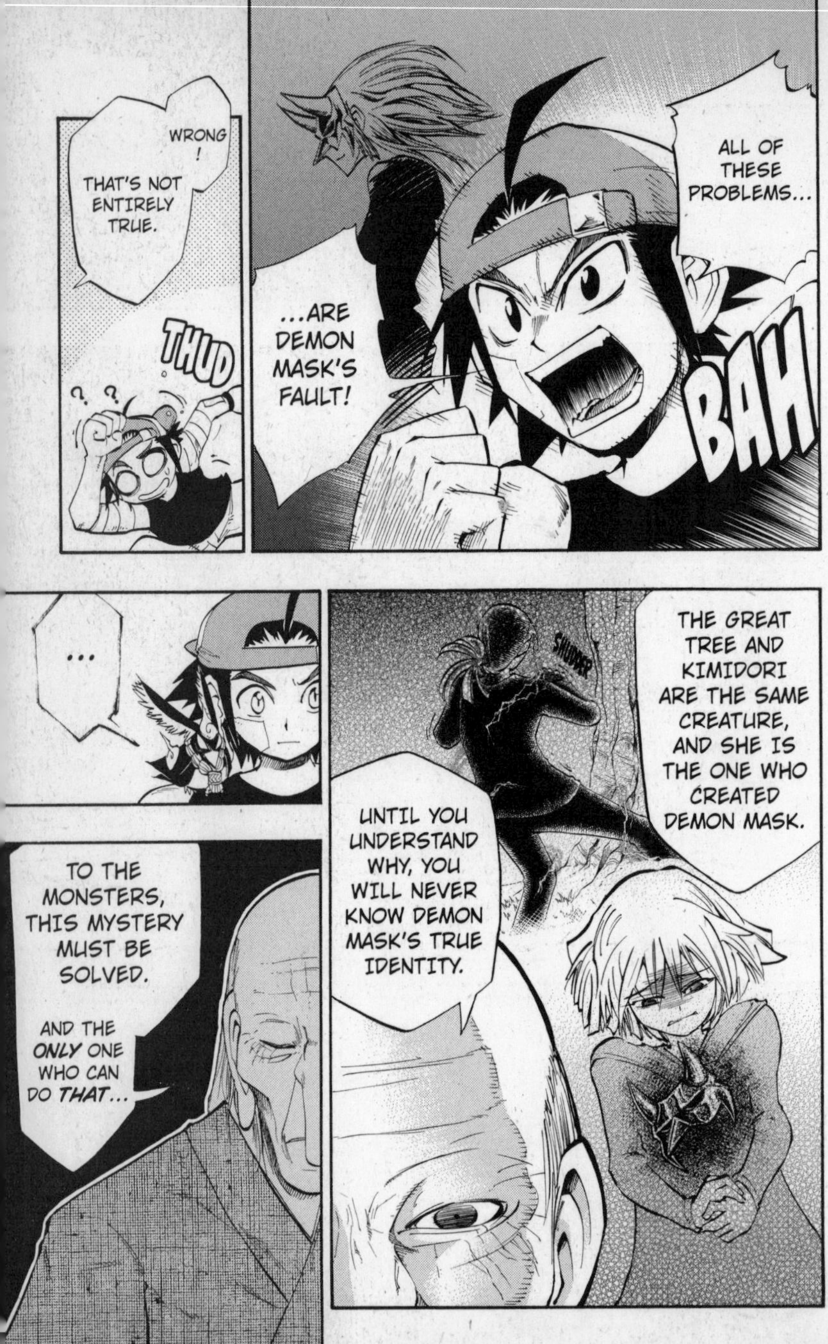
ALL OF THESE PROBLEMS...
...ARE DEMON MASK'S FAULT!
BAH
WRONG!
THAT'S NOT ENTIRELY TRUE.
THUD
? ?
THE GREAT TREE AND KIMIDORI ARE THE SAME CREATURE, AND SHE IS THE ONE WHO CREATED DEMON MASK.
SHUDDER
UNTIL YOU UNDERSTAND WHY, YOU WILL NEVER KNOW DEMON MASK'S TRUE IDENTITY.
...
TO THE MONSTERS, THIS MYSTERY MUST BE SOLVED.
AND THE *ONLY* ONE WHO CAN DO *THAT*...

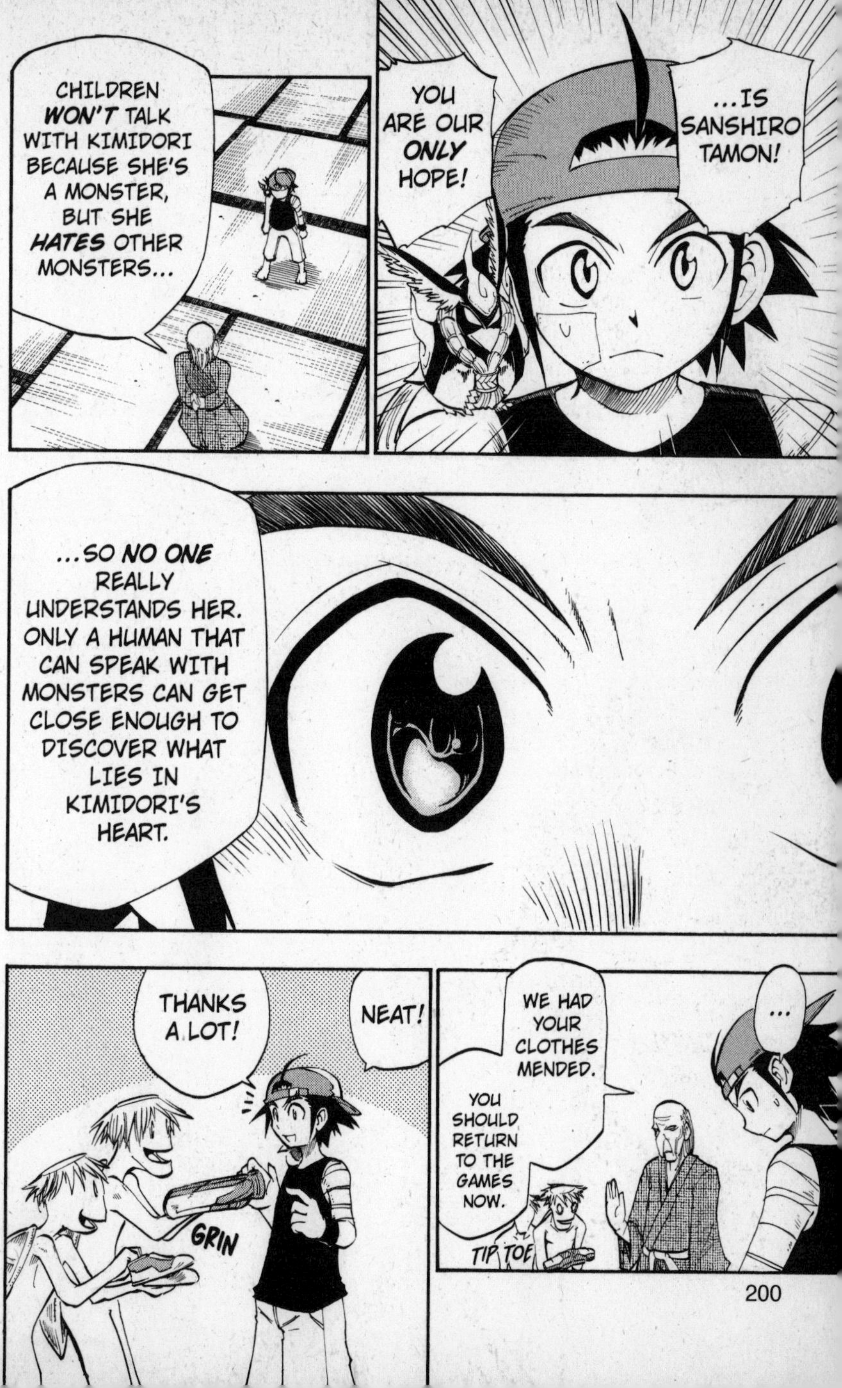
...IS SANSHIRO TAMON!
YOU ARE OUR ONLY HOPE!
CHILDREN WON'T TALK WITH KIMIDORI BECAUSE SHE'S A MONSTER, BUT SHE HATES OTHER MONSTERS...
...SO NO ONE REALLY UNDERSTANDS HER. ONLY A HUMAN THAT CAN SPEAK WITH MONSTERS CAN GET CLOSE ENOUGH TO DISCOVER WHAT LIES IN KIMIDORI'S HEART.
...
WE HAD YOUR CLOTHES MENDED.
YOU SHOULD RETURN TO THE GAMES NOW.
TIP TOE
NEAT!
THANKS A LOT!
GRIN

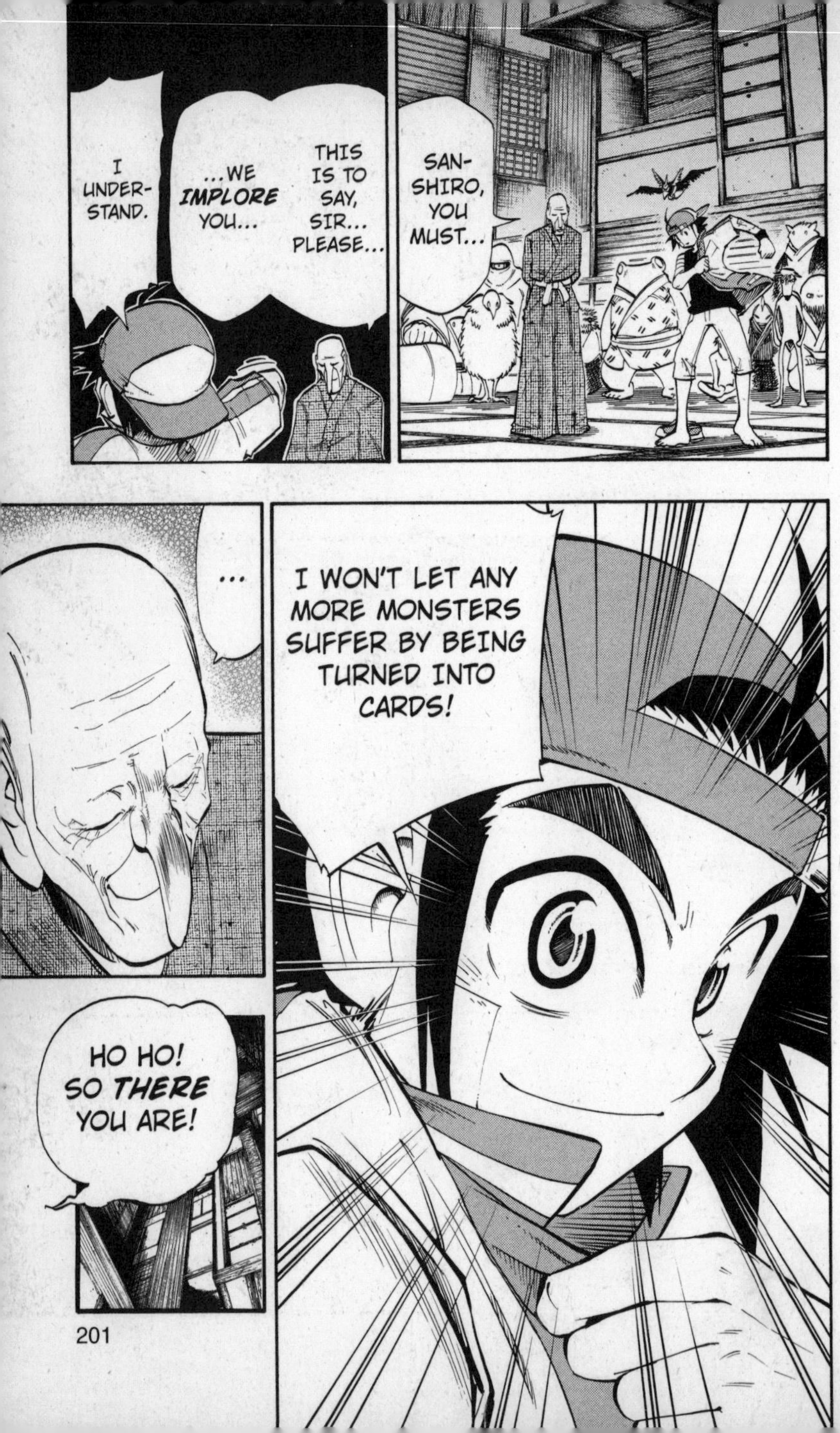
SAN-SHIRO, YOU MUST...
THIS IS TO SAY, SIR... PLEASE...
...WE IMPLORE YOU...
I UNDER-STAND.
I WON'T LET ANY MORE MONSTERS SUFFER BY BEING TURNED INTO CARDS!
...
HO HO! SO THERE YOU ARE!

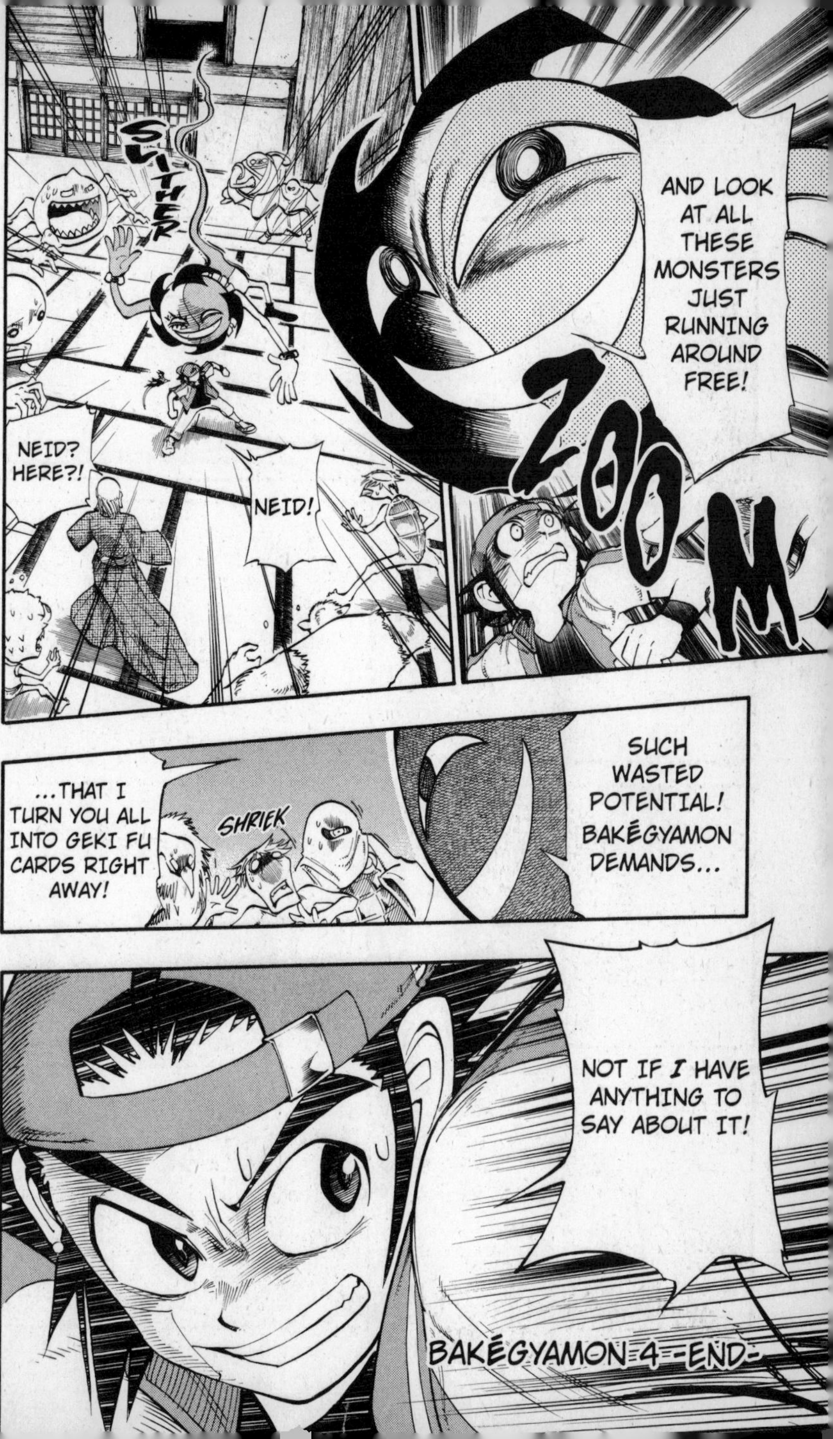
AND LOOK AT ALL THESE MONSTERS JUST RUNNING AROUND FREE!
ZOOM
SLITHER
NEID!
NEID? HERE?!
SUCH WASTED POTENTIAL! BAKĒGYAMON DEMANDS...
SHRIEK
...THAT I TURN YOU ALL INTO GEKI FU CARDS RIGHT AWAY!
NOT IF *I* HAVE ANYTHING TO SAY ABOUT IT!
BAKĒGYAMON 4 -END-

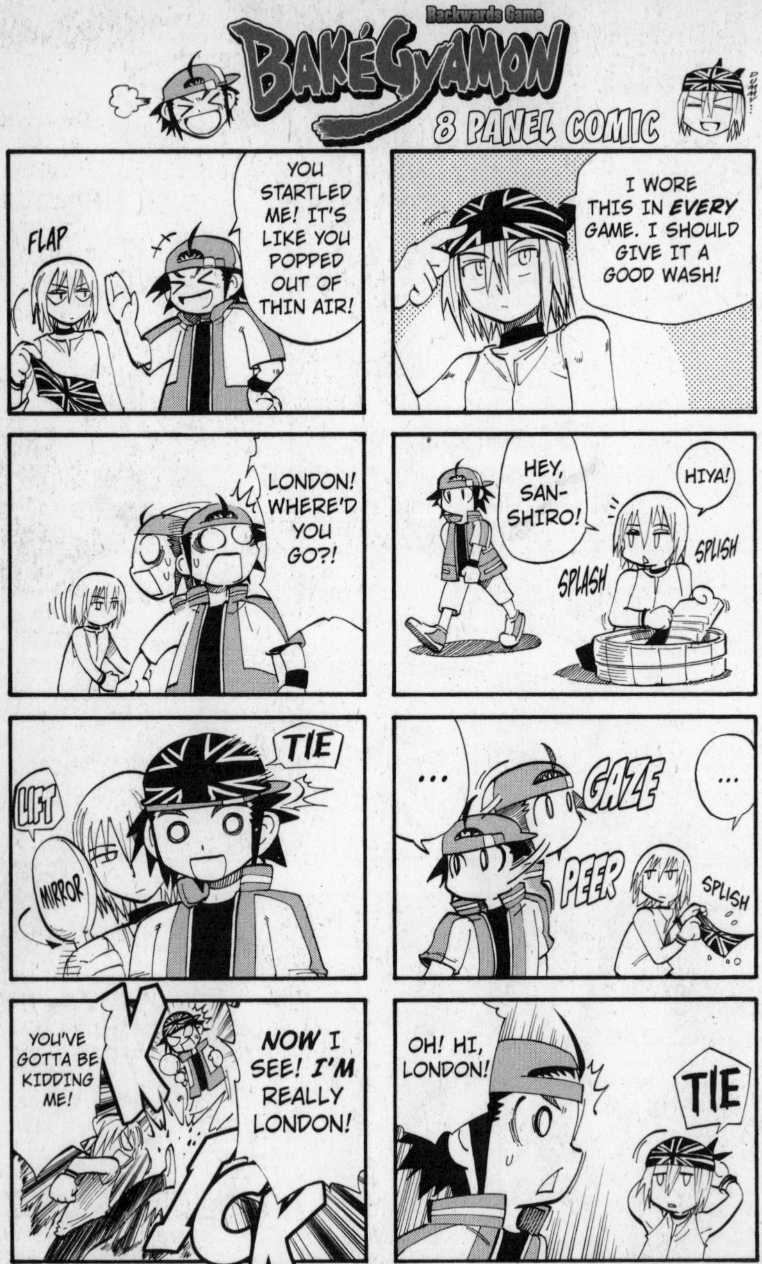
Backwards Game
BAKÉGYAMON
8 PANEL COMIC
I WORE THIS IN *EVERY* GAME. I SHOULD GIVE IT A GOOD WASH!
YOU STARTLED ME! IT'S LIKE YOU POPPED OUT OF THIN AIR!
FLAP
HIYA!
HEY, SAN-SHIRO!
SPLISH
SPLASH
LONDON! WHERE'D YOU GO?!
...
GAZE
...
PEER
SPLISH
TIE
LIFT
MIRROR
TIE
OH! HI, LONDON!
NOW I SEE! *I'M* REALLY LONDON!
YOU'VE GOTTA BE KIDDING ME!
KICK

BAKÉGYAMON DIARY DIETING

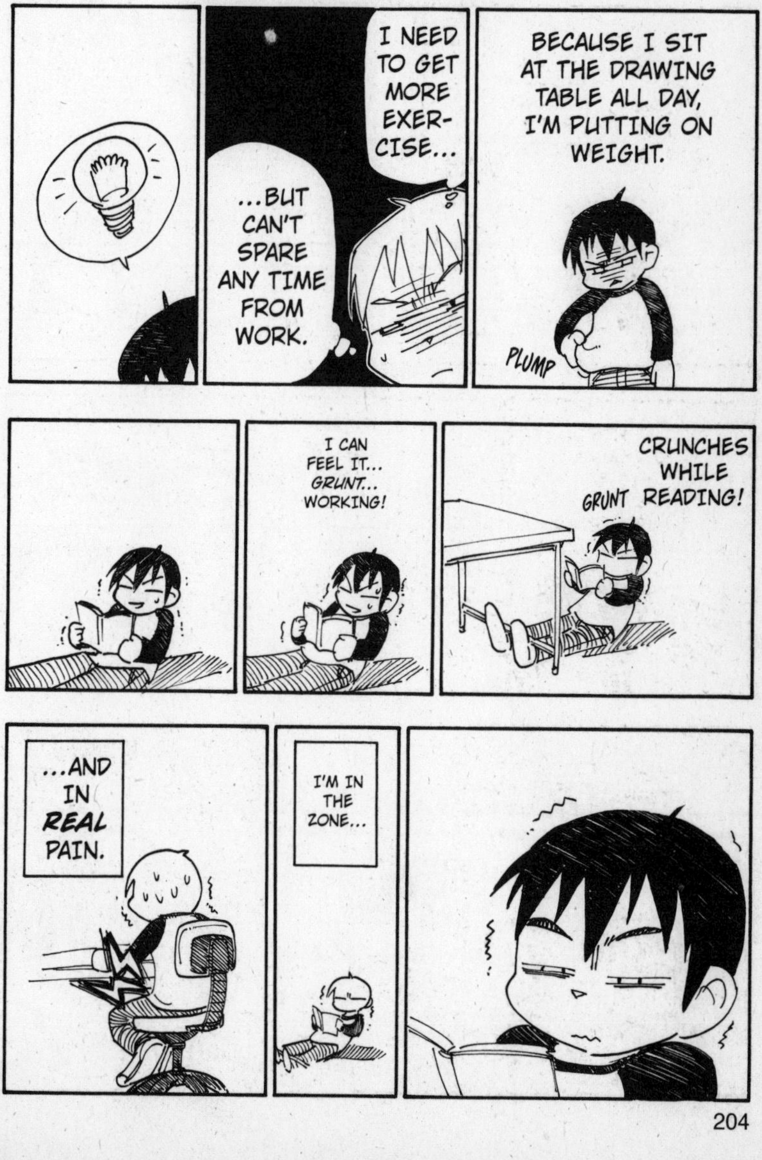
BECAUSE I SIT AT THE DRAWING TABLE ALL DAY, I'M PUTTING ON WEIGHT.
PLUMP
I NEED TO GET MORE EXER-CISE...
...BUT CAN'T SPARE ANY TIME FROM WORK.
CRUNCHES WHILE READING!
GRUNT
I CAN FEEL IT... GRUNT... WORKING!
I'M IN THE ZONE...
...AND IN REAL PAIN.

BAKÉGYAMON DIARY A FUN WORKPLACE

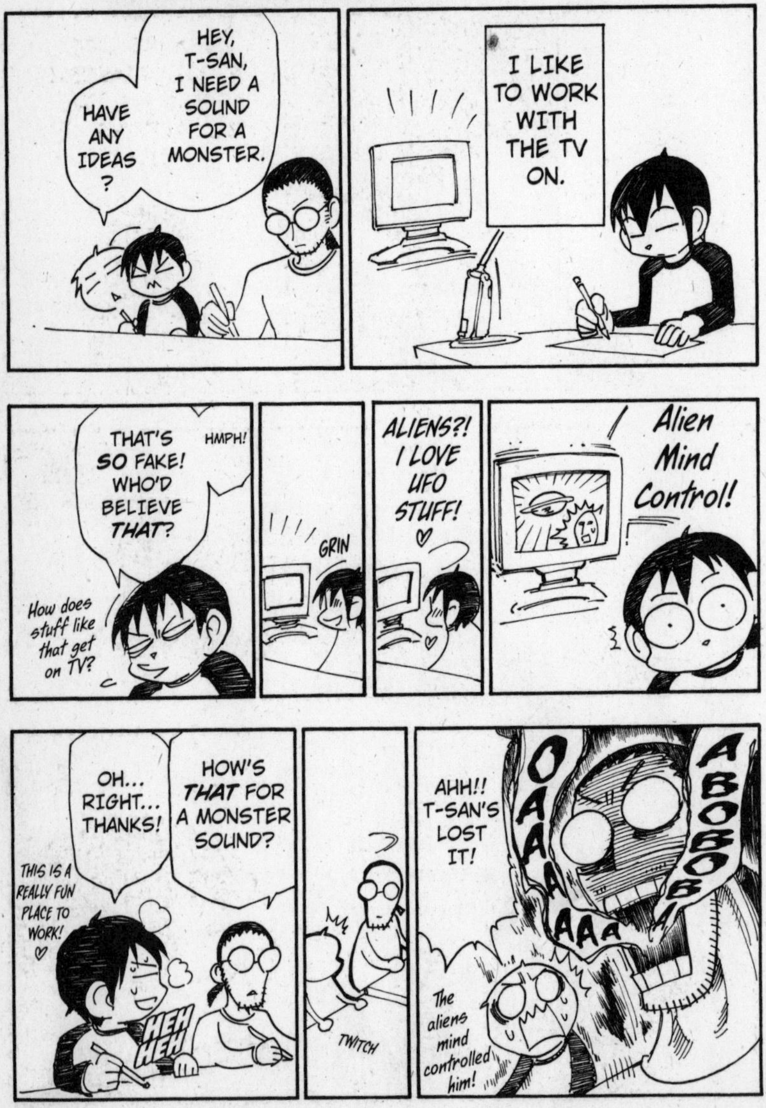

I LIKE TO WORK WITH THE TV ON.
HEY, T-SAN, I NEED A SOUND FOR A MONSTER.
HAVE ANY IDEAS?
Alien Mind Control!
ALIENS?! I LOVE UFO STUFF!
GRIN
HMPH!
THAT'S SO FAKE! WHO'D BELIEVE THAT?
How does stuff like that get on TV?
ABOBOBA
AHH!! T-SAN'S LOST IT!
OAAAAAAAA
The aliens mind controlled him!
TWITCH
HOW'S THAT FOR A MONSTER SOUND?
OH... RIGHT... THANKS!
THIS IS A REALLY FUN PLACE TO WORK!
HEH HEH

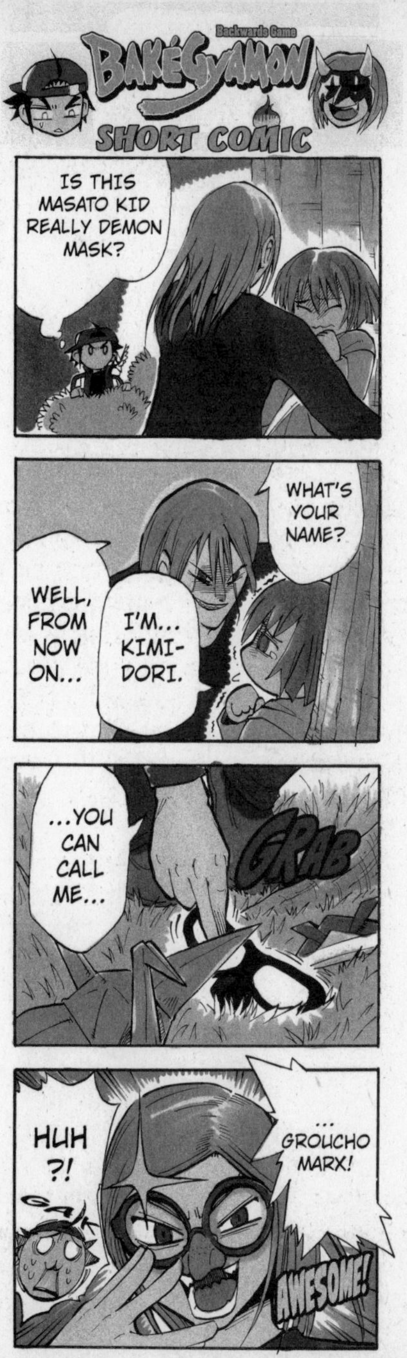
Backwards Game
BAKÉGYAMON
SHORT COMIC
IS THIS MASATO KID REALLY DEMON MASK?
WHAT'S YOUR NAME?
I'M... KIMIDORI.
WELL, FROM NOW ON...
...YOU CAN CALL ME...
GRAB
...GROUCHO MARX!
AWESOME!
HUH ?!
GAK

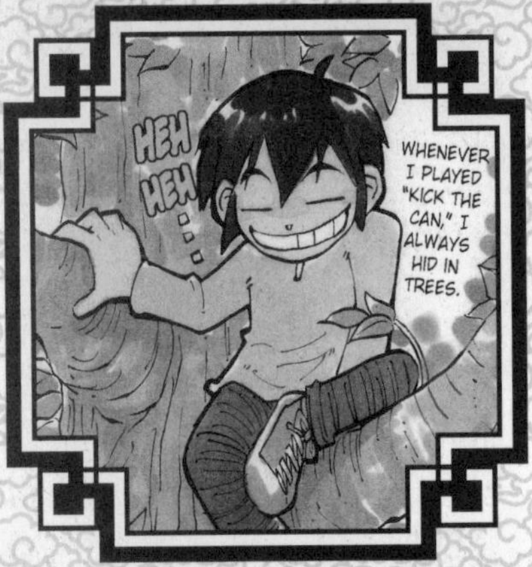
HEH HEH
WHENEVER I PLAYED "KICK THE CAN," I ALWAYS HID IN TREES.

Adults always say, "Stop playing around, study more." But I think we learn a lot more by going out to play than by opening up a textbook and being forced to study. That's why everyone should go out and play more! Play and play until you can't play no more! Chances are, you'll see and do things that you wouldn't have been able to by sitting at a desk!

-Mitsuhisa Tamura, 2007

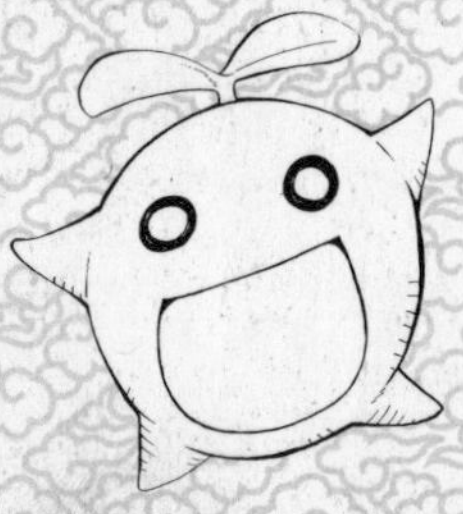

Mitsuhisa Tamura debuted in 2004 with "Comical Magical," a one-shot manga in *Shonen Sunday R. BakéGyamon* is his first serialized manga. His favorite foods are cutlet curry and chocolate snacks.

BakéGyamon Vol. 4
Backwards Game

VIZKIDS Edition

STORY AND ART BY MITSUHISA TAMURA
Original Concept by Kazuhiro Fujita

Translation/Labaaman, HC Language Solutions, Inc.
English Adaptation/Stan!
Touch-up Art & Lettering/Primary Graphix
Design/Sean Lee
Editor/Alexis Kirsch

VP, Production/Alvin Lu
VP, Publishing Licensing/Rika Inouye
VP, Sales & Product Marketing/Gonzalo Ferreyra
VP, Creative/Linda Espinosa
Publisher/Hyoe Narita

BAKEGYAMON 4 by Mitsuhisa TAMURA, Kazuhiro FUJITA
© 2007 Mitsuhisa TAMURA, Kazuhiro FUJITA
All rights reserved. Original Japanese edition published in 2007
by Shogakukan Inc., Tokyo.
The stories, characters and incidents mentioned in this
publication are entirely fictional.

Printed in the U.S.A.

Published by VIZ Media, LLC
P.O. Box 77010
San Francisco, CA 94107

VIZKIDS Edition
10 9 8 7 6 5 4 3 2 1
First printing, October 2009

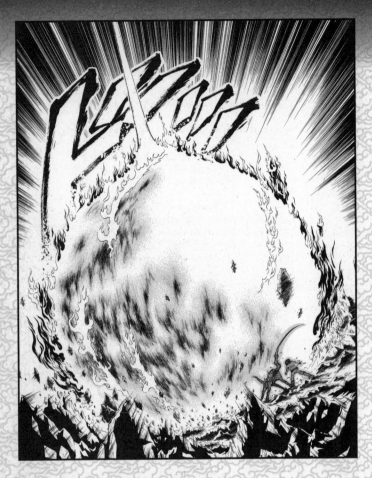

Coming Next Volume

Sanshiro's been knocked out of the competition, but now the monsters that saved his life are in danger! Fue makes the ultimate sacrifice to send him back into the game so he can take down Demon Mask, but does Sanshiro have what it takes to save everyone?!

Coming December 2009!

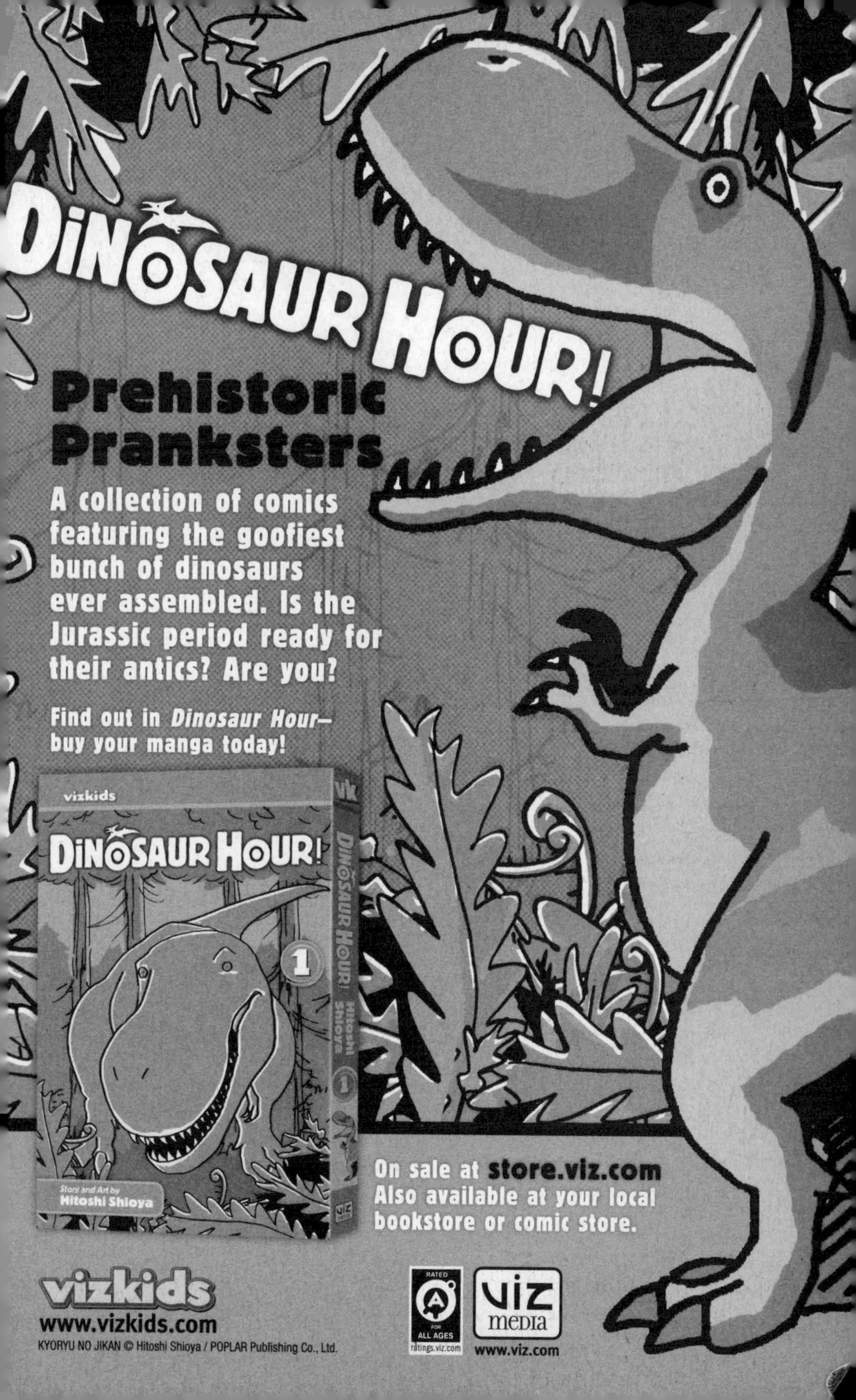
DINOSAUR HOUR!
Prehistoric Pranksters
A collection of comics featuring the goofiest bunch of dinosaurs ever assembled. Is the Jurassic period ready for their antics? Are you?
Find out in Dinosaur Hour—buy your manga today!
vizkids
DINOSAUR HOUR!
1
Story and Art by Hitoshi Shioya
On sale at store.viz.com
Also available at your local bookstore or comic store.
vizkids
www.vizkids.com
KYORYU NO JIKAN © Hitoshi Shioya / POPLAR Publishing Co., Ltd.
RATED A FOR ALL AGES
ratings.viz.com
VIZ media
www.viz.com

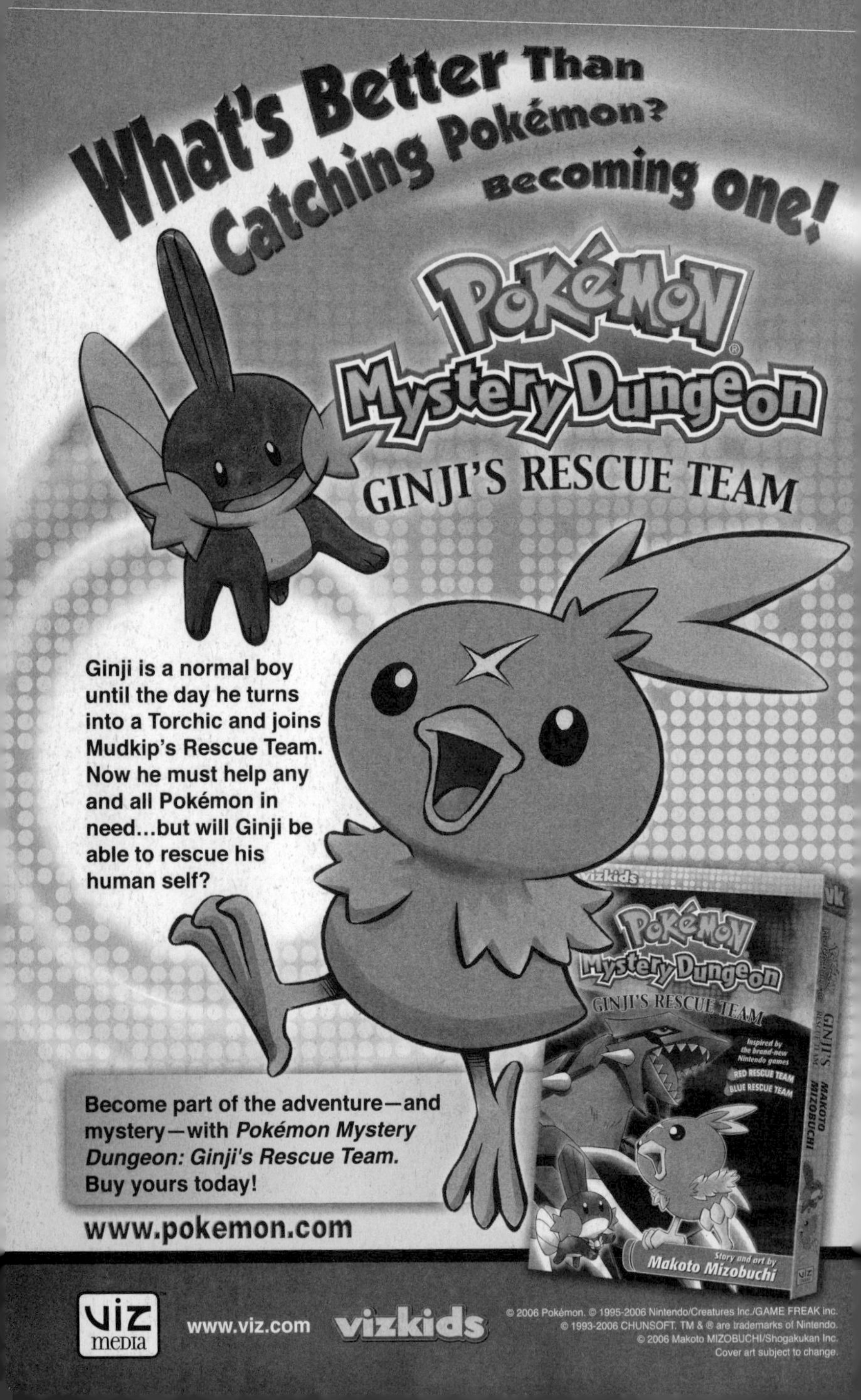
What's Better Than Catching Pokémon?
Becoming one!
Pokémon® Mystery Dungeon
GINJI'S RESCUE TEAM
Ginji is a normal boy until the day he turns into a Torchic and joins Mudkip's Rescue Team. Now he must help any and all Pokémon in need...but will Ginji be able to rescue his human self?
Become part of the adventure—and mystery—with Pokémon Mystery Dungeon: Ginji's Rescue Team. Buy yours today!
www.pokemon.com
vizkids
Pokémon Mystery Dungeon
GINJI'S RESCUE TEAM
Inspired by the brand-new Nintendo games
RED RESCUE TEAM
BLUE RESCUE TEAM
Story and art by Makoto Mizobuchi
GINJI'S RESCUE TEAM
MAKOTO MIZOBUCHI
VIZ media
www.viz.com
vizkids
© 2006 Pokémon. © 1995-2006 Nintendo/Creatures Inc./GAME FREAK inc.
© 1993-2006 CHUNSOFT. TM & ® are trademarks of Nintendo.
© 2006 Makoto MIZOBUCHI/Shogakukan Inc.
Cover art subject to change.

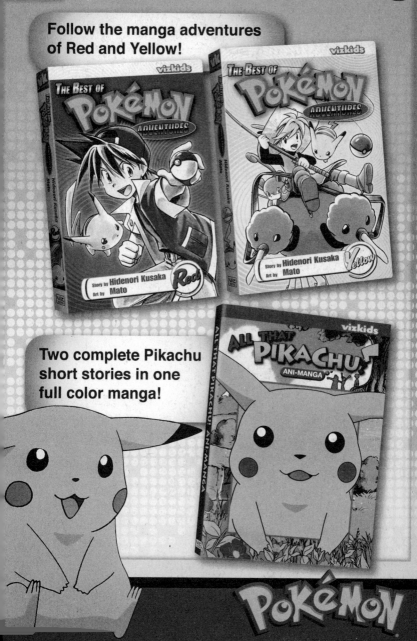

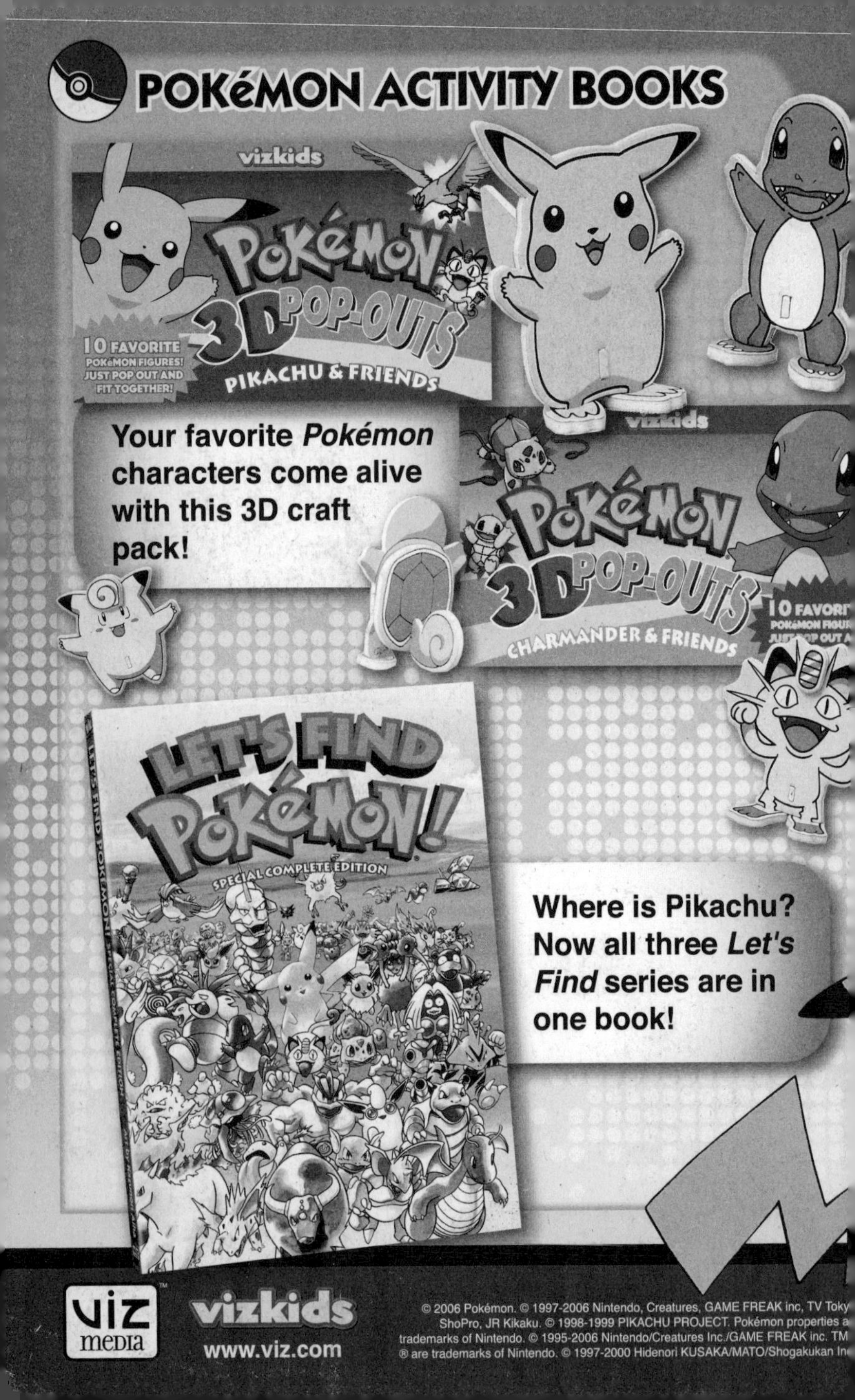
POKéMON ACTIVITY BOOKS
vizkids
POKéMON 3D POP-OUTS
PIKACHU & FRIENDS
10 FAVORITE POKéMON FIGURES! JUST POP OUT AND FIT TOGETHER!
Your favorite Pokémon characters come alive with this 3D craft pack!
vizkids
POKéMON 3D POP-OUTS
CHARMANDER & FRIENDS
LET'S FIND POKéMON!
SPECIAL COMPLETE EDITION
Where is Pikachu? Now all three Let's Find series are in one book!
VIZ MEDIA
vizkids
www.viz.com
© 2006 Pokémon. © 1997-2006 Nintendo, Creatures, GAME FREAK inc, TV Toky
ShoPro, JR Kikaku. © 1998-1999 PIKACHU PROJECT. Pokémon properties a
trademarks of Nintendo. © 1995-2006 Nintendo/Creatures Inc./GAME FREAK inc. TM
® are trademarks of Nintendo. © 1997-2000 Hidenori KUSAKA/MATO/Shogakukan In

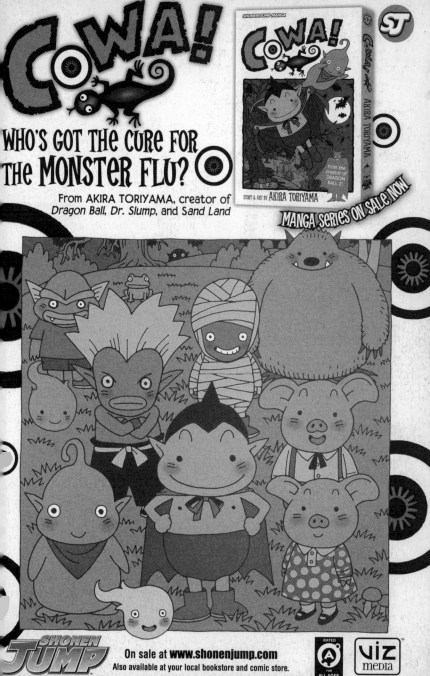

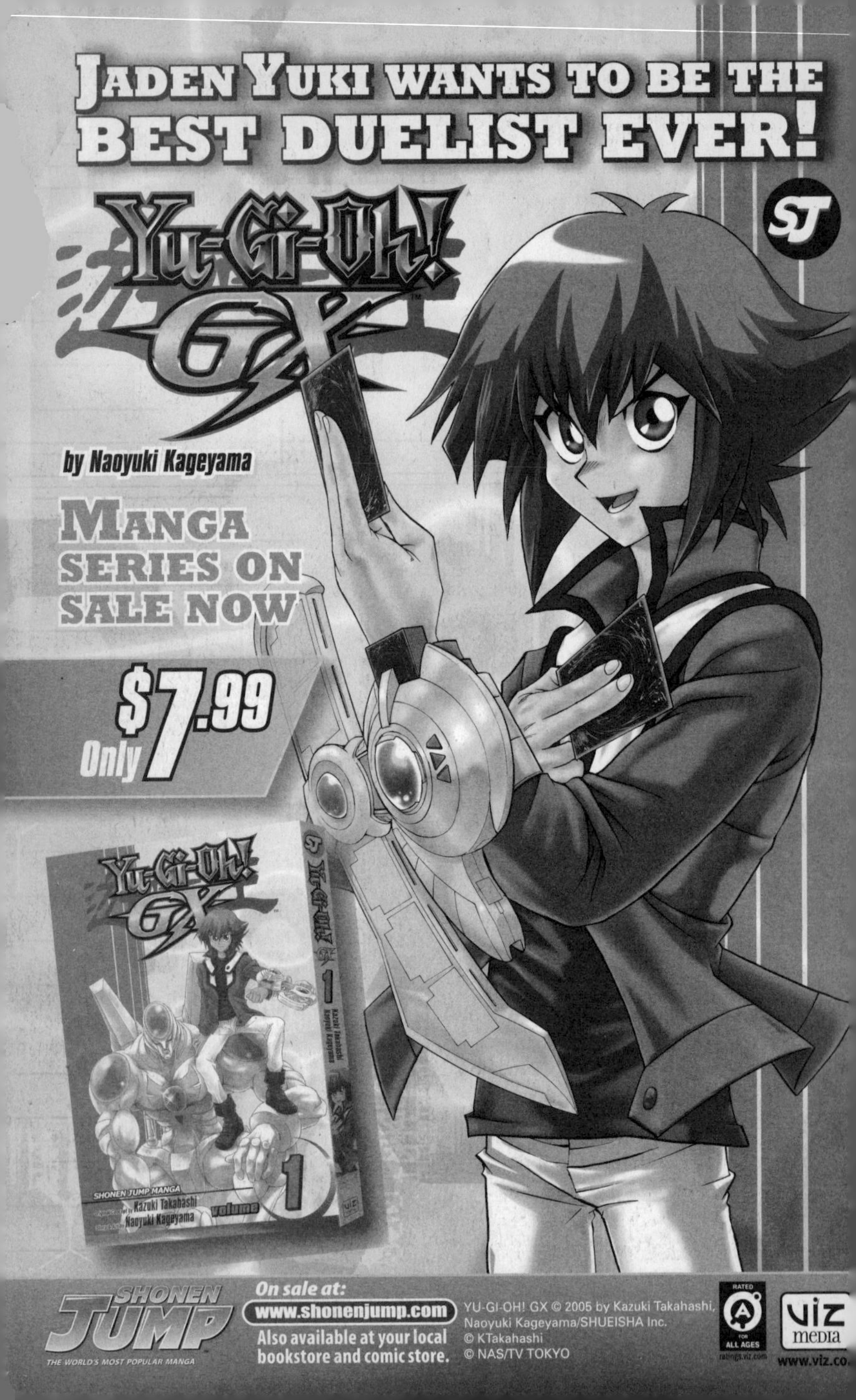
JADEN YUKI WANTS TO BE THE BEST DUELIST EVER!
SJ
YU-GI-OH! GX
by Naoyuki Kageyama
MANGA SERIES ON SALE NOW
Only $7.99
YU-GI-OH! GX
1
SHONEN JUMP MANGA
Kazuki Takahashi
Naoyuki Kageyama
volume 1
SHONEN JUMP
THE WORLD'S MOST POPULAR MANGA
On sale at:
www.shonenjump.com
Also available at your local bookstore and comic store.
YU-GI-OH! GX © 2005 by Kazuki Takahashi, Naoyuki Kageyama/SHUEISHA Inc.
© KTakahashi
© NAS/TV TOKYO
RATED A FOR ALL AGES
ratings.viz.com
VIZ media
www.viz.co

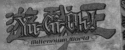
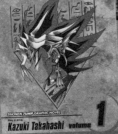